Sustainability in Question

ADVANCES IN ECOLOGICAL ECONOMICS

General Editor: Robert Costanza, *Director, University of Maryland Institute for Ecological Economics and Professor, Center for Environmental and Estuarine Studies and Zoology Department, USA*

This important series makes a significant contribution to the development of the principles and practices of ecological economics, a field which has expanded dramatically in recent years. The series provides an invaluable forum for the publication of high quality work and shows how ecological economic analysis can make a contribution to understanding and resolving important problems.

The main emphasis of the series is on the development and application of new original ideas in ecological economics. International in its approach, it includes some of the best theoretical and empirical work in the field with contributions to fundamental principles, rigorous evaluations of existing concepts, historical surveys and future visions. It seeks to address some of the most important theoretical questions and gives policy solutions for the ecological problems confronting the global village as we move into the twenty-first century.

Titles in the series include:

Sustainability in Question

The Search for a Conceptual Framework

Edited by

Jörg Köhn
Assistant Professor, Department of Economics, Rostock University, Germany

John Gowdy
Professor of Economics, Rensselaer Polytechnic Institute, USA

Friedrich Hinterberger
Senior Economist, Wuppertal Institute for Climate, Environment and Energy, Germany

Jan van der Straaten
Senior Lecturer, Department of Leisure Studies, Tilburg University, The Netherlands

ADVANCES IN ECOLOGICAL ECONOMICS

Edward Elgar
Cheltenham, UK • Northampton, MA, USA

Published by
Edward Elgar Publishing Limited
Glensanda House
Montpellier Parade
Cheltenham
Glos GL50 1UA
UK

Edward Elgar Publishing, Inc.
6 Market Street
Northampton
Massachusetts 01060
USA

A catalogue record for this book
is available from the British Library

Library of Congress Cataloguing in Publication Data

Sustainability in question: the search for a conceptual framework /
    edited by Jörg Köhn . . . [et al.].
        (Advances in ecological economics)
    Includes index.
    1. Sustainable development. I. Köhn, Jörg, 1959–
II. Series.
HC79.E5S8665 1999
338.9—dc21   98–45764
                                                                        CIP

ISBN 1 84064 050 2

Printed and bound in Great Britain by Bookcraft (Bath) Ltd.

Contents

List of Figures

List of Tables

List of Contributors

Frank J. Dietz is affiliated, as an economist, to the Department of Public Administration at Erasmus University, Rotterdam. His main interests of research are welfare economics, environmental economics, and law and economics. He has written textbooks in Dutch, and co-edited several volumes on environmental issues. His paper, 'Environment, Incentives and the Common Market', has been published in international journals, and contributed to various volumes, among which is the forthcoming *Handbook of Environmental and Resource Economics* (Edward Elgar, together with J.C.J.M. van den Bergh).

Aldo Femia graduated in 1991 in Economics (Bocconi University, Milan), obtained a Master of Sciences in Economics and Econometrics (1994, Southampton University), and a Ph.D. in Political Economy (1996, Ancona University). Current employment: researcher at the Environmental Accounting Unit of the Italian National Institute of Statistics (Istat). Main interests: material flows and ecological economic policy.

Maria-Elisabeth Fischer, born in 1973, studied economics, especially environmental economics at the universities of Bonn/D and Lausanne/CH (1993-1998). She was involved in several projects at the Wuppertal Institute and obtained a grant from the "Cusanuswerk".

John Gowdy is Professor of Economics at Rensselaer Polytechnic Institute in Troy, New York; and Director of the Graduate Ph.D. program in Ecological Economics. His recent books include *Economic Theory for Environmentalists* (with Sabine O'Hara), *Limited Wants, Unlimited Means: A Reader on Hunter-Gatherer Economics and the Environment*, and *Full Circle: Back to Sustainability* (with Carl McDaniel).

Julia Haake is a Ph.D. Student at the C3ED, Université de Versailles/St. Quentin-en-Yvelines, France. Her work is financed through a scholarship of the ADEME (Agence de l'Environnement et de la Maîtrise de l'Energie), and co-financed by the CEA (Commissariat à l'Energie Atomique).

Friedrich Hinterberger studied economics at the Johannes-Kepler-Universität in Linz/Austria, and obtained a Ph.D. from Justus-Liebig-Universität in Gießen. Following Post-Doctoral visits to universities in Roma, Firenze, New York and Berkeley, he has been working at the Wuppertal Institute for Climate, Environment and Energy. He is currently officer-in-charge of the division for eco-efficiency, material flows and structural change. Main research interests: ecological economic policy, sustainability and evolutionary economics.

Wander Jager is a researcher at the Centre for Environmental and Traffic Psychology, University of Groningen. He is working with the project 'Simulating Consumer Behaviour'. He has special interest in multi-disciplinary research.

Melinda Kane is currently completing her Ph.D. in Ecological Economics at Rensselaer Polytechnic Institute in Troy, New York. Her research interests include economic valuation, environmental sustainability and community sustainability initiatives.

Jörg Köhn, born in 1959, is Assistant Professor at the University of Rostock. He studied ecology, and is currently teaching regional and ecological economics. He was visiting professor at the Rensselear Polytechnic Institute Troy, New York, and the University of Bremen, Germany. He has published approximately 60 scientific papers, including 10 books.

Michael Kuhndt is researcher for the working group 'Sustainable Enterprise', in the Department for Material Flow and Structural Changes, at the Wuppertal Institute. He holds a Master's degree in Chemical Engineering and Environmental Management and Policy, from the University of Dortmund, Germany and the University of Lund, Sweden. Currently, he is working on his Ph.D., focusing on the development of toolboxes, in order to evaluate, improve and communicate the environmental and economic performance of enterprises towards the goal of sustainable development.

Christa Liedtke, born in 1964, has studied biology and theology at the University of Essen and Bonn, Germany. She is working as a project-manager at the Wuppertal Institute for Climate, Environment and Energy, in the division for material flows and structural change, working group 'Sustainable Enterprise'. Her main research areas are material flow accounting, environmental management and resource management.

Fred Luks is a socio-economist. He is co-founder and member of the research field 'Globalisation and Ecological Discourse' at the Hochschule für Politik und Wirtschaft in Hamburg. He is also a contributor to the material flows division of the Wuppertal Institute. Major research interests are sustainable development, ecological economics, steady-state and globalisation.

Richard B. Norgaard is Professor of Energy and Resources, and of Agricultural and Resource Economics, at the University of California at Berkeley (USA). He obtained a Ph.D. in Economics from the University of Chicago; contributes to environmental economic theory through general equilibrium models; participates in the development of co-evolutionary understandings of our environmental dilemmas; and also writes in the fields of environmental epistemology and sociology. Norgaard is currently the President of the International Society for Ecological Economics, and serves on born the U.S. Committee of the Scientific Committee on Problems of the Environment (SCOPE), and the Board of Directors of Redefining Progress.

Thomas Orbach, born in 1968, has studied economics, environmental economics, at the University of Siegen, Germany. Since 1996, he has worked as a freelance researcher at the Wuppertal Institute for Climate, Environment and Energy, in the division for material flows and structural change, working group 'Sustainable Enterprise.' His main research field is environmental management accounting.

David Pimentel received his BSc degree from the University of Massachusetts, and Ph.D. from Cornell University. He is currently Professor of Ecology and Agricultural Sciences in the Department of Entomology, and Section of Ecology and Systematics, at Cornell University. He has published 475 scientific papers, including 20 books.

Andreas Renner, born 1967 at Freiburg, Germany. Studied from 1988 until 1994 economics, roman languages and geography, in Tübingen (Germany), Pavia (Italy) and Brussels (Belgium). He has been the research assistant at the Walter Eucken Institute (Freiburg, Germany) since 1995. Fields of research: Constitutional Political Economy, Institutional Economics, Jurisdictional Competition and Sustainable Development. He received the Walter-Eucken-Award 1996 of the University of Jena.

R. Bruce Rettig is Professor of Agricultural and Resource Economics at Oregon State University, where he teaches marine fishery economics, and environmental economics and policy. His research currently focuses on the relationship between private property rights and environmental regulations. He has participated in many international fishery management discussions and is currently studying the influence of U.S. policies on investment in fisheries. Rettig received his Ph.D. in economics from the University of Washington in 1969.

Holger Rohn, born in 1965, is an engineer and works as an independent scientist with the Department of Material Flows at the Wuppertal Institute for Climate, Environment and Energy. His research concentrates on environmental and resource management, environmental information systems, participatory processes and environmental education at the firm level.

Inge Røpke is an economist, Associate Professor at the Department of Technology and Social Sciences, Technical University of Denmark. Her main field of research is socio-ecological economics. She has written on a number of issues in relation to the environment: cleaner technologies, growth, trade, technology optimism, socio-structural perspectives on environmental problems, consumption and everyday life.

Jan Rotmans is Professor at the International Centre for Integrative Studies, University of Maastricht. He was formerly working at the Dutch National Institute for Public Health and Environmental Protection, Bilthoven, The Netherlands, and at the Department of Policy Co-ordination and Sustainable Development, United Nations, New York. He is a leading scientist in the field of integrated assessment.

Erik C. Schmieman, born 1968, studied Agricultural and Environmental Economics at Wageningen Agricultural University. At present, he is working as a Ph.D. student, focusing on the economics of acidification and tropospheric ozone in Europe.

Joachim Schütz is a human ecology economist. He received his education at the universities of Mannheim, Ann Arbor, Bonn and Cologne, focusing on economic theory and social policy. Currently, he is in the process of formulating a framework for economic analysis based on co-evolutionary systems-theory, in (bio)diversity and contextual ethics.

Thomas Sikor is a Ph.D. candidate at the Energy and Resources Group of the University of California at Berkeley. His dissertation examines the economic and environmental effects of decollectivisation in Vietnam. Sikor's broader research interests lie in the political economy of rural resource use and environmental change. He has pursued such research in Vietnam, Chile and Nicaragua.

Peter Söderbaum is professor of Economics in the Department of Business Studies and Informatics, at Mälardalen University, Sweden. He is responsible for the undergraduate programme in Ecological Economics the first Ecological Economics programme in Sweden where a large part of courses in economics, business and environment, ecology etc. have been designed specifically for the purpose of the programme.

Clive L. Spash is a lecturer in environmental economics in the Department of Land Economy, at the University of Cambridge, where he is also Director of Cambridge Research for the Environment (CRE). He has been Vice-President of the European Society for Ecological Economics since 1996. In recent years his work has focused on economics and ethics, with regard to the environment, and environmental values.

Marjolein van Asselt is a researcher at the International Centre for Integrative Studies, University of Maastricht. She is working in the field of integrated assessment with special interest in uncertainty and risk analysis.

Jan van der Straaten is a senior lecturer at Tilburg University. He focuses on tourism and the environment, EU policy, and ecological economics theory. He is a member of the Editorial Board of Environmental Politics, the Journal of Sustainable Tourism, Business Strategy and the Environment, and Milieu. He has published many books and articles.

Ekko C. van Ierland, born 1953, is Professor of environmental economics at Wageningen Agricultural University in The Netherlands. He worked for UNESCO as a lecturer of Economics at the University of Malawi in Africa, and at the Foundation for Economic Research (SEO) of the University of Amsterdam. Currently, he is working on the economics of global warming, acidification, nature conservation, and biodiversity.

Charles Vlek is Professor at the Centre for Environmental and Traffic Psychology, and Social and Organisational Psychology, University of Groningen. He is working in the field of risk analysis and behaviour and environment. He has large expertise in multidisciplinary research.

Nese Yavuz holds a Master's degree in economics. She is an independent consultant and has set up ECOBUILD Yavuz + Partner for economic and ecological housing-management in Essen, Germany. Her research priorities are marketing-management, development of organisational structure towards an improved information flow, ecological housing-management and life-styles, eco-efficient consumption and services.

Preface

The term sustainability has evolved over the years as we have learned more and more about the complexities of the social, economic and biological worlds. We now recognise that sustainability does not mean perpetuating the status quo; this is an impossibility because it would neglect change as a stabilising mechanism in an ever changing (evolutionary) world. Moreover, sustainability actually incorporates a variety of concepts operating on different regional scales, different time scales, and on different levels of human action. Ironically, a constituent property of sustainability is change. Change is the context of policy responses to the human-environment conflict; it is a constitutional property of all systems. This implies that sustainability does not belong exclusively to the realm of policy–environment interactions. Sustainability is a process which takes place in systems which themselves induce changes and are subject to change. Sustainability, then, does not mean perpetuating a system in static equilibrium, but rather maintaining the resilience of social and environmental systems. It is the outcome of self-organisation and self-regulation which allows a system to respond effectively to changing conditions. It cannot cope, however, with processes of change which are out of the scope of systems resilience. Once a system loses its capacity to absorb turbulence then the system flips to another state and cannot steered by any human action. This is why sustainability policies only can aim at encouraging processes of safeguarding system resilience.

As the twentieth century closes, the entire planet is now under human domination. Sustainability depends as never before on human actions. Much of the writing about sustainability makes the point that all human activity takes place within the geophysical and biological systems that make up planet Earth. All human action also takes place within the 'lifeworld;' the cultural beliefs, institutions, knowledge and traditions that encapsulate all individuals. Another essential component of sustainability, then, is maintaining the ability of humans to create institutional and social arrangements which are able to adapt to changing conditions.

The papers in this volume take as their starting point the environmental and institutional context of economic activity and public policy. There is a recognition that some basic economic notions such as universal substitutability, methodological individualism, and the superiority of the price mechanism over all other methods of economic allocation may be misplaced in the case of environmental protection. Sustainability does not

xv

aim solely at protection of the environment. It is a unifying principle which is based upon and brings together environmental and social systems resilience. We hope that the papers in this volume will encourage theoretical and policy responses that are capable of coping with the uncertainties inherent in dynamic, self-organising systems.

We gratefully acknowledge the cooperation from all contributors. We also like to express our gratitude to Edward Elgar and his team for continuous support for this book. Last but not least we thank Antje Köhn who arranged the final version of the text.

PART I

Introduction

1. The Imperative of Sustainability: Introduction

Jörg Köhn, John Gowdy, Friedrich Hinterberger and Jan van der Straaten

The economist Herman Daly (1996), drawing on his experiences at the World Bank, uses the term 'pre-analytic vision' to distinguish between traditional environmental economists and ecological economists. Traditional environmental economists begin their analysis of environmental problems with a view that the natural environment is only a source of inputs to be allocated for economic production. Ecological economists, on the other hand, begin their analysis with a pre-analytic view of the economy as a sub-system of the larger human society and institutions and of the still larger biophysical world.

These two pre-analytic views imply two very different approaches to the theory and practice of sustainability. If the natural world is merely a collection of resource inputs ('natural capital') to be used to fuel economic activity, then the policy goal is to make sure these resources are used in the most economically beneficial way possible. Policies following from this vision include extending more complete property rights to environmental resources, making sure that the prices of goods and services reflect their environmental costs and benefits, and educating the public about these environmental costs and benefits.

If, on the other hand, features of the natural world are more than mere economic inputs, but rather essential and irreplaceable requirements for human existence, it is not enough to assign property rights or find the proper set of taxes and subsidies. Some environmental features simply cannot be assigned a meaningful price. This implies a different agenda for environmental education and a more complex one. As discussed in the essays in this volume, it means broadening the economists' concept of value to include not only market prices but also unpriceable and even unquantifiable human cultural and environmental features.

The essays in this volume arise from the conviction that the current level of human impact on the natural world is unsustainable. A variety of indicators show that the Earth's biological systems are under increasing stress

3

and that the geochemical and atmospheric conditions under which humans evolved are undergoing rapid, but largely unpredictable, change. A number of seemingly unrelated 'movements' will eventually, we believe, change the way the economic profession views the economy and the natural world. All of these will challenge basic economic notions of how to value nature's attributes:

- Re-examination of the foundations of utility theory. There is an exponentially growing literature exploring the philosophical, psychological, and ethical foundations of neoclassical theory (Dasgupta, 1998; Bromley, 1998). New ideas broadening the economic concept of value are beginning to show up in mainstream economic journals.
- Re-examination of the 'microfoundations' controversy. The past twenty years or so has seen the ascendancy of the view that the macro economy can be explained by the same principles that govern economic behaviour at the micro level (as in the 'weak sustainability concept'). This view has always been controversial within the profession, but the challenges now seem to be on a firmer footing and are being reinforced by the growing evidence of the negative effects of economic activity on the Earth's atmospheric, biological, and geochemical systems (Bromley, 1989; Colander, 1996; Hodgson, 1993).
- Re-capturing the commons. There has been an explosion of literature in recent years challenging the sanctity of individual choice and arguing for new institutional arrangements protecting future generations and environmental integrity (Bromley, 1989, 1998; Norton *et al.*, 1998; Sen, 1987).
- Corporate responsibility. There are encouraging signs that the corporate world is moving away from Friedman's position that the only social responsibility of the firm is to maximise profits. Corporations such as Monsanto and British Petroleum have taken leading roles, not only in promoting sustainable production practices, but also in addressing the major environmental issues of our time, biodiversity loss and global climate change.

As Jane Lubchenco (1998) so eloquently argued in her outgoing address as American Association of the Advancement of Science (AAAS) president, there is an increased realisation of the connections between the economy, the biosphere, and human social systems. A new social contract is needed committing scientists to work toward solving the pressing problems we face. Solving these problems will require unprecedented interdisciplinary cooperation and understanding. To be successful, interdisciplinary work requires more than merely assembling specialists from a variety of relevant disciplines. It requires that each discipline's practitioners have some understanding of the other's relevant findings and approaches. Economists must learn the rules by which ecosystems operate and biologists must learn the rules by which markets operate. It should not be assumed, as is too often the case, that these rules are in harmony with each other. Biologists are perhaps in a better position than economists to understand principles of self-organisation, self-regulation and evolution.

CONCEPTUAL FRAMEWORKS REVISITED

The purpose of the first part of the book is to clarify, to the greatest extent possible, the meaning of the terms *sustainability* and *sustainable development*, and to illuminate some related considerations such as the social context of sustainability and the role of hierarchical process and coevolutionary development.

As Melinda Kane argues in Chapter 2 the definition and conceptualisation of sustainability has come a long way since it was formalised in the Brundtland report, *Our Common Future*, in 1988. After the initial euphoria wore off it became apparent that there exists deep theoretical divisions among those who embrace the term 'sustainable development'.

In Chapter 3, Jan van der Straaten asks the question 'What type of environmental economic theory do we need?' He argues that certain economic theories are already applicable to environmental issues. Although many concepts have been developed, the problem of an unpriced environmental scarcity of the environment and in particular nature cannot be solved within the context of 'normal' economic paradigms. Dealing with the environment requires a broader understanding of the social context within which economic decisions are made.

Thomas Sikor and Richard Norgaard argue in Chapter 4 that sustainability should be seen as an on-going outcome of appropriate social processes. The traditional approach assumes that sustainability can be defined by an 'objective' function independent of historical and social factors. By contrast, Sikor and Norgaard shift the emphasis of policies for sustainability from *a priori* goals to the basic conditions under which appropriate goals can be constantly and systematically assessed. They also recognise that sustainability implies regulating large-scale economic, environmental, and socio-economic forces as well as determining appropriate local policies. They illustrate these basic concepts with the examples of forest policy in Vietnam, agroecological research and extension in Latin America, and cooperation between researchers and farmers in Chile.

In Chapter 5, John Gowdy draws upon an evolutionary perspective of economic theory. Humans and with them their economic systems are part of a hierarchy of complex interactions. The economy cannot perpetuate itself without self-regulation between complex and dependent systems. It becomes more and more clear that the standard economic concept of value, as expressed in relative market prices, and the economic paradigm of 'efficiency' cannot guide sustainability policies, and nor are they consistent from a systemic point of view.

In Chapter 6, Jörg Köhn discusses the context for sustainability policies in terms of the interaction between ecological, cultural, and economic systems. He argues that sustainability is a concept that is closely related to the ability of systems to evolve and co-evolve in challenging and responding to corresponding systems. Sustainability relates to systems' resilience. Sustainability in a systemic and evolutionary perspective is the ability to absorb disturbance and to reorganise, self-regulate and evolve. Whereas the capacity to absorb disturbances clearly relates to the carrying capacity concept, the reorganisation, self-regulation and evolution principles relate to change and more importantly to the diversity aspects of systems that enable them to adapt to change and survive. Sustaining a system's capacity to survive clearly means in this respect that diversity is of indispensable value and a constitutional parameter of sustainability.

Joachim Schütz uses a philosophical perspective in Chapter 7 to analyse concepts of systems identity and ethics in the human-environment relationship. He calls for mutuality, understanding, plurality, balance and systemic competence as guiding principles for sustainability. His analysis clearly shows that in the long run all individual interests must be integrated into a systems point of view, and that systems efficiency is built upon diversity and cooperative behaviour that currently needs cultural adaptation.

In Chapter 8, Fred Luks argues that the concept of 'scale' can play an important role in ecological economics. Although scale may be a metaphor, like the 'invisible hand', it can play an important heuristic role in depicting the economy as embedded in the larger ecosystem. Luks relates, in his section on the notion of scale to industrial metabolism, the set of physical and chemical transformations that convert the raw material entering the economic process into manufactured products and waste. The concept of scale is operationalised into policy through measures of resource intensity developed by the Wuppertal Institute in Germany. Luks argues that only by explicitly recognising the importance of the scale of economic activity *vis-à-vis* the carrying capacity of the planet, can we address the real issue of sustainability, namely that the total human impact is too great and should be reduced. If we focus only on a narrow industrial metabolism perspective, we run the risk of merely shifting waste emissions from one medium to another without reducing the total.

Clive Spash explores in Chapter 9 the thesis that an ethical perspective is central to any economic theory which tries to predict human behaviour. An ethical perspective is necessary to support policies whether or not policy aims at sustainability. Following Smith and Sen he argues that economic behaviour is always part of a broader social context in which moral considerations play an important role. Spash uses the example of environmental valuation to verify his analysis of economic theory. His example clearly shows that the environment cannot be transformed into a commodity. Economic thinking does not solely determine decisions. He concludes that ethics, trust, romance, emotions, and so on have serious implications for economic decisions.

SUSTAINABLE PRODUCTION

There has been much interest in the past few years in what has variously been called sustainable production, green production, or industrial ecology. Several major firms, such as Mansanto and British Petroleum, are attempting to translate the vague notion of sustainability into practical management and monitoring principles. The essays in this section discuss the theory and strategy of making production sustainable.

David Pimentel, in Chapter 10, discusses the environmental and economic benefits of sustainable agriculture. It is often overlooked that agriculture is the most critical production activity and is one of the most vulnerable to mismanagement and the effects of global environmental change. Pimentel points out that, under current unsustainable practices, soil is being lost from croplands 20 to 40 times faster than it is being replaced by natural forces. Likewise, the wasteful use of water by industrial agriculture has resulted in salinisation of vast areas and the depletion of aquifers. Even though massive amounts of pesticides are applied each year to crops, the percentage of crops lost to insect pests has been increasing as they become more and more pesticide resistant. Pimentel presents calculations showing the benefits of sustainable management in agriculture. These include reductions in energy use, reduction in soil erosion, the elimination of the need for insecticides, and the recycling of manure, which replaced all the nitrogen and most of the phosphorous and potassium fertiliser.

In Chapter 13, Rettig discusses sustainable production in the case of the Pacific Salmon and Global Fishery industries. The case of collapsing fishing stocks worldwide is interesting to ecological economics for at least two reasons. First of all, the fishery was one of the first resource industries to be theoretically examined by economists, and secondly, policies advocated by economists have come under fire from several quarters. Rettig discusses trends in global fisheries, the apparent sources of fishery declines, and the issues surrounding the establishment of fishing quotas. He then turns to the case of Pacific salmon as an example of how endangered species are treated in theory and in policy. Rettig argues that policy responses to date have not been cost effective nor economically efficient. The conclusion is that decisions about the sustainable use of fish and wildlife requires the resolution of conflicts between traditional users, regulatory agencies and conservation advocates.

In Chapter 12, Haake, Kuhndt, Liedtke, Orbach and Rohn advocate sustainable development through dematerialisation. They emphasise the need for specific firm-level information in order to measure material flows. Material input into the production process is summarised in five categories: abiotic raw material, biotic raw material, soil displaced by agricultural and forestry use, water, and chemically or physically transformed air. They define a measure to describe material input called MIPS, material input per unit of service. Dematerialisation in theory is described in terms of product and process innovation. A practical example of a dematerialisation policy is given by the German furniture producing firm Kambium, which re-engineered its production process to reduce its material flow from cradle to grave.

Ekko van Ierland and Erik Schieman analyse the case of air pollution and abatement strategies in Europe. They put a special emphasis on The Netherlands' mitigation targets, which are part of The Netherlands Environmental Plan Plus. They point to trade-off effects between mitigating different pollutants in isolation. It might happen that reducing a target pollutant causes an increase in discharging another pollutant. Such trade-offs have to be taken into consideration when designing models that should support policies designed to have a net benefit for the environment. Van Ierland and Schieman design a model that assumes that the changes in the discharges will gradually diminish. Although such models can hardly cope with threshold effects along a mitigation path, they support understanding of a complex phenomenon such as air pollution. Moreover, the different scenarios the authors' build clearly shows that joint efforts of industries and countries are necessary to treat the air pollution problem.

SUSTAINABLE CONSUMPTION

It is widely recognised that the major threats to the global environment, global warming, biodiversity loss, chemical residues in land and water, to name a few, are the result of unsustainable consumption patterns, particularly in Northern countries. No environmental policy that fails to address the issue of unsustainable consumption patterns can hope to be successful. The essays in this section address this problem in a variety of ways.

Jager, van Asselt, Rotmans, and Vlek, in Chapter 14, present a model of consumer behaviour in the context of an integrated assessment of global change. They point out that, contrary to prevailing opinion, a growing body of archeological research shows that many past civilisations overshot their natural resource bases and collapsed. This research is increasing our awareness of the interconnections between environmental degradation and socio-economic systems. Integrated assessment attempts to capture the complex relationships between environmental change, patterns of consumption, and the institutional framework. Their model characterises these relationships in terms of the impact system, the response system, and mechanisms to promote behavioural change.

Inge Røpke, in Chapter 15, links the discussion on sustainable consumption to the dynamics and pressures behind the unsustainable growth path with the quality of life concept. She first argues from the perspective of individual perception and behaviour in the industrialised world. She opens this view to consumption as a space of collective action and indicates pressures behind consumption. Røpke argues consumption is a social process that cannot be conceptualised in a means-ends perspective. Moreover, it is impossible to develop a concept of sustainable consumption within the traditional concept of welfare economics.

In Chapter 16, Hinterberger, Femia, Fischer, Luks and Yavuz design a research agenda for sustainable consumption. They develop a taxonomy of different socio-economic approaches and perspectives on that issue and link these findings to political discourse on consumption. The authors develop a catalogue of unresolved questions on the consumption issue that emerge if one takes a systemic analytical perspective.

SUSTAINABILITY AND POLITICAL ECONOMY

Sustainability can be understood as a process of regulatory decision-making. In the opinion of the authors of this volume, sustainability cannot be split into economic, social or environmental categories. On the contrary, sustainability is a unifying and guiding principle of social and social-environmental interaction. Therefore, sustainability cannot be an issue for a solely social or natural science. The call for a post-normal science that relates science to decision-making within the social context requires designing a political economy of sustainability.

In Chapter 19, Peter Söderbaum argues that neoclassical economics is of little help in understanding the phenomena basic to sustainability policies, such as the value orientation of individuals, and of social and economic institutions, and the motivations of businesses. He argues that there is an important tradition in Europe, namely, a European Institutional Economics, that is particularly relevant to the issue of environmental sustainability. Following in the tradition of the German Historical School, the American Thorstein Veblen, Swiss economist William Kapp, and of course the Swedish economist Gunnar Myrdal, Söderbaum argues that we must consider the motivations of the 'Political Economic Person' (PEP) as well as the neoclassical 'Economic Person'. Drawing on the European Institutional tradition, Söderbaum outlines a conceptual framework for environmental policy. In his PEP formulation, humans are actors with many, sometimes conflicting, roles rather than being exclusively consumers and wage earners. Going beyond the methodological individualism of neoclassical economics allows the development of a realistic theory of the political, social and institutional framework within which policies for sustainability can be formulated.

Frank Dietz and Jan van der Straaten, in Chapter 18, analyse European environmental policy. They, like van Ierland and Schieman, exemplify their analysis with the air pollution issue. They apply the concept of environmental utilisation space to show the 'space' within which standard economic approaches can support an environmental policy that aims at environmental impact mitigation. However, once a certain level of pollution mitigation is achieved, institutional and distributional barriers may appear that resist further mitigation. Dietz and van der Straten argue that environmental policies must take into account 'solving' not only the environmental but the social question in the context of the environmental problem at hand.

In Chapter 19, Andreas Renner proposes the linking of ecological and constitutional economics. He draws on the findings of the recommendations of the Freiburg School and the Virginia School – mainly on Walter Eucken's Policy of Institutional Design and James Buchanan's Constitutional Political Economy, respectively. The idea of linking constitutional Economics to sustainability policies makes transparent normative assumptions so that alternative policy proposals can be rationally discussed. This may open the floor for a democratisation of decision-making but more importantly it creates a decision-making space within which sustainability can develop as a guiding principle for decision-making to regulate policies.

REFERENCES

Bromley, D. 1989. 'Entitlements, Missing Markets, and Environmental Uncertainty.' *Journal of Environmental Economics and Management* 17, 181–94.

Bromley, D. 1998. 'Searching for Sustainability: The Poverty of Spontaneous Order.' *Ecological Economics* 24, 231–240.

Colander, D. 1996. *Beyond Microfoundations*. New York: Cambridge University Press.

Daly, H. 1996. *Beyond Growth*. Boston: Beacon Press.

Dasgupta, P. 1998. 'Population, Consumption and Resources: Ethical Issues.' *Ecological Economics* 24, 139–151.

Hodgson, G. 1993. *Economics and Evolution*. Ann Arbor: University of Michigan Press.

Lubchenco, J. 1998. 'Entering the Century of the Environment: A New Social Contract for Science.' *Science* 279, 491–497.

Norton, B., Costanza, R. and Bishop, R. 1998. 'The Evolution of Preferences: Why "Sovereign" Preferences May Not Lead to Sustainable Policies and What to Do About It.' *Ecological Economics* 24, 193–211.

Sen, A. 1987. *On Ethics and Economics.* Oxford: Blackwell.

PART II

Conceptual Frameworks Revised

2. Sustainability Concepts: From Theory to Practice

Melinda Kane

INTRODUCTION

Since the early 1970s, environmental issues have come to the forefront of the debate over how we, as humans, should inhabit this planet. The debate has, at various times, centred around whether there are limits to the growth of our population and our level of activity, whether there are moral considerations in living on the planet the way we do, whether we owe anything to future generations, and whether there is an absolute tradeoff between the level of economic activity and environmental quality. These questions are all wrapped into the debate on sustainability. What is it? How can it be achieved? How do we know if we are moving towards that state? Is there a conflict between economic and environmental sustainability? What are the links between environmental sustainability and the uneven distribution of economic benefits? Should it be a goal whose scope is local, regional or global, and is local sustainability even possible without a sustainable global system? These are the questions raised by other authors in this volume, and which I briefly review here. I focus on three broad areas of discussion: grappling with the as yet elusive definition of sustainability, unravelling the layers of hierarchy which form the systems we are trying to sustain, and measuring our progress towards the goal of a sustainable world.

WHAT IS SUSTAINABILITY?

The term 'sustainability' itself has been the subject of much debate in recent years. Although a popular concept in general terms, it lacks a precise definition or set of criteria by which to judge our actions. In conceptualising what sustainability might be, we often go through a process of deciding what sustainability is *not*. Indeed, the basic motive behind the sustainability discussion is the perception that our current manner of living is not sustainable. Beyond the major media issues of global warming and biodiversity loss are others such as rising atmospheric mercury levels, health impacts from synthetic chemicals like dioxin, falling sperm counts and a host of other indicators which lead many to believe that human impact on the natural environment is having unpredictable but adverse consequences which are likely to seriously impact the quality of human and non-human life all over the globe in the next few decades. This discussion begs an answer to the question: 'What can we do to avert problems caused by human impacts on the natural environment?' The broadness of the concept has led many researchers and practitioners to search for details which might give us the answer to the original question of how we should inhabit the planet.

The roots of the sustainability debate can be found in several places. The sustainability discussion can be traced back to basic resource management decisions of how to manage renewable resources such as forests, fisheries or clean water for sustained yields. The field of natural resource economics often focuses on the optimal use of resources to ensure availability far into the future. These resources, if they continue to be available, sustain the economies which are based on them. More generally, outside of a strict economic sustainability and before the popularisation of resource economics, resource managers and conservationists such as Gifford Pinchot and Aldo Leopold wrote of the importance of conservation for protecting the services provided by nature. The current sustainability debate raises once again some of the arguments brought forth by Pinchot and the early resource managers who favoured a sustained pattern of resource exploitation in contrast to John Muir and the early preservationists who focused on the aesthetic and spiritual benefits of resource protection (Leavenworth, 1991).

As the adverse consequences of human impact on the natural environment became more widely recognised, more serious inquiry into the limits of the planet's ability to deal with these impacts came to the fore. The controversial Club of Rome study, *Limits to Growth*, (Meadows *et al.*, 1972) illustrated the overshoot-and-collapse scenario which we would follow, according to the authors, if we did not significantly change our actions and control our population. While *Limits to Growth* focused exclusively on physical ecological limits to economic growth, many authors argue that the limits to growth may also be social. For example, Paul Ekins (1993) argues that there might also be social limits to economic growth and/or limits to welfare which might be derived from such growth, while the work of Homer-Dixon (1994) and others focuses on the repercussions of societal conflicts resulting from environmental degradation contributing to the unequitable distribution of resources or wealth.[1] In fact, Ekins (1993, p. 269) argues that sustainability

---

[1] See, for example, articles on limits to the use of national income accounts as measures of welfare, for example Daly and Cobb, 1989. Typical arguments against this include the inclusion of defensive expenditures, or the exclusion of natural resource depletion.

(or alternatively, sustainable development, as the two terms are used somewhat interchangeably in the literature) is actually a way of presenting an acknowledgement of the limits to economic throughput in a more palatable manner.

> The 1970s' limits to growth critiques, both physical and social, failed to dent the social consensus in favour of economic growth, so that by the time the Brundtland Commission produced its report, *Our Common Future*, on environment and development, the emphasis was placed on a perceived complementarity between growth and environment.

Ekins refers to the first widely recognised definition of sustainability published by the World Commission on Environment and Development in 1987. According to that report, commonly referred to as the Brundtland Report after WCED's chair, Gro Harlem Brundtland, sustainable development is that which "meets the needs of the present without compromising the ability of future generations to meet their own needs."

This definition is obviously very broad and could have many different interpretations. If one were to believe that future generations will be able to meet their needs by inventing new technologies and reinventing or recreating ecosystems, there is no need to conserve any ecosystems; economic sustainability will suffice (Solow, 1992). On the other hand, we could assume that technology and ecosystem services are not substitutable and, since ecosystem services are essential to human existence, we should act so as to preserve as much of the biosphere as possible. Thus, the definition, and more importantly, the interpretation of sustainability, hinges on underlying assumptions of what is important for the continued existence and happiness of the human species, and the possibility for substitution of those things which contribute to our welfare. Ekins (1993) argues that there is consensus that current economic development patterns are not ecologically sustainable, but the core of disagreement is on the extent to which new technologies can resolve problems of ecological unsustainability by replacing certain ecosystem functions while permitting continuing growth of the gross national product. He concludes that this is essentially an empirical question, which cannot be answered theoretically. This leaves us with the question others have raised, namely, do we now have enough time to work out the details of those empirical answers, or have we already depleted our options by destroying both natural and institutional resources?

Duchin (1996) would somewhat agree with Ekins in terms of his argument that our best chance at finding solutions is through empirical testing. She argues that the next step in finding the possible paths to sustainability is to design a theoretical quantitative framework from which to predict some of the consequences of various technological and/or policy changes. It is a process of building scenarios for particular geographical and societal contexts and then testing them in the real world. This, she states, will require two components (1) coming up with concrete strategies about ways for people to make their livelihoods in particular physical and cultural settings, and (2) creating a framework and tools for evaluating alternative strategies from environmental, economic, and social points of view.

Redclift (1996) has pointed out the problems of operationalising the Brundtland definition given the changing meaning or interpretation of current and future 'needs'. The concept of needs, he argues, is no longer based on survival but on accepted norms. He argues for the need to integrate biophysical limits with sociological constructions of nature. Sustainable development is a hard concept to base on needs because development itself, whatever form it takes, contributes to the changing perception of what is a need.

The vagueness inherent in the Brundtland definition, however, need not be the downfall of the concept. Lélé (1991) points out that while operationalising the concept of sustainability has been problematic due to its vague definition, there is some value in its broadness. It has allowed those with seemingly irreconcilable differences of opinion within the 'environment versus development' debate to look for commonality among themselves without appearing to compromise their positions. Others would argue, however, that if the concept of sustainability were to ever be operational, the broadness would have to give way to more specificity.

Like the limits to growth arguments, the Brundtland definition of sustainability is still focused on constraints, but now the constraints focus more on the type of activity rather than purely on the scale of activity. This fits with recent studies that highlight the differences between environmental problems which result from poverty and which might be somewhat alleviated by proper economic development, and those which result from overconsumption and are only exacerbated by more growth of the same type. Shafik and Bandyopadhyay (1992) made an empirical contribution to this debate with their econometric study of the relationship between economic growth and various environmental quality variables for a cross section of country-specific time series data. Their results show that environmental problems resulting from poverty, like access to safe water and urban sanitation, can be improved by economic growth, while other problems like air and water pollution or deforestation are exacerbated by an increase in economic activity. Arrow *et al.* (1995) also argue for caution in making the argument that economic growth can help alleviate environmental problems. This has been shown to be true, they note, for problems of pollutant emissions but not generally for resource stock depletion. Additionally, the relationship may only hold for those pollutants involving concentrated short-term costs (for example sulphur, particulates, or fecal coliforms) but not for those involving long-term or more dispersed costs. Perhaps most importantly, Arrow *et al.* (1995) also argue that in most cases where pollution has declined with an increase in income, the reductions have not occurred automatically, but rather, they have been the result of local institutional reforms whether via direct regulation or market-based incentive.

Since the Brundtland Report, sustainability has been defined variously as (1) maintaining intergenerational welfare, (2) maintaining the existence of the human species, (3) sustaining the productivity of economic systems, (4) maintaining biodiversity, and (5) maintaining evolutionary potential (Tisdell, 1991). These various meanings lead to a wide range of sometimes conflicting policy proposals, which may or may not contribute to sustainability.

Lélé (1991) shows how the term 'sustainable development' has been interpreted in different ways which can either lead to contradictory or meaningful policy suggestions. Interpreting the concept as a justification for sustaining anything and advocating development merely as a process leading to a changed state is, according to Lélé, "contradictory or trivial." On the other hand, interpreting the concept in terms of sustaining the social and ecological basis of life and defining development according to its objectives (for example, meeting basic needs), leads to a more meaningful interpretation, one that might help us develop criteria to determine what kinds of activities are, indeed, sustainable.

The difficulty in defining sustainability often comes down to a disagreement on exactly what can or should be maintained. For example, if one were to argue that sustainability means maintaining intergenerational welfare, one would also have to ask what things contribute to welfare and how they can be maintained. If all human wants are commensurable, that is, all wants can be reduced to a monetary metric, then maintaining the ability of the economy to generate income will maintain intergenerational welfare (see Bromley, 1998). If wants are lexicographic, meaning that non-substitutability exists between some categories of goods, then a money metric is insufficient for gauging sustainability. Finally, if economic sustainability is inconsistent with maintaining the long-term capacity of the biosphere to support human life, there is obviously a problem. It is useful to examine the several layers of the hierarchical systems in which human activity takes place in order to develop further these ideas.

LAYERS OF SUSTAINABILITY

The biosphere itself is made of components which operate on very different scales of geographic scope and time. Add to that the complex nature of human societies with all their various layers, whether social, economic, ethical, technological or biological, and it is easy to understand why the general notion of sustainability has been difficult to operationalise. Each layer of human existence takes on its own dimensions of time and spatial impact, and decisions made with respect to one layer may have unpredictable consequences for others. Environmental problems which have recently come to fuel the urgency of the sustainability debate, such as global warming or tropical deforestation, are often traced back to economic decisions made by actors who evaluate their own actions based on decision criteria from only one or two of these layers. In order to reach a general state of sustainability, all of these layers must be included in our individual and collective decisions.

How do we evaluate whether an activity is sustainable or not? By evaluating it from several different viewpoints (say, for example, an ecological, economic and social analysis), we can gain more insight than if we were to evaluate it from only one of these lenses. Those who have been researching sustainability have found themselves crossing disciplinary borders, sometimes somewhat uncomfortably. Jane Lubchenco (1998), in her Presidential Address to the American Association for the Advancement of Science, noted (1) the massive uncertainty associated with all aspects of the sustainability debate, (2) the increasing need for scientists from various disciplines to work together and (3) the need for both individual researchers, as well as universities and agencies, to cooperate to "construct more effective bridges between policy, management, and science, as well as between the public and private sectors." Economists and non-economists alike, including biologists, social theorists, industrial ecologists, and others with a wide range of backgrounds have adopted the new field of ecological economics, claimed by some to be the 'science of sustainability'. Each of these specialists, and many more, will likely be able to contribute some insight to an appropriate path towards sustainability.

Whether an activity is sustainable or not depends on its motivations or inputs (links to society and ecological sources) and output or results (links to society and ecological sinks) as well as other characteristics. Operationalising sustainability using these links leads us to a hierarchical view of the world in which problems are approached from their various layers, and the solutions may present themselves by looking at the various links between these layers.

In some of the recent literature, the sustainability of the whole system has been confused with the sustainability of one or more layers. Some authors have recently started to differentiate between a partial and total sustainability analysis (see, for example, Lélé, 1991), but a potential weakness of the sustainability debate is that it does not adequately characterise the relationships between these different layers in relation to the problems it is trying to address. Take the case of the linkages between poverty and environmental degradation, one example of which might be that of shifting or 'slash-and-burn' agriculture. The two are often envisioned as being connected via a downward spiral, one reinforcing the negative effects of the other. This may in fact be true, but telling the poverty-degradation story in this way leaves it without context. If we were to envision it as a consequence of all the social, environmental and ecological pressures associated with it, we might find an appropriate context from which to draw our policy decisions. An examination of the social context of 'slash-and-burn' agriculture will make the concept more concrete.

The practice of shifting cultivation is responsible for the loss of untold acres of tropical forests. Soil fertility is rapidly depleted, water quality often suffers and the biodiversity of the ecosystem is greatly simplified, both from the loss of habitat and the introduction of a monocultured crop. This is the ecological reality of this process. But there are social conditions underlying this method of agriculture which serve to reinforce the problems. In many tropical countries, farmers use this 'slash-and-burn' method because they are desperate for food and income. Considered from a strictly economic lens, these people have no monetary income and so to find income, they farm in areas which are not already taken by other farmers, probably the least productive lands, as both economic theory and common sense would tell us that the most productive plots would already be in use.

But what of the social and ecological causes and impacts of this agriculture? These are marginalised people, those without access to other sources of income and who are not provided for by some sort of social safety net. They usually own no land and are thus left with whatever land is unwanted by those with the resources to own and cut off access to the better-suited agricultural lands. The shifting farmers are marginalised because of their economic situation but this may happen in other circumstances as a result of cultural, religious, or other reasons as well.

As this case illustrates, there are layers of reality which must be observed together in context in order to gain a full understanding of the root causes of environmental problems, as well as in order to appreciate how difficult it is to develop solutions to these problems. There is an ecological layer (the loss of soil fertility and other impacts from deforestation), a social layer which underlies the ecological unsustainability (the common practice of shifting areas of cultivation without adequate time for the forest to go through the necessary successional stages), and perhaps a strictly social layer which underlies the whole (for example, a history of conflict with nearby communities).

Now let us return to the idea of separate layers of activity, each with its own sustainability criterion. Ecological problems caused by human activity have sometimes led to the suggestion that the way to solve the problem is to remove the people from the area. Environmental groups from the industrial world, in seeking to protect forests and wildlife, especially in less developed tropical countries, have often tried, and in some cases are still trying to establish national parks and/or forest preserves to keep people out in an effort to protect the natural resources. Some have gone so far as to relocate people from their traditional homes to new locations. Africa and South America are full of stories of these failed plans, with poachers coming in to preserves to collect wildlife which would fetch them a month's wages and the desperately poor ignoring or unable to read signs which implore them to keep out. Making the situations doubly complicated are the policies of global lending institutions that place restrictions on the spending activities of these governments, in many cases adding to the pressure on the local population. The social and economic pressures contributing to the ecological problem are too great to make a successful policy based on a strictly ecological view of the problem.

The field of economics is perhaps most guilty of considering only its own scope of activity, assuming other layers will operate by the same rules because actors will always be rational in their decision-making and will have all the information they need to do so. Welfare is considered to derive from consumption and as such can be adequately measured by national income figures. Thus, it is barely surprising that a notion of sustainability that comes from a strictly neoclassical economic analysis will involve a simple rule like maintaining the total capital stock at a level that will maintain consumption of goods and services far into the future (see Solow, 1992). Some economists have argued that in order to make up for some acknowledged externalities, we must stabilise the level of natural capital. The former approach is known as a weak sustainability criterion (Pearce and Atkinson, 1993), while the latter is referred to as strong sustainability (Goodland *et al.*, 1993). The crux of the difference between the two relates to the substitutability of one type of capital for another. This returns us to the argument mentioned earlier, that is, the question of whether technology can adequately replace ecosystem services. Even if it were found to be technologically possible, the question remains as to whether there are other attributes of nature which cannot be replaced by technology, for example aesthetic or recreational services.

The notion of a strictly social sustainability is somewhat more recent than the notion of either a strictly ecological or economic sustainability and is much less well articulated (see, for example, Barbier, 1987). Some recent examples in the literature do focus on the notion of an intertwined environmental and social sustainability. Often these works focus on the social upheaval which comes from being in competition for scarce resources (see, for example, Homer-Dixon, 1994; Dasgupta, 1995). Alternatively, there is consideration of the impacts of globalisation on recent economic and social phenomena. John Cobb (1998) considers the impact of globalisation on those in the U.S. who make their living from various kinds of capital (for example financiers, bankers, lawyers, technical experts) and those who earn their living from labour. He argues that as global markets expand, increasing the gap between those who live from capital and those who live from labour, the many associated negative social impacts are exacerbated.

Much work remains to be done in fusing the research on layers of hierarchy to determine what is sustainable for a whole system. The need remains to adequately characterise the links between the various layers and to design methods which help us resolve the tension between the layers. We need to ensure that our institutions sustain both social and ecological attributes. We need technologies which meet strict technical efficiency criteria and which protect ecosystem services. We need an ethic which promotes care of both social and ecological resources when they serve as inputs and as waste assimilators for economic processes. This will involve designing new technologies, policies, institutions, and lifestyles and implies the need for new methods of manufacturing, education, governance, and management. These requirements are by no means easy to fulfill as O'Hara (1998) points out:

> The provision for basic physical needs, the support of social relationships and the preservation of ecological functions all place constraints on economics activity, yet at the same time they provide the very basis for economic activity. Sustaining individuals, social relationships and ecosystems require three kinds of services: technological, relational and ecosystem but their provision "is not mutually compatible but in tension.

Nevertheless, they are necessary requirements if we are to reach a true state of sustainability. The question still remains of how to determine whether we are moving in that direction.

INDICATORS

Given the severity of environmental problems and the complexity of the world, it is often difficult to know whether our collective actions are solving problems or just further contributing to them. Are we moving towards or away from sustainability? Without some way of discovering the answers to these seemingly simple questions, we can make few decisions about how to proceed. Indicators provide some way of discovering the state of the world around us. The necessity for indicators of sustainable development was set forth in *Agenda 21*, the document produced at the UN Earth Summit in Rio de Janeiro, Brazil. This document set forth an agenda for coming to and maintaining a state of sustainability and pointed out the data gap which exists with respect to the state of the environment and society.

Indicators are meant to convey information which is otherwise too complicated to understand. They are, by their very nature, reductions of information. A good indicator will convey information easily without losing too much information or creating too much distortion. But in reducing information to a manageable level, we necessarily lose some in the process. In deciding which indicators to keep track of, we, as a society, make decisions on what information is important enough on which to base our decisions.

Indicators may measure, among other things, stocks or flows, current conditions or changes in those current conditions, or responses to those changes. The OECD set of Core Indicators for Environmental Performance Review (OECD, 1993), for example, seeks to measure three things: the pressure placed on the environment (for example pollutant emissions and other flows), the current condition of the environment (for example atmospheric concentrations of greenhouse gases or other stocks), and the responses of society to these problems (expenditure on air pollution abatement or other such defensive expenditures, for example). While these focus on the integration between economic and environmental layers, indicators from other sources may describe any or all of a set of proxies for economic, environmental or social conditions.

Not only can indicators give a sense of the state of the world, but they also bring attention to certain phenomena and create a context in which they can be considered by policymakers and the general public. An excellent example of this is the body of economic indicators. New economic data of all kinds are generated and reported on with remarkable regularity and in great quantities. Consider the ubiquitous reports of the Consumer Price Index, leading and coincidental indicators of the business cycle, consumer confidence, unemployment, GDP, stock indices, and many others. Not only is each of these indicators reported regularly and widely, but they serve to create a context for each other so that each indicator contributes a piece to a larger picture of the economy. Economic indicators are highly visible and accessible and this makes the information they convey recognisable as important. O'Hara (1995) has pointed out the importance of creating a context for evaluating all data, but especially the economic data we, as a society, are so intent on collecting.

In contrast to economic indicators, social and environmental indicators appear much more sporadically and are not given as much publicity. There is no regular widespread publication of homelessness or illiteracy rates. Crime trends and pollution data do not appear on the nightly news as does the Dow Jones Industrial Average. As a consequence, when data are made available, we tend to portray the trends they suggest as crises rather than as part of a larger picture. These problems may in fact be crises, but the point is that we lack a context with which to put them in perspective. A more regularly constructed view of social and environmental phenomena would provide such a context and some necessary public attention for these problems, as well as add to the context in which we perceive the economy and other layers of our lives. There is a clear need to place our picture of the economy within a context of other ecological and social trends, and vice versa.

All of the industrialised nation-states of the world, except the United States, have at least the beginnings of such a system of indicators for social data. The UK's is entitled *SOCIAL TRENDS*. France has *DONNÉES SOCIALES*. The Netherlands and Italy have *SOCIAAL EN CULTUREEL RAPPORT* and *SINTESI DELLA VITA SOCIALE ITALIANA* respectively (Miringoff, 1995). While the content, frequency and quality of such reports vary, they represent a commitment by those governments to periodically investigate the state of social health in their respective countries. The United States continues to track its economic indicators and leaves much of the social and environmental data collecting and reporting to individual researchers. When agencies like the Environmental Protection Agency or the Office of Health and Human Services publish their findings, they are not nearly as widely publicised, nor are their findings reported nearly as regularly as those of the Commerce Department or the Bureau of Labor Statistics.

Part of the gap in the U.S. data is being filled by the Fordham Institute for Innovation in Social Policy's Index of Social Health for the United States (Miringoff, 1995). The index summarises data on 16 component indicators chosen to represent social problems faced by people at various ages. The indicators are broken down into impacts on five age groups (children, youth, adults, the aged, and all ages) and include such information as statistics on infant mortality, the incidence of child abuse, unemployment, teen suicide, health care coverage and access to affordable housing. Looking at both these data and the economic data that is already collected on a regular basis, we might begin to observe many of the reasons why increases in Gross Domestic Product (GDP) do not always lead to an improved quality of life.

Many authors who have examined the issue have written extensively on the shortcomings of the GDP as a quality of life indicator.[2] Ekins and Max-Neef (1992) summarise three approaches towards finding an appropriate quality of life indicator: (1) adjustment of GDP to account for its shortcomings, to move it closer to an indicator of true welfare or perhaps of sustainable production; (2) another single index measure to replace GDP, for example the Index of Sustainable Economic Welfare, the Gross Progress Indicator, or the Physical Quality of Life index, as an indicator of development; (3) a framework of several indicators to replace the single index approach, for example the UNICEF Basic Indicators, or the set adopted by the Sustainable Seattle initiative. These approaches apply not only to

---

[2] See, for example, Daly and Cobb (1989), and Cobb et. al. (1995).

quality of life indicators but also to any indicator which seeks to look at a phenomenon with many components, for example a general indicator of 'environmental health'.

Each approach has it own set of advantages and shortcomings. While single-index measures are attractive for their conciseness, the amount of information reduction involved in getting to an aggregate indicator makes them too broad for some applications. These are also questionable when looked at from the hierarchy approach developed earlier. Reducing information about different hierarchies to a single aggregate hides key information which may be necessary to adequately address problems at various levels. Ekins and Max-Neef (1992) argue against using an aggregate index because the reduction of information often involves somewhat arbitrary assumptions, though they admit that these aggregates are useful for showing counter trends between GDP and a 'corrected' or new index.

A framework or set of more specific indicators, however, does not solve all the issues addressed with aggregate indices. Using a set may solve the problem of incommensurability but policy makers and researchers are now faced with the choice of which indicators to include. Often there are limits to the time and resources available for data collection and these must be balanced against the need for an adequate representation of the 'big picture'.

The challenge facing those trying to implement sustainability policies is to choose among these approaches and to find appropriate indicators for the phenomena they attempt to study.[3] There is a need to develop some criteria by which to judge indicators. There has been a recent explosion of literature on this topic and this treatment of it shall not be considered a final statement of what is most appropriate but a summary of some of the important issues raised.

As mentioned briefly above, when it comes to sustainability indicators, a tension often exists between the availability of data and the contextual framework in which the data should fit. This framework of indicators must incorporate ecological, social and ethical issues and information as well as economics. Methodologically, Ekins and Max-Neef (1992) argue that it is preferred to have:

---

[3] There are some cases in which some combination of the three approaches listed is possible, for example the United Nations Development Programme's Human Development Index which uses a combination of certain national statistics to develop an index of development and then ranks 175 countries by their HDI score. See, for example, articles on limits to the use of national income accounts as measures of welfare, for example Daly and Cobb, 1989. Typical arguments against this include the inclusion of defensive expenditures, or the exclusion of natural resource depletion (see, for example, Daly and Cobb, 1989, and Cobb et. al., 1995).

1.   an accurate framework with omissions rather than a wrong framework which appears complete but actually excludes important variables. With such a framework one can at least be aware of the omissions and can seek to allow for them and minimise them.

2.   a framework whose structure is accurate but which embodies imprecisions in its components rather than one which achieves detailed precision at the cost of structural distortions or omissions.

Several other authors have also suggested criteria for indicators of sustainable development. In order to be good indicators, they must be:

• applicable to scale;
• appropriate to their audience;
• appropriate to the layers of sustainability which they address;
• applicable to place/location.

Once again, a few examples may serve to illustrate the importance of these criteria.

Applicability to scale. Over the past decade, many organisations have been established on local, regional and global levels to attempt to define or operationalise the notion of sustainability. Each has recognised the importance of having some metric with which to gauge their progress. As discussed above, there are two main approaches to establishing such a metric: (1) broad single metric indicators such as the Gross Domestic Product, the ecological footprint concept (Wackernagel and Rees, 1996) or the Index of Sustainable Economic Welfare, and (2) indicator sets which seek to combine data on many phenomena. While broad indicators might be useful to track trends on a global or regional basis, they would hardly provide adequate information for efforts to achieve local sustainability. On the other hand, it would be a daunting task to create and gather information for an indicator set which would be applicable on a global scale. Even on a local basis, there is often trouble finding the time and resources to gather all the selected data.

Appropriateness for audience. An indicator or set of indicators should be tailored for those who will receive and use the information. While policymakers or planners might be in need of more technical information, the general public would likely appreciate a less technical approach.

Timeliness is another important issue for audience. While researchers or policy analysts might want the same level of technicality, they may be interested in different indicators based on the timeliness of the data or with respect to the information it provides. In particular, regulators who are going to periodically review policies might want a leading indicator which provides information as to what will happen in the future while others might be interested in coincidental indicators which focus on the current state of the world (see, in particular, Azar *et al.*, 1996, for a further discussion of indicator temporality).

Appropriateness for the layers of sustainability. In looking at indicator sets in particular, one would want to have a group of indicators which addresses all the layers of sustainability. For example, Sustainable Seattle's set includes five categories of indicators which address the Environment, Population and Resources, the Economy, Youth and Education, and Health and Community. This emphasises the importance of context which I discussed earlier. Aggregate indices may be applicable to only one layer of the hierarchy, or they may attempt to find a single indicator which merges information about all the layers.

Applicability to place/location. In looking at local sustainability, there may be measures specific to place which would serve to help identify how well the community is progressing in its efforts toward reaching its goals. An example of this, again from the Sustainable Seattle set, is the number of wild salmon returning to King's County each year to spawn. Biodiversity indicators especially, such as the presence or number of keystone species, should be applicable to place when considering local cases. Additionally, local and urban communities will likely need different metrics to gauge their success or failure.

CONCLUSION

With the explosion of literature surrounding the many aspects of the sustainability debate, it is easy to see why there seems to have been little progress in the way of operationalising the concept. Theoretical arguments and technical uncertainties continue to limit the progress we make. Political maneuvering on the part of all stakeholders and resistance to a widespread change in the way we think about the environment also plague even the most consistent and thorough efforts at implementation.

Eventually though, we must make the leap from debating sustainability to implementing strategies to move towards it. Although we are faced with an enormous amount of uncertainty, only through testing our theories will we find ways to truly make progress towards the goal. This is perhaps a grand experiment, but we can hardly afford to continue with the current experiment which looks at just how far we can push the earth's systems before we irrevocably ruin the planet. We need common sense efforts at making progress and we need to redefine what we consider to be real 'progress'. It must be measured considering all the layers of sustainability discussed above, not just economic layers.

Through local projects, we can attempt to pinpoint the conflicts between economic activity and social and environmental quality. There is much progress to be made by questioning the traditional tools of economic development which are based on a single-layer view of economic activity (for example, strengthening a region's export base or enticing large firms to relocate). It is time to re-examine the connections between environmental sustainability and people's livelihoods, so we may begin to forge new tools which allow us to monitor and care for all the layers.

REFERENCES

Arrow, K., Bolin, B, Costanza, R., Dasgupta, P., Folke, C., Holling, C.S., Jansson, B., Levin, S., Mäler, K., Perrings, C. and Pimentel, D. 1995. 'Economic Growth, Carrying Capacity, and the Environment.' *Science* 268, 520–521.

Azar, C., Holmberg, J. and Lindgren, K. 1996. 'Socio-ecological Indicators for Sustainability.' *Ecological Economics* 18, 89–112.

Barbier, E.B. 1987. 'The Concept of Sustainable Economic Development.' *Environmental Conservation* 14, 2, 101–110.

Bowers, J. 1995. 'Sustainability, Agriculture and Agricultural Policy.' *Environment and Planning* A, 27, 8, 1231–1243.

Bromley, D. 1998. 'Searching for Sustainability: The Poverty of Spontaneous Order.' *Ecological Economics* 24, 231–240.

Cobb, C., Halstead, T. and Rowe, J. 1995. 'If the GDP is Up, Why is America Down?' *The Atlantic Monthly* 276, 4, 59–78.

Cobb, John, Jr. 1998. 'The Threat to the Underclass.' In Dobkowski, M. and Walliman, I. (eds.) *The Coming Age of Scarcity: Preventing Mass Death and Genocide in the Twenty-first Century.* Syracuse: Syracuse University Press, 25–42.

Costanza, R., Segura, O. and Martinez-Alier, J. (eds.) 1996. *Getting Down to Earth: Practical Applications of Ecological Economics.* Washington D.C.: Island Press.

Daly, H. and Cobb, J., Jr. 1989. *For the Common Good.* Boston: Beacon Press.

Dasgupta, P. 1995. 'Population, Poverty, and the Local Environment.' *Scientific American* 272, 40–45.

Dobkowski, M. and Walliman, I. (eds.) 1998. *The Coming Age of Scarcity: Preventing Mass Death and Genocide in the Twenty-first Century.* Syracuse: Syracuse University Press.

Duchin, F. 1996. 'Ecological Economics: The Second Stage.' In Costanza, R., Segura, O. and Martinez-Alier, J. (eds.) 1996. *Getting Down to Earth: Practical Applications of Ecological Economics.* Washington D.C.: Island Press, 285–299.

Ekins, P. 1993. "Limits to Growth' and 'Sustainable Development:' Grappling with Ecological Realities.' *Ecological Economics* 8, 269–288.

Ekins, P. and Max-Neef, M. (eds.) 1992. *Real-life Economics: Understanding wealth creation.* New York: Routledge.

Goodland, R., Daly, H. and El Serafy, S. 1993. 'The Urgent Need for a Rapid Transition to Global Environmental Sustainability.' *Environmental Conservation* 20, 297–309.

Homer-Dixon, T. 1994. 'Environmental Scarcities and Violent Conflict: Evidence from Cases.' *International Security* 19, 1, 5–40.

Leavenworth, W.B. 1991. 'Roosevelt to Roosevelt: Foundations of American Environmentalism.' unpublished.

Lélé, S. 1991. 'Sustainable Development: A Critical Review.' *World Development* 19, 6, 607–21.

Lubchenco, J. 1998. 'Entering the Century of the Environment: A New Social Contract for Science.' *Science* 279, 491–497.

Meadows, D., Meadows, D., Randers, J. Behrens III, W. 1972. *The Limits to Growth.* New York: Universe Books.

Miringoff, M. 1995. 'Toward a National Standard of Social Health: The Need for Progress in Social Indicators.' *American Journal of Orthopsychiatry* 65, 4, 462–7.

O'Hara, S. 1995. 'Sustainability: Social and Ecological Dimensions.' *Review of Social Economy* 53, 4, 529–550.

O'Hara, S. 1998. 'Internalizing Economics: Sustainability Between Matter and Meaning.' forthcoming.

Organization for Economic Co-operation and Development 1993. 'OECD Core Set of Indicators for Environmental Program Reviews: A Synthesis Report by the Group on the State of the Environment.' *Environment Monographs* 83.

Pearce, D.W. and Atkinson, G.D. 1993. 'Capital Theory and the Measurement of Sustainable Development: An Indicator of Weak Sustainability.' *Ecological Economics* 8, 103–108.

Redclift, M. 1996. 'Sustainability and Sociology: Northern Preoccupations.' presented at the UNESCO Management of Social Transformations conference *Sustainability as a Concept for the Social Sciences.* Frankfurt, Germany, November 23–25, 1996.

Shafik, N. and Bandyopadhyay, S. 1992. 'Economic Growth and Environmental Quality: Time Series and Cross-Country Evidence.' *World Bank Working Paper Series* 904, June 1992.

Solow, R.M. 1992. *An Almost Practical Step Toward Sustainability.* Washington, D.C.: Resources for the Future.

Tisdell, C.A. 1991. *Economics of Environmental Conservation.* New York: Elsevier.

Wackernagel, M. and Rees, W. 1996. *Our Ecological Footprint*. Philadelphia: New Society Publishers.

World Commission on Environment and Development 1987. *Our Common Future*. Oxford: Oxford University Press.

3. What Type of Economic Theory Dealing with the Environment Do We Need?

Jan van der Straaten

INTRODUCTION

It can make sense, from a theoretical point of view, to investigate to what extent a certain economic theory dealing with environmental problems is 'true' or 'correct'. Many publications on that topic have appeared during the last decades. A debate has also been going on about the question whether environmental economics can describe and analyse environmental problems better than ecological economics; the type of instruments to be used in environmental policy has been disputed in many articles; and the controversy between weak and strong sustainability is still being discussed by many scientists and political scientists. In nearly all these cases, the debate has been on an abstract and theoretical level.

In this paper, we will follow different lines. We are of the opinion that the differences between scientists sketched above, are not in the first place caused by theoretical differences but by differences in perception and societal choice. This means that a debate along these lines, in general, cannot be very fruitful, as researchers are inclined, in that case, to continuously repeat the same type of arguments without being able to give full attention to the argument of others. It is the paradigmatic difference which counts. Therefore, other approaches may have more effect on the debate if they are based on the arguments related to environmental problems themselves. Therefore, the question we address in this paper is which type of theory can be useful to solve our environmental problems. We assume that there is some relationship between economic theory, on the one hand, and environmental policy on the other. Every policy with economic characteristics needs to be based on a certain economic theory. This is normal practice, for example, when employment policies, currency rate policies, and industrial policies are at stake. When we take as a starting-point that environmental problems are, in fact, economic problems, such a relationship also needs to be found.

Furthermore, we assume that there is a relationship between environmental policy on the one hand, and environmental problems on the other. Environmental policies can only have a certain meaning if the intention is to overcome certain well-defined environmental problems. It is within the realm of environmental policies that environmental problems have theoretical economic starting-points. It is from this confrontation that environmental policies result. As was stated earlier, we will follow the line from environmental problems via environmental policies to economic theories. By doing so, we can perhaps provide more insight into the relevance of current economic theories.

THEORETICAL INTERMEZZO

Before starting with the main current environmental problems, we will give a short overview of the economic relevance of environmental problems and policies. In traditional neoclassical economics, the standard criterion is that economic relevance is measured on the market. It is the revealed preference that counts, which finds its way on the market, resulting in a market price. It is this market price which is taken as a reflection of the demand for the good as well as that of the price of the production factors used in the production process. In this well-known neoclassical model, the market price is, in principle, always an optimal price, as this price guarantees an optimal use of production given consumers' demand.

Of course, this model has come in for various forms of criticism, even from traditional neoclassical economists, demonstrating that in many cases the outcome of this process cannot be an optimal situation. Pigou (1920/1952) used the concept of negative external effects to make it clear that the market price could not generate an optimal situation if significant environmental problems occur. In this view, environmental problems are negative side effects of the market process, which have to be corrected by the government by implementing a tax to be paid by the polluter. It has been demonstrated by many authors (among others Baumol and Oates, 1988; Dietz and Van der Straaten, 1992; Norgaard, 1984) that this approach is not appropriate in many cases, as environmental costs often cannot be calculated. It is mainly for that reason that the approach of the critical load was launched (Ciriacy Wantrup, 1963). Later on, this method was widely accepted, even in neoclassical circles (Baumol and Oates, 1988).

However, environmental economists of the neoclassical school hardly paid any attention to the immanent friction in this approach. In a neoclassical world, prices are the obvious signals for the economic process. In all elementary textbooks, three production factors are recognised, usually labour, capital and natural resources. Sometimes other names are used for the same concept, such as nature, environment, land, and so on, but in all cases, it is taken for granted that three production functions can be recognised: we cannot produce using only labour and capital. Natural resources are, in one way or another, a *conditio sine qua non* when we want to produce. Labour and capital have a price on the market, as do some natural resources, such as natural gas, iron ore, crude oil, and fertile land. However, many natural resources, such as clean water, a certain climate, and fresh air, do not have a price as such, which means that the use of these resources does not react to the 'normal' price signals. Then the question arises what the internal consistency of such a theoretical system can be. Is it possible to have, in the same theoretical system, production factors which have prices via the market process, and others that do not? And what could be the effect of having two types of economic goods in one theoretical framework? From many publications, one gets the impression that there are two options: one is the 'normal' Pigovian approach, and, when this is not possible, we use the critical-load concept. By doing so, all theoretical problems are solved. We have various instruments for different situations. We can, in principle, solve every environmental problem by using one of the two types of instruments. In this view, politicians need only to follow the advice of environmental economists.

On the other side, there is the reaction of ecological economists. They are, in general, fully aware of the shortcomings of this neoclassical approach; they argue that economic theory should integrate the ecological argument. Many proposals in this field have been articulated. Some of the ecological economists argue that critical loads should be the answer to environmental problems. This approach, however, does not differ from many neoclassical contributions. Others introduce concepts, such as Sustainable Development (World Commission on Environment and Development, 1987; Van den Bergh and Van der Straaten, 1997; Pearce *et al.*, 1990), Ecological Footprint (Wackernagel and Rees, 1996), Environmental Utilisation Space (Opschoor and Weterings, 1994), Plimsol Line (Daly and Cobb, 1989), Sustainable Indicators (Kuik and Verbruggen, 1993), etc. In all these cases, something is taken as an instrument that differs from a price impetus. The general presumption in all these cases is that we need a certain type of physical entity which can be put in opposition to price signals: against the 'incorrect' price signals, physical entities can correct the economic process. But again the crucial question is: can we have a theoretical framework with an internal consistency when in the system we have price signals as well other concepts?

Perhaps for that reason, some ecological economists prefer to work on the other side of the spectrum. They argue, for example, that the calculation of the Gross Domestic Product (GDP) should be corrected, as in the current calculation environmental costs are neglected and sometimes even booked as final consumption (Hueting, 1991; Repetto *et al.*, 1989). Therefore, we should reduce the level of the GDP to a green one. By doing so, the wrong results of the traditional practice will be corrected and we have a green GDP. However, on further analysis, this option is not so different from the concepts mentioned previously. When we correct the calculation of the GDP, we need to have certain safe standards and sustainable indicators, which can be used as reference points in the calculation. In this case we use the physical indicators as instruments to correct the price signal. Therefore, we have here the same question regarding the internal consistency of these approaches.

Another line of reasoning is the use of the contingent valuation method (CVM).[1] This approach differs, in principle, from the previous concepts, as the method aims to construct 'new' prices for environmental issues. People are asked, in a pseudo-market situation, what they are willing to pay to protect nature and the environment in one way or another. We cannot discuss all the pitfalls and barriers of this method; they are sufficiently discussed in the existing literature. We only want to underline that this method takes another line of approach than all the previous ones. The intention is to put forward new prices, which results in a situation in which all economic goods have a price. The use of labour, capital and priced natural resources are calculated using market prices, while the unpriced natural resources are priced by a CVM. By doing so, the internal consistency is strengthened: we have only price signals as relevant instruments, and additionally, it is again only revealed preference that counts, as in a CVM the revealed preference – resulting from a questionnaire – is taken as fact. In this case, the crucial question is whether we have restored a real internal consistency in the theoretical framework. Are the prices resulting from the market operation the 'same' as those resulting from the CVM? When this is the case, we have a real internal consistency.

Summarising, we may conclude that in an ecological-economic approach, the crucial question is what the meaning of a theoretical system can be when we have different measures indicating economic scarcity: one is realised by the market in market prices, the other is derived from physical standards and entities. Can such a system work in reality when no explicit attention is paid to the possible friction in these systems?

ENVIRONMENTAL PROBLEMS

Some Further Theoretical Considerations

There are many terms used to indicate the 'third' production factor. Some of them have only a semantic meaning, but others do not. Regarding our starting-point – the relevance of economic theories – the division between nature and the environment is very relevant. In many publications, these terms and concepts are

---

[1] There exists a wealth of literature dealing with CVM. In the last decade, this method has been propagated by environmental as well as ecological economists. For an overview, see Hanley and Spash, 1993; Navrud, 1992; Hoevenagel, 1994.

used as if they are similar, which is not the case. Nature deals with the biotic part of the ecosystem whereas the environment refers to the abiotic part. This implies that a forest as such is nature, while its destruction by acid rain is an environmental phenomenon due to acid particulars (the abiotic part). However, for the tourist and the ecologist it does not make any difference whether the forest is cut down by paper mill companies or ruined by acid precipitation. In both cases the forest is gone. Therefore it is understandable that many authors do not make sharp distinctions between the two concepts.

However, from the point of view of economic theory, these differences are relevant. In general, the analysis of environmental problems is easier, as in the case of nature. It is relatively easier to relate environmental problems, such as water pollution and air pollution, to a cost structure than nature as such. Though many substantial problems can be recognised, one cannot overlook the fact that, for example, air pollution results in higher costs in many production processes, so that these costs can, in principle, be calculated. If this is not the case, it is possible to introduce a safe standard or a critical load, as has been done in the case of acid rain and the pollution of the river Rhine.

However, what are the costs of the declining quantity and quality of nature? They can hardly ever be connected with cost structures in production processes. What is the economic value of significant ecosystems which are not used in production systems, such as the mountain tops of the Alps, the Rocky Mountains, or the raptors of Spain? There is no trade in these ecosystems and no monetary costs can be recognised in production processes when these ecosystems are deteriorating. Furthermore, it is not possible to arrive at indisputable safe standards. How much of the Brazilian rain forests or of the Mediterranean wetlands should be protected and maintained in a sound ecological condition? Nobody is able to give a clear answer to these questions. This implies that the economic characteristics of nature problems differ considerably from environmental problems. They behave differently as regards the internal consistency we have discussed previously. Generally speaking, environmental problems can cope more easily with the demand for internal consistency than nature problems. This, as will be demonstrated later on, has serious effects on the protection of nature.

Concrete Environmental Problems

From official reports, such as the UNEP Environmental Data Report (GEMS, 1991), Europe's Environment, The Dobríš Assessment (Stanners and Bourdeau, 1995), and Environment in the European Union 1995 (Wieringa, 1995), the conclusion can be drawn that the condition of the environment is still deteriorating in many parts of the world. Indeed, in some cases environmental policies did have substantial positive effects, such as the collection of garbage, the quality of the Rhine and Thames rivers, the level of air pollution. However, many parts of the environment are suffering from significant threats. In this respect, negative developments still are: the ongoing rise in the use of fossil energy; the effects of intensive agriculture on the quality of soil, surface water, ground water due to the emissions of acidifying substances, the use of pesticides and high amounts of fertiliser; the increasing demand made by traffic, accompanied by an increase in the emission of greenhouse gasses. Policies have not been able to curb these pressures on the environment.

Concrete Nature Problems

Higher emissions of substances alien to the ecosystem have negative effects on the quality of nature. Environmental pollution increases the pressure on ecosystems; in particular, vulnerable ecosystems such as peatbogs, mountains, and coasts can be severely affected by these phenomena. However, there are many other ways to reduce the quantity and quality of ecosystems. The most significant of these are:

- An increase in the intensity with which soils are used for agricultural purposes. This intensification process is often accompanied by a range of factors, such as increasing the size of the parcels, the lowering of the water table, a decrease in the number of hedges, groups of trees, and extensively used land, a reduction in the number of pools and agricultural paths, restructuring of the regimes of brooks, rivers and ground water streams, a shift in the direction of more intensive crops, regional specialisation in types of crops, and so on. On the other hand, this intensification process is often accompanied by an extensification of agriculture in certain parts of the region. In many mountain valleys, for example, an intensification of the bottom of the valley can be observed, while at the same time the use of the slopes is extensified. This means that, in many cases, the traditional agricultural practices on these slopes are no longer continued. As these traditional agricultural activities resulted in high levels of biodiversity, the restriction of this use is detrimental to nature. Summarising, one may conclude that the typical ecological framework of traditional agriculture, leading to high levels of biodiversity, are more and more being eroded by the introduction of increasingly modern types of agriculture.
- Industrialisation and the concentration of economic activities in the existing centres of economic activities, have had a negative effect on the quantity and quality of many coastal wetlands and deltas, such as the Camarque, the Rhine Delta, many Mediterranean wetlands, the Danube Delta, and so on.
- This process of concentrating economic activities in the core regions, requires the expansion of the infrastructure. The expansion of airports, harbours, main roads, trading facilities, and parking places needs space which has often had a high nature value. These core regions need to be

connected again, which means that new infrastructure will be constructed. The fragmentation of many ecosystems and habitats is the result of this process.

- Though the impact of tourism on nature is, in most cases, quite low, the effect of the infrastructure is often significant. This is particularly valid in the case of ribbon development along coasts and beaches. Skiing in the mountains often results in building transport facilities above the tree line, which implies that these areas are not attractive to visitors in the summer season.

Surprisingly, information regarding the quantity and quality of nature is often lacking in the official documents. It is conservationist groups like WWF, Greenpeace, and national conservation organisations which inform the general public. For example, in the Report Europe's Environment, the Dobríš Assessment of the European Union (Stanners and Bourdeau, 1995), only a few chapters give information regarding nature, while the environment is given a high profile.

THE UNDERLYING CAUSES OF THE DECLINE OF NATURE AND THE ENVIRONMENT

One cannot argue that the decline in quality and quantity of nature and the environment is caused by a lack of laws and initiatives of national and international authorities. For many decades now, all Western and former East block countries have had significant protection levels with respect to nature and the environment. However, generally speaking, these laws and initiatives are not fully equipped to neutralise all the negative effects. What are the reasons for this?

It is not possible to investigate all the effects of all the policies on all emissions in all countries. Therefore, we restrict ourselves to the analysis of European acid rain policy, which is important for nature as well as the environment. This analysis can provide insight into the complexity of the international policies in this field.

The damage caused by acid rain includes:

Acidification of Lakes

In particular those lakes which are located in regions where soils do not contain alkaline components. In that case, acid rain can easily mobilise heavy metals in the soils. In spring, when snow layers which are contaminated with acid substances melt, these heavy metals are washed out into little streams and lakes.

Fish such as salmon and trout spawn at this time of year; they are heavily affected by this influx of heavy metals. Other animals and plants in the lakes are affected when acidity in the lakes surpasses certain levels. The end result of this acidification process is that living organisms are no longer found in these lakes. Many lakes in Southern Scandinavia hardly contain any living organisms.

The Effect on Forests

Forests are affected in two different ways. In the first place, the acid precipitation changes the acidity of the soil. When the soil has a high percentage of alkaline components, this acidification can be neutralised fairly easily. This is not the case in vast parts of the Alps, the mountain ranges of Central Europe and the Scandinavian region. In these soils, the micorrhizas which are vital to the functioning of the roots of trees, are damaged by an increase in acidity. The result is that trees can no longer obtain the necessary nutrients.

Even when alkaline soils are abundant, trees can be affected by the influence of the acidity on their needles and leaves. This damage negatively influences the use of carbon dioxide and oxygen from the air, both of which are needed for growth.

In most cases, it is not acid rain which kills the trees. Acid rain will make trees more vulnerable to various types of diseases and insects. Owing to acid rain, trees cannot cope with many otherwise normal environmental influences. The result is that trees die on a massive scale as has occurred in the Schwarzwald and the Harz in Germany, in many parts of the Northern and Central Alps, and the forests of Slovakia, Poland and East Germany.

Public Health

Air pollution will have a negative effect on the respiratory organs of people living in areas affected by it. In Western Europe, air pollution from industries located in the neighbourhood of residential areas has been diminished since the 1960s. However, in many areas in Central and Eastern Europe, where traditional industries are still discharging high levels of emissions in the vicinity of residential areas, the negative influence on people's health can be demonstrated.

Monuments

Acid rain affects the surfaces of monuments such as old churches, houses, statues and bridges. In particular, in areas where a type of stone which is extremely vulnerable to acidity was used in construction, as in Vienna, the negative effects are considerable.

Nature Reserves

As was argued previously, acidity affects the functioning of the soil. In nature reserves a correct functioning of the soil is important. Additionally, nature reserves receive a high level of nutrients from acid rain. Nitrogen oxides contain nitrogen, which is a nutrient for all types of vegetation. In particular, in nature reserves where the level of the nutrients is normally low, this influx of nutrients will ruin their ecological value.

Ground Water Bodies

It is nitrogen oxide which can increase the nitrogen content of ground water bodies to a level which is dangerous to public health. In particular, in regions in which traffic and intensive cattle breeding are mainly responsible for acid rain, this threat is serious. In the Netherlands, for example, an increasing number of wells used for drinking water purposes have recently been closed due to unacceptable levels of nitrogen.

Agricultural Crops

Acid rain affects the crops of vegetables. It is, in particular, acidity which is responsible for this problem. It has been demonstrated that in many parts of Europe this influence on crops is considerable.

One of the most important causes of acid rain is the emission of large quantities of sulphur dioxide. Some 20 years ago, the first measures were taken in European industrial areas to reduce the harmful effects of sulphur dioxide on public health. These measures included the increased use of natural gas and nuclear energy and, in particular, the construction of tall chimneys. It seemed that adequate measures had been taken, because air pollution in urban and industrial areas did decrease. However, the tall chimneys only dispersed the acidifying substances over large parts of Europe. Acid deposition beyond industrial areas increased rapidly, affecting forests in particular, in Central Europe and Scandinavia. The acidification of ecosystems was probably foreseeable. Biologists warned at an early stage that tall chimneys would at best shift the problem to elsewhere. Society, however, could easily dismiss these warnings as exaggerations, because it was not known for certain what the effects on nature would be.

If the effects of so many interventions in, and influences on, nature are not sufficiently known or are consistently disregarded, the optimum use of natural resources for human production and consumption, presupposed by neoclassical analyses and policy recommendations becomes a problem. The point is that neoclassical optimisation requires insight into the effects of alternative behaviour towards nature with a probability bordering on certainty, or at least with a probability that can be calculated using the theory of probabilities. The former is the familiar assumption of the existence of fully-informed agents, which simply neglects the problem of inadequate ecological knowledge.

In general, processes in nature, and, hence, human interventions in these processes, appear to be extremely difficult to predict for at least three reasons. First, synergetic effects increase the impact of separate emissions on the environment. For example, laboratory experiments have made clear that the combined impact of the acidifying substances SO_2, NO_x, NH_3, and O_3 on plant growth is substantially more significant than the linear total would be of the impacts of each of these substances separately (Tonneijk, 1981). Second, thresholds are very common in ecosystems. Again acidification serves as an excellent example. The sudden acceleration of the deterioration of forests and the subsequent dying off of large tracts of European forest in the early 1980s for most people came like a bolt from the blue. It appeared that the buffering capacity of the soil had protected trees from serious damage for decades. Once a saturation point had been reached, acidifying substances could damage trees considerably and kill them within a couple of years. Third, many emissions have a delayed effect on the environment. It takes decades, for example, before the nitrogen from manure and chemical fertilisers is washed from the top soil into deeper layers, causing severe nitrate pollution of the ground water, which in most countries serves as drinking water. Even if nitrogen leakages into the ground water could be stopped, nitrate pollution of ground water would still continue to increase considerably well into the next century.

In short, thresholds, synergetic effects and delayed reactions cloud the issue of the relations between emissions and the deterioration of nature. It must be concluded that, as a result of human actions, ecosystems can change far more capriciously than economists normally assume. The neoclassical approach to optimising the use of the natural resources available is senseless as long as the quantity of the natural resources available cannot be accurately assessed. In other words, we cannot optimise our ecological utilisation space without knowing the concrete limits that must not be crossed if irreversible effects on nature are to be avoided. The construction and the recent implementation of the RAINS model which describes the relationship between emission levels, depositions, and cost and benefits of abatement policies (Alcamo *et al.*, 1990) made it possible to solve the main part of these problems.

In many cases, it is argued that environmental measures should not be taken at present, as not all cause–effect relations are known in detail. When not all effects are clear, the implementation of environmental measures may prove counterproductive in the future, when new facts and relations will be known. In nearly all cases, these arguments are used by those groups or sectors in society which reap the benefits of the present environmental pollution.

These problems are, on the one hand, connected to the field of environmental issues. On the other hand, one should not fail to see that the implementation of instruments which aim to reach a certain well-defined economic target is always difficult in the context of a policy. For instance, an increase in the exchange rate of a certain currency is always surrounded by numerous pros and cons argued by different economic actors. In addition, the effect of the implementation of a certain economic instrument cannot be predicted with absolute certainty. This implies that all economic policy is accompanied by some degree of uncertainty. This uncertainty is always given full attention by economic agents who benefit or suffer from the measures to be taken.

However, environmental issues are accompanied by more complexity. Firstly, there is the still widely accepted idea that environmental problems are not real economic problems. In this view, economic issues always deal with problems connected with market transactions in one way or another, and economic problems are reduced to problems of labour and capital. In this approach, there is no recognition whatsoever of the fact that modern environmental problems are closely connected with the market process. Although, for instance, the economic losses to the natural assets of countries such as Switzerland, Sweden, Austria, the Netherlands, and Germany caused by acid rain, are difficult to calculate, it is clear that the economies of these countries suffer losses of many billions of dollars. The same type of argument can be used when discussing measures to reduce the greenhouse effect, deforestation, the use of pesticides, the pollution of rivers, seas and oceans, nuclear pollution, and so on. These environmental phenomena are accompanied by high costs. This is the reason why environmental policy will result in substantial benefits. Nevertheless, the prevalent opinion in the economic literature and in the public debate is that we have 'the economy' on one side, and the environment on the other. In this view, the implementation of strict environmental standards or norms will hurt the economy. It is this type of uncertainty and the traditional economic arguments which are used primarily by economic vested interests to neutralise the implementation of instruments in environmental policy. If this way of reasoning is dominant, it is difficult to bring environmental problems to the centre of the public debate. This is, in particular, the case when traditional economic problems such as unemployment are relevant. The public debate will then be concentrated on these issues.

When measures are proposed, this can result in a certain reduction of the emissions in polluting sectors. However, it is not clear in advance that all sectors will reduce their emissions by an equal percentage. Some sectors will have better access to the centres of decision making. Hence, they will be better able to articulate their interests when decisions are made. This is, in particular, true when international bargaining processes take place. When a polluting industry in a certain country has in the past been able to build up a comfortable competitive position by discharging polluting substances in the air free of charge, such an industry will put pressure on the national authorities in order not to lose this position.

The argument of scientific uncertainty is a very effective instrument in the hands of the polluting sectors. As soon as they are confronted with calculations about the monetary costs resulting from pollution, these calculations are always weaker than the costs of the environmental measures to be taken in the polluting industries. Against the 'weak' calculations of environmental groups or the Ministry of the Environment the vested economic interests bring forward the 'strong' calculations of the costs which should be taken when strict environmental norms would be implemented.

Furthermore, when authorities prefer not to publish calculations of environmental costs, they often articulate the option of critical loads. This also brings the polluting sectors into a comfortable position. These strict norms are always based on certain investigations in the ecosystems. The results of these research projects are nearly always accompanied by a host of scientific uncertainties. And what is the level of ecological damage which can confidently be accepted without any danger in the future? These questions cannot be answered in a clear way. This means that polluting industries have many opportunities to nullify the arguments to accept a certain ecological standard.

Regarding nature, the position of polluting industries is relatively easy, as nobody can define which level of ecosystem we really need. How many wetlands should be conserved? And what about small-scale agricultural landscapes with a high level of biodiversity in Italy, Greece, and Spain? To what extent must they be preserved? There are no costs and benefits of nature protection as in the case of environmental protection.

AGAIN, WHAT TYPE OF THEORY DO WE NEED?

From the previous discussion some conclusions can be drawn regarding the theoretical starting points. To mention the most important ones:

1.   In principle, the problem of the unpriced scarcity of the environment and, in particular, nature, cannot be solved within the context of the 'normal' economic paradigms. Ecological economics and environmental economics have here more or less the same position. There is a difference in awareness of the problem; most ecological economists know what the shortcomings are, while most environmental economists believe that an optimal allocation of production factors can be reached.

       This brings us to the point that it is better to accept the immanent shortcomings of economic theories when nature and the environment are at stake. It makes more sense to discuss the opportunities for economists to contribute to a solution of the societal environmental problems. Such an approach puts economic science in a complete other position. Economic science is then no longer a theory outside the societal reality which can provide solutions for societal problems, but economic science tries to investigate which type of environmental problems occur and to what extent it can help to improve the environmental quality.

One could argue that this will give the opportunity to mix science with subjective opinions regarding what should be done with nature and the environment. In principle, this in true, but when economists will stay at the current quite well-accepted starting points, they have to be aware that this theory will lose all predictive power. With the help of economic theories and instruments, they cannot give clear answers to societal questions. They can, however, help and facilitate the discussion and solution of societal environmental problems. That is a complete other starting-point for economists.

2. This does not mean that calculations of costs and benefits of environmental policies do not make sense. On the contrary, as in many cases, economists can calculate the extremely high costs of ground water pollution, dying off of forests due to acid rain, nuclear pollution, and the effects of air pollution on health. By doing so, they can make it clear that a neglect of the damage to nature and the environment will result in high future societal costs.

    Economists can stress the point that high levels of societal costs are currently shifted away to future generations or other countries. We have to maintain the nature capital, this is a normal economic practice. The discussion on weak and strong sustainability contributes to these issues, as is the case with the discussion on greening the National Account. However, in principle, nobody knows what in reality a green BNP is, as we are not able to calculate *all* environmental costs. So, we do not know whether or not a green BNP is in reality a green BNP. Again, it is better to accept the shortcomings of our economic theoretical system than to go on with sub-optimal ideas from which we do not know the real shortcomings.

3. In particular in the case of the value of nature, calculations demonstrating the significance of nature for tourism, recreational opportunities, and calculations on the quality of housing and dwelling areas can provide helpful insight into the societal economic value of nature. Of course, CVM can provide more insight to the levels of willingness to pay. However, the outcome of these investigations will always be regarded as the outcome of a pseudo-market approach, which do not have the same power as the arguments from the market. CVM can help to underline the economic value of nature.

4. Perhaps the most important theoretical point is the acceptance of the fact that economics is a societal science. As we learned from the previous discussion, polluting sectors often use the shortcomings of the theoretical framework to nullify or to attack the implementation of strict norms. Furthermore, they often stress their significance on the outcome of the economic process. Polluting sectors such as intensive agriculture in the

Netherlands, and motorcar industries in Germany, France, Italy and Great Britain put pressure on their governments using the arguments of export benefits and their contribution to employment. In most cases, these polluting sectors have built up a better position in the state machinery than environmental pressure groups.

The previous arguments bring us to the conclusion that nature and the environment are, just as many other topics, a normal part of political controversy. Theoretical principles, starting-points and instruments which are often seen as objective, are, in fact, a part of the political debate. Therefore, economists dealing with nature and the environment should not neglect this political component. Their arguments are always value-loaded, in particular when they do not prefer that. It is the vested economic interests who are perfectly able to use the weakness of all economic concepts to their own benefit, which is in most cases not the benefit of society.

Finalising, it has to be underlined that a theoretical economic framework is always a part of society. In that case, it is better to investigate to what extent theoretical concepts can contribute to a better environmental policy and better results of existing environmental policies, than to discuss the question of which theoretical starting-point is better than others from a theoretical point of view.

REFERENCES

Alcamo, J.R.S. and Hordijk, L. (eds.) 1990. *The RAINS Model of Acidification.* Dordrecht: Kluwer Academic Publishers.

Baumol, W.J. and Oates, W.E. 1988. *The Theory of Environmental Policy.* Cambridge: Cambridge University Press.

Bergh, van den C.J.M. and van der Straaten, J. (eds.) 1997. *Economy and Ecosystems in Change; Analytical and Historical Approaches.* Cheltenham: Edward Elgar.

Ciriacy Wantrup, S.V. 1963. *Resource Conservation: Economies and Policies.* Berkeley: University of California Division of Agricultural Science.

Daly, H.E. and Cobb, J.B. Jr. 1989. *For the Common Good: Redirecting the Economy toward Community, the Environment, and a Sustainable Future.* Boston: Beacon Press.

Dietz, F.J. and van der Straaten, J. 1992. 'Rethinking environmental economics: Missing links between economic theory and environmental policy.' *Journal of Economic Issues* 26, 27–51.

GEMS Monitoring and Assessment Research Centre, London, 1991. *Environmental Data Report.* Oxford: Basil Blackwell.

Hanley, N. and Spash, C. 1993. *Cost-Benefit Analysis and the Environment.* Aldershot: Edward Elgar.

Hoevenagel, R. 1994. *The Contingent Valuation Method: Scope and Validity.* Amsterdam: Free University.

Hueting, R. 1991. 'Correcting National Income for Environmental Losses; a Practical Solution for a Theoretical Dilemma.' In Costanza, R. (ed.) *Ecological Economics: The Science and Management of Sustainability.* New York: Columbia University Press, 194–213.

Kuik, O. and Verbruggen, H. 1993. *In Search of Sustainable Indicators.* Dordrecht: Kluwer Academic Publishers.

Navrud, S. (ed.) 1992. *Pricing the European Environment.* Oslo: Scandinavian University Press.

Norgaard, R.B. 1984. 'Coevolutionary Development Potential.' *Land Economics* 60, 160–173.

Opschoor, J.B. and Weterings, R. 1994. 'Environmental utilisation space: an introduction.' *Milieu* 5, 198–205.

Pearce, D.W., Barbier, E.B. and Markandya, A. 1990. *Sustainable Development.* London: Earthscan.

Pigou, A.C., 1920/1952. *The Economics of Welfare.* London: Macmillan.

Repetto, R., Magrath, W., Wells, M. Beer, C. and Rosini, F. 1989. *Wasting Assets: Natural Resources in the National Income Accounts.* Washington, D.C.: World Resources Institute.

Stanners D. and Bourdeau, P. (eds.) 1995. *Europe's Environment, The Dobriš Assessment.* Copenhagen: European Environment Agency.

Tonneijk, A.E.G. 1981. *Research on the Influence of Different Air Pollutants Separately and in Combination in Agriculture, Horticulture and Forestry Crops.* Wageningen: IPE Report No. R 262.

Wackernagel, M. and Rees, W. 1996. *Our Ecological Footprint.* Washington: New Society Publishers.

Wieringa, K. (ed.) 1995. *Environment in the European Union.* Copenhagen: European Environment Agency.

World Commission on Environment and Development 1987. *Our Common Future.* Oxford: Oxford University Press.

4. Principles for Sustainability: Protection, Investment, Co-operation, and Innovation

Thomas Sikor and Richard B. Norgaard[1]

INTRODUCTION

'Managing Sustainability,' the theme of the conference leading to this book, suggests that sustainability is a matter of implementation. If we had an 'objective' definition of sustainability agreed to and understood by all, we could employ technology, institutions, and moral appeals to 'manage sustainability.' Technologists could design environmentally benign technologies. Institutionalists could change rights and obligations so that people face the right incentives. Moralists could appeal to people's collective sense of moral responsibility to behave in the right way. The literature on sustainability broadly reflects these technological, institutional, and moral emphases.

There is considerable frustration, however, that the technological, institutional, and moral approaches largely remain inoperable because the presumption of an 'objective' definition of the goal of sustainability has not been met. Sustainability cannot be determined objectively because defining sustainability involves value judgements with respect to which qualities of which resources should be sustained by which means, as well as for and by whom. Differences in human values make people's answers to these questions, and hence their definitions of sustainability, differ. In addition, social contexts shape our different understandings of the environment. Even scientific characterisations of qualities and the relationships between them depend upon historical and social factors. We can therefore not presuppose an 'objective' definition of sustainability. Thus the challenge of sustainability

[1] Our work has been supported by a grant from the World Environment and Resources Program of the John D. and Catherine T. Mac Arthur Foundation. We gratefully acknowledge comments by Dara O'Rourke and Katja Schumacher.

cannot be to define and implement *the* sustainable world, Germany, or Berkeley.

The challenge of sustainability is to develop social processes that integrate diverse views of sustainability and create sufficient opportunities to satisfy future demands on resources. The conditions of all natural and environmental resources have strongly been influenced by how people's values and understanding have affected how they have interacted with natural processes in the past. And this will continue to be so in the future. Sustainability therefore rests on the contextual social processes that modify, conserve, augment, and replace qualities of resources.

This chapter begins with a critique of attempts to define sustainability objectively. We briefly summarise a series of articles initiated by Norgaard, in which he explores an emerging environmental epistemology that is transforming how we think about science and practice. In the main part we discuss the principles of sustainability through four empirical cases from our work in Vietnam and Latin America. We conclude with a brief summary of our argument and its implications for the role of external expertise in achieving sustainability.

SUSTAINABILITY QUESTIONS, SUBJECTIVITY, AND SOCIAL CONTEXT

If we had an objective definition of sustainability, then we could devise technologies, change people's rights and obligations, or appeal to people's collective sense of moral responsibility to implement sustainability. Ecologists, economists, and others concerned with sustainability usually propose technological, institutional, and moral approaches or a combination of them. Nearly all bemoan in common, however, that we still must *scientifically* define the goal of sustainability so that one preferred path or the other can be identified and taken. Thus, at one international conference after another, there have been clarion calls for sustainability to be defined. For example, scientists have been called upon to:

> agree on a *scientific* definition of biophysical sustainability ...
> [and] to recommend ... a *scientifically sound* and practical
> index of biophysical sustainability... the ecological equivalent
> of the Gross National Product ... [that] reflect[s]... net primary
> productivity, biological diversity and perhaps other factor (De
> Souza 1992, emphasis ours).

The technological, institutional and moral approaches assume that we can define sustainability objectively. By objectively, we mean that the knowledge of what sustainability is, exists as some truth apart from society. Of course, this does not mean that people and their behaviour do not figure prominently in the definition of sustainability. Rather, by apart from society, we mean that the answer to 'what is sustainability?' is 'out there,' available to be discovered. Also, as the answers have been believed to exist as some truth apart from society, we have traditionally thought of science as an individual process. The important point is that, in the conventional understanding, the answer we strive for: (1) exists apart from the process of the implementation of the answer, and (2) its discovery does not depend on the social context of the individual or the social processes of the research groups.

In the dominant, Western view of science, the definition of sustainability is free from history and culture. Only implementation must be adjusted for cultural differences, and even this concession to history and culture is only being won after a century of development disasters. This 'apartness,' 'separability,' or 'existence out there' is the essence of objective knowledge, a key premise of Western science. It is this premise that underlies the Western tradition of keeping science separate from the implementation of scientific knowledge. And it is this premise that some of us are now convinced has become an obstacle to both understanding and achieving sustainability.

Within the broad search for sustainability and the means for implementing it, a significant number of theorists and practitioners are emerging who are developing different approaches to how they think about science and social change. This emergence is occurring on many fronts in diverse and complementary ways. In agricultural development, it is participatory research. In philosophy, it comes, in part, from the realisation that what we understand of reality is intimately tied to the history of how we have used words in the past and hence our understandings in the past. In ecology, we have theorists who argue that learning about ecology and managing ecosystems must be a mutual, on-going, process of adaptive environmental management (Walters, 1986).

Few of the new scientists–implementers are particularly conscious of how the transition they are making complements the procedural adjustments being made by others. But in each case, the different approach entails a shift from thinking about knowledge as consisting of true statements to which our behaviour must conform to thinking about knowing and conforming as an interactive social process. The premise that knowledge can be objective or apart from the social processes of implementation is being dropped. Rather, learning and implementing are merging in creative ways.

The second author of this chapter has explored how our growing awareness of systems and complexity, new developments in the philosophy of knowledge, and increasing concern with the cultural and ecological sustainability of development are merging into an environmental epistemology that is transforming how we think about science and practice.

In 'The Case for Methodological Pluralism', Norgaard (1989) argued that since interactions between economic and ecological systems are clearly complex and since every method of understanding is a simplification of reality, then multiple methods should be maintained as we develop the field of ecological economics. Fortunately ecology and economics already have multiple frames of analysis, each with different strengths and weaknesses depending on what they emphasise and what they leave out. Ecological economics should be a search for the methods from the existing fields that are compatible, a search for new methods emphasising the phenomena existing frameworks ignored, and a broad discourse between the participants sharing insights between their respective findings. The resulting collective understanding is different from an aggregate of information presented in the individual papers they prepare for journals. Indeed, no such aggregate can be derived for the knowledge from the separate models are built around incongruous assumptions and patterns of relationships.

In 'Environmental Science as a Social Process', Norgaard (1992) develops the cosmological and epistemological arguments for why understanding environmental systems must be a collective learning process between scientists with different specialities. That paper further emphasises that the resulting scientific knowledge is the collective understanding of the group. We fall short of adequate collective understanding and fail to use what we have, however, because now historic, modern assumptions about the nature of reality, as well as about the nature of knowledge and knowing, impede the collective learning and application process. Disciplines themselves are an outgrowth of our assumption of atomism, that the parts of systems can be understood apart from the system, and assumption of monism, that our knowledge of the separate parts of systems will aggregate into a single, coherent understanding of the system as a whole. Together, these assumptions justify individual efforts and the accumulation of disciplinary findings in journals rather than a discursive shared-learning approach. These and other assumptions prevent us from gaining and implementing an understanding of complex social and environmental problems.

In 'Sustainability and the Scientist's Burden', Lélé and Norgaard (1996) document why scientific knowledge is never apart from values and hence why scientists need to work with local people when contemplating how sustainability might be achieved. The argument here shows how sustainability policies derived from frameworks which gave little emphasis to particular phenomena necessarily gave little value to those phenomena. The problem is not simply that the values of biologists lead them to pick particular biological models and the values of economists lead them to pick particular economic models and that these models then emphasise different things. The problem is also that the models of Western biologists and economists may give scant attention to what are critical ecological and economic variables given the behaviour and values of the local people. The 'objective' information derived from the scientists' models may be absolutely correct from a modern scientific perspective, but it will also quite likely be irrelevant or erroneous from the local perspective, from the perspective of the people whose actions may or may not need to change to promote sustainability. Thus framework selection, modelling, data collection, and parameter estimation need to be undertaken in collaboration with the people whose ecosystems and livelihoods are being modelled.

While the community of scholars and practitioners addressing sustainability issues have increasingly recognised the subjectivity and social embeddedness of our knowledge, these ideas are by no means well understood. Further, the community has expanded rapidly over the past two decades by an infusion of natural scientists seeking to promote sustainable development, tipping the cosmological and epistemological consciousness back to where it was at the beginning of the 'green revolution.' Thus the technological, institutional, and moral prescriptions are still the predominant approaches taken in the attempt to achieve sustainability.

PRINCIPLES FOR SUSTAINABILITY

In contrast to the technological, institutional, and moral approaches, we argue for an approach that recognises sustainability as an on-going outcome of appropriate social processes. Clearly, what are 'appropriate' processes can only be judged by the quality of the outcome, so we have not got around the definition problem. But we do think it is important to shift the emphasis from the goal of sustainability defined *a priori,* and that is presented as timeless and universal across people, to the conditions under which appropriate goals can be constantly assessed and worked toward by the people involved. Sustainability results from social processes that integrate diverse perspectives of sustainability and create sufficient opportunities to satisfy future demands on the resource. Following Romm (1993), the following four general principles seem to be necessary for sustainability:

- protection of resource users from large-scale forces which discourage or prevent them from improving resource qualities,
- investment for future resource opportunities,
- co-operation among diverse interests, and,
- innovation.[2]

---

[2] Romm (1993) develops five elements of sustainable forestry, including the four used here. His

For example, take a hypothetical forest where the logging industry, environmentalists, and local communities have different visions of the desirable qualities of the forest. The industry's interests focus on exploiting the value of the standing timber in a way that yields optimal profits as represented by net present values. Environmentalists emphasise the qualities of the forest that make it a habitat of a diversity of biological species and a place of recreation for visitors from urban areas. The concerns of local communities are centred around the effects of the forest on community development, emphasising the generation of a sustained stream of revenues, employment, and other benefits, such as watershed protection. Forestry is then the regime of actions by which the different actors modify the forest. Sustainable forestry demands the protection of the industry, environmentalists, and local communities from large-scale forces, which prevent or discourage them from improving desirable forest qualities. For example, a national policy of high interest rates increases pressures for large-scale cutting in the presence of strong demands for wood. Investment, such as afforestation, preserves the desired qualities of the forest and creates opportunities to satisfy future demands on the forest. Co-operation among industry, environmentalists, and communities, for example through forest management advisory boards, facilitates accommodating and satisfying diverse interests in the forest. Innovation creates new technical and institutional options to protect logging industry, environmentalists, and local communities from detrimental large-scale forces, to preserve and enlarge forest resources for future demands, and balance the different interests in the forest. Thus if social processes of protection, investment, co-operation, and innovation are in place, forestry will be sustainable.

In the following sections, we discuss and illustrate the principles through cases drawn from Sikor's work in Vietnam and Latin America. In Vietnam, Sikor analysed how macroeconomic reforms are affecting the use of natural and environmental resources, and how forestry reforms changed the conditions of investment in the forestry sector. In Latin America and specifically in Chile, he investigated how agro-ecological research and extension projects undertaken by non-governmental organisations (NGOs) found new ways to facilitate co-operation between farmers and researchers and produce technical and institutional innovation.

---

fifth principle, complementation among different levels and scales of forest governance, adds an important dimension that we have chosen to leave undeveloped in this paper. Note that we have indicated that our criteria are necessary. Such a fifth criteria also seems necessary but may not be sufficient.

PROTECTION: ECONOMIC AND ENVIRONMENTAL EFFECTS OF MACROECONOMIC REFORM IN VIETNAM

The conditions of natural and environmental resources not only depend on the actions of immediate resource users, but also depend on large-scale forces. Large-scale forces influence the patterns of resource use by influencing the environmental and socio-economic possibilities for resource use. Changes in these forces redefine the possibilities for resource use and may thus either augment or reduce the prospects for sustainability. The search for sustainability therefore implies finding ways to regulate large-scale forces as much as look for sustainable resource management practices on the ground.

The influence of large-scale economic forces on resource use are rarely as sharp as currently in Vietnam, where economic reforms are transforming the basic structure of the economy.[3] By changing economic activities, the reforms are exerting a profound effect on Vietnam's environment. For example, shifts in the allocation of capital and in control over production decisions are changing pressures on resource use and the environment through modifications in the scale of economic activities, changes in efficiencies, and changing social control over impacts. Sectors that offer low profitability are losing capital sources, decreasing the scale of activity, and reducing demands for resources. Pressure is also decreasing for activities in which economic reform facilitates increased efficiencies of resource use and where reform reduces conflicts between interests in short-term resource exploitation and environmental objectives. On the other hand, pressure on the environment is increasing in sectors expanding in scale due to their profit potentials for private investment. Pressure is also intensifying for activities in which resource use is becoming less efficient, such as in sectors that rely on the availability of public access to capital for efficient resource utilisation. Economic reform further increases pressure where it widens conflicts between private interests in resource exploitation and environmental objectives.

These dynamics are visible in Vietnam's agricultural sector. Competitive allocation of capital and greater household control over production decisions are increasing regional differences in land use, intensity, and productivity. For example, while Mekong Delta farmers drove the record growth in rice production between 1985 and 1992, per capita production of rice did not grow significantly in other regions. Competitive allocation of capital and increased household control over production are also increasing the pressure for resource strategies that yield sizeable returns in the short-term, at the cost of long-term and public sector investment. Households applying increasing

---

[3] This section is based upon Sikor and O'Rourke (1996).

amounts of current inputs, such as chemical fertiliser have facilitated rapid output increases in rice. At the same time, state investment in irrigation decreased substantially, and many water control projects could not be completed due to funding shortages. Competitive capital allocation is also homogenising resource use on land that was previously under relative household control. Previously self-sustaining, highly diverse home gardens are being expanded and transformed toward orchards of high-value fruit trees that require the use of additional fertiliser.

The consequences of economic reform have been particularly drastic in the case of mangrove forests. The high cost of capital has discriminated against forestry in favour of shrimp farming, which can generate substantial financial gains in the short-term. Furthermore, capital scarcity has favoured shrimp farming techniques that require low levels of investment, but which cannot sustain viable yields in the long run. As a result, vast areas of mangrove forests have been converted to extensive shrimp ponds over the past decade.

Policy that recognises the larger economic dynamics impacting on the environment can help shift Vietnam towards a more sustainable development path. Counteracting the detrimental large external forces would challenge the Vietnamese government to formulate policy that mediates between growth and environmental goals. Policy for sustainable development would strengthen the role of the public sector in capital accumulation and more strictly define the rights and responsibilities of private investors. Mobilising capital for the supply of public goods, providing capital at adequate terms to shift private initiative toward national objectives, and taxing highly profitable private activities that threaten social and future interests, helps to reduce pressures on natural resources. Policy for sustainable development would also strengthen existing mechanisms of control over economic activity or develop new mechanisms to safeguard environmental objectives against private interests of resource exploitation.

The dynamics of resource use in Vietnam demonstrate how large-scale economic forces affect the use of natural and environmental resources. The effects of external forces on local resource use dynamics are particularly sharp in Vietnam because, of the drastic shift in macroeconomic policy and the associated increased interest by foreign investors and multilateral development agencies in working with the Vietnamese. But macro-scale forces affect resource use in every country and may discourage or prevent resource users from improving resource qualities, such as in the case of Vietnam's mangroves. Sustainability therefore entails the need to protect resource users from detrimental large-scale forces through macro policy that balances economic and environmental goals.

INVESTMENT: VIETNAM'S FORESTRY SECTOR IN TRANSITION FROM THE STATE TO FOREIGN DONORS AND FARM HOUSEHOLDS

Sustainability requires the investment of resources that go beyond those needed to satisfy immediate needs. Sustainability depends on the generation of surplus resources and the capturing of those by resource users, as they allow people to protect and augment resource qualities they would otherwise deplete. Investment, however, also rests on assurances that resource users can enjoy the future benefits of their investment. Those benefits may accrue to them directly, such as in the case of short-rotation trees, or may be transferred to future generations, such as in the case of ameliorating global warming. Managing sustainability thus requires attention to the conditions of investment in resources.

As in other sectors, Vietnam's forest sector has experience of drastic changes in policy over the past decades, from a policy centred around direct state control over forests to one that allows direct forest management by households.[4] The Vietnamese government nationalised forest land in the early 1960s and founded numerous State Forest Enterprises to manage forests and forest land. Though the enterprises were independent in day-to-day management affairs, they had to follow forest exploitation and afforestation targets set by the Ministry of Forestry and received funding from the central government. The enterprises were expected to serve as rural growth poles and provide employment for rural people, who were excluded from access to Vietnam's forests.

Though State Forest Enterprises undertook significant investments in afforestation, they could not prevent a drastic decline in forest cover. Between 1961 and 1985, more than one million hectares of concentrated forest and three billion scattered trees were planted. Afforestation activities, however, fell drastically short of preventing a decline in the country's forest resources. By the 1980s, the decline in forest cover had reached an annual rate of 300,000 hectares. The areas of annual forest lost were particularly high in and around more densely populated areas, along the coast, and in more accessible mountainous regions. Only forest in more remote highland regions or in priority areas, such as mangrove forests in the Mekong Delta, increased or remained stable. By the late 1980s, the Ministry of Forestry classified more than half of designated forest land as 'barren' because of its degraded status or use for the cultivation of food crops and livestock grazing.

Vietnam's forest cover declined because capital for investment was limited and there was no assurance of claims over future benefits. The capacity of the forest sector itself to generate funds was weak. Charges

---

[4] This section is based on Sikor (1998).

collected for forest exploitation amounted to only a small part of total investment as the state-administered price system assigned a low value to wood and wood products. The central government discriminated against forest investment in favour of industry and infrastructure projects, sometimes, as in the case of large-scale hydropower projects, with detrimental consequences for Vietnam's forests. Local authorities often managed local forests to satisfy immediate needs of revenue generation and income creation. For example, they used a large share of the funds made available by the central government for the construction of a massive number of small-scale wood processing plants. Rural people often saw little value in protecting forests managed by the state as they would not be able to claim future benefits. On the other hand, investment by farmers into tree planting around houses and fields and along roads and canals received little attention and no support by the state.

The conditions of investment in Vietnam's forestry sector have fundamentally changed over the last decade as forest policy has been changing towards a management regime based upon farm households. Farm households have received direct control over forest land by receiving long-term land use rights or signing contracts with State Forest Enterprises for the management of forests. State forest enterprises have been converted to service units, which support households with technical extension, marketing, and processing. Households also receive assistance from the state through a national program for land use intensification and specialised agencies, such as the Agricultural Bank and local extension services. The state has retained direct control only over some forest areas of particular value for watershed protection or biodiversity preservation. In addition, Vietnam's forest sector has also benefited from large amounts of international donor assistance that is specifically targeted to forest investment.

The change in policy appears to have halted deforestation and even facilitated increases in forest cover in some regions, though not in others. Farmers in relatively well-off regions with access to urban and industrial markets have expanded forest plantations, particularly if they have received support under internationally-assisted projects. For example, forest plantations now cover barren hills in the Northern Midlands, once a symbol of land degradation in Vietnam. Forest cover is also increasing in better-off regions where land allocation or forest management contracts have increased household control over the benefits from forest investment. In addition, international support has facilitated the state to achieve effective control over certain areas, which are of international interest for their biodiversity value. Forest cover has, however, been decreasing in regions in more remote and poorer regions where local people and authorities have continued to cut the forest for the satisfaction of immediate needs. Particularly in cases such as the above-mentioned mangrove forest in southern Vietnam, where there are highly profitable alternatives to forestry, local interests in income and employment have led to a dramatic decline in forest resources.

Forest policy in Vietnam is in transition to a policy regime that recognises forest planting and protection as investments by rural people, which depend on broader rural socio-economic conditions. In some regions, Vietnam's forest cover has already increased because capital for investment has become increasingly available from domestic and international sources and the reform in forest tenure rights has improved the security of claims over future benefits. Vietnam faces a double challenge in these regions. First, high rural interest rates currently discriminate against more valuable tree species with longer rotation cycles in favour of fast-yielding tree species. The challenge is to create conditions under which farmers invest in a broader array of tree species. Second, Vietnam's forest sector needs to increase its capacity to generate its own funds to reduce its dependence on external funds, both from international and central government sources, and vulnerability to changes in their availability. In less well-off regions, deforestation is progressing, because urgent needs of subsistence and income generation and insecure claims over future benefits forbid investment in the forest. The challenge here is to facilitate broad economic development that can satisfy immediate subsistence and income needs and, at the same time, generate additional resources for forest investment. Managing Vietnam's forests thus requires explicit attention to the conditions of investment in forestry. Protecting and planting trees are investments by people that are affected by the availability of capital for forestry and the security of claims upon future benefits. Managing Vietnam's forests in a sustainable way will involve finding ways to increase people's investment in the forest. People will invest if the resources available to them in excess of the demands of immediate needs expand, if they can capture those resources, and have assurances that they will enjoy the benefits of their investment.

INNOVATION: AGRO-ECOLOGICAL RESEARCH AND EXTENSION IN LATIN AMERICA

Sustainability does not only include principles of protection, investment, and co-operation. Sustainability also needs the continuous search for new technical and institutional options to protect resource users from detrimental large-scale forces, to invest into future resource possibilities, and to balance different interests in resources. Innovation is crucial to better fit resource use practices to heterogeneous ecological and socio-economic conditions and adjust them to changes in these conditions.

Latin American non-governmental organisations (NGOs) following an agro-ecological approach have been radically innovative in comparison to conventional agricultural research and extension programs.[5] Conventional agricultural development efforts have rarely been able to improve the living conditions and farming systems of the rural poor in Latin America. Technological improvements brought increases in farm productivity and earnings, but only for some farmers with adequate amounts of land. Peasants without sufficient access to land and other productive resources remained outside the dynamics of rural development. Around 1980, approximately two thirds of the rural population in Latin America was poor, and around 40% was not even able to cover basic food needs. The Latin American food sector had become highly dependent on imports of agricultural products, inputs, and machinery for food processing. Conventional agricultural development also entailed massive environmental damage, such as deforestation, soil degradation, fertiliser and pesticide pollution, and erosion of genetic resources.

NGOs following an agro-ecological approach have been innovative because agro-ecologists have conceptualised the field as an ecological system. They have conducted research on ecological phenomena in the field, at the same time paying attention to economic, social, and cultural factors motivating agricultural practices. On the basis of the research, agro-ecologists have elaborated guidelines for economically viable and ecologically sustainable farming systems. For example, on the basis of case studies on weed management, agro-ecologists have determined general ecological principles regulating weed dynamics and interactions in agrarian ecosystems. The findings helped establish approaches to analysing specific crop–weed assemblages in specific local agrarian ecosystems and developing flexible guidelines for the design of farming systems. For each application, agro-ecologists then translate the general principles regulating weed dynamics into appropriate recommendations for specific local conditions. In this way, agro-ecologists are truly innovative, not only for their theoretical approach to agriculture but also for their concrete approach to applying general knowledge to specific circumstances.

Latin American NGOs following an agro-ecological approach have produced new institutional and technical options for research and extension projects for the continent's resource-poor farmers. From an institutional perspective, agro-ecological NGOs have developed novel strategies for integrating farmers into research agendas through activities such as on-farm research and farmer evaluation of new technologies. They have also functioned as intermediary institutions that forge links between resource-poor farmers, on the one side, and government agencies and international donors, on the other. From a technical perspective, agro-ecological NGOs have designed farming systems that meet the needs of many of Latin American resource-poor farmers. For example, a Bolivian NGO promotes small-scale

---

[5] This section is based upon Norgaard and Sikor (1995).

vegetable production in protected beds that withstands harsh environmental constraints, such as low temperatures, seasonal water scarcity, and low soil fertility, predominant in the Altiplano. A Chilean NGO developed gardening techniques for rural and semi-rural dwellers with only small pieces of land to reduce their food expenditures and improve diets.

Innovations by agro-ecological NGOs have improved the prospects for sustainable rural development in Latin America. Agro-ecological NGOs have developed institutional innovations, which provide new forms of co-operation between different interests in rural development. They have also successfully experimented with and disseminated new farming systems, which fit the conditions of resource-poor farmers in Latin America. Given the ecological, economic, and cultural heterogeneity of rural conditions in Latin America, agro-ecological NGOs have been more successful – both economically and ecologically – because they have emphasised local innovation and technology adaptation rather than wide dissemination of technology packages developed at centralised research stations.

CO-OPERATION: THE CHILEAN NGO CENTRO DE EDUCACIÓN Y TECNOLOGÍA

The conditions of natural and environmental resources rarely express the goals of one particular interest. In contrast, they usually attest to influences of different interests, and to compromises and trade-offs negotiated among competing interests. Resource conditions express the forms and degrees of co-operation among different interests. Sustainable resource use thus depends on forms of co-operation that are flexible enough to accommodate competing interests and prevent situations in which opposing interests obstruct negotiation of the goals and means of their co-operation, accelerating environmental degradation.

The Chilean Centro de Educación y Tecnología (CET) is one of the Latin American NGOs following an agro-ecological approach discussed in the previous section.[6] Research undertaken in CET's programs has produced a variety of technological improvements for farmers who had not benefited from the output of conventional research before. For example, research in Colina has found ways to increase soil fertility through green manure and control pests in vegetable without the use of chemical pesticides. In Temuco, CET researchers and Mapuche farmers have established contour lines and planted trees to reduce erosion rates and augment soil fertility. Research in Yumbel has investigated and introduced methods to conserve water during

---

[6] This section draws from research that Sikor conducted in 1992 and 1993 and is partially summarised in Sikor (1994).

the dry season to extend the growing season.

The centrepiece of CET's work has been experimentation with new ways of co-operation between researchers and farmers. The NGO is convinced that farmer participation in research is a crucial component of any attempt to improve the economic viability and ecological sustainability of farming systems. Co-operation has facilitated the identification of both constraints on and opportunities for agricultural improvements. Research therefore combines experiments in controlled environments at regional research centres with on-farm trials managed jointly by CET's staff and local farmers. Co-operation with rural people has, however, shown that people's participation depends on social conditions in rural areas and past experiences with participation in development projects. CET's strategy to work with rural people thus provides for an initial state that concentrates on activating and mobilising local people. The following stages of co-operation proceed from activities undertaken by individual farmers to group efforts and from projects internal to communities to their relations with external actors and institutions.

That co-operation between farmers and researchers can take different forms becomes clear when we look into developments during two five-day workshops on Participatory Rural Appraisal methods. These particular workshops, observed by Sikor in 1993, were organised by teams working in the two regions of Temuco and Yumbel. Farmer participation in the two workshops differed. Farmers assumed a much more active role in the workshop in Temuco than in Yumbel. For example, community leaders participated in the research team in Temuco but not in Yumbel. An additional meeting with the community at the beginning of the workshop allowed farmers in Temuco to influence the research agenda, while there was only a single final meeting in Yumbel to present research results. The final meeting in Temuco ended with the community deciding upon an agenda for action, while decisions about future actions were postponed in Yumbel.

Interactions between CET's staff and farmers during the workshops reflected different preconditions for co-operation. The long-term strategies that guided each teams' interaction with farmers and social conditions in communities were different. The team in Temuco had dedicated significant effort in their past work to integrate non-agricultural aspects into a more holistic development approach. The team pursued a strategy that views people's own initiatives and capacities as driving forces and building blocks of rural development. It recognised the relatively cohesive social organisation of local communities and worked to strengthen community organisations over several years. When more funds became available from the government, the team used those community organisations as intermediaries between the NGO and local communities.

The team in Yumbel had just recently begun to work in villages that possess only weak community organisations. Its members were driven by the desire to research and test a set of low-input technologies for resource-poor farmers. The team followed an approach that combines appropriate technology with sophisticated pedagogical methods to disseminate new technology to farmers. The team mainly integrated staff with technical backgrounds and focused on improving agricultural technology. When receiving a large grant for the dissemination of their technological innovations, they decided to divide research and extension into separate units and hired young extensionists as intermediaries between themselves, the researchers, and farmers.

The different forms of co-operation in Temuco and Yumbel have shaped local technologies and farming systems. Project activities in Temuco have covered a much broader set of rural livelihood needs. Extension efforts in Yumbel have focused on a few specific technological improvements, driven by what the team perceived as economically beneficial and transferable to farmers. The team in Yumbel may achieve more rapid dissemination of new technology than in Temuco. Yet it will face the challenge to find ways to ensure that people's interests, needs, and perspectives are expressed, heard, and reacted upon. Otherwise, proposed technological improvements may not meet the communities' most urgent needs and not solve the most critical resource use problems.

CET, along with many other NGOs, demonstrates forms of co-operation for sustainable agricultural and resource development projects. Integration of basic research, applied research, adaptive trials, technology dissemination, and technology use, facilitate more co-operation between researchers and farmers than conventional agricultural research. Sustainability depends on forms of co-operation which accommodate different interests and prevent situations in which different interests stop negotiating the goals and means of their co-operation.

CONCLUSIONS: A ROLE FOR EXTERNAL EXPERTISE

Sustainability depends on social processes that integrate diverse interests in natural and environmental resources and create sufficient opportunities to satisfy future resource demands. In this contribution we have tried to demonstrate the importance of social processes that protect resource users from detrimental large-scale forces, support investment for future resource possibilities, provide avenues for co-operation among diverse interests in resources, and encourage innovation. Processes of protection, investment, co-operation, and innovation help people to conserve and augment environmental resources in generally beneficial ways.

Though we have drawn our cases from agriculture and forestry, the four principles equally apply to industry. For example, take a hypothetical industrial plant. Plant managers want to maximise profits. Workers emphasise job security and workplace conditions. Local communities are concerned about the quality of a lake next to the factory. The actions of managers, workers, and communities shape water conditions. Sustainable industrial production requires the protection of the industry and communities from detrimental large-scale forces, such as unfettered global competition. Investment such as improved technology that reduces water usage preserves the desired qualities of the lake and creates opportunities to satisfy future demands on the lake. Co-operation among managers, workers, and communities, for example through community development boards, facilitates accommodating and satisfying the different interests in the lake. Innovation creates new technical and institutional options for industrial management.

Understanding sustainability as an outcome of social process requires re-conceptualising the role of external expertise. The technological, institutional, and moral approaches are flawed as they presuppose an 'objective' definition of the goal of sustainability that is impossible. Yet external expertise can help achieve sustainability if external experts acknowledge the social processes that shape the use of natural and environmental resources.

Understanding sustainability as an on-going outcome of appropriate social processes has two implications for the role of external expertise. It requires understanding people's behaviour, motivations, and values. Understanding why people act the way they act allows external experts to not only understand the current conditions of natural and environmental resources but also hypothesise on the effects of proposed courses of action on people and resource conditions in the future. If external experts are truly concerned about people then they have an obligation to try to understand why they act the way they act.

Understanding sustainability as a social process also brings experts to view their role as 'external facilitators.' If people shape the conditions of natural and environmental resources, if people have different values and interests, and if knowledge depends on the social context, then external experts can only facilitate social change and achieve sustainability in close interactions with people. External facilitators can introduce new ideas to the process, but they have to be prepared to watch those ideas be reinterpreted and modified by people until they are the people's own ideas. Experts without a vested interest in their expertise may seem like a contradiction, but this is where we come out.

REFERENCES

De Souza, H.G. 1992. 'Inaugural Address at International Conference on the Definition and Measurement of Sustainability: The Biophysical Foundations.' Washington D.C.: The World Bank.

Lélé, S. and Norgaard, R.B. 1996. 'Sustainability and the Scientist's Burden.'

Conservation Biology 10, 354–365.

Norgaard, R.B. 1989. 'The Case for Methodological Pluralism.' *Ecological Economics* 1, 37–57.

Norgaard, R.B. 1992. 'Environmental Science as a Social Process.' *Environmental Monitoring and Assessment* 20, 95–110.

Norgaard, R.B. and Sikor, T. 1995. 'The Methodology and Practice of Agroecology.' In Altieri, M. (ed.). *Agroecology: The Science of Sustainable Agriculture.* Boulder: Westview Press, 21–39.

Romm, J. 1993. 'Sustainable Forestry, an Adaptive Social Process.' In Aplet, G., Johnson, N., Olson, J., and Sample, V.A. (eds.). *Defining Sustainable Forestry.* Washington D.C.: Island Press, 280–293.

Sikor, T. 1994. 'Participatory Methods and Empowerment in Rural Development: Lessons from Two Experimental Workshops with a Chilean NGO.' *Agriculture and Human Values* 11, 2/3, 151–158.

Sikor, T. 1998. 'Forest Policy Reform: From State to Household Forestry.' In Poffenberger, M. (ed.). *Stewards of Vietnam's Upland Forests.* Berkeley: Asia Forest Network, 18–37.

Sikor, T. and O'Rourke, D. 1996. 'Economic and Environmental Dynamics of Reform in Vietnam.' *Asian Survey* 36, 6, 601–617.

Walters, C.J. 1986. *Adaptive Environmental Management of Renewable Resources.* New York: Macmillan.

5. Hierarchies in Human Affairs: Microfoundations and Environmental Sustainability

John Gowdy

INTRODUCTION

Complex systems are made up of nested levels of stable and discrete sub-systems. The term hierarchical organisation usually refers to an arrangement of descending order, with the higher levels having control over those directly under them. However, this subordination between levels is always incomplete and each level has its own rules of behaviour and its own specific concerns (Vrba and Eldredge, 1984). Such hierarchies exist in a variety of physical and social systems. Physicists arrange the world in levels of detail from sub-atomic particles to galaxies, biologists move comfortably from genes to ecosystems. In the field of physics the articulation between spatial and temporal hierarchies has been explored for well over 100 years. In evolutionary biology the discussion of hierarchies is more recent but potentially more relevant to economics.

Economic systems differ from biological systems and any appeal to biology for insights into how economies work must be done with caution. However, the field of evolutionary biology is today a major centre of activity in the philosophy of science, much as classical physics was the centre for most of this century. There is one common reality that is divided for convenience by various fields of science. If some fields of study are further along in their understanding of this reality, other fields should make sure that their explanations are consistent with the latest discoveries and insights. Just as classical mechanics gave birth to the positivist philosophy of neoclassical economics, so can evolutionary biology be the guide for a new economics relevant to the overwhelming social and environmental challenges that will undoubtedly confront us in the 21st century.

Neoclassical economics sees all attributes of social and biological reality from the viewpoint of one level in the many hierarchies enveloping our species, namely, the level of market exchange. *Homo economicus* (economic

67

man) has no social context and *Fabrica economicus* (the economic firm) has no physical context. Neoclassical theory offers an inadequate framework for a general theory of economic behaviour relevant to the total environmental context and the social institutions essential for the long-term survival of the human species (Gowdy and McDaniel, 1995; Gowdy and O'Hara, 1995). It is a theory of isolated exchange in markets and, like the markets it describes, it homogenises space and time. As Altvater (1994, p. 76) puts it, markets treat ecological modalities as economic modalities. A relevant theory of economic change and the environment must begin with the realisation that ecosystems, social systems, and markets are discrete elements in a system of hierarchical structures and that each element has its own, sometimes conflicting, rules that differ across space and time.

The system of market exchange, the subject matter of neoclassical economics, is contained in the higher order system comprised of various human societies and institutional arrangements. In turn, all human activity ultimately depends upon resources taken from the natural environment. The biosphere, geosphere, and atmosphere contain all human systems and provide the material conditions necessary for human existence. Until quite recently, a few hundred years ago at most, human societies were comprised of a very large number of quite different societies, each having its own unique rules of kinship, distribution, power sharing and so on. The economies of different societies were keyed to specific ecosystems. This was much more true of hunter-gatherers than of early agriculturalists, and more true of early agriculturalists than of industrial societies. Today, the relentless rules of the logic of market exchange are eliminating differences between various human cultures, and are also simplifying and homogenising the world's ecosystems. How can it be that one lower level system in this nested hierarchy, the system of market exchange, can have such widespread detrimental effects, which threaten the stability of all higher order systems in the hierarchy? This is the key question that has to be answered if we are to have any hope of moving towards a sustainable economic system.

The extreme reductionism of standard economics has its counterpart in evolutionary biology, although the micro–macro controversy in evolutionary biology is much further along, spurred by the 'punctuated equilibrium' revolution which began in the 1970s (Eldredge and Gould, 1972). The punctuated equilibria protagonists successfully challenged the dominant notion in biology that all features of an organism were the result of 'micro' adaptations at the margin (Gould and Lewontin, 1979). The recognition of punctuations in evolutionary history also led to the recognition of hierarchies of selection (Vrba and Gould, 1986) and the realisation that these hierarchies may not fit together as seamless integrated systems (Eldredge 1995, p. 177). Again, it is not the intention here to argue for the wholesale importation into economics of detailed biological metaphors. However, if biologists have acquired insights into the common world we inhabit we should make sure our scientific explanations of reality are consistent with these new discoveries.

THE MICROFOUNDATIONS DEBATE: DENIAL OF HIERARCHY

The idea of hierarchies in human social systems is certainly not a new one, but it is an idea, which is yet to be operationalised in economics into a coherent research program. The nearest economists have come to dealing with the problem of hierarchies is the 'microfoundations' controversy; that is, whether the neoclassical theory of the firm should be the basis for a theory of macroeconomics. Standard theory answers this question with a resounding 'yes,' arguing that the microeconomic principle of constrained optimisation should not only be the basis for macroeconomics but also provides a general theory for all social and biological phenomena (Hirshleifer, 1977). In the decades since World War Two, there has been a steady erosion in the distinction between micro and macroeconomics. The rules of behaviour describing the lowest level in the economic hierarchy, market exchange, have been used to describe all economic activity. After years of this trend towards reductionism by Monetarists, the Rational Expectations Hypothesis, and New Classical Economists, to mention a few, the tide seems to be turning and new, more realistic theories of macroeconomics seem to be emerging. Within ecological economics, influenced by the entropy metaphor of Georgescu-Roegen (1971), exciting work is being done applying theories of self-organisation and chaos to examine the behaviour of whole economic systems (Hinterberger, 1993; Foster, 1994; Perrings, 1987). More mainstream work is being done in what has been called 'Post Walrasian' macroeconomics (Colander, 1996).

Niles Eldredge (1995, p. 176) describes his early difficulty in dealing with hierarchical structures as he tried to force them into one seamless integrated system. Hierarchical organisation in ecosystems became easier to describe when he realised that hierarchies are independent systems. There is no smooth articulation between hierarchies and there may be contradictions. There are hints of the recognition of conflicting hierarchies in economic theory but they always seem to be papered over. Economists from Mandeville to Keynes have discussed the paradox of thrift, persistent involuntary unemployment, and oscillating price systems, which never reach equilibrium. Rather than seeing these phenomena as indicative of different hierarchies at the micro and macro level, economists usually force them into a general equilibrium framework and analyse them as intervention failure, coordination failure, or an imperfect property rights regime.

Coordination failure can be interpreted in a way such that the notion of hierarchies can be included. Van Ees and Garretsen (1996, p. 224) write:

> In fact, the assumption of full coordination leaves the analyst no other possibility than to ground the performance of the aggregate economy upon the individual responses to exogenous states of nature. On the other hand, the (macro)foundations of Post Walrasian economics starts from the notion that the aggregate state of the economy affects the behaviour of the individual decision unit in a way that cannot completely be reduced to given individual preferences, technology, and endowments. Individual behaviour is contextual or social behaviour (Bryant, 1993), conditional on time and place and on the physical as well as the social environment.

The Post Walrasian school recognises conflicts in valuation between markets, society and ecosystems. This approach could be enriched by incorporating metaphors from evolutionary biology and extending the micro–macro distinction to include more hierarchical levels.

The microfoundations position in economics has the same problem that ultra-Darwinism has in biology: it is not that it is wrong, but that it is incomplete. It is a description of only part of economic reality, namely market exchange. Having a well-developed, stylised description of market exchange is essential to understanding how markets interact with social and environmental systems. Understanding how market exchange works, and how markets force substitution and discounting the future, is crucial, but there are limits to the applicability of the theory and there are contradictions between the rules of markets and the rules by which larger systems operate. Markets are driving the loss of biodiversity, climate destabilisation and most of the other perhaps insurmountable environmental problems we face. Taken in context, neoclassical theory can be a useful tool for analysis of the detrimental effects of market outcomes.

HIERARCHIES IN THE ECONOMIC WORLD: MECHANISMS OF EVOLUTIONARY CHANGE

When Gould and Eldredge first proposed the theory of punctuated equilibria they simply argued that the evolutionary record was characterised by stasis interrupted by episodes of rapid change (Eldredge and Gould, 1972). This theme is potentially consistent with the Modern Synthesis in biology, that is, natural selection of individual organisms is the only driving force in evolutionary change. It was only later that they came to believe that periods of punctuation are driven by higher order selection. According to Gould and Eldredge (1986) it is the notion of hierarchical selection that really constitutes the radical content of punctuated equilibrium. Briefly, punctuated equilibrium theorists make a distinction between *sorting* and *selection* (Gould and Vrba, 1982; Vrba and Eldredge, 1984). Sorting is a broad term that simply means differential survival rates. At time *t* there is a certain array of species present, and at time *t+1* there is a different array. Some species have survived and others have not for whatever reason. One mechanism for sorting is selection, that is, Darwinian selection due to competitive pressure. Selection is a *cause* while sorting is merely an *outcome*. A hierarchical approach to the study of the evolution of complex systems involves, above all, an explicit analysis of the sorting mechanism, that is, the mechanisms involved in survival through time.

In an earlier paper (Gowdy, 1992) I proposed a simple system of three economic hierarchies. At the lowest level, survival of an economic feature depends on efficiency. Given an array of firms in a given industry, the firms which most efficiently allocate resources to maximise profit will survive. This is the process of rationalisation so eloquently described by neoclassical economics. At another level, a firm may survive not because it is more efficient, but because of historical accident, path dependence, or by being at the right place at the right time. The well-known example of the QWERTY keyboard (David, 1985) is a case in point. In an environmental application of the path dependence idea, Cowan and Gunby (1996) argue that this phenomenon explains why chemical pest control in agriculture is the dominant technology even though integrated pest management is superior. Inferior and inefficient techniques may also be developed and adopted because they favour the dominant economic powers, as in the case of hybrid corn. The seeds of hybrid corn cannot be planted to get new hybrid corn and so farmers must buy new seeds from the producers every year. In effect, the producers of hybrid corn have a built-in copyright protection (Lewontin, 1992, p. 54). According to Lewontin (1992, p. 56) it is possible, given enough time and effort, to develop high-yielding varieties of corn by the method of simple direct selection of high yielding plants in successive generations. No company will undertake this effort, however, since there would be no profit in it. As soon as these kinds of high-yielding seeds were on the market anyone could produce more.

Another case of this kind of sorting would be an unforeseen revolutionary breakthrough in one industry which gives an unexpected advantage to some firms, but not others, in a related industry. This is a kind of sorting which does not depend upon the competitive ability or the internal efficiency of the indirectly benefiting firm. Differential survival is merely an accident of history. At a higher hierarchy there exist *macro shocks* arising from such diverse causes as wars, energy shortages, financial crises, or perhaps global climate change. For example, many very efficient firms went bankrupt after the stock market crash of 1987 just because they picked the wrong time to be heavily leveraged. So a firm, or technique, or 'microinvention' (Mokyr, 1990), like an organism, can be at the right place at the right time or at the wrong place at the wrong time.

Once different hierarchies are delineated, the task of modelling economic change becomes more manageable. A far broader range of phenomena can be judged as directly relevant and different techniques of analysis may be developed and applied to different hierarchies. As Eldredge argues (1985, p. 11), hierarchies deal with complexity by "teasing it apart". This approach offers a more honest and direct approach than one seeking unity by forcing all phenomena into one simple system as neoclassical theory does. The seemingly complex models of the firm that grace the leading journals of our profession are based on a rather crude notion of social Darwinism. For example, Geroski (1989, p. 572) begins an analysis of market entry and innovation activity with an explicit statement of a Spencerian survival of the fittest viewpoint: "It is widely believed that competition promotes efficiency, that a vigorous competitive process throws up alternatives in the form of new firms and new ideas, and that selection amongst them induces movements to, and movements of, the production frontier." Likewise Telser (1996) writes: "It has become nearly an article of faith that unlimited competition brings about efficient outcomes in the sense of eliminating deadweight losses. It is also widely believed that the associated prices are capable of guiding individuals not only to choices they consider as best for themselves but also to results that are best for the whole economy." By this view whatever exists is best. Whatever outcome the market dictates, it must be the best since it was chosen through competitive selection.

Deep down, many economists have such an antipathy to government involvement in the economy because of the belief that if interferes with 'natural' selection, hindering the progressive drive towards increased efficiency inherent in the workings of the system. Even though it is generally accepted that the market works imperfectly, there is a pervasive attitude that governmental interference will make the selection process more inefficient. Among many economists there exists a pervasive attitude that if the result of government involvement in the economy is different than the non-interventionist outcome would be, this in itself is proof of inefficiency. To the extent that changes in the economy are driven by higher level sorting, the antipathy to government involvement in economic activity is at least partially unwarranted. Neoclassical economic policy ignores other forms of sorting and focuses policy recommendations entirely on 'selection.' Firms, techniques, and routines which appear to be successful because they have won the struggle for existence, may in fact exist for reasons unrelated to efficiency.

The preoccupation with market efficiency also denies a role for the government in dealing with economic outcomes which are acceptable in the framework of competitive markets but which may have adverse effects on social and environmental systems. It is by now well-known that rational markets may result in species extinction, and that free market policies may result in social disruption if they do not take into account social context (Norgaard, 1994).

Just because certain techniques 'survive', does not mean they are the most efficient in a strictly neoclassical sense. Likewise, just because market economies 'survive' and expand even though they are drawing down ecological and social stability does not mean that they are the 'best' forms of economic organisation for human societies. Decisions made on the timescale of market exchange may limit future choices in a matter, which we will later come to regret. This has happened in a variety of societies in a variety of social and ecological contexts. Since the wide-spread adoption of agriculture civilisations as varied as the Sumerians, Maya, and Easter Islanders have drawn down their resource bases and gradually limited their choices until their societies disintegrated (Gowdy, 1997a).

INTERACTIONS BETWEEN HIERARCHIES: SELF-ORGANISATION AND CHAOS

The first revolutionary challenge to economic theory from natural science since the mechanical and energetic metaphors of the nineteenth century came from the field of thermodynamics. Thermodynamics entered economic theory with a bang in 1971 with the publication of Georgescu-Roegen's *The Entropy Law and the Economic Process*. The Entropy Law as a powerful metaphor challenging the mechanical, reversible, static world of neoclassical analysis, was quickly adopted by a new generation of environmentally minded economists. In contrast to the circular flow of economic activity depicted by almost all economic texts, the economic system began to be seen as a one-way flow of low-entropy energy and raw material going into the economy and then leaving it as high entropy waste and dissipated energy.

The adoption of the entropy metaphor by a variety of alternative schools of economic thought led naturally to a consideration of theories of self-organising systems and their relevance to the economic process. This in turn led to the examination of markets, social systems, and biophysical systems as interconnected hierarchies each operating on different scales of time and space. The study of hierarchical systems is now a central feature of the science of ecology and some simple observations from this field have great relevance for the study of economic systems.

(1) Entropy in one hierarchy can decrease only by taking low entropy

from another. An obvious example is the dependence of economic activity on fossil fuels (Georgescu-Roegen, 1976). The market economy extracts carbon stored up over millions of years during the Permian age and expels it as atmospheric gas and heat within a period of a few decades. Our industrial economy depends on a steady and apparently increasing flow of raw materials and biological inputs from the lithosphere, atmosphere, and biosphere. On the output side of the economy, discharges back into the environment disrupt and destabilise natural biological and atmospheric systems. If entropy is viewed as information, there is a staggering loss of low entropy as genetic information is lost through the destruction of individual organisms, species, and ecosystems. We are losing information, which may be critical to the long-term stability of the natural systems of the planet which ultimately support all human activity, in order to subsidise the temporary growth of economic markets.

The idea of entropic drawdown may also be extended to social support systems; the institutions which have evolved over hundreds of years to support and stabilise human activity. In the present age of increasing scarcity and falling profit rates, economic growth may be maintained by drawing down the stability of social systems. A number of social scientists argue that with increasing scarcity income distribution becomes more unequal as the upper classes seek to maintain their income growth rates by taking from the bottom, with the consequent social instability. The phenomenon of social disintegration seems to be now happening world-wide (Kaplan, 1996; Mayumi, 1993; Weiskel, 1989).

(2) Different levels in hierarchical systems operate on different time scales. This is a phenomenon frequently observed in ecosystems. Periodic fires, for example, may have devastating local temporary effects on individual organisms, but are crucial to the long run stability of certain kinds of ecosystems. Examining the hierarchy of a tree shows the different timescales involved (O'Neill *et al.* 1986, p. 78). At a lower hierarchy, the sunlight striking the leaves fluctuate on a 24 hour timescale, at a higher level of organisation, we find tree growth registered as annual tree rings which are a kind of average of the daily activity over the course of a year, and the tree may be part of a forest ecosystem that evolved over hundreds of years. A timescale relevant to the analysis of one level may be of little or no use when applied to another.

An economic example is the vast difference between the time scale on which markets operate versus the time scales of social and political institutions, and even more so compared to the time scales on which ecosystems operate. These differences in time scales means that information about increasing instability of ecosystems may not enter day-to-day market calculations. Goodall (1974) notes that information flows in a nested hierarchical system can be completely blocked because the differences in scale are too great. This idea, or finding, from studies of hierarchies in ecology, points out the inherent danger of relying on market signals (from a level low on the hierarchy) to give adequate information about what is happening on higher levels. Formulating 'environmental' policies based on market or pseudo-market outcomes may be non-sensical; equivalent to trying to save a forest by saving individual leaves.

(3) Hierarchical systems probably arose because they offered evolutionary advantages. Herbert Simon (1962), among others, uses the example of two watchmakers, Hora and Tempus, to illustrate the advantages of hierarchical ordering. Imagine these two watchmakers each assembling a watch with 1000 parts. One watchmaker must work steadily assembling the watch from the first to the last part. If he is interrupted, even if he has 999 parts in place, he must start the process over from the beginning. The other watchmaker is able to subdivide the process of watch building into 10 operations working with 100 parts each, and then subdivide each those 10 operations into another 10 working with 10 parts each. If this watchmaker is interrupted, only a small part of his work is lost. In evolutionary systems in biology there may be advantages to blocking out information (or perturbations) between hierarchies. Allen and Starr (1982, p. 112) write: "Because scale differences can completely block information flow, the environment is compartmentalised with respect to the biotic experience. By accentuating steep portions of the scale gradient from its base to its apex, the biotic hierarchy can present separate biotic compartments to the environment. Thus, when there is a perturbation in one environmental compartment, only the holons in that compartment are destroyed." We have seen a parallel example in Herbert Simon's two watchmakers. The interruptions are the perturbation; the assembled subunits represent holons in safe compartments with which the disturbance cannot communicate.

Again, the separation of information between hierarchies of ecosystems has a parallel with what is happening between economic markets and the biosphere. Great chunks of information are being destroyed at the biosphere level, but the physical and time scales are so different, that this information is not feeding back into the economic subsystem (or at least feeding back in a very limited way). Allen and Starr, although they are biologists, recognise that the market economy is really a self-replicating hierarchy, like a virus. They point out (1982, p. 112) that such self-replicating hierarchies achieve a particularly high level of resilience. They write:

In general, only a self-replicating hierarchy can destroy another. We have a name for that: competition. Parasitism and predation destroy entire hierarchies less frequently, for the tendency to self-damping is greater (host and prey become harder to find, and the parasite or predator tends to decline). The wave of extinctions associated with human intrusion into natural ecosystems would seem to be peculiar to modern times.

The term 'coevolutionary economics' coined by Richard Norgaard (1984) and used widely now (Gowdy, 1994) was chosen to describe the reciprocal, mutually reinforcing relationship between the economy and the environment. The term is somewhat flawed, however, since it implies a mutually beneficial relationship, as in the coevolutionary relationship between butterflies and plants for which the term coevolution was first used (Ehrlich and Raven, 1964). What we have in the current economy–environment relationship is two self-replicating hierarchies, one of which is expanding by degrading the other. Over the past 100 years or so, and especially since World War Two, a variety of biological indicators show varying degrees of stress and decline. Economic indicators, however, show vigorous growth (Gowdy and McDaniel, 1995). This vigorous economic growth has only in rare instances been impeded by environmental degradation. If the only criteria for assessing environmental damage is whether or not it affects the economy, including non-market measures of economic value, there is little hope for solving problems such as biodiversity loss or global climate change. How can we begin to get a handle on the seeming absence of information flowing from environmental health to economic indicators? A fruitful way to approach this is to return to one of the basic ideas in economic theory, namely, the distinction between macro and microeconomics. If we can drive a wedge between theories of efficiency at the firm level, and theories of macroeconomic behaviour, perhaps another wedge can be driven between the macro economy and its surrounding social and environmental systems.

Interestingly, some of the most innovative work linking self-organisation, punctuated equilibria, and the notion of hierarchies is being done in the field of management. Baum and Singh (1994), Gersick (1991), Hannan and Freeman (1984) and Wollin (1995) have used the idea of nested hierarchies in models of organisation, which can account for both incremental self-organisation and punctuated change.

HIERARCHIES, VALUATION AND SUSTAINABILITY: THE CASE OF BIODIVERSITY PRESERVATION

The issue of biodiversity loss divides standard economists and most biologists perhaps more than any other environmental issue. Biologists warn that we are now in the middle of one of the five or six major extinction episodes in the half billion year history of complex life on earth (Leakey and Lewin, 1995; Ward, 1994). Pimm *et al.* (1995) estimate that current rates of extinction are 100 to 1000 times higher than their pre-human levels, and that this rate is expected to increase 10 fold in the next century. Biologists point to the value of biodiversity in ecosystem stability and in the ability of the biological world to adapt to inevitable environmental change. Economists, on the other hand, see biodiversity as being just another 'good' which yields utility to humans, and which can be substituted for and traded in markets just as any other economic good (Solow, 1993). The conflicting views of the value of biodiversity arise from looking at it from the point of view of its values in different hierarchies, such as market value, total value to humans, and its value to ecosystems.

Several studies have shown that biological resources as raw material can have considerable market value. Peters, Gentry, and Mendelsohn (1989) estimated that the economic value of a hectare of forest in the Peruvian Amazon, based on the yield of various forest products was $422 per year after deducting transport and harvesting costs. Mendelsohn and Balick (1995) estimated the potential value of all yet-to-be-discovered rainforest drugs to be between $3 and $4 billion to a private pharmaceutical company and $147 billion to society as a whole. There is also a substantial and growing value of biodiversity for ecotourism. Geist (1994) estimates that the direct economic benefit of Wyoming's big game animals, from tourism and hunting is about $1 billion per year or about $1000 per large animal. Studies like these show that biodiversity *in situ* can have substantial market value, but in many cases its value is probably not great enough to insure its preservation on economic grounds alone. The very narrow and ephemeral framework of market-based valuation can hardly begin to take into account the total value of biodiversity to the human species. As long as we remain in the one-dimensional, timeless and spaceless hierarchy of market exchange, even the destruction of resources essential to the long-term survival of our species can be justified. O'Connor (1994, p. 144) writes:

> What does it matter if some genes, Indians, tropical forests, urban environments and their inhabitants, and so on, are, along with the firms forced to the wall, lost in the rush. These losses are of little consequence as long as the outcomes and decisions can be *re-presented* as the *rational use* of the available capital: that is, at some moment in time, by somebody's calculus, on whatever shifting-sands evaluation baseline, allocated to their highest value on the margin use.

In the realm of market exchange, the valuation framework forces the following assumptions, (1) a meaningful price can be put on biodiversity, (2) biodiversity is a substitutable market good just like any other, and (3) it is socially desirable to use up biodiversity in the pursuit of market-determined goals.

What is the difference between market values and value to the human species? An example by Sagoff (1988) helps to clarify this point. In the 1960s Walt Disney Enterprises proposed to develop a ski resort in the Mineral King Valley in Sequoia National Park in California. In an informal survey of his students, Sagoff found that his students were almost unanimous in their opposition to the project. However, when asked whether they would visit the park to ski if it were developed the vast majority answered 'yes.' The simple explanation of this seeming contradiction is that people make different decisions as members of a society than they do in the restricted realm of markets. Markets limit choice. Again, past societies, particularly hunter-gatherers, had a variety of rules, customs, totems, traditions and religious beliefs that enabled individuals to be part of a larger social system which worked to ensure the long-term preservation of natural systems essential for the sustainability of the group. In these societies there was no contradiction between economic sustainability and ecological sustainability (Gowdy, 1997c).

Neoclassical theory is a theory of market exchange, that sees all values arising from the desires of isolated individuals at a particular point in space and time. Most economists believe this approach is 'value-neutral' on their part. Randall (1988, p. 217) writes: "The mainstream approach is doggedly nonjudgmental about people's preferences: what the individual wants is presumed to be good for that individual." The mainstream approach is actually very judgmental. What is good for the individual must be determined by choosing alternatives in a restricted market or pseudo-market framework where all goods are substitutable, there is no social context, and the needs of future generations count only to the extent that accounting for them gives utility to individuals in the present. Eckstein (1957, p. 75) is explicit on this last point: "...a social welfare function based on consumers' sovereignty must accept people's tastes, including their intertemporal preferences." If consumers choose to leave a biologically impoverished planet to future generations, standard economists have no choice but to accept that result as rational, and not only rational for the individual but rational for the human species.

Even if we could properly take into account social context by allowing people to make collective as well as individual decisions, there is still the problem of discounting the future. The choice made by a representative of the human species not present in any given time period could differ from a fully informed, democratic, discursive choice made at a point in time. Price (1993, pp. 102–103) writes:

> There is a fatal weakness in the parallel between contemporary and intertemporal choice. Consumers may choose between two

goods at one point in time on an equal footing (if similar information is given about each): they do not so choose between two time periods, for the choice is made *from within one of those time periods*. This asymmetry may make irrationality and misinformation more serious in intertemporal choice than in choice between contemporary acts of consumption.

The seriousness of this difficulty can be seen in a brief look at the value of biodiversity at a still higher hierarchical level, that of the ecosystem. It is only recently that the value of biodiversity to ecosystems has been demonstrated. Tilman and Downing (1994) found that biodiversity plays a crucial role in maintaining the resilience of ecosystems to environmental shocks. In a study of Minnesota grasslands they found that primary productivity in more diverse plant communities is more resistant to drought and recovers faster. Alarmingly, in view of the predicted sharp increase in extinction rates, they found that each additional species lost in the grasslands they studied had an increasingly greater negative impact on drought resistance. In another controlled experiment Naeem *et al.* (1994) also found that declining biodiversity adversely affected the performance of ecosystems in terms of plant productivity, nutrient retention, water retention, and decomposition. Tilman *et al.* (1994, p. 65) warn of an 'extinction debt.' They argue that, primarily because of habitat fragmentation, the stage is set for a sharp increase in extinction rates in the near future. They write:

> Even moderate habitat destruction is predicted to cause time-delayed but deterministic extinction of the dominant competitor in remnant patches. Further species are predicted to become extinct, in order from the best to the poorest competitors as habitat destruction increases. Moreover, the more fragmented a habitat already is, the greater is the number of extinctions caused by added destruction. Because such extinctions occur generations after fragmentation, they represent a debt – a future ecological cost of current habitat destruction. (Tilman *et al.* 1994, p. 65)

Perhaps the most important ecological value of diverse ecosystems is the preservation of evolutionary potential. Species diversity, as well as genetic diversity within species, allows species and ecosystems to adapt to environmental changes. Natural systems are not in a 'state of equilibrium' as economists use the term equilibrium. Economic theory refers to an equilibrium system as one that returns to its initial state after a disturbance. When ecosystems are disturbed, depending on the nature and extent of the disturbance, they do not necessarily revert to their initial state when the disturbance is removed, because the initial state is no longer the same. This flexibility to adapt to different environmental conditions has evolved over eons. Geological records show that the Earth is a constantly changing system. Mountains are formed and eroded, ice sheets expand and contract, and volcanoes disrupt climate patterns. Genetic diversity, as well as higher orders of biological diversity, gives ecosystems the ability to adapt to, and coevolve with, these changing systems. When we reduce the variability within the biological world through habitat destruction, ecosystem modification, extinction and genetic erosion we limit the possible responses to future environmental change. Evolutionary potential has obvious 'value' to ecosystems, but we cannot meaningfully quantify its value to the human species (Gowdy, 1997b).

CONCLUSION

Humans are part of the natural world and any damage humans do to that world has the potential to increase the risk to ourselves. Many economists counter that humans are fundamentally different from other species. We are unique and not subject to the same laws of nature as other species. It is hard to answer this because it is not a testable scientific argument, merely a statement of optimism: "we'll think of something." To counter this argument one can only point to past and present cases where human society did not think of anything clever to save them in the face of self-inflicted environmental disaster. There is mounting evidence that almost every civilisation since the adoption of agriculture some 10,000 years ago has overshot and collapsed, most of them because of the misuse of their natural resource base. Of course the cause of the collapse of past civilisations is a complex mix of rapid environmental change, resource degradation, including biodiversity loss, social instability and unresponsive political institutions. In view of the history of our species, the argument that humans do not need to conserve biodiversity because we are so resourceful and intelligent seems imprudent at best.

The problems with the standard economic concept of value as expressed in relative market prices are becoming increasingly clear. The "ideology of efficiency" (Bromley, 1990) is coming under increasing attack within the economics profession even as it extends its political dominance. Difficulties with the neoclassical theory of value include problems in cognition, the incongruity problem, indivisibilities and complementary of ecosystem functions, and pure time preference. Attempts to duplicate market values for environmental attributes through contingent valuation suffer from these same difficulties. It is clear both from theoretical considerations and scientific evidence about the nature of biodiversity, that economists need to broaden their concept of value beyond that determined in the narrow hierarchical level of market exchange. Such a broad concept of value leads inevitably to the need for a broader array of policy options for the protection of biodiversity beyond those based on simple cost benefit calculations.

REFERENCES

Allen, T. and Starr, T. 1982. *Hierarchy: Perspectives for Ecological Complexity.* Chicago: University of Chicago Press.

Altvater, E. 1994. 'Ecological and Economic Modalities of Time and Space.' In O'Connor, M. (ed.), *Is Capitalism Sustainable?* New York: Guilford Press, 76–90.

Baum, J.C. and Singh, J.V. 1994. *Evolutionary Dynamics of Organizations.* New York: Oxford University Press.

Bryant, J. 1993. 'Coordination, the Stag Hunt and Macroeconomics'. In Friedman, J.W. (ed.) *Problems of Coordination in Economic Activity.* Boston: Kluwer.

Colander, D. (ed.) 1996. *Beyond Microfoundations: Post Walrasian Macroeconomics.* New York: Cambridge University Press.

Cowan, R. and Gunby, P. 1996. 'Sprayed to Death: Path Dependence, Lock-in and Pest Control Strategies.' *The Economic Journal* 106, 521–542.

David, P. 1985. 'Clio and the Economics of QWERTY.' *American Economic Review* 75, 332–337.

Eckstein, O. 1957. 'Investment Criteria for Economic Development and the Theory of Intertemporal Welfare Economics.' *Quarterly Journal of Economics* 71, 56–84.

Ehrlich, P. and Raven, P. 1964. 'Butterflies and Plants: A Study in Coevolution.' *Evolution* 18, 586–608.

Eldredge, N. 1985. *'Unfinished Synthesis.'* New York: Oxford University Press.

Eldredge, N. 1995. *Reinventing Darwin: The Great Debate at the High Table of Evolutionary Theory.* New York: John Wiley.

Eldredge, N. and Gould, S. 1972. 'Punctuated Equilibria: An Alternative to Phyletic Gradualism.' In Schopf, T.J.M. (ed.) *Models in Paleobiology.* San Francisco: Freeman, Cooper, 82–115.

Foster, J. 1994. 'The Self-organization Approach in Economics.' In Burley, S. and Foster, J. (eds.) *Economics and Thermodynamics: New Perspectives on Economic Analysis.* Boston: Kluwer, 183 202.

Geist, V. 1994. 'Wildlife Conservation as Wealth.' *Nature* 368, 491–492.

Georgescu-Roegen, N. 1971. *The Entropy Law and the Economic Process.* Boston: Harvard University Press.

Georgescu-Roegen, N. 1976. *Energy and Economic Myths.* San Francisco: Pergamon Press.

Geroski, P.A. 1989. 'Entry, Innovation and Productivity Growth.' *Review of Economics and Statistics* 71, 555–564.

Gersick, C.J.G. 1991. 'Revolutionary Change Theories: A Multilevel Exploration of the Punctuated Equilibrium Paradigm.' *Strategic Management Journal* 16,1, 10–36.

Goodall, D. 1974. 'Problems of Scale and Detail in Ecological Modelling.' *Journal of Environmental Management* 2, 149–157.

Gould, S. and Eldredge, N. 1986. 'Punctuated Equilibrium at the Third Stage.' *Systematic Zoology* 35, 143–148.

Gould, S. and Lewontin, R. 1979. 'The Spandrels of San Marco and the Panglossian Paradigm: A Critique of the Adaptationist Programme.' *Proceedings of the Royal Society of London* B 205, 581–598.

Gould, S. and Vrba, E. 1982. 'Exaptation – A Missing Term in the Science of Form.' *Paleobiology* 8, 4–15.

Gowdy, J. 1992. 'Higher Selection Processes in Evolutionary Economic Change.' *Journal of Evolutionary Economics* 2, 1, 1–16.

Gowdy, J. 1994. *Coevolutionary Economics: Economy, Society and Environment.* Boston: Kluwer.

Gowdy, J. 1997a. 'The Industrial Bubble and Biophysical Limits: Prospects for the 21st Century.' In Dobkowski, M. and Walliman, I. (eds.) *The Coming Age of Scarcity: Preventing Mass Death and Genocide in the 21st Century.* Syracuse: Syracuse University Press.

Gowdy, J. 1997b. 'The Value of Biodiversity: Markets, Society and Ecosystems.' *Land Economics* 73, 1, 25–41.

Gowdy, J. (ed.) 1997c. *Limited Wants, Unlimited Means: A Hunter-Gatherer Reader on Economics and the Environment.* Washington, D.C.: Island Press.

Gowdy, J. and McDaniel, C. 1995. 'One World, One Experiment: Addressing the Biodiversity-Economics Conflict.' *Ecological Economics* 15, 181–192.

Gowdy, J. and O'Hara, S. 1995. *Economic Theory for Environmentalists.* Delray Beach FL: St. Lucie Press.

Hannan, M.T. and Freeman, J. 1984. 'Structural Inertia and Organizational Change.' *American Sociological Review* 29, 149–164.

Hinterberger, F. 1993. 'On the Evolution of Open Socio-economic Systems.' In Mishra, R. (ed.) *Self-Organization as a Paradigm in Science.* Heidelberg: Springer.

Hirshleifer, J. 1977. 'Economics from a Biological Viewpoint.' *The Journal of Law and Economics* 20, 1–52.

Kaplan, R. 1996. *The Ends of the Earth.* New York: Random House.

Leakey, R. and Lewin, R. 1995. *The Sixth Extinction.* New York: Doubleday.

Lewontin, R. 1992. *Biology as Ideology.* New York: HarperCollins.

Mayumi, K. 1993. 'Development, Ecological Degradation and North-south

Trade.' Proceedings of the International Conference: *Training of Experts for European Cooperation on Protection of the Environment and Promotion of Sustainable Development.* University of Mining and Metallurgy, Kraków, Poland.

Mendelsohn, R. and Balick, M. 1995. 'The Value of Undiscovered Pharmaceuticals in Tropical Forests.' *Economic Botany* 49, 223–228.

Mokyr, J. 1990. *The Lever of Riches.* New York: Oxford University Press.

Naeem, S., Thompson, L., Lawler, S., Lawton, J. and Woodfin, R. 1994. 'Declining Biodiversity Can Alter the Performance of Ecosystems.' *Nature* 368, 734–737.

Norgaard, R. 1984. 'Coevolutionary Development Potential.' *Land Economics* 60, 160–173.

Norgaard, R. 1994. *Development Betrayed.* London: Routledge.

O'Connor, M. 1994. 'On the Misadventures of Capitalist Nature'. In O'Connor, M. (ed.) *Is Capitalism Sustainable?* New York: Guilford Press.

O'Neill, R., DeAngelis, D., Waide, J. and Allen, T. 1986. *A Hierarchical Concept of Ecosystems.* Princeton: Princeton University Press.

Perrings, C. 1987. *Economy and Environment: A Theoretical Essay on the Interdependence of Economic and Environmental Systems.* Cambridge: Cambridge University Press.

Peters, C., Gentry, A. and Mendelsohn, R. 1989. 'Valuation of an Amazonian Rainforest.' *Nature* 339, 655–656.

Pimm, S., Russell, G., Gittleman, J. and Brooks, T. 1995. 'The Future of Biodiversity.' *Science* 269, 347–350.

Price, C. 1991. *Time, Discounting and Value.* New York: Basil Blackwell.

Randall, A. 1988. 'What Mainstream Economists Have to Say about the Value of Biodiversity.' In Wilson, E.O. (ed.) *Biodiversity.* Washington, D.C.: National Academy Press, 217–226.

Sagoff, M. 1988. *The Economy of the Earth.* New York: Cambridge University Press.

Simon, H. 1962. 'The Architecture of Complexity.' Proceedings of the American Philosophical Society. Cambridge, Massachusetts MIT Press.

Solow, R. 1993. 'Sustainability: An Economist's Perspective.' In Dorfman, R. and Dorfman, N. (eds.): *Economics of the Environment.* New York: W. W. Norton.

Telser, L. 1996. 'Competition and the Core.' *Journal of Political Economy* 104, 85–107.

Tilman, D. and Downing, J. 1994. 'Biodiversity and Stability in Grasslands.' *Nature* 367, 363–365.

Tilman, D., May, R., Lehman, C. and Nowak, M. 1994. 'Habitat Destruction and the Extinction Debt.' *Nature* 371, 65–68.

van Ees, H. and Garretsen, H. 1996. 'An Annotated Bibliography on the

(Macro)foundation of Post Walrasian Economics.' In Colander, D. (ed.) *Beyond Microfoundations: Post Walrasian Macroeconomics.* New York: Cambridge University Press.

Vrba, E. and Eldredge, N. 1984. 'Individuals, Hierarchies and Processes: Towards a More Complete Evolutionary Theory.' *Paleobiology* 10, 2, 146–171.

Vrba, E. and Gould, S. 1986. 'The Hierarchical Expansion of Sorting and Selection: Sorting and Selection Cannot Be Equated.' *Paleobiology* 12, 217–228.

Ward, P. 1994. *The End of Evolution.* New York: Bantam Books.

Weiskel, T. 1989. 'The Ecological Lessons of the Past: An Anthropology of Environmental Decline.' *The Ecologist* 19, 104–109.

Wollin, A.S. 1995. *A Hierarchy-Based Punctuated Equilibrium Model of Emergence and Change of New Rural Industries.* Unpublished Ph.D. thesis, Griffith University, Brisbane, Australia.

6. System Hierarchy, Change and Sustainability

Jörg Köhn[1]

INTRODUCTION

The context for sustainability policies is the interaction among ecological, societal, political, cultural and economic systems, the structural and functional connections between them, and how changes in a subsystem affect the general system. Account also has to be taken of how different rates of change affect these interconnected systems.

The paper begins with a discussion of sustainability policies, focussing on some of the shortcomings in the sustainability literature. The concepts of the 'maximum sustainable yield' (MSY) and material-energy balances are discussed in detail. Next the contributions of Boulding, Georgescu-Roegen and Daly are considered, focusing on the thermodynamic and societal aspects of sustainability, and the relations between material, energy and information in system evolution. Much of the sustainable development literature has focused on material and energy approaches (Ayres and Simonis, 1996; Faber and Proops, 1991; Hannon and Ruth, 1994). Next, the discussion turns to information and its institutional context. Dawkins' (1989) concept of information replicators (genes and memes) and the 'dual inheritance theory' (gene pools and cultures) of Boyd and Richerson (1985) are integrated with systems evolution. Taken together, these concepts allow the development of a model of system hierarchy. Finally, rates and sensitivity to change of natural, social, cultural, political and economic systems are compared.

[1] This chapter is part of a project "Conflict resolution strategies by discourse" supported by the German Marshall Fund of the United States (Grant No. A−0374−01).

CONCEPTS OF SUSTAINABILITY

For most human history, our species lived in ways that were environmentally sustainable. Gowdy (1997) describes how the survival of hunter–gatherer communities depended on the sustainable way in which they used their resources. Ponting (1993) points to the Nile valley cultures that developed (and depended on) an intricate system using natural resources in a sustainable way. The Nile River floods provided farmlands with soil nutrients but at the same time harmed humans perishing in the floods. The supply of nutrients, however, was the result of erosion of soils as a consequence of clearing the forests in Ethiopia and Uganda. Thus the sustainable economy in the Nile valley was non-sustainable on a wider scale. The Nile valley economy, however, lasted for almost 7,000 years. The people observed the extension of the annual floods and built on these observations a flexible tax system: low floods – low taxes; high floods – high taxes. Although the political system changed several times in the Nile valley the economic principles remained adapted to the natural conditions. There are many more examples in the literature of the use of scarce resources through local communities that protected their resources with socio-cultural institutions (Ostrom, 1990; Keohane and Ostrom, 1995).

Goodland (1995) points out that the concept of a sustainable use of resources was first mentioned in the writings of Malthus (1798) and Mill (1848). As early as 1849 Faustmann used a similar concept to calculate the forest rotation period needed to maximise returns in German forests (Ludwig, 1993). Forestry was one of the first domains in which scientists developed concepts of sustainable resource use. As early as in the second half of the nineteen century concepts of sustainable forest management began to consider the forest ecosystem as a resource supplier for timber. This over-rode other economic functions a forest has for humans – providing fuel, food, shelter, clean water, oxygen production, air cleaning, etc.

Separating one resource function from a set of multiple uses and putting the only emphasis on this use is, from a systemic point of view, a step towards making a system vulnerable. In line with these earlier approaches, economists developed the concept of the 'Maximum Sustainable Yield' (MSY, see for instance Pearce and Turner, 1990) to manage renewable resources. This concept, however, is strongly reductionist in its treatment of environmental variability since it separates a single commodity from its wider ecological and economic context. Environmental services of forests are no longer taken into consideration. The MSY concept supports sustainability with the 'carrying capacity' and the 'non-overexploitation' rule.

Goodland (1995) summarises the discussion on sustainability and distinguishes 'economic sustainability' from its more comprehensive social and environmental counterparts (pp. 2ff). He recognises the varying degrees with which sustainability can be understood and implemented, classifying them as weak, strong, and absurdly strong sustainability. In this classification, one may associate economic sustainability with weak sustainability; with social and environmental sustainability being stronger concepts. In a political sense, however, it is hard to separate social and environmental sustainability from economic sustainability.

The lack of a universally accepted definition of sustainable development has led to a dispute in economic science marked by widely differing viewpoints – usually dictated by different goals. An important issue is the substitutability of various kinds of capital (Hartwick, 1977). Economists following the neoclassical approach believe that technological progress and markets will continue to mitigate scarcity (see for instance Solow, 1974; Herfindahl and Kneese, 1974; Dasgupta and Heal, 1979). Another approach is based on the belief that natural capital stock should be maintained intact. A third approach links natural with social sciences in an attempt to apply the laws of physics to economics via biophysical constraints to economic activity. The latter approach also includes intergenerational and global justice as societal constraints (Victor, 1991).

The first two approaches seem to be compatible with the growth of economic wealth, the 'sustainable growth concept.' Proponents of these approaches assume that the present generation is entitled to consume more resources than future ones, because coming generations will be better off owing to their greater technological knowledge. Both schools assume that progress in science and technology will provide adequate opportunities for the substitution of resources.

The third approach denies that 'natural capital' can be substituted by manufactured capital, because nature sustains human systems with environmental commodities, amenities and services for which there are no substitutes. Victor (1991) quotes Marshall (1920) on this point: "a far-seeing statesman will feel a greater responsibility to future generations when legislating as to land than as to other forms of wealth; and that from the economic and from the ethical point of view, land must be everywhere and always be classed as a thing by itself." Victor (1991, pp. 210–211) shows that the environment cannot be regarded as 'capital'. Referring to the first approach, Victor wrote: "In referring to the environment as capital, there is an implicit assumption that it can be substituted by other forms of capital, that is reproducible and that it is there to be managed in much the same way as manufactured capital ...", and regarding the second: "The efforts of those engaged in extending the system of national accounts to incorporate the depletion of natural resources and the degradation of the environment and of others to monetarise environmental quality are worth pursuing though, in this author's opinion, they will fall short until a more appropriate conceptualisation of the interdependency of the economy and the environment is achieved."

Victor's approach takes into account the fact that both social and natural systems evolve and, therefore, the endogenous (system inherent) and exogenous (external) variables and processes, regulated by system adaptation and evolution, are themselves the products of change (Norgaard, 1975). In this context, the sustainability concept implies coping with change, uncertainty and irreversibility and taking self-regulating and self-organising processes within natural and social systems into account (Ayres, 1988).

Finally, in its political context, sustainability may be regarded as a set of political actions aimed at "development that meets the needs of the present without compromising the ability of future generations to meet their own needs." (WCED, 1987). This necessarily implies other targets than simply maintaining the capital stock. It implies that social (intra- and intergenerational) and environmental equity, ethics, social institutions, conservation of cultural diversity and biodiversity are all components of the sustainability goal.

TOWARDS SUSTAINABILITY CONCEPTS BASED ON THINKING IN TERMS OF SYSTEM HIERARCHY

The Contributions of Kenneth Boulding

One may describe the interrelations between social systems as functions of the rate of exchange of material, energy, and information between systems.[2] This leads to a stock-flow approach that explains the development of both natural and social systems in terms of 'birth', 'self-generation' and 'ageing' (Boulding, 1966, pp. 4–5). The exchange of material, energy, and information seems to be a necessary condition for the survival of living systems. Measuring the stock of material, energy, and information in a system, and the rates at which they are exchanged, to identify input-throughput-output relations permits the stability and velocity of processes taking place within the system to be assessed and any deviations from a state of equilibrium to be detected. The rate of 'acceleration' at which a stock is

---

[2] This chapter uses the information as a category. Information may be in some respect a misleading term since it has been used extensively in many other respects. The term as it is used here refers in the biological sense to the genome of a system, and in a social system to knowledge, cultural values, beliefs and behaviour encoded in social institutions (Cable and Cable, 1995, p. 10).

exchanged corresponds to the rate of growth (Boulding, 1966, p. 8) or, under certain circumstances, a deviation from a state of equilibrium. In essence, Boulding's work draws attention to several important aspects of system sustainability.

Development is a process that takes place in open systems. System inherent processes may sustain a particular subsystem at least within certain limits. Systems exchange matter, energy and information at specific rates. One may describe the rate of exchange in terms of stocks and funds, fluxes and flows (Georgescu-Roegen, 1971). Matter, energy, and information are the crucial structural classes of systems. Although matter and energy only enter the socio-economic system after they become an object of human interest, the self-generation of information and its codified forms constitute 'culture', for example, a 'set of common values' defining specific social systems. The values defining a particular social system are subject to 'mutation and selection.' Boulding distinguished three types of 'social organisers' that differ in their institutional arrangements:

- the threat system (policy),
- the exchange system (economy),
- the integrative system (culture).

Boulding (1969, p. 4) states that "these systems are linked together dynamically through the process of human learning, which is the main dynamic factor in all social systems." One may conclude that all three subsystems (policy, economy, and culture) are components of a more comprehensive social system and that social evolution is based on learning.

The Contribution of Nicholas Georgescu-Roegen

Georgescu-Roegen (1971) pioneered the use of thermodynamic principles in considerations of the exchange of matter – 'matters matters too' (Georgescu-Roegen, 1977b) – and energy in system development. He argues that the economic system is subject to the rules of thermodynamics. This may support the idea that the economic system is nested in a higher ranked system, 'nature'. The economic system extracts from nature low entropy matter–energy and converts it into high entropy matter–energy waste. Since the economic system exchanges matter and energy with this higher system, it is an open system. The system to which the economic system is open may be a source of negative feedback to the economic system.

Faber *et al.* (1987, p. 13) adopted this approach. They consider the economic system a subsystem of the higher system 'nature.' One may simulate both the material and energetic aspects of the two-system case if entropy can be quantifiable as a measure of degradation. The interdependence of the two systems varies with the intensity of the exchange processes – transfer of matter and energy. Both systems are in a state of constant evolution, but the subsystem 'economy' has to adapt to the evolution of the higher system. Spontaneous evolution of the higher system 'nature' is governed by, among other things, the laws of thermodynamics, and these laws must also apply to the subsystems, including the subsystem 'economy' (see Georgescu-Roegen, 1971, p. 57).

The Contribution of Herman Daly

Daly (1973, 1977) introduced the concept of a steady-state economy as a 'physical concept' (1977, p. 17) that can be used as a basis for sustainable development. It is based on the assumption of "physical populations – people and artefacts – existing as elements of a larger environmental system." (1977, p. 15). Daly observes that, "[o]rganisms cannot survive in a medium consisting of their own final outputs. Neither can economies" (1977, p. 22, his Figure 3; p. 35).

Daly applies the concept of scale to economic systems, an idea crucial for explaining interrelations in multi-hierarchical and complex systems (O'Neill *et al.*, 1989). Daly writes: "The growth of the economic subsystem is limited by the size of the overall system..., and by the intricate ecological connections which are more easily disrupted as the scale of the economic subsystem grows relatively to the total system." (1987, p. 324). The scale concept provides at least three methodological advantages. First, one may measure the dynamics and direction of the adaptation process (coevolution in resilient systems) in terms of the intensity of matter and energy flows within and between systems. Second, it fits the input–output(–throughput) or stock-flow concepts used in natural science and economics. Third, it permits inclusion of interrelated conditions such as complex interdependence, and time and space vectors in the analysis of a system's adaptation and evolution.

In addition, Daly's 'steady-state concept' links biophysical constraints (1977, p. 17) with societal ones (ibid., p. 16): "culture, genetic inheritance, knowledge, goodness, ethical codes, and so forth embodied in human beings." Whereas the sustainability discussion uses biophysical limits (for example, in material–energy balance analyses) as 'indicators' of sustained socio-economic development, the second group ('societal limits') are not operationalised for the discussion and even appear unsuitable for the purpose.

INFORMATION, REPLICATORS AND HUMAN SOCIETIES

Systems develop on the basis of the information they possess.[3] Boulding (1969, p. 6) states that "the larger amount of information and knowledge is self-generated by human society." Georgescu-Roegen (1977a, p. 363) sees the evolution of the human species as being "to live in society as the result of exosomatic evolution." Gathering and capturing information is a process of transforming free energy into information, but also one of generating entropy (uncertainty, see my second contribution in this volume).

Gene pools store genetic information, whereas humans are able to capture and store information externally in the institutions and organisational structures of society (Ayres, 1988). The information pool consists of a set of 'frozen knowledge' which human society generates by individual and social learning (Boulding 1969, p. 6) during processes that are part of human (genetic) evolution. Social learning processes play an important role in the evolution of institutional arrangements (Young, 1995, pp. 41–42). The human information pool consists of various forms of information, for instance technological and traditional knowledge, social norms, rules and taboos or even knowledge about these components, etc. The information pool is the structural frame for relations within a society; it is the potential (genotype) of a particular society to express itself as a distinct phenotype. Conservation of traditional knowledge, the creation of new knowledge, mutation and selection by learning are essential for human survival in different cultures (phenotypes).

In nature, information is pooled for each population, species and living components of natural systems in the genotype. The genotype is the potential actually expressed in a given phenotype, thereby creating individuals, populations and the system itself. In the short run, individuals adapt to the random conditions of the system they are part of, individuals adapt in relation to the population to which they belong, populations adapt to other populations and the ecosystem they live in, the ecosystem to the geographic region and climate, and so on. Feedback modulates these processes: each individual and population change the structural and functional constraints of the system surrounding it. Conversely, the system will influence the selection process down to the population and individual levels (co-evolution). This later process is intertemporal. The changes taking place as parts of the long-term process include changes in the structure of the replicators (evolution). The long-term process therefore leads to structural

[3] I use the term information in its largest sense. In this respect information means that an ecosystem is built on the pools of genes expressed under certain environmental conditions as societies possess data, knowledge, norms, regulations, and so on which determine the phenotype of a society actually to be seen.

and functional changes within the information pool (mutation) that vary in space and time. These processes take place on different scales.

This description, however, is only part of the truth. The information pool is also subject to erosion (internal changes within the system concerned), for instance the extinction of species and dissipation of information (Arrow, 1987, p. 223). Variations may occur gradually but they may be sudden. Systems may flip when they loose their capability to buffer shocks caused internally or externally. Flips may be caused either internally or externally. A flip may result in a new resilient state, which is distinct from the preceding state. It may take a long time until a new resilient state is established by the survivors of the preceding state or by their descendants, as demonstrated, for instance, by the five great extinctions that have occurred during the history of life on earth (Lovelock, 1995). Moreover, the velocity of evolution following such catastrophes is probably much higher than during 'normal' evolution. Rates of evolution vary in both natural and social systems. Brief spurts may appear between periods of resilient equilibrium or immediately after such periods have been established, with the rate diminishing as such periods draw to a close.

Naturally, one has to be careful when drawing conclusions based on analogy to human society and human information pools. Fischer (1996) shows that complex changes within society are also strongly related to changes in the information pool. Once a social process has been set in motion, for example, be changes within the economic system such as (a) price increase, the political and cultural systems are affected by instabilities of the former system. The process may result in a general crisis of society. The subsequent periods of equilibrium, which may have begun with a fall in prices, and the recovery of stability, had a distinct cultural character. New ideas and institutions emerged because the new equilibrium supported a high level of cultural, technological and scientific prosperity. Furthermore, the structures of both the political and economic systems change with the institutional arrangements. Fischer describes these processes as autogeneous and self-generating, driven by human will and chains of individual decisions.

Boyd and Richerson (1985, p. 281), however, in their 'dual inheritance theory', showed that genetic and cultural evolution is simultaneous and inseparable. They write: "Human beings are biological *and* cultural organisms. Systems of inheritance have internal structure *and* relationships to the external world. Individuals are the products of gene pools *and* cultures; they are loci of natural selection *and* decision making. ... [t]he presence of two systems of inheritance leads to complex evolutionary problems and possibilities."

Learning from natural systems and their 'information processing' raises questions concerning the structures on which cultural evolution is based. Dawkins (1989, p. 192) compares human culture to a 'soup' consisting of human needs, technical and social knowledge and knowledge, about rules and norms, preferences, etc. The 'soup' is the superstructure, the metaphor to which all human information belongs. It refers to the genome, that is, the pool of information that humans have created in their history and now possess. This 'genome' is the 'potential' to create, manage and sustain social structures. Dawkins, however, describes evolutionary processes as involving both gene transfer from parents to offspring (genetic evolution) and individual learning by offspring from their parents (individual learning by imitation as symmetric transmission). Furthermore, in cultural evolution socialisation processes play an important role.

Boyd and Richerson (1985, p. 130, p. 292) emphasise the importance of group behaviour. Groups are subject to selection

> [b]ecause the cultural population is affected by both forces of
> selection and guided variation ... cultural transmission creates
> heritable variation between individuals and groups. ... direct
> bias and guided variation would act to increase the frequency
> of individually advantageous beliefs within groups, while
> selection between groups would act to decrease the frequency
> of such beliefs to the extent to which self-interest conflicts
> with co-operative activities.

This, however, relates cultural inheritance to social learning processes in which 'asymmetric transmission' may sometimes be the preferable strategy. However, both processes – individual and social learning – are usually intertwined and forced by the pressures of selection and decision making.

NEW THINKING IN TERMS OF SYSTEM HIERARCHIES

Models used in economics portray relations between the systems 'nature' and 'economy' in various ways. Neoclassical economics considers and treats the problem of the environment as external to the economic system (see Siebert, 1994), but evolutionary economists regard the two as coexistent and coevolutionary (for example, Norgaard, 1975).

Faber and Proops (1991, pp. 75f) describe the rapid and unpredictable formation of the 'genotype' of the physical system. They postulate a 'unique genotype' for physical systems and increasing diversification for natural systems (corresponding in this case at least to the genetic potential of all species) and economic systems. The 'genomes' of economic systems determine such things as preference orders of the economic subjects, technology, the legal system and economic and social institutions. They are stocks of information. On this basis, the economic 'phenotype' is the expression of a 'memone', to use Dawkins' term, under given conditions (technologies in current use, capital consumption per unit good, quantities and prices of goods, market structures, and so on).

Analysis of the economic system proposed by Faber *et al.* (1987, p. 13) and the economic genome of Faber and Proops (1991, p. 76) leads to a modification of the system-hierarchic view. As a first step, one may separate the economic parts of the memone related to financial capital stock (preference orders of the economic subjects, technologies, economic institutions) from the economic genome. They form the memone of the economic system. Secondly, one may regard jointly the organisations or institutions of the state and its legal system as the memone of the political system (institutional non-transferable stock). Finally, one may put together history, beliefs, and values apart from the consolidated preference orders to form the cultural memone. National or ethnic traditions are part of this system model. The cultural system is decisive for the inertia of social systems, and forms the ethical backbone of a society. However, clear-cut separation between the subsystems seems impossible or even inappropriate to systems thinking.

The three newly formed systems are part of the social system. They develop partly independently of each other owing to the accumulation (and erosion) of the information stock (evolution of their distinct memones). Information flows between their memones balance the subsystems. The information pools create local, regional, national or continental phenotypes. Feedback controls the rates of development of the subsystems at some stages, that is, each subsystem must have time to adapt to the development of the others. Trigger and carrier feedback mechanisms analogous to those of enzyme cycles could serve as regulating instruments. We know little about such mechanisms in social systems. Ever since the division of labour, and certainly since the Industrial Revolution, evolutionary and coevolutionary processes in the social system have been taking place at a substantially faster pace than in nature (see for instance, Boyd and Richerson, 1985, p. 130). As a result, the uncertainty and unpredictability on paths of development have increased.

The social system replaces the economic submodel in the considerations of Faber *et al.* (1987, p. 13). That is, an additional coevolutionary process takes place between the social and natural system (Figures 6.1–6.3). This process is inevitably slower than processes between subsystems of the social system, but is strongly influenced by their rates. Rates of evolution depend on the genetic resistance of the various attributes and on factors outside the system concerned, such as those exerted by systems in which the system concerned is nested (Table 6.1). In contrast to the models discussed earlier, the model considered here expands to form a three-level hierarchy. Feedback takes the form of adaptation of the phenotype of a system within the existing hierarchy and relative to the source reference system.

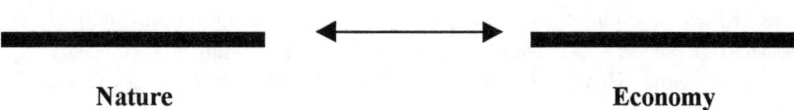

Figure 6.1. A One-Level Hierarchy and possible feedback between systems.

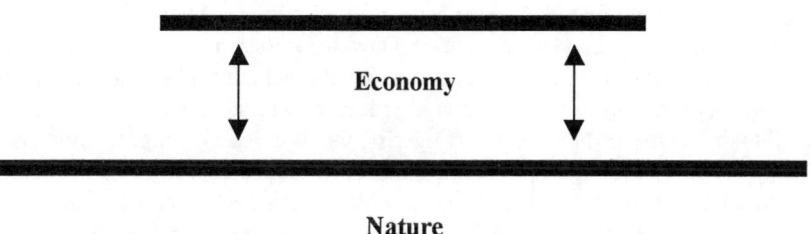

Figure 6.2. A Two-Level Hierarchy and possible feedback between systems.

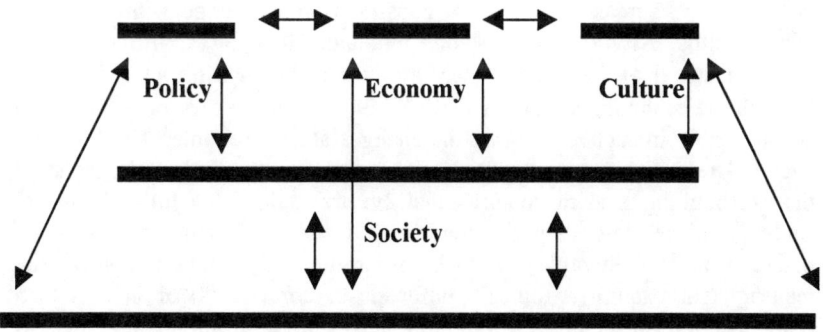

Figure 6.3. A Three-Level Hierarchy and possible feedback between systems.

VELOCITY OF SYSTEM CHANGE

One cannot assume rates of change to be constant. Even during periods in which a system seems to be in equilibrium, the rates of adaptation, co-evolution and evolutionary processes are not uniform. Moreover, it is impossible to measure the absolute rates of evolutionary processes since clear-cut physical indicators are lacking and fixed reference points do not exist. However, one may compare rates of change between systems in relative terms. Rates of change within social systems are all the more unequal, as historical processes are usually diachronic, whereas natural processes are more synchronic (Boyd and Richerson, 1985, p. 290), at least for systems in an equilibrium phase. Holling (1995, p. 24, p. 27) shows, however, that in natural systems the larger, slower levels set constraints within which smaller, faster levels operate. Conversely, smaller, faster systems may drive dynamic processes in the system in which they are part of, if the larger system is vulnerable to small disturbances at certain critical times (Lovelock, 1995).

Georgescu-Roegen (1977a, p. 366), Dawkins (1989, p. 194), Ayres (1988, p. 21) and Fischer (1996, p. 241) show that the velocity of social processes has increased owing to self-reinforcing processes within society's information pool in the course of history. The triggering factor at least during, say, the last 150 years of technological capability, has been technological 'progress', "an output of the economic system." (Ayres 1988, p. 25) Technological capability depends on investment in R&D, which is a function of private and state investment and state regulations. Boyd and Richerson (1985, p. 191) show that "Cultural transmission leads to persistence of behavioral traits through time." One may measure the time required for cultural change in terms of generations, whereas technological constraints may change within years or even months. All three subsystems, although changing at different rates, change faster than the social system they are embedded in, but – especially through the economic system as Fischer (1996) shows – they may change the social system in such a way that the changes are irreversible, therefore non-cyclic. The social system, however, not only depends on, but also changes, the surrounding system 'nature' that, in the sense of Holling's (1995) findings, is the slowest in the hierarchy concerned. On the regional scale, nature is most vulnerable where the environmental system is approaching maturity (for example, tropical rainforests or coral reefs) or in a state of reorganisation (farmland; restoration of landscapes after mining activities, for instance). It is more resistant to disturbances caused by the lower level (social, cultural, political, economic) systems, if both the social and the natural system are in a co-evolutionary process. These findings strongly support Fischer's (1996) analysis on 'great waves' in which newly established equilibria are characterised by inventions, cultural progress and economic stability.

Table 6.1. Velocity and sensitivity to change of resilient systems.

	velocity of change	sensitivity to change
Natural systems	very slow	extremely low
Social systems		
• Cultural systems	slow	low
• Political systems	medium	low
• Economic systems	fast	medium

VALIDITY FOR SUSTAINABILITY POLICIES

One can set the system bounds of the hierarchy model described above at a local, regional, national, continental or global decision-making level. The determinants set by the supersystem 'nature' consist of climate, biogeographic features, and the resource stock. The social system also develops against its historical background. The evolution of the social system is the result of the development of the memones of its subsystems, the expression of specific (for instance local community or national) phenotypes and the adaptation of the subsystems to each other and to hierarchically equal and higher systems (coevolution). The expression of its information stock (potentials) characterises the degree of development of a system. The model may also point to a new way of thinking about sustainability since it assumes that the economic system is nested in the social system that also consists of the cultural and political system. Together, these systems are parts of the natural life supporting system on which they depend.

Decisions, however, are made individually and also in social contexts. Decision making processes and a changing set of technological capabilities include gathering, evaluating and storing information, but they also involve social interaction: conflicts, learning and co-operation (Boyd and Richerson, 1985, pp. 292–293). Since conflict resolution processes and learning are subject to, but also drive, social evolution, policies for sustainability can no longer rest on material-energy-balance approaches. To illustrate this point, the model demands that sustainability be a more unifying concept than it has hitherto been considered. There is no need to distinguish between different kinds of sustainability, for example, environmental, social and economic. According to the model, environmental sustainability has to include social sustainability. If we accept this, economic sustainability is part of social sustainability. Hence, there is no longer any point in considering economic sustainability as a superfluous category since the economic system cannot act separately.

Sustainability policies should be orientated towards safeguarding and using the information stock. One may evaluate inputs (flows such as technical knowledge) in terms of their suitability and adaptability to the cultural and political system. Globally free transferability of technical knowledge, preference hierarchies or economic institutions may cause unpredictable changes within the (local, regional, national) social system and even in the natural system concerned.

As early as 1966 (p. 5) Boulding stated that three classes – matter, energy, and information – must be taken into account, implying that sustainability policies ('stewardship' on earth) will involve more than the bare necessities matter and energy. The problem of sustainability can be solved only by encouraging "synergetic feedbacks between human societies and their environment" (Berkes and Folke, 1994, p. 134). Such feedback consists in the information affecting expression of the phenotype (Boyd and Richerson, 1985, p. 283) of an individual and social system. This is especially due to the cultural sphere, capacity building by processes of social learning, strengthening institutional and organisational capabilities. These processes will capture and store human information for sustainable policies and will also support the sustainable use and conservation of resources. This clearly shows that sustainability policies, although also focusing on 'sustainable management' in production, product and service development and availability, consumption, recycling and reintroduction to 'natural' material fluxes, have to have a much wider scope. In addition, appropriate capacities and institutions may also cope with uncertainty stemming from and generated by social processes.

REFERENCES

Arrow, K.J. 1987. 'Oral History I: An Interview.' In Feiwel, G.R. (ed.), *Arrow and the Ascent of Modern Economic Theory*. Basingstoke: Mcmillan.

Ayres, R.U. 1988. 'Self-organisation in Biology and Economics.' International Institute for Applied Systems Analysis, Laxenburg.

Ayres, R.U., and Simonis, U.E. 1996. *Industrial Metabolism. Restructuring for Sustainable Development*. Tokyo: United Nations University Press.

Berkes, F., and Folke, C. 1994. 'Investing in Cultural Capital for Sustainable Use of Natural Capital.' Stockholm: *Beijer Reprint Series* 22, 128–149.

Boulding, K.E. 1966. 'The Economics of the Coming Spaceship Earth.' In Jarrett, H. (ed.) *Environmental Quality in a Growing Economy.* Baltimore: John Hopkins University Press, 3–14.

Boulding, K.E. 1969. 'Economics as A Moral Science.' *American Economic Review* 59, 1–12.

Boyd, R. and Richerson, P.J. 1985. *Culture and the Evolutionary Process.* Chicago: The University of Chicago Press.

Cable, S. and Cable, C. 1995. *Environmental Problems. Grassroots Solutions.* New York: St. Martin's Press.

Daly, H.E. 1973. 'Introduction to the Steady-state Economy.' In Daly, H.E. (ed.) *Toward a Steady-state Economy.* San Francisco: W.H. Freeman, 1–32.

Daly, H.E. 1977. *Steady-state Economics. The Economics of Biophysical Equilibrium and Moral Growth.* San Francisco: W.H. Freemann.

Daly, H.E. 1987. 'The Economic Growth Debate: What Some Economists Have Learned But Many Have Not.' *Journal for Environmental Economics and Managemaent* 14, 323–336.

Dasgupta, P. and Heal, G. 1979. *The Economic Theory and Exhaustible Resources.* London: Cambrigde University Press.

Dawkins, R. 1989. *The Selfish Gene.* Oxford: Oxford University Press.

Faber, M., Niemes, S. and Stephan, G. 1987. *Entropy, Environment, and Resources.* Berlin: Springer.

Faber, M. and Proops, J.L.R. 1991. 'Evolution in Biology, Physics and Economics: A Conceptual Analysis.' In Saviotti, P. and Metcalfe, S. (eds.) *Evolutionary Theories of Economic and Technological Change: Present Status and Future Prospects.* Manchester: Harwood Academic Publishers, 58–87.

Fischer, D.H. 1996. *The Great Wave. Price Revolutions and the Rhythm of History.* New York: Oxford University Press.

Georgescu-Roegen, N. 1971. 'The Entropy Law and the Economic Problem.' In Daly, H.E. 1973 (ed.) *Toward a Steady-state Economy.* San Francisco: W.H. Freeman, 49–60.

Georgescu-Roegen, N. 1977a. 'Inequality, Limits, and Growth From a Bioeconomics Viewpoint.' *Review Social Economics* 35, 361–375.

Georgescu-Roegen, N. 1977b. 'Matter Matters Too.' In Wilson, K.D. (ed.) *Prospects of Growth: Changing Expectations for the Future.* New York: Praeger Books.

Goodland, R. 1995. 'The Concept of Environmental Sustainability.' *Annual Review of Ecological Systems* 26, 1–24.

Gowdy, J. (ed.) 1997. *Limited Wants, Unlimited Means: A Reader on Hunter-gather Economics and the Environment.* Washington D.C.: Island Press.

Hannon, B. and Ruth, M. 1994. *Dynamic Modeling.* New York: Springer.

Hartwick, J.M. 1977. 'Intergenerational Equity and the Investing of Rents from Exhaustible Resources.' *American Economics Review* 66, 972–974.

Herfindahl, O. and Kneese, A.V. 1974. *Natural Theory of Natural Resources.* Columbus: Charles E. Merle.

Holling, C.S. 1995. 'What Barriers? What Bridges?' In Gunderson, L.H., Holling, C.S. and Light, S.S. (eds.) *Barriers and Bridges to the Renewal of Ecosystems and Institutions.* New York: Columbia University Press, 3–34.

Keohane, R.O. and Ostrom, E. 1995. *Local Commons and Global Interdependence.* London: Sage.

Lovelock, J. 1995. *The Ages of Gaia.* New York: W.W. Norton and Company.

Ludwig, D. 1993. 'Uncertainty, Resource Exploitation and Conservation: Lessons from History.' *Science* 260, 17–53.

Malthus, T.R. 1798. *An Essay on the Principle of Population.* London.

Marshall, A. 1920. *Principles of Economics.* London: Macmillan.

Mill, J.S. 1848. *Principles of Political Economy with Some of Their Applications to Social Philosophy.* London.

Norgaard, R.B. 1975. 'Scarcity and Growth: How Does It Look Today?' *American Journal for Agricultural Economics* 810–814.

O'Neill, R.V., Johnson, A.R. and King, A.W. 1989. 'A Hierarchical Framework for the Analysis of Scale.' *Landscape Ecolology* 3, 193–205.

Ostrom, E. 1990. *Governing the Commons: The Evolution of Institutions for Collective Action.* New York: Cambridge University Press.

Pearce, D.W. and Turner, R.K. 1990. *Economics of Natural Resources and the Environment.* New York: Harvester Wheatsheaf.

Ponting, C. 1993. *A Green History of the World.* New York: Penguin Books.

Siebert, H. 1994. *The Economics of the Environment.* Berlin: Springer.

Solow, R. 1974. 'The Economics of Resources or the Resources for Economics.' *American Economic Revue* 15, 1–14.

Victor, P.A. 1991. 'Indicators for Sustainable Development: Some Lessons from Capital Theory.' *Ecological Economics* 4, 191–213.

World Commission on Environment and Development 1987. *Our common future.* Oxford: Oxford University Press.

Young, O.R. 1995. 'The Problem of Scale in Human/Environment Relationships.' In Keohane, R.O. and Ostrom, E. (eds.) *Local Commons and Global Interdependence.* London: Sage, 27–45.

7. Organising Diversity

Joachim Schütz

INTRODUCTION

A growing body of research, both in natural and social sciences, conceives the world as interconnected systems (See Capra, 1996; Clark and Munn 1986; Checkland, 1993; Luhmann, 1987). From a system perspective the world is not only an assemblage of objects, but its elements contain multiple mutual relations. Coevolutionary systems theory shifts the focus from intrinsic properties of objects or elements to their relations; more precisely, to the quality of their relations, to the quality of the resulting net, to the environmental context, and to the various degrees of freedom systems may have (Churchman, 1979; Norgaard, 1994; Boulding, 1981; Costanza, 1991; Schütz, 1997). Regarding human systems, or systems where humans are involved, at least three strategies to deal with diversity and heterogeneous interests in a systemic environment can be recognised. The first is to consider self-organisation an end in itself, and thus not to interfere with any self-organising process taking place (Anderson et al., 1988). The second is to integrate the wide variety of interests into one common denominator or process leading to a unique solution; be it by virtue, by majority voting or by the market process (Feldman, 1980). Finally, we may observe and influence systems by multi-dimensional sets of indicators (Bossel, 1994). The first part of the paper goes one step further by giving the multi-dimensional indicator approach a 'structure' through balancing and focusing essential qualities of a system within bipolar fields. It is suggested that various viewpoints should be acknowledged as expressions of essential qualities of a system, and that they should be to consciously balanced and focused. Thus it is argued that although plurality is necessary, it is not sufficient. From a systems point of view, plurality still has to make sense. It is shown that it is a functional necessity for responsible human behaviour to assign (human) systems an identity, and thus, at least indirectly, a system purpose. This identity will be reflected by the behaviour of the system and vice versa, giving rise to the concept of systems guided by meaning. The second part of this chapter comments on economic, institutional and individual consequences of pursuing a wise form of production relying on genuine (bio)diversity. The key issue seems to be the capability of the individual to balance his or her personal interest with the systemic purpose of the larger system she or he belongs to.

MAKING SENSE OF PLURALITY

Autopoietic Systems

The concept of autopoietic systems was coined in the research of living systems (Maturana, 1980; Maturana and Varela, 1980; Capra, 1996). The key element and the new quality autopoiesis introduces into the scientific explanation of the world is the capacity of living systems to react, to influence, and to establish relationships with their surroundings. Thus, besides the precisely measured objects and fluxes within the physical plane we may, for analytic purposes, identify a set of relations within an informational plane that organises the physical reaction and controls the energetic and material fluxes between objects, groups and their environment. Both analytic planes are connected through a circular feedback structure, the 'autopoietic dialogue.' (Schwarz, 1996).

Following critical systems theory (Churchman, 1979), I assume that especially for human systems these organisational relationships do not only reflect the laws of the physical plane, but also a unique, though arbitrary element of choice. This element of choice may be expressed as a third element within a third plane, the identity plane. If a system wants to be identified as a unique phenomenon within its environment, it must be able to distinguish between inside and outside of itself. Or as Maturana and Varela (1980) put it, it must be able to read and to evaluate its surroundings in the energy–matter plane. To do so, it must have the capacity to realise itself as different from its environment, and it must have a notion of its system limits. But realising and establishing ones outer border requires an identity concept. In that respect it is important to note that any system may not only cease to exist if it cannot adjust to changing circumstances, but also, if it can not integrate any partial differentiation taking part, it will simply fall apart, or change its identity. This has two important consequences. First, in an open dynamic context, a system must have at least implicitly a notion of an overriding system identity; and second, in an open evolutionary environment following a laissez-faire concept towards change may put the survival of the system at risk.

Systems and Meaning

By explicitly recognising the additional analytic dimensions of the autopoietic system approach as portrayed above, one obviously loses the possibility of holding an indisputable viewpoint in any scientific analysis. The multitude of interconnected circular causal structures opens a vast array of potential starting points for argumentation. For the majority of scientists the capacity to recognise and the capacity to handle material or energy flows simply co-emerge simultaneously within the physical world (Maturana and Varela, 1980; Capra, 1996). The various planes may be identified during analysis, but any argument must have its basis within the energy–matter plane. In this view any autopoietic systems has – due to functional specialisation – a comparative advantage over single objects

- with respect to obtaining and consuming resources,
- with respect to handling waste,
- with respect to evaluating and responding to outside impulses,
- with respect to handling non-linear dynamics of various fluxes, as well as
- concerning the capability of actively changing the environment according to its necessities.

The identity plane and its content may vary according to the capacities of a system to be aware and conscious, but any perceived systemic identity results only from its physical existence, the physical body, the neurological system including the brain, its neurological ego called the mind, and from its physical relations with the global ecosystem. Thus any system's identity concept should be totally expressible within the discovered laws of natural science (for example, to minimise the consumption of negative entropy). In that way autopoiesis is quite compatible with traditional concepts of 'hard' science.

This might be a valid position either if there is no possibility for choice – if it is all in the genes and chance (Monod, 1971) –, or as long as non-physical elements of identity are not relevant or even existential for objects or systems within the energy–matter plane. But if they do, as it is the case in selection processes of human beings with respect to feasible behaviour within the biosphere and culturally designed systems, or whenever elements of a system creatively use any degree of freedom beyond the laws of the energy–matter plane, the evaluation of a specific question under the former or latter rationale will lead to qualitatively very different answers.

Systems guided by meaning

There seems to be no way of avoiding the question of systemic orientation. As different actions will lead to different structures, to different system states, to different system paths, and thus to different futures of the world, so too will different concepts of identity define different arrays of feasible actions, leading to a different world. Even 'hard' science may no longer provide us with a 'neutral' position where we could take a refuge. The drive to enlarge the field of science to widen the base for objective knowledge has effectively undermined the possibility of achieving objective knowledge at all. By defining the outer limits of a system we belong to wide enough, it becomes impossible to adopt an objective outside position. If we grant human beings some degree of autonomy beyond their genetic code and chance, how can we responsibly decide without any objective outside point of reference? One possible reaction would be to reject the problem. Either by arguing that any result of self-organisation is optimal, or by arguing that any 'material edition' of the world is simply irrelevant. A qualitatively different reaction would be to consciously design an artificial outside-position. If we acknowledge the necessity to assign systems designed or severely influenced by human beings with an identity, knowing about the impossibility to scientifically prove any position held, and if we would thus decide to construct an artificial outside position, I can see three principal directions a (sustainable) society may pursue: first, minimal interference with individual decision-making. Second, adopt an artificially constructed outside position based upon global spiritual insights. Third, to organise a social process in order to define principal elements of the identity of their system.

The identity concept fulfils at least four important functions: first, at the systems level, it serves as a criterion for balancing the various interests of the system elements against each other, and concerning the interests of the system itself. Second, as soon as the potential to react upon a stimulus offers some degree of freedom beyond natural laws, the identity concept is the relevant 'guide' for action. Third, by at least partially guiding the action of a system, the identity concept shapes the appearance and the role of the system both in the material as well as in the informational plane. It thus effectively 'co-creates' the world. Finally, even before any action is taken, the identity concept calls our attention to issues of systemic interest. Even if current scientific knowledge will subsequently identify the specific 'problems' the system will focus upon, the identity concept guides autopoietic systems within the principles of the energy–matter–plane. The identity concept is thus the central concept for systemic orientation.

Whenever we meet co-ordinated processes across all three analytic planes, we refer to such actions, resulting from co-ordinated overlapping of the identity of subsystems and the larger system, as 'meaningful behaviour.' Thus by assigning a system with a certain identity and by securing a continuous interrelated flow of information across all three analytical planes, we actually create meaning: meaning as a balanced answer between individual freedom and systemic requirements; meaning as a concept of limits one consciously places upon her- or himself; meaning as an integrative explicit or at least implicit answer to Why, What, and How; meaning as an important prerequisite for current and future system states, for pursuing unknown paths, for unleashing unknown creative potentials, and as general guidelines for human behaviour; meaning as the synthesis of understanding the world including and beyond the natural sciences. It is in this sense, that we can think of systems as being guided by meaning (Schütz, 1997).

Assigning a system, a purpose within the theoretical framework presented so far should not be confused with unjustified attempts to conclusively determine 'the one and only' purpose. Any purpose assigned to a system is inherently relative, both substantial and timewise. What may be unique, is the quality in the relationship and the degree of integration between the identity of the total system, and the identity of its various subsystems, but never any idea specifically. Thus the call for a system purpose makes only sense in an atmosphere of tolerance. Consciously adopting an identity in the above sense is more like growing up. We should decide what we want to do, and coherently restrict ourselves if necessary according to the system purpose we recognise and assign. At the same time we should always be aware that any purpose is only one of numerous other possibilities.

Balance instead of security

If we continue to assume that we are able to exert a decisive influence upon our world, a responsible decision would ideally require knowing ex ante all consequences of the decision to be made. But in a coevolutionary framework we are never able to know all consequences in advance. Nevertheless we are forced to decide. The decisions have to be made, not only under uncertainty, but the longer the time horizon and the more complex the issue, the more they have to be taken under real ignorance (Knight, 1921). Under these conditions it seems wise to refrain from establishing any specific physical structure or set of relations, but to look for ways to identify and maintain qualities independent of any physical appearance. A system and its elements should be preoccupied with establishing qualities in the set of relations the identity plane considers as desirable. In that respect the physical plane becomes nothing more and nothing less than a contingency plane. The task of a system is to look for processes that are both compatible with the desired quality of the relations of a system, and with the principles of the physical plane. It is like digging 'a tunnel from two sides at once.' Priorities may rotate, but the final product is not pure chance within a given physical context, but is consciously self-imposed.

To be able to pursue such a strategy, the overriding quality is to maintain the capacity of a system to endogenously react upon as many impulses or circumstances conceivable, and to secure potential evolution in as many ways as possible. Especially for open systems, like the biosphere or any economic system, the capacity to react with structural changes to external or internal impulses is vital. It is thus essential for any system not only to maintain the variety of qualities as broad as possible, but also to maintain them in qualitatively opposing ways. If the required state of the system is not confined to a specific *status quo* or constant change, resilience and cumulative dynamics have to be permanently present, at least potentially. This calls for maintaining as wide a spectrum of behaviour as possible, and for multiple feedback structures leading to circular causality, since that secures the capacity of a system to endogenously overcome otherwise meaningful inertia.

A first theoretical consequence would be to stop the futile fight of proving supremacy of any partial point of view. The coexistence of opposing viewpoints is simply a sheer necessity for survival. The 'solution,' if we want to use this expression, can neither be absolute hierarchy nor synthesis; at least not in the Hegelian sense of effectively dissolving the unique qualities of any single perspective. It cannot be an undifferentiated plea for plurality either. Instead what is needed, is an analytical structure that allows or even needs the coexistence of qualitatively opposing arguments, like the idea of bipolar fields. If we express circular causality structures and possible venues within bipolar fields, it would be possible to retain both the unique quality of each pole and the complementary character of its opposing point of view. A concept that is not only close to field theory in science, but also to Daoistic, Buddhist, and American Indian teachings (Deng, 1993; Macy, 1991; Storm, 1994).

The challenge would no longer be to overcome or suppress any one pole, but, given the circumstances, to consciously find a position of balance within such a polarity field, knowing that both poles are equally necessary for the very existence of the field. Striving for balance explicitly recognises the necessity to decide and to select, but avoids denouncing any polar quality, since the supreme strategy is neither dominance, nor exclusion of one perspective, nor dilution of all perspectives in one grand synthesis, but a meaningful integration of coexisting polarities. The resulting 'normal optimal position' is the centre. It holds the greatest degree of freedom, since it allows the maximum capability to react. It also maintains the potential of switching priorities, allowing a temporary move into an asymmetric position, if considered necessary.

The decisive questions are then: What are the fields to be considered? What are the polar qualities? Which position is adequate, given the current circumstances? Why should we take it? What for? It is immediately obvious that these questions cannot be answered without referring to the assumed or assigned system purpose, thereby touching the identity plane again. Actually, whenever balance is to be used as a concept beyond formalistic or numerical equity, a conscious decision for a system purpose or identity is a necessity, since the selection of the qualities to be considered as well as the final position in the required balancing process will depend on the respective (sub)system purposes. Thus, once again, even though a system purpose might never be objectively determined beyond any doubt, it is functionally necessary.

ORGANISING SYSTEMIC WEALTH

More and more evidence urges us to realise that there is no indisputable unique reality out there to discover, neither a unique *Gestalt* nor a unique process, only a potential to be determined and to be used in order to 'create' a process, a way towards a vision of identity. Therefore we have to change the focus of sustainable sciences from determining limits towards describing the potentials and visions for co-creation. In that sense, we should be preoccupied with the meaningful organisation of diversity, both in the biosphere and in human systems. But what is needed to establish balance within human systems and towards the biosphere when the dominant culture no longer appreciates systems both in terms of wealth and in terms of awe? Even though individuals hold a key position in the puzzle of an ecological future, the capacity to organise the wealth of biodiversity depends crucially on the willingness and capability of our culture to explain and justify the systemic perspective, or what may be called a culture of social efficiency (Schütz, 1997).

Regarding biological evolution it has been argued that to be efficient means to compete with your fellow citizens. Yes, there are different species competing for the same niche or resources. Yes, the physically more efficient ones will succeed. But it is a competition at a less threatening level than in economics. Efficiency in ecology is never reached through partial analysis alone, but by integrating individual efforts within a systemic purpose (see Brown, 1991; Holdgate, 1996; Naeem *et al.*, 1994, 1996; Odum, 1971; Tilman, 1987; Schütz, 1998). All arguments so far suggest that only such a strategy secures a high diversity, and is thus feasible in the long-run.

Not the partial perspective *per se* is problematic, but the extent to which a partial viewpoint is considered as the most relevant point of view. It is immediately obvious that in our analytic framework a dominating partial analysis perspective tends to underestimate the organisational venue, the environment, and the interdependencies arising among all three venues.

Looking back it seems as if our Western societies have gone too far in the reasonable process to induce individual improvements and to instrumentalise the biosphere. Concerning society, this attitude tends to disintegrate communities, and concerning the biosphere, tends to push us, despite continuous technical progress, far beyond the space within which a sustainable existence seems feasible. Vital interests of various systems have been undermined to such an extent that some have lost their capability to reproduce a healthy *status quo*. Previously carefully balanced human systems, as the economy or the civil society, are at the verge of being tipped. Combined with a lack of appreciation for biospherical systems as such, unbalanced behaviour has exhausted and overloaded many buffers in our biospherical environment. We are just about to realise again, that individual well-being depends not only upon the capability to control resources, but also on the performance of the larger systems the individual belongs to.

We suggest as an alternative strategy neither the rejection of individual improvements nor the rejection of the marginal perspective *per se*. Individual improvements are still necessary and welcome, but they should not extensively interfere with the assigned system purposes. We should focus on finding and establishing the balance and organisation of the individual purposes within an agreed system purpose, as well as to strengthen the well-being of the environment the system belongs to. This would require first, to accept the functional necessity of a system purpose, second, to institutionalise the process of determining and assigning such a system purpose, third, to institutionalise a balancing procedure, and finally, to respect and honour the larger system we are a part of, the biosphere.

Systemic Competence

A partial perspective tends to reduce diversity to raise efficiency, while a systemic perspective tends to improve efficiency by raising diversity. Thus there is a fundamental qualitative tension between a partial and a systemic viewpoint about how to raise efficiency and its entailing dynamic tendencies. This principal difference in evaluation carries over to the field of organisation. From a partial point of view, co-operative structures hamper individual efficiency, while from a systemic point of view, co-operative structures are significant for raising the efficiency of a system. The capability to understand the superiority of the systemic viewpoint without giving up individual interests, is what we call systemic competence.

Systemic competence, co-operative structures, and (bio)diversity are in various ways mutually interrelated. Systemic competence may be seen as being fostered by three somewhat interdependent sources. The first is the positive practical experience of diverse systems and co-operative behaviour.

The second is the rationale of systems thinking. And the third is spiritual identification with other elements of the biosphere. While (bio)diversity is certainly positively influenced by co-operative structures and systemic competence, co-operative structures do not necessarily preclude systemic competence. Many forms of 'win-win' constellations, especially assurances, may be explained by pure individualistic reasoning. But the extent and the quality of co-operation will always be limited by partial reasoning, or the prisoner's dilemma (Axelrod, 1984). Not only that the marginal perspective forgoes the potential synergetic effects built on trust, more important, it will forgo the evolutionary chances a creative interplay of the system elements may hold beyond a given *status quo*. Thus it may be said, that a high degree of systems efficiency is always contingent upon a high degree of (bio)diversity, wide co-operative behaviour, and a high standard of systemic competence.

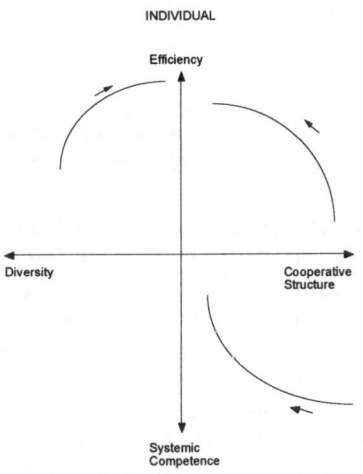

Figure 7.1. The individual view.

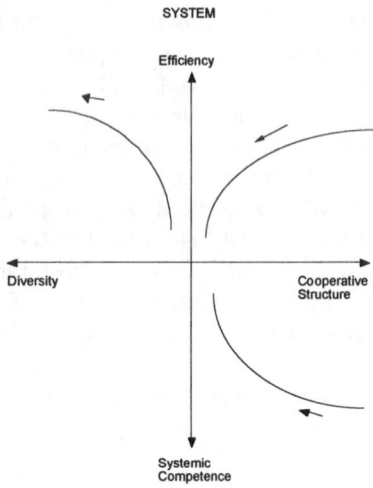

Figure 7.2. The systemic view.

But it seems as if efficient systemic configurations are not inherently stable. The dynamic tendencies are indicated by the arrows in Figures 7.1–7.2.

Systemic competence has to be maintained by positive experience, by continuous education, and if you may, by spiritual insight. Co-operate structures are also very delicate. They depend on constant approval through its members to be maintained. If systemic competence is not high enough, or if a sufficient number of individuals take advantage of co-operative structures, co-operative behaviour may break down, leading to reinforced tendencies of maximising individual behaviour (Figure 7.3, $A_0 \Rightarrow A_1$). In such instances there is the risk that a human system might become locked in a configuration of low (bio)diversity, low system efficiency, low co-operative behaviour, and a low standard of systemic competence (A_1, D_1, E_1, S_1).

Our current economic system of private goods in competitive markets asks for significantly less systemic competence than club goods, public goods, commons or even global commons do. According to the previous reasoning there seems to be no way to achieve a high level of system efficiency under conditions of low (bio)diversity, non-cooperative behaviour, and a low standard of systemic competence, as it is proposed by currently favoured economic reasoning. By the same argument, any politically intended increase in biodiversity will only be successful if systemic competence rises accordingly, and an adequate co-operative structure is established. If not, all attempts to raise biodiversity should not be very successful.

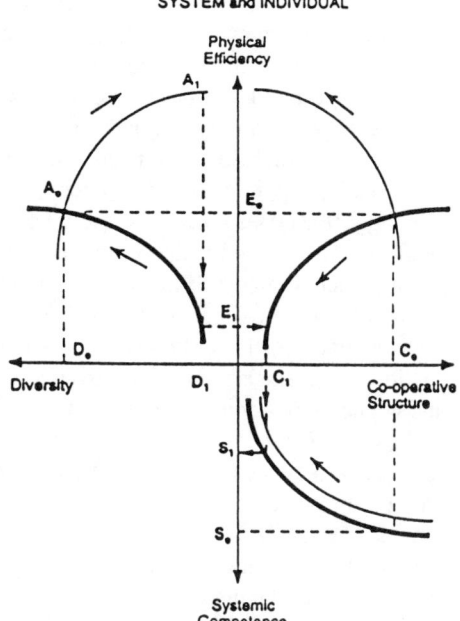

Figure 7.3. The cleavages between individual and systems thinking.

It is obvious by now that it is not at all safe to confine integrative reasoning to human societies. Systemic competence must include the biosphere (Stokes, 1992). If the biosphere is instrumentalised for group interests in much the same way as for individual interests, a collapse of an ecosystem seems unavoidable. If this happens, the sudden massive decline of the material basis for the human system will severely test the capability of its members to subsume their individual interests to a common purpose at a substantially lower material level. It is not inconceivable that social institutions of a co-operatively organised society may break down in the aftermath of an ecological collapse. Thus disregarding the biosphere might have as severe consequences as the neglect of establishing a sufficient standard of co-operative structures and systemic competence.

Economic Efficiency and (Bio)Diversity

Important subsystems in society, like the economy, should be able to resonate systemic reasoning and any determined systems purpose. Mainstream economists are quick to point out that cost minimisation and the international division of labour is both physically and costwise efficient and ecologically beneficial since it tends to reduce net material flows. Certainly, if monetary surcharges for the sake of the environment change relative prices in favour of environmentally less damaging production and consumption, and if one can assume, that there is a close correspondence between prices and the physical content of materials, work, energy or entropy in goods and services, it makes perfect sense to consider cost minimisation a rational procedure to achieve economic efficiency, as well as approaching ecological sustainability by reducing throughput (Young, 1992). But that is not the whole story. On the contrary, to rely only upon ecologically motivated economic surcharges might turn out to be a Mephistophelen strategy. While environmental surcharges will increase the relevance of ecological considerations relatively speaking, price tags on environmental goods will not interfere at all with the usual partial analysis evaluation mechanisms or the striving for unfettered expansion. Conventional economic wisdom will still hold: more consumption is better than less. This principal is not at all challenged through environmental pricing. And a key contradiction between economic and ecological reasoning remains unsolved.

While both ecology and economics strive for the best performance possible, and both refer to their striving as efficiency, ecology builds on diversity while economics builds on homogeneity. Within a dynamic market economy the normally employed partial analysis in economics eventually leads to numerous replacements of all machines, processes, and people that are not considered to be efficient enough compared to cheaper ones. Since according to economic theory a system is nothing but the sum of its members, any system will be the more efficient the more it uses those most efficient machines, processes, and persons. Thus our current socially legitimised strategy to become ever more efficient by cost minimisation leads, in the currently practised unbalanced way, through diffusion of the cheapest production processes, and its inherent bias for mass application, to a homogenisation and reduction of diversity within production processes, human artefacts, resources being used, biodiversity being maintained, know how in general, and types of labour employed. Provocatively, it could be said that economic efficiency is achieved by the exclusion of the inefficient from productive economic processes, and by copying the remaining. The quest for ecologically safe limits and ecologically true prices in mainstream economics seems therefore to be driven more by the need for monetary compensation of any damage being done to individual property rights than by ecologically based insights. It is essential to realise that environmentally correct prices are necessary, but not sufficient, since it is exactly the unrestrained cost-minimisation approach that hinders economic reasoning to see the ecological point: efficiency of natural ecosystems is not achieved by a reduction of diversity, but rather through interrelated, maintained diversity. Thus even with environmentally correct prices, an unreflected cost-minimisation exerts an inevitable tendency towards homogenisation by exclusion, which will continue to erode both ecological diversity and social integration, the pillars any society rests upon in the longrun (Costanza, 1991; Daly, 1991).

Maintaining Balance in Organising Society

In recent decades, our cultures have transformed various hierarchical structures into weblike structures without obvious centres, spreading power from the head to the elements (Habermas, 1985). If we accept the functional necessity of a system purpose, these transformations equally transfer the necessity to adopt a holistic point of view from the head-position of the former hierarchical structures to each element of the net. While it is undisputed that any head of a hierarchical structure must hold a holistic perspective, we still seem to reject the necessity to hold any kind of common holistic perspective at the individual level (Beck, 1988). It is not the multitude of competing values on the level of the individuals that is giving us trouble, but the unbalanced nature of our currently held common ground in Western societies. The problem is not that we all believe in personal freedom for the sake of individual self-realisation, but how we interpret the intended self-realisation: go for the maximum *possible* instead of what should be jointly determined as *feasible*.

It is becoming increasingly apparent that our current Western societies do wrong if they assume that any disintegrating forces set free within a system will automatically be sufficiently counterbalanced by some other integrative forces. The historically unique combination of liberation of the individuals from patronising regulations through churches, absolutism, nationalism, or other political ideologies, and the institutionalisation of a dominating economic market system based upon individual preferences have weakened the integrative forces in various systems to such an extent, that extensive disintegration started to take place. But, who is to blame for the current system state, the idea of a market system or the way our culture handles it? I admit, the market mechanism reduces everything – human beings, the environment or technological risks – to a comparable singular pecuniary number. It is obvious that even without questioning the specific procedures how this is beeing done, the reduction into one dimension contrasts sharply with the quest for a kind of holistic decision making especially in context with the human being or the environment. But is it necessary to conceive the price of a good or service as a kind of absolution for any consequences that are connected with the production and consumption of it?

The challenge for us, and especially for economics as a discipline, is to learn from our current experiences to balance individual freedoms against systems priorities, like differentiation and integration, or partial and total analysis within and between various efficiency concepts. In doing so, we should not blame the past for supporting the differentiating forces at the expense of integrative forces, we should rather realise where we still follow outdated, unbalanced reasoning. We should also realise from hindsight why this unbalanced strategy had been bound for failure, as any evolutionary system needs both opposing qualities to survive. Successful development of a system is always characterised by two complementary aspects: growing differentiation and a shift of integration on a hierarchically higher, maybe abstract level. But economics for example has no concept of reintegrating any differentiation processes taking place within the system towards a common purpose. This lack of systemic perspective, other than pure summing up, leads to a continuous crumbling of the system as a whole. For example, the currently praised productivity strategy, which means to produce more with fewer people, does not have an integral system perspective. Without such a perspective we should not be surprised that employment will become the major social problem in the future.

Certainly, separateness and connectedness are coexisting features in any systemic model. Elements are only perceived if they are identifiable. They must be differentiable from their immediate context, and elements must be connected in multiple ways to react as a whole. However, the relative position between these two equally necessary but still opposing qualities is not predetermined. Should we maximise separateness and limit connectedness to the essentials, or should it be the other way round? Luhmann (1986, 1987) has shown that it is theoretically possible and 'logically correct' to consider separateness instead of connectedness as the 'conditio sine qua non' for an element or a subsystem of a larger system. If we follow Luhmann and ignore the complementary view, that the system enables the individual's existence, we will get more of what we already have. The other elements of the system are needed only as a differentiating background for reaching and maintaining one's identity. Any element will try both to hold on to whatever he accrued, and to shape the conditions such that a maximum unfolding of oneself will be possible with minimal consideration for others (Daly and Cobb, 1989).

FINAL STATEMENT

Following the arguments put forth so far, I take a somewhat opposing position to Luhmann. Our societies should strive for conditions that enable everybody to unfold oneself for and beyond individual interests within a reassuring circular systemic structure. Impossible? Cultural experience and spiritual knowledge hold that it is not impossible, but it is easy to fail. Considering the state of the environment, do we really have an alternative but to try again? To be successful, it certainly takes both scientific insights and aspects of meaning. The biosphere may be seen as a vital regenerating system, but if it has no meaning, we or the respective human system will not care. There will be no interest in its well-being other than to secure its capability to provide any currently recognised vital services. For the biosphere to improve significantly, it must have meaning for both individual human beings and various human systems. Thus a deep appreciation and understanding of the logic in going beyond what is necessary, might be a necessary condition for the biosphere to improve. Otherwise, any technical and legal regulations concerning the biosphere will only be considered as cost factors to be minimised, or restrictions to be circumvented. The same is true for altruistic behaviour. If it has no meaning to us, we just will not do it.

The willingness to redistribute resources seems to be an implicit lesson of the reasoning advocated so far. Of course, one can argue about where and when to stop redistributive processes, but one cannot reject the necessity of redistribution as such. Pursuing a balanced integrative approach would thus, contrary to currently dominating economic wisdom, strengthen not weaken the chances for future survival and development of any human society. By developing a societal infrastructure capable of focusing and integrating continuously existing differentiation processes and (bio)diversity, any economic system may reach a higher level of efficiency than otherwise. It should therefore be no surprise, if many spiritual traditions hold that a human society may grow from a crippling state of collective mutual competition to an enabling state of future development, if individual human beings are capable of seeing their own interests also in the systems they belong to, especially in the well-being of the biosphere (Pojman, 1994; Teilhard de Chardin, 1961; Deng, 1993; Buber, 1923). Any individual approving would then fully unfold her or his potential beyond one's necessities within, and for the sake of, a self-reproducing net that keeps the circle running and the system prosperous. But the insight that in the long run all individual interests must be integrated in a systems point of view, and that systems efficiency is build upon diversity and co-operative behaviour, is subject to decay and needs constant cultural work to maintain a certain level of competence over generations. A concept to compete and at the same time to do whatever one knows best beyond ones own necessity seems to be the prerequisite for integrating individual competition and differentiation taking place in a 'circle of mutual feeding.' It is this balance of coexisting individualistic and altruistic behaviour at the individual level integrated in a working circular system structure that forms the basis for a level of efficiency no individual is able to achieve on their own.

Maybe we human beings are, as some American Indian cultures claim (Storm, 1994), the only species in the biosphere, which does not have a natural feeling for an adequate balance between egocentric and altruistic behaviour, and therefore lack the respect of diversity and the biosphere. According to their teachings, we have to rediscover and appreciate diversity, to practise balance over and over again, to discover the meaning in doing so. Thus it should come as no surprise that they consider the deep understanding and the subsequent behaviour, to work with the biosphere in a respectful way, and to 'give-away' whatever one achieves beyond ones own needs to those in need, as holy. In the case of our society let's call it an attitude of mutual caring; caring about our fellow citizens, caring about other forms of life on earth, caring about our planet earth. A consciously determined cultural way to systemic efficiency is not easy, but it is not impossible either. Maybe Callenbach's (1995) convincing call for the return of the buffalo in the Great Plains shows how to align management and spiritual awareness to see both beauty and economic wealth in a diverse biosphere.

REFERENCES

Anderson, P., Arrow, K.J., and Pines, D. (eds.) 1988. *The Economy as an Evolving Complex System.* Redwood City, California: Addison-Wesley.

Axelrod, R. 1984. *The Evolution of Cooperation.* New York: Basic Books.

Beck, U. 1988. *Gegengifte. Die organisierte Unverantwortlichkeit.* Frankfurt: Suhrkamp.

Bossel, H. 1994. *Modelling and Simulation.* Wellesley: A K Peters.

Boulding, K.E. 1981. *Evolutionary Economics.* Beverly Hills: Sage.

Brinkman, R.L. 1981. *Cultural Economics.* Portland: Hapi Press.

Brown, J.H. 1991. 'Species Diversity.' In Myers, A.A. and Giller, P.S. (eds.) *Analytical Biogeography.* London: Chapman and Hall, 57–89.

Buber, M. 1923 (1997). *Ich und Du.* Stuttgart: SVK.

Callenbach, E. 1995. *Bringing Back the Buffalo.* Washington D.C.: Island Press.

Capra, F. 1996. *Lebensnetz.* Bern: Scherz.

Checkland, P. 1993. *Systems Thinking, Systems Practice.* Chichester: Wiley.

Churchman, C.W. 1979. *The Systems Approach and Its Enemies.* New York: Basic Books.

Clark, W.C. and Munn, R.E. (eds.) 1986. *Sustainable Development of the Biosphere*. Cambridge: Cambridge University Press.

Costanza, R. (ed.) 1991. *Ecological Economics*. New York: Columbia University Press.

Daly, H.E. 1991. *Steady State Economics*. Washington D.C.: Island Press.

Daly, H.E. and Cobb, J.B. Jr. 1989. *For the Common Good*. Boston: Beacon Press.

Deng, Mind-Dao 1993. *Chronicles of Tao*. San Francisco: Harper.

Feldman, A.M. 1980. *Welfare Economics and Social Choice Theory*. Boston: Nijhoff.

Habermas, J. 1985. *Die neue Unübersichtlichkeit*. Frankfurt: Suhrkamp.

Holdgate, M. 1996. 'The Ecological Significance of Biological Diversity.' *Ambio* 25, 409–416.

Knight, F.H. 1921 (1971). *Risk, Uncertainty, and Profit*. New York: Kelley.

Luhmann, N. 1986. *Ökologische Kommunikation*. Opladen: Westdeutscher Verlag.

Luhmann, N. 1987. *Soziale Systeme. Grundriss einer allgemeinen Theorie*. Frankfurt: Suhrkamp.

Macy, J. 1991. *Mutual Causality in Buddhism and General Systems Theory*. Albany: SUNY-Press.

Maturana, H.R. 1980. 'Biology of Cognition.' In Maturana, H.R and Varela, F.J. (eds.) *Autopoiesis and Cognition: The Realisation of the Living*. Boston: Reidel, 1–58.

Maturana, H.R. and Varela, F.J. (eds.) 1980. *Autopoiesis and Cognition*. Boston: Reidel.

Monod, J. 1971. *Zufall und Notwendigkeit*. München: Piper.

Naeem, S., Hakansson, K., Lawton, S.P., Crawley, M.J. and Thompson, L.J. 1996. 'Biodiversity and Plant Productivity in a Model Assemblage of Plant Species.' *OIKOS* 76, 259–264.

Naeem, S., Thompson, L.J., Lawler, S.P., Lawton, J.H. and Woodfin, R.M. 1994. 'Declining Biodiversity Can Alter the Performance of Ecosystems.' *Nature* 368, 734–736.

Norgaard, R.B. 1994. *Development Betrayed*. New York: Routledge.

Odum, E.P. 1971. *Fundamentals of Ecology*. Philadelphia: W.B. Saunders Company.

Pojman, L.P. (ed.) 1994. *Environmental Ethics*. Boston: Jones and Barlett.

Schütz, J. 1997. 'Systems Guided by Meaning.' Paper presented at the First European Dialogue Conference on Science for a Sustainable Society, Roskilde, Denmark.

Schütz, J. 1998. 'Dreamtime Economics 101.' *Human Ecology Review* 4, forthcoming.

Schwarz, E. 1996. 'Systems Thinking, World View and Principles of Action.' In Pessa, E., Penna, M.P. and Montesanto, A. (eds.), *Third European Congress On Systems Science.* Rome: Kappa, 255–259.

Stokes, K. 1992. *Man and the Biosphere.* New York: Sharpe.

Storm, H. 1994. *Lightningbolt.* New York: Ballantine Books.

Teilhard de Chardin, P. 1961. *The Phenomenon of Man.* New York: Harper and Row.

Tilman, D. 1987. 'Secondary Succession and the Pattern of Plant Dominance Along Experimental Nitrogen Gradients.' *Ecological Monographs* 57, 189–214.

Young, M.D. 1992. *Sustainable Investment and Resource Use.* Paris: UNESCO.

8. Throughput, Scale, Material Input

Fred Luks

INTRODUCTION: ECOLOGICAL ECONOMICS, ITS SECOND STAGE AND ITS META-ECONOMICS

It has been argued that the concept of scale will not be very helpful for the 'second stage' of ecological economics (Duchin, 1996b), that is,for the further development of the field in order to deliver its potential for contributing to sustainable development. In the following it is argued that scale *can* contribute to scientific work as well as to the development of policy instruments aimed at sustainable development. While scale is certainly also a metaphor (like the invisible hand, industrial metabolism, natural capital, and so on), it is just as much a heuristic device for depicting the embeddedness of the economy into the larger ecosystem. The recognition of this embeddedness is of course one of the cornerstones of ecological economics, which is concerned with nature's household (ecology) and humankind's household (the economy). Ecological economics is therefore in general sceptical of economic growth, a goal universally accepted in mainstream economics and even more so in practical politics.

The notions of scale and throughput are thus an important part of the meta-economics of ecological economics. Meta-economics refers to a "set of first principles or basic assumptions" upon which economic analysis is founded (Underwood and King, 1989, p. 317). This notion is obviously closely related to what Schumpeter called 'preanalytic vision.' Another basic principle of ecological economics is what can be called 'prudent technological scepticism.'

> Given our high level of uncertainty about this issue, it is irrational to *bank on* technology's ability to remove resource constraints. If we guess wrong then the result is disastrous – irreversible destruction of our resource base and civilisation itself. We should, at least for the time being, assume that technology would *not* be able to remove resource constraints. If it does, we can be pleasantly surprised. If it does not, we are still

left with a sustainable system. (Costanza *et al.*, 1991, p. 7; emphases supplied).

Led by Funtowicz and Ravetz, there is a lively discussion about the idea of a post-normal science, and many ecological economists agree that ecological economics should be such a science (Funtowicz and Ravetz, 1991, 1994; Costanza, 1994; Duchin, 1996a, 1996b; Viederman, 1994; Luks, 1996). From a post-normal scientific perspective, "uncertainty and ignorance can no longer be expected to be conquered; instead, they must be managed for the common good" (Funtowicz and Ravetz, 1991, p. 146). In a situation characterised by global environmental problems,

> scientific problems, which are addressed, can no longer be chosen on the basis of abstract scientific curiosity or industrial imperatives. Instead, scientists now tackle problems introduced through policy issues where, typically, facts are uncertain, values in dispute, stakes high, and decisions urgent. ... *On the basis of such uncertain inputs, decisions must be made, under somewhat urgent conditions* (Funtowicz and Ravetz, 1991, pp. 138f; emphasis added).

The issue of scale is related to all this. It emphasises the embeddedness of the economy, and it is derived from recognition of knowledge problems, which relate to technological scepticism and post-normal science. In the following, it will be argued that scale is an important concept of ecological economics and that it will remain crucial to our vision of the economic process. As ecological economics enters its second stage, it will be important to further develop this heuristic concept. The operationalisation of scale is an important task in this respect. The concept of material input (MI) is presented as a tool that allows this operationalisation.

THE THROUGHPUT OF THE INDUSTRIAL METABOLISM

The concept of throughput is crucial for the ecological economic perspective of the economic process and was key for early expressions of this view (Boulding, 1973 [1966]; Georgescu-Roegen, 1971). In his seminal paper on 'The Economics of the Coming Spaceship Earth,' Boulding emphasises the crucial importance of throughput for a spaceship perspective. Throughput is both the input and the output of a system; it is necessary for the maintenance of its structure. Throughput consists of matter, energy and information (Boulding, 1973 [1966], pp. 122f.). While Boulding (1973 [1966], p. 124) holds that information is most important from a human point of view, with respect to the ecological impact of economic activities, what counts is the throughput of materials and energy. Georgescu-Roegen, as is well known, has pointed out the entropic nature of the throughput.

The throughput concept is closely related to the notion of industrial metabolism, which is a metaphor borrowed from biology. The anthroposphere as part of the larger ecosystem can be viewed as an industrial metabolism (Baccini and Brunner, 1991; Ayres and Simonis, 1994). The economy as a metabolic process depends upon the import and export of energy and materials. According to the first law of thermodynamics, neither matter nor energy can be destroyed. Consequently, the mass of the intake of the metabolism is equal to its output plus the accumulation of stocks (for example, houses, roads, and so on). The throughput, however, is subject to the second law of thermodynamics: this implies that the metabolism's input and output differ in quality. More precisely, the second law of thermodynamics implies a directionality of the economic process. "The matter–energy going in is useful raw material, while that coming out is useless waste. The flowthrough, or throughput of matter–energy that maintains the funds of artefacts and people, is entropic in nature. Low entropy inputs are imported and high entropy outputs are exported." (Daly, 1991b, p. 15f)

According to Ayres and Simonis (1994, p. xi), "industrial metabolism, by analogy, is the set of physico-chemical transformations that convert raw materials (biomass, minerals, metals) into manufactured products and structures (that is,'goods') and wastes." This set of transformations is moving the throughput of matter–energy from the environment into the anthroposphere and back to the environment. The materials balance approach, which basically is an analysis of throughput, "shows that the external costs phenomena which economists have written much about are not isolated and somewhat freakish aberrations but are inherent in the production and consumption activities of modern economies" (Kneese *et al.*, 1972, p. v; see also Ayres and Kneese, 1969). Therefore, acknowledging the importance of the throughput of the economy is a perspective quite different from the mainstream view in environmental economics. Considering the scale of the throughput is a distinguishing feature of ecological economics. The limits to (physical) growth, for example, only enter the stage from a metabolic perspective: 'Limits to growth' has been called 'the first metabolic study' (Baccini and Brunner, 1991, p. 6). What, then, is scale?

THE NOTION OF SCALE

Herman Daly's Concept of Scale

Herman Daly is one of the most influential authors in the ecological economics discourse. His major theme is the issue of economic growth. Since the late

1960s, Daly has argued that a growing economy is a long run impossibility within a limited environment. To put it in modern terminology: in order to be sustainable, an economy must be a steady-state economy. An idiosyncratic feature of Daly's work is the extensive use of metaphors. The metaphor which has become a core of ecological economics is that of scale, and related to that, the boat metaphor:

> When the watermark hits the Plimsoll line the boat is full, it has reached its safe *carrying capacity*. Of course, if the weight is badly allocated, the water line will touch the Plimsoll mark sooner. But eventually as the absolute load is increased, the watermark will reach the Plimsoll line even for a boat whose load is optimally allocated. Optimally loaded boats will sink under too much weight – even though they may sink optimally! It should be clear that optimal allocation and optimal scale are quite distinct problems. The major task of environmental macroeconomics is to design an economic institution analogous to the Plimsoll mark – to keep the weight, the absolute scale, of the economy from sinking our biospheric ark. (Daly, 1991a, p. 35; emphasis supplied; see also Daly, 1996, chapter 2).

Daly defines scale, as applied to the anthroposphere, as "the physical scale or size of the human presence in the ecosystem, as measured by population times per capita resource use" (Daly, 1991a, p. 35; see also Daly, 1992b, p. 337). In another context, Daly states that scale "refers to the *physical volume of the throughput*, the flow of matter–energy from the environment as low-entropy raw materials, and back to the environment as high-entropy wastes" (Daly, 1992a, p. 186; emphasis added). Scale, then, is the dimension of the throughput of the industrial metabolism; it is the burden put on the carrying capacity of the planet or single ecosystems.

Daly's notion of scale is closely related to his concept of a steady-state economy, which he defines as "one whose *throughput remains constant* at a level that neither depletes the environment beyond its regenerative capacity, nor pollutes it beyond its absorptive capacity." (Daly, 1992b, p. 333; emphasis added). It is evident today to most ecological economists (including Daly) that before throughput can remain constant, it has to be reduced, i.e. what is needed before a steady-state is a declining state (Gowdy, 1994, p. 14). From this perspective, "the central policy issue is to limit scale – preferably at the optimal scale of course, but for a start any sustainable level will do very nicely" (Daly, 1992b, p. 337). Sustainability, then, implies the necessity of throughput–scale reduction.

The concept of scale has become a "central concept to debates on economic growth" (Harris, 1995, p. 98) and is much emphasised by ecological economists (Krishnan *et al.*, 1995, p. xxxvi). Daly, however, does not offer a practical method of operationalising scale. 'Population times per capita resource use' of course resembles the often-quoted IPAT-formula, popularised by the Ehrlichs (see, for example, Ehrlich and Ehrlich, 1991). Obviously, this equals the 'physical volume of throughput' of the economy, but it remains an open question how this throughput can be measured. This is where Duchin's critique sets in.

Critique of the Scale-concept

In a paper on the development of the field of ecological economics, Faye Duchin points out that theory is needed in order to evaluate different development strategies and that the theory should serve as a framework to carry out quantitative calculations "since the tradeoffs among strategies require an empirical analysis and not just an application of abstract principles." (1996b, p. 286). Duchin examines Daly's environmental macroeconomics and critisises that "rather than providing a conceptual framework for analysing the underlying reality, Daly as a theorist is putting the burden of interpreting what scale really means in any concrete situation on the empirical analyst" (Duchin, 1996b, p. 289). Duchin holds that scale is not a useful concept for ecological economics. While it is true that Daly does not come up with a theory of how the economy 'works,' it is questionable whether a theorist can be criticised for not doing empirical work. As economists are well aware, a division of labour can contribute to an increase in productivity (in this case: the productivity of the community of ecological economists). Of course, empirical work depends on theoretical frameworks and vice versa. 'Scale' is a powerful metaphor, even if there would be no way of depicting it empirically.[1] It can be shown, however, that scale can be described in an empirically meaningful way.

A crucial problem associated with Daly's use of the scale concept, however, lies in his definition of the 'optimal scale,' as Daly calls it. While the scale can indeed be measured, the natural processes are much too complex to find out what scale can be allowed without putting excessive pressure on the natural sources and sinks. This is because, as for carrying capacity, "no one knows what that is, and attempts to measure it must rely on very gross assumptions." (Underwood and King, 1989, p. 333). Obviously, "we will only know what the carrying capacity *was* after we have passed it. By then it will be

---

[1] As for the metaphorical character of concepts such as throughput and scale, I have argued in another paper that ecological economics should continue to provide metaphors (and visions) that can inspire scientific inquiry and can serve in the political discourse on sustainable development. In other words: metaphors are important for both the 'internal' and the 'external' rhetoric of ecological economics (Luks, 1998). Moreover, it is exactly the openendedness of metaphors that makes them useful to scientific work: "New concepts do not come to us ready made; their novelty defies our existing language and conceptual schema. Science needs metaphor since it provides the cognitive means to chart the unknown." (Klamer and Leonard, 1994, p. 31; see also Lakoff and Johnson, 1980; McCloskey, 1995; Norgaard, 1995)

too late, but optimally, of course." (Underwood and King, 1989, p. 333; emphasis supplied). The complexity of natural processes makes predictions in this respect impossible (Gowdy and McDaniel, 1995, p. 187). This problem is closely related to what Vatn and Bromley (1994, p. 133) call 'functional transparency,' that is, the fact that many environmental assets are "characterised by their quintessential invisibility." Thus, there is no way of finding out what the optimal scale of the economy in relationship to its environment would be. To use Daly's terms (1992b, p. 337), neither an 'anthropocentric optimum' (equating marginal costs and benefits) nor a 'biocentric optimum' (taking into account intrinsic and instrumental value of other species) can be calculated. One faces a critical knowledge problem here. If a 'prudently sceptical' stance and a precautionary principle are adopted, this leads to the call for reducing the scale, that is, reducing the throughput of the economy. This notion of reduction of course implies an idea of a standard of living that should be kept – otherwise, the extinction of the human race would be a strategy to minimise throughput.

The shortcomings of the scale-concept, then, are both of theoretical and practical-political nature. As for theory, a further elaboration of the scale concept implies the need for operationalisation. On the policy level, operationalising scale is of equal importance, for to design instruments for reducing the scale, some measure of it is needed. How, then, can scale be operationalised?

MATERIAL INPUTS – AN OPERATIONALISATION OF SCALE

The Concept of Material Inputs

The division for Material Flows and Structural Change at the Wuppertal Institute for Climate, Environment and Energy is developing a concept to estimate the resource intensity of products as well as of economies in a Material Input Analysis framework (MAIA) (Schmidt-Bleek, 1996). This framework builds on the material input approach developed by Schmidt-Bleek (1994). Material inputs (MI) include all the materials displaced by human activity, for example, overburden, minerals, ores, oil, water, air, biomass, and so on, that are needed over the entire life-cycle of a product or service. All materials used for production (energy carriers, natural materials used for auxiliary material production, transportation, infrastructures, factories, and so on) are added up as the material input from nature to the anthroposphere (in metric tons). Hence, all the inputs of the industrial metabolism are taken into account *including* the so-called 'ecological rucksacks,' that is, those materials that are moved but not used in the economic process. Generally, all products can be analysed with respect to their material intensity throughout their entire life cycle, that is, step by step from the extraction of raw-materials, the production process, during usage, disposal or recycling phases. By relating the material input to the service delivered by a product, the material input per unit of service (MIPS) can be calculated. This 'micro-economic' applicability is important for the issue of 'ecological decision-making' by households, firms and policy-makers. For our purposes, the macro-dimension – the material input of a region or an economy – is crucial. The framework can also be used to analyse the ecological impacts of interregional trade. Waste flows *per se* are not accounted for in this approach, since they are outputs, not inputs. Since matter cannot be destroyed, all inputs into the economy will eventually be turned into outputs. As for material streams of secondary materials, only the natural materials used for the secondary processing are counted in order to avoid double counting.

Why Material Input Can Operationalise Scale

Several attempts have been made to show the physical scale of the economy. Templet (1995) uses the energy use of economic activities as a proxy for the scale. Vitousek *et al.* (1986) estimate the human appropriation of the products of photosynthesis. Wackernagel and Rees (1996) calculate the 'ecological footprint,' a concept closely related to the use of land. Such approaches are important in showing the move to a 'full world' in terms of the utilisation of natural sources and sinks. In this respect, these approaches are particularly important to building public awareness about the threats to sustainability. So far, however, it seems hard to conceive how such indicators can be 'translated' in order to serve as policy instruments or building blocks of environmental macroeconomics.

The concept of material input can serve as an operationalisation of throughput–scale. Recalling Daly's definitions of scale as 'population times per capita resource use' and 'the flow of matter–energy from the environment as low-entropy raw materials, and back to the environment as high-entropy wastes.' It is evident that resource use, if it is to have any sensible meaning, includes not only the utilisation of source functions but also the pressure put on ecological sinks. Moreover, to be meaningful from an ecological point of view, it must also include the anthropogenic material movements that do not enter the economy. The entropic nature of throughput is of course not explicitly taken into account by the MI-framework. Nor are the outputs considered. Yet, measuring material inputs is exactly an operationalisation of scale, since material input minus stock accumulation equals the output of the industrial metabolism. Hence, with material input figures for, say, regions, at hand, we can determine the scale of the throughput of an economy (for an application of material input analysis to economies see Adriaanse *et al.*, 1997; Behrensmeier and Bringezu, 1995; Femia, 1996). Note that by including ecological rucksacks, MI includes not only the materials converted within the economy but also those 'left aside,' for example at mining sites. From an ecological point of view, this broad concept of scale is clearly beneficial. Nonetheless, this approach is of course not without its shortcomings, which will now be elaborated.

Energy, Land Use, Biodiversity, and Toxicity

As for the treatment of energy in the material input framework, it has been noted that energy carriers are included. This can be problematic if the qualitative differences between matter and energy are neglected. Production obviously needs not only materials but also energy and information, and Christensen (1989, p. 28) reminds us of Boulding's famous dictum that the inputs of traditional theory (land, labour, capital) are 'hopelessly heterogeneous aggregates.' Apparently, from this perspective, the preoccupation with material input is misdirected. However, considering only the material aspects of energy use is justified by the fact that it is not the energetic but the material dimension of energy that burdens the carrying capacity of the environment. Moreover, "we can never handle energy without a material lever, a material receptor, or a material transmitter" (Georgescu-Roegen, 1981, p. 57). In other words, just as energy is needed to move materials, material input of some form is always needed to utilise energy. This is not to say that an ecological economic theory should not take into account dissaggregated inputs (differentiating between energy and different materials). However, in the context of a conceptualisation of throughput–scale on the level discussed here, material input seems to be a concept with a great potential and with the great advantage that it can actually be measured.

Material input analysis does not include the use of surface and the loss of biodiversity. This is of course also true for the notions of throughput and scale. Land use certainly does not belong to the category of throughput, but it is nevertheless important for the sustainability of economic activities. As noted before, the 'ecological footprint' (Wackernagel and Rees, 1996) emphasises the issue of land use. The loss of biodiversity cannot be accounted for in a throughput measure such as MI, but it is sensible to assume that there is a close relationship between the intensity of resource use and the threat to plant and animal species (Schmidt-Bleek, 1994, p. 121). However, while the use of renewable resources requires more land than utilising non-renewable resources, land use remains a problem that cannot directly be taken into account by the concept of scale/MI. As sustainable development requires a move towards less dependence on non-renewable resources and the use of more renewables, the effects of this requirement on land use and biodiversity must be taken into account. This problem has to be dealt with *in addition* to the throughput-problematic.

Two cornerstones of the material input approach are the acknowledgement of ignorance with respect to natural processes and the application of a precautionary principle. Of course the MI-concept is criticised for not taking into account the quality (for example, toxicity) of substances. The use of the material input framework might involve consideration of all known eco-toxicities of the material flows associated with a good or service. But reduction of material input would 'automatically' lead to a considerable reduction of toxic chemical and waste flows through the technosphere and into the environment. What is more, in most cases it is impossible to distinguish between 'good' and 'bad' throughput. There are, however, cases in which it is obvious that such a differentiation is feasible – plutonium, for example, has a toxic quality that is, very different indeed from, say, sand.[2] But very often it is not possible to anticipate the impacts human activities have on the natural environment. Besides that, it is of course not only the quality but also the quantity of throughput that disturbs natural systems. To make this clear one could think of an industrialised economy that does not produce toxic substances at all – just 'good' throughput at today's level. Would that imply that environmental problems would be solved? The answer is clear: no, it would not. The waste problems, the greenhouse effect (CO_2 is not a toxic substance in the traditional sense), soil erosion, the threat to biodiversity – none of those problems would be solved if we just 'clean up our throughput' but let it continue to grow. Reducing scale means reducing the *potential* ecological impacts of economic activities. A policy of dematerialisation would therefore decrease the potential disruptive effects of economies.

THEORETICAL AND POLITICAL IMPLICATIONS

Ecological Macroeconomics and Material Input

As for Daly's concept of scale as a part of ecological macroeconomics, what is indeed problematic is the fact that "rather than being impressed by the strong interdependencies among policies and their effects" (Duchin, 1996b, p. 288). Daly argues that a separate policy instrument is needed for each separate goal. One could say that this position does not show enough awareness of the complexities of socio-economic processes, which is the bottom line of Duchin's critique. If one views socio-economic development as a coevolutionary process – as many ecological econonmists do (see, for example, Gowdy, 1994; Norgaard, 1994; Hinterberger *et al.*, 1996) – simple

---

[2] Biotechnology may be a material-extensive technology with possibly disastrous effects. These dangers have, of course, to be taken into account. A low MI cannot *per se* serve as an argument for the desirability of a technology (Hinterberger *et al.* 1996, pp. 89ff.). *Biotechnology is an obvious case.*

recipes such as "determine scale, care for the community and let the market do the rest of the job" do not seem convincing (see also Prakash and Gupta, 1994; Stewen, 1998). Duchin correctly points out that "we cannot afford to accept simplistic answers to complex questions" (Duchin, 1996b, p. 297).

It is, however, important to distinguish between Daly's use of the scale concept and his belief that the market is the best institution to deal with allocation. His treatment of allocative problems does not result from his argument that scale is important. Daly's point is to emphasise that the scale-problematic is very different from the issue of allocation. Viewing environmental problems purely as a matter of allocation is of course the hallmark of neoclassical environmental economics. Daly's aim is to show that this is a crucial problem for policies for sustainable development. Agreeing with this does not imply that one has to be in favour of his view that after determining scale, the market should do the job.

The upshot is that the throughput–scale–material input perspective does not imply the notion of separability of the economic problems of allocation, distribution and scale. Daly's idea is an important contribution to the question of ecological macroeconomics. As is well known, environmental economics so far is basically *micro*economics, with the concept of external effects at its core. Acknowledging the importance of throughput and scale inevitably leads to the issue of how environmental problems can be treated at the macro level. This is the point Daly makes. It is necessary, however, to go beyond the mere recognition that scale is important: in order to incorporate scale into macroeconomic analysis, a measure is needed. Therefore, the material input framework can serve as a building block of macroeconomic analysis of environmental problems. The further collection of MI-figures and possibly its partial dissaggregation (for example, abiotic and biotic materials, water, and air) could contribute to such work. For example, for the issue of delinking environmental pressure and national product – a vital question for sustainable development – the MI-concept can be used to analyse past trends as well as to analyse the potential for future delinking (Femia *et al.*, 1996). First attempts have been made to use the material input approach for the theory of economic policy, its relation to institutions and to (co)evolutionary economics (Hinterberger *et al.*, 1996).

Dematerialisation as a Policy for Sustainable Development

With the recognition of Daly's scale concept, a policy of limiting throughput gains additional support on the political agenda. Conventional environmental policy in the past has been output oriented and was concerned with the resolution of single problems (Hinterberger and Welfens, 1996). From the industrial metabolism perspective, "narrowly conceived environmental policies over the past 20 years and more have largely shifted waste emissions from one form [and medium] to another, *without significantly reducing the totals.*"

(Ayres, 1994, p. 17; emphasis added). 'Reducing the totals' of course, means reducing the scale. From this perspective, the reduction of material input can be presented as an alternative management rule for sustainable development (Hinterberger *et al.*, 1997). The rationale behind this view is that the material inputs of the industrial metabolism must be reduced in order to achieve a socio-economic development path that is,ecologically sustainable. More and more studies conclude that in order to restabilise the ecosphere, roughly a 90 per cent reduction of the material flows induced by the industrialised economies is necessary, that is, a reduction by a factor of 10 (see for example Spangenberg, 1995; Weterings and Opschoor, 1992). The goal of a *dematerialisation (that is, the reduction of material input)* by a factor 10 takes into account the present inequity of the use of sinks and sources between North and South. The concept is therefore based on a principally equal right of humans for using environmental resources.

As for the problem of toxicity, society can, at least theoretically, 'decide' to not use certain substances about which dangers are known. This is what happens in environmental policy practised so far. But decisions about the treatment of specific substances require knowledge, and this knowledge is frequently not available. Legislative measures have been taken to ban DDT, CFCs and other substances. But all this happened after the impact of these substances became known – and how could it be otherwise? With some 100,000 chemicals being produced within the industrial metabolism, society cannot be expected to ever get a handle on all the possible dangers by tracing individual problems. This is the rationale for the dematerialisation approach and of course one motivation for the call for scale reduction.

The goal of dematerialisation (reduction of material input in the industrialised countries by 90 per cent) is not based on exact calculations. Because of the complexities of natural processes such calculations are impossible. The basis for dematerialisation thus is its plausibility. We do not – and cannot – know whether a reduction of the material input by a factor of eighteen or seven is necessary for a development that is,ecologically sustainable. Factor 10 as a goal for the industrialised countries gives a plausible direction in which socio-economic change should move in order to reach sustainability. Note that in this respect, dematerialisation differs from Daly's ideas in that it does not imply the idea of an 'optimal' level of material input into the economy.

The MI-concept can contribute to the implementation of instruments for an ecological economic policy, on a macro- well as on a micro-level. And it is exactly the complexity and interwovenness (or the general interdependency, as Duchin calls it) of socio-economic and natural processes that makes this approach feasible for policies aimed at sustainable development. Thus, the concept of scale, operationalised by the MI-approach, can be used for practical steps to promote sustainable development. The recognition that scale matters, combined with the material input approach, leads straightforwardly to instruments of ecological economic policy. Ecological economic policy, defined as the sum of measures directed towards the reduction of material input (that is, of the scale) can offer a way to deal with the complexities of socio-economic development (Hinterberger *et al.*, 1996). The combination of environmental macroeconomics as envisioned by Daly and the approach of ecological economic policy can show the way for a policy of scale reduction (Luks, 1997, pp. 57ff).

CONCLUSION: WHY SCALE IS KEY

Throughput and scale are more than 'mere' metaphors that have a symbolic value for the development of ecological economics. Contrary to Duchin, I hold that as we move toward the second stage of our field, the MI-approach can serve as a tool that can help to do theoretical as well as empirical work on the scale issue. As Duchin argues, ecological economists will have to come up with situation-specific strategies in order to contribute to sustainable development. The question remains, however, how 'concrete' these scenarios can be. Ecological economics as a 'post-normal science' requires at least an awareness of the importance of ignorance. The material input approach can operationalise scale, and, since it is based on the acknowledgement of systemic ignorance, it represents a case of 'post-normal science' – if not in a fully developed sense, at least with respect to the 'management' of ignorance (Luks, 1996). A crucial issue that is,not taken into account by the scale-concept is the use of land, which must be considered in addition to the throughput.

To sum up, the throughput of the industrial metabolism is a crucial factor for the sustainability of economies. The scale metaphor, which refers to the volume of this throughput, has provided important insights into this question and has contributed to the acknowledgement of the importance of the quantity of matter and energy used in the economic process. The concept of scale, however, must be operationalised in order to contribute to practical policy measures. The concept of material inputs can provide such an operationalisation. It can be a building block of an ecological macroeconomics as well as of an ecological economic policy that is, aimed at the reduction of matter–energy–throughput. While this reduction is not sufficient for sustainability, it is certainly a necessary condition for a socio-economic development that does not proceed at the expense of future generations.

Acknowledgements

Major parts of this text were developed during my stay at the Institute for Economic Analysis, New York University. I thank Faye Duchin for advice and very helpful discussions. I am grateful to Herman Daly and Glenn-Marie Lange for discussing themes of this chapter with me and to Ute Brümmer, Reuben

Deumling, Peter Fuchs, John Gowdy, Fritz Hinterberger, Jörg Köhn and Maggy Winslow, who all made helpful comments on an earlier version. I also thank Silke Schuback for her help. The support of the Friedrich-Ebert-Foundation for my doctoral thesis, of which this chapter is a part, is appreciated. The usual disclaimer applies, that is, I am solely responsible for the views expressed and for any shortcomings.

REFERENCES

Adriaanse, A., Bringezu, S., Hammond, A., Moriguchi, Y., Rodenburg, E., Rogich, D. and Schütz, H. 1997. *Resource Flows: The Material Basis of Industrial Economies*. Washington D.C.: World Resources Institute.

Ayres, R.U. 1994. 'Industrial Metabolism: Theory and Policy.' In Ayres, R.U. and Simonis, U.E. (eds.) *Industrial Metabolism: Restructuring for Sustainable Development*. Tokyo: United Nations University Press, 3–20.

Ayres, R.U. and Kneese, A.V. 1969. 'Production, Consumption, and Externalities.' *American Economic Review* LIX, 3, 282–297.

Ayres, R.U. and Simonis, U.E. 1994. 'Introduction.' In Ayres, R.U. and Simonis, U.E. (eds.): *Industrial Metabolism: Restructuring for Sustainable Development*. Tokyo: United Nations University Press, xi-xix.

Baccini, P. and Brunner, H. 1991. *Metabolism of the Anthroposphere*. Berlin: Springer.

Behrensmeier, R. and Bringezu, S. 1995. 'Zur Methodik der volkswirtschaftlichen Material-Intensitäts-Analyse: Ein quantitativer Vergleich des Umweltverbrauchs der bundesdeutschen Produktionssektoren.' *Wuppertal Paper* 34, Wuppertal Institut.

Boulding, K.E. 1973 [1966]. 'The Economics of the Coming Spaceship Earth.' In Daly, H.E. (ed.) *Toward a Steady-State Economy*. San Francisco: Freeman, 121–132.

Christensen, P. 1989. 'Historical Roots for Ecological Economics – Biophysical Versus Allocative Approaches.' *Ecological Economics* 1, 17–36.

Costanza, R. 1994. 'Three General Policies to Achieve Sustainability.' In Jansson, A.M., Hammer, M., Folke, C. and Costanza, R. (eds.) *Investing in Natural Capital. The Ecological Economics Approach to Sustainability*. Washington D.C.: Island Press, 392–407.

Costanza, R., Daly, H.E. and Bartholomew, J.A. 1991. 'Goals, Agenda, and Policy Recommendations for Ecological Economics.' In Costanza, R. (ed.) *Ecological Economics. The Science and Management of Sustainability*. New York: Columbia University Press, 1–21.

Daly, H.E. 1991a. 'Elements of Environmental Macroeconomics.' In Costanza, R. (ed.) *Ecological Economics. The Science and Management of Sustainability.* New York: Columbia University Press, 32–46.

Daly, H.E. 1991b. *Steady-State Economics.* Washington D.C.: Island Press.

Daly, H.E. 1992a. 'Allocation, Distribution, and Scale: Towards an Economics That Is Efficient, Just, and Sustainable.' *Ecological Economics* 6, 185–193.

Daly, H.E. 1992b. 'Steady-State Economics: Concepts, Questions, Policies.' *GAIA* 1, 6, 333–338.

Daly, H.E 1996. *Beyond Growth. The Economics of Sustainable Development.* Boston: Beacon Press.

Duchin, F. 1996a. 'Ecological Economics: The Research Challenge.' *The Ecological Economics Bulletin.*

Duchin, F. 1996b. 'Ecological Economics: The Second Stage.' In Costanza, R., Segura, O. and Martinez-Alier, J. (eds.) *Getting Down to Earth: Practical Applications of Ecological Economics.* Washington, D.C.: Island Press, 285–299.

Ehrlich, P.R. and Ehrlich, A.H. 1991. *Healing the Planet. Strategies for Resolving the Environmental Crisis.* Reading: Addison-Wesley.

Femia, A. 1996. 'Input–output analysis of material flows: an application to the German economic system for the year 1990.' *Quaderni di Ricerca* 82, Università degli Studi di Ancona, Dipartimento di Economia, Ancona.

Femia, A., Hinterberger, F. and Luks, F. 1996. 'Ecological Sustainability, Economic Growth, Individual Well-Being ... and Dematerialization.' Wuppertal Institut: Mimeo.

Funtowicz, S.O. and Ravetz, J.R. 1991. 'A New Scientific Methodology for Global Environmental Issues.' In Costanza, R. (ed.) *Ecological Economics. The Science and Management of Sustainability.* New York: Columbia University Press, 137–152.

Funtowicz, S.O. and Ravetz, J.R. 1994. 'The Worth of A Songbird: Ecological Economics as a Post-normal Science.' *Ecological Economics* 10, 197–207.

Georgescu-Roegen, N. 1971. *The Entropy Law and the Economic Process.* Cambridge: Harvard University Press.

Georgescu-Roegen, N. 1981. 'Energy, Matter, and Economic Valuation: Where Do We Stand?' In Daly, H.E. and Umana, A.F. (eds.) *Energy, Economics, and the Environment. Conflicting Views of an Essential Interrelationship.* AAAS Selected Symposium 64, Boulder: Westview Press, 43–79.

Gowdy, J.M. 1994. *Coevolutionary Economics: The Economy, Society and the Environment.* Boston: Kluwer Academic Publishers.

Gowdy, J.M. and McDaniel, C.N. 1995. 'One World, One Experiment: Addressing the Biodiversity-economics Conflict.' *Ecological Economics* 15, 181–192.

Harris, J.M. 1995. 'Theoretical Frameworks and Techniques. Overview Essay.' In Krishnan, R., Harris, J.M. and Goodwin, N.R. (eds.) *A Survey of Ecological Economics.* Washington D.C.: Island Press, 97–105.

Hinterberger, F., Luks, F. and Schmidt-Bleek, F. 1997. 'Material Flows vs. 'Natural Capital'. What Makes an Economy Sustainable?' *Ecological Economics* 23, 1–14.

Hinterberger, F., Luks, F. and Stewen, M. 1996. *Ökologische Wirtschaftspolitik. Zwischen Ökodiktatur und Umweltkatastrophe.* Basel: Birkhäuser.

Hinterberger, F. and Welfens, M.J. 1996. 'Warum input-orientierte Umweltpolitik?' In Köhn, J. and Welfens, M.J. (eds.) *Neue Ansätze in der Umweltökonomie.* Marburg: Metropolis, 21–44.

Klamer, A. and Leonard, T.C. 1994. 'So What's an Economic Metaphor?' In Mirowski, P. (ed.) *Natural Images in Economic Thought: 'Markets Read in Tooth and Claw'.* Cambridge: Cambridge University Press, 20–51.

Kneese, A.V., Ayres, R.U. and d'Arge, R.C. 1972. *Economics and the Environment – A Materials Balance Approach.* Baltimore: Johns Hopkins University Press.

Krishnan, R., Harris, J.M. and Goodwin, N.R. 1995. Preface. In Krishnan, R., Harris, J.M. and Goodwin, N.R. (eds.) *A Survey of Ecological Economics.* Washington D.C.: Island Press, xxxv–xxxvii.

Lakoff, G. and Johnson, M. 1980. *Metaphors We Live By.* Chicago: University of Chicago Press.

Luks, F. 1996. 'Post-Normal Science, Dematerialisierung und die Ökonomie - Über den (wirtschafts-)wissenschaftlichen Umgang mit Umweltproblemen.' In Köhn, J. and Welfens, M.J. (eds.) *Neue Ansätze in der Umweltökonomie.* Marburg: Metropolis, 89–108.

Luks, F. 1997. 'Herman E. Dalys Steady-State Economics – Ursprünge, Bedeutung und Perspektiven.' In Köhn, J. and Gowdy. J. (eds.) *Implikationen der Ökologischen Ökonomie für die Regionalökonomie.* Rostock: Rostock University Press, 40–69.

Luks, F. 1998. 'The Rhetorics of Ecological Economics.' *Ecological Economics,* forthcoming.

McCloskey, D.N. 1995. 'Metaphors Economists Live By.' *Social Research* 62, 2, 215–237.

Norgaard, R.B. 1994. *Development Betrayed. The End of Progress and a Coevolutionary Revisioning of the Future.* London: Routledge.

Norgaard, R.B. 1995. 'Metaphors We Might Survive By.' *Ecological Economics* 15, 129–131.

Prakash, A. and Gupta, A.K. 1994. 'Are Efficiency, Equity, and Scale Independent?' *Ecological Economics* 10, 89–90.

Schmidt-Bleek, F. 1994. *Wieviel Umwelt braucht der Mensch? MIPS – Das Maß für ökologisches Wirtschaften.* Basel: Birkhäuser.

Schmidt-Bleek, F. 1996. 'MAIA. Einführung in die Materialintensitätsanalyse nach dem MIPS-Konzept.' Wuppertal Institut: Mimeo.

Spangenberg, J. (ed.) 1995. *Towards Sustainable Europe. The Study*. Brussels: Friends of the Earth.

Stewen, M. 1998. 'On the Interdependence of Allocation, Distribution, and Scale – A Comment on Herman Daly's Extension of Neoclassical Economics.' *Ecological Economics*, forthcoming.

Templet, P.H. 1995. 'Economic Scale, Energy and Sustainability: An International Empirical Analysis.' *International Journal for Sustainable Development and World Ecology* 2, 153–165.

Underwood, D.A. and King, P.G. 1989. 'On the Ideological Foundations of Environmental Policy.' *Ecological Economics* 1, 315–334.

Vatn, A. and Bromley, D.W. 1994. 'Choices Without Prices Without Apologies.' *Journal of Environmental Economics and Management* 26, 129–148.

Viederman, S. 1994. 'Public Policy: Challenge to Ecological Economics.' In Jansson, A.M., Hammer, A., Folke, C. and Costanza, R. (eds.) *Investing in Natural Capital. The Ecological Economics Approach to Sustainability*. Washington D.C.: Island Press, 467–478.

Vitousek, P.M., Ehrlich, P.R., Ehrlich, H. and Matson, P.A. 1986. 'Human Appropriation of the Products of Photosythesis.' *BioScience* 36, 6, 368–373.

Wackernagel, M. and Rees, W. 1996. *Our Ecological Footprint. Reducing Human Impact on the Earth*. Philadelphia: New Society Publishers.

Weterings, R.A.P.M. and Opschoor, J.B. 1992. 'The Ecocapacity as a Challenge to Technological Development.' Rijswijk, Advisory Council for Research on Nature and Environment, Publication RMNO 74a.

9. Reflections Upon the Role of Moral Sentiments in Economics

Clive L. Spash

INTRODUCTION

The viewpoint I wish to explore in this chapter is that an ethical perspective is central to any economic model which tries to predict human behaviour and inform policy. This position contrasts with the separation of economic analysis into normative and positive and implies that such a division is artificial and misleading. The artificial aspect might be dismissed along the methodological lines of Friedman (1953), although the inability to describe behaviour as a result of the abstract should be recognised as a serious drawback rather than dismissed as long as behaviour can be accurately predicted. More than this, the interconnections between the positive and normative mean that a purely positive model of human behaviour is unable to predict in as far as the normative aspects influence economic choice. Thus, concentration upon an ethics free version of economics will fail the empirical test, which Friedman's argument requires.

In order to approach the issue of what role ethics plays in economics the investigation can be split into a theoretical discussion and an empirical analysis. The theoretical aspect requires reflection upon human nature, as well as over the extent to which the motivation for actions can be reduced down to individual preferences. This reductionism, which is present in current economic thinking, is where the classical economists have been left behind. In trying to distil some essence of human behaviour, modern economics has lost sight of the broad social context within which humans operate, the importance of a range of motives to action and the range of ethical value systems. In the context of environmental policy the approach has direct relevance because of the limited concept of environmental values which modern economics regards as rational.

An empirical approach to these theoretical ideas might propose a general hypothesis such as: individuals are motivated to action not purely from a selfish interest but also by wider ethical concerns. This begins to link economics and ethics with individual and social psychology. One current area in which economists and psychologists sometimes work together has been contingent valuation of the environment and this method has provided an opportunity to test such hypotheses (Spash, 1998; Spash and Hanley, 1995). While some mainstream economists argue that contingent valuation is problematic and should be dropped, because it fails to allow for arbitrage and is therefore a poor imitation of an actual market, there is little reflection upon what respondents are actually telling economists about their value systems in these surveys. The serious description and treatment of actual policy scenarios and extensive attention to survey design and conduct make totally dismissing the results of well conducted studies only tenable by the arrogant and narrow minded. There are of course many badly conducted studies, but rather than throw all the work into this category attention should be paid to the results from the well conducted studies and what it is they tell us about environmental valuation.

In this chapter, I explore some of these ideas and concentrate on the theoretical aspects by considering the foundations for the moral considerability of others in an individual model of human behaviour. In the first part of this chapter the moral sentiments to action are discussed. That is, why and how are we motivated to act and how does this affect the way in which we value our environment? This can then be used to draw out how specific valuation issues are moulded by different institutional arrangements proposed to address environmental policy problems. For example, cost-benefit analysis as an institution makes certain claims on an individual's framing of the policy context and implies a social framework within which the problem at hand should be considered. If the case can be made that ethical positions have specific implications for behaviour then empirical evidence should show moral sentiments arising in supposedly neutral economic decisions. For example, individuals refusing to play the contingent valuation method game may signify moral repulsion at an institution reducing diverse values into money with regard to the particular environmental attribute under consideration. These instances of moral indignation may be associated with specific aspects of the environment or be more general.

SOCIAL VERSUS SELFISH INTEREST

Adam Smith's work in the *Wealth of Nations* tries, in part, to explain economic growth via the division of labour (Smith, 1776). This has come to imply that individuals, as units of production, can largely be separated from their social context and treated as uniform units only differentiated by their embodied capital, as if machines. Beyond this, humans as individual units, operating for self interest, are essentially co-ordinated via the mechanism of market trading. Specialisation of individual functions is linked to co-operation with others via the price mechanism. Thus, while Smith would disagree with the modern interpretation and synthesis of his work, the outcome has been for social contracts, historical associations and cultural ties to become excluded from considerations of what makes economic systems successful. Neoclassical theory in particular has reduced the production and exchange process down to a mechanical process where high marginal productivity is the best attribute of a unit of labour and profit the only serious consideration in production. Selective reading of Smith's work has allowed his name to be used as an icon for the laissez-faire free market philosophy which is the current political vogue.

This use of Smith is apparent in both the selection of passages quoted from the *Wealth of Nations* and the monograph to which economists mostly refer, that is, the *Wealth of Nations*. An often neglected side of Smith is his work as a moral philosopher and the considerable attention he paid to the role of moral judgement in society. His previous work to the *Wealth of Nations* was *The Theory of Moral Sentiments*, his first book (Smith, 1759). In that work the idea of a social context in which humanity operates comes to the fore. Modern economists have tried to adopt a positivist position and remove moral considerations from economic science, but for Smith the selfish role of individuals and their moral sentiments were the two parts which make a human being whole. They are two parts of one human nature.

Now, for modern analysts there seems to be a problem here. Models based upon ignoring individuals acting socially and emphasising only self interest have become dominant. A society based upon the model of selfish individuals is attributed to Smith and there is then no need for fellow feeling towards others which is an unnecessary complication. So the only problem then is to explain why Smith wasted his time on moral issues. This has been termed 'the Adam Smith problem'. A simple explanation is that Smith was a misguided youth and later came to his senses when he wrote the *Wealth of Nations*. However, Smith spent the last years of his life revising *The Theory of Moral Sentiments* and its sixth edition came out in 1790, some years after the *Wealth of Nations*. In the sixth edition, Smith stuck by his story that there was an important role for 'sympathy' and that the nature of moral judgement was central to an explanation of how humans operate and value the world around them. The origin and nature of moral judgement was of deep concern to Smith – judgements over whether an action is right or wrong. The problem then lies not with Smith but with the failure of modern economics to provide a more complete model of human behaviour. Thus, these moral writings cannot be dismissed out of hand, and further consideration of Smith's own position can show where the gaps have grown.

Sympathy

Smith explains morality through a concept he calls 'sympathy'. There are two principal parts to his explanation of whether an action is right or wrong. First, the reasoning behind the motive for the action must be considered by placing oneself in the position of the person initiating the act. Second, the person on the receiving end of the act must be considered. For example, seeing a blind person at the side of the road another person may decide to be benevolent and help them cross. However, the blind person may be frustrated and annoyed by the intervention when they were perfectly in control of their own situation and, worse still, may well have wanted to go in the other direction.

An act cannot be judged as good purely from one perspective. That is, if an act is to be judged as good, the concept of 'sympathy' must operate by placing oneself in the position of the initiator and the recipient. Reflecting upon the motive of the initiator of an act, or upon one's own actions, is only part of the process. Thus, maintaining growth of Gross National Product may be motivated by a concern that material objects be increased in quality and number to improve the position of others both current and future. However, the position of those others must also be considered and the loss of cultural and historical values may be deemed worse by the intended recipients of the supposed material benefits. Much cultural imperialism has been based upon good intentions. For example, the spread of Christianity through Africa and North America was in part justified in terms of saving the savages from eternal damnation, even if they rejected salvation and preferred their traditional lifestyles.

There is a similarity in these examples with the way in which future generations are entered into the current policy debate on environmental problems. Rather than trying to place ourselves in the position of future generations and considering whether we would appreciate say nuclear waste, the tendency has been to justify the creation of potentially long term problems by restricting our vision. In the moral context of 'sympathy' providing justifications for why our actions have good motives has been sufficient.

Another important aspect of 'sympathy', as described by Smith, is the requirement for imagination. You have to imagine yourself to be the actor and the recipient of an act, but from an impartial perspective. The idea of the impartial spectator is to allow an individual to step outside of their own immediate motives and circumstances. In considering the propriety of actions the impartial spectator reflects upon the likely results, the circumstances and the intentions of the actors. This develops what we might now term a social conscience, and leads to a social psychology: people try to imagine themselves in a wider social role.

Commonly referred to sympathy is compassion. The motive to action in this case being sharing the burden of others. Economists have made much of adopting this motive as 'altruism' by allowing one individual's utility function to include the consumption of goods by others (Becker, 1976). As social creatures humans are concerned about others and show sympathy. However, for Smith 'sympathy' is a much broader concept – a social bond – and it requires motivation on the grounds of seeking the approval of others and avoiding their disapproval. As Elsner (1989) points out, this "principle of self-approbation" fails to supply information on whether other individuals actually will approve or disapprove, but rather requires that the individual confirm the morality of behaviour from the position of an individual perception of the impartial spectator.

Unfortunately, the social psychology of the individual is absent from modern economic models. However, the recognition of the missing social context has been evident and a prominent exponent of the problem has been Amartya Sen. What Adam Smith called 'sympathy' Sen (1985) calls 'commitment' – the importance of social relationships, the idea of duty without the intention of personal gain, the role of ethical judgement in our decisions. These considerations bring forward the role of the wider context within which humans operate, and also emphasise that the current economic model of a rational individual misses out on a whole range of motives to action which actually maintain a social structure. The rationality implied by the selfish individual at the centre of the modern economic model of human behaviour leads at best to foolish behaviour and at worse anarchy. So, for example, rather than exploiting our own position of superior knowledge to gain payments when a stranger asks directions in our town we give information freely and as accurately as possible (Sen, 1977). We try and treat others as we would wish to be treated. More generally, business exchange operates upon trust rather than complete information with well defined contracts. Where this trust breaks down society also can be seen to decay because resources are then devoted to move and counter move in a game of deceit. The failure of modern economics is then to pretend the winner of such a game is rational and society better-off when all individuals act in a similarly self-centred fashion. Political adoption of regard to the selfish motivation to the exclusion of all else leads to a society dependent upon litigation and contract law to conduct even simple exchange.

Motives to Action

So, where does the role of self interest fall in our concerns about what motivates individuals? For Smith self interest can only be a primary motive to action if it is regarded in terms of 'prudence'. Self interest should be qualified by self command and the sacrifice of immediate pleasure for long term happiness. In fact, self command, a sense of duty, and regard to justice are the higher virtues for Smith. Such things as the meditative virtue of avoiding

harm is seen to be above self interest or acting as a control upon the actions
motivated by self interest. As Smith (1759, p. 53) states:

> Generosity, humanity, kindness, compassion, mutual friendship
> and esteem, all the social and benevolent affections, when
> expressed in the countenance or behaviour, even towards those
> who are not peculiarly connected with ourselves, please the
> indifferent spectator upon almost every occasion.

This then leads to the consideration of social bonds. Sympathy and
imagination are required in order for a system of political economy to
operate. This is evident in the code of ethics and law which help define how
far selfish interests are operative in society, but regard for others without law
is a higher virtue. Reliance upon the higher motives to action and
benevolence actually reduces the need for recourse to legal codes. Functional
human societies recognise mutual dependence and therefore self-interest is
bounded; economic transactions and exchange operate by respecting personal
duties and the rights of others (and not merely legally defined rights). In fact,
the prime motive to do best for oneself is something which can only be
sustained when individuals have self command and are prepared to recognise
a sense of duty and regard for natural justice.

Yet the reader should avoid falling into the trap of assuming that modern
economics has no moral philosophy. Modern economics shares with Smith a
world description in which the origin of moral judgement is explained by
individual psychology. Smith spends much time giving examples of
individual behaviour and appealing to his reader to consider these examples
in a way that suggests how humans operate. In modern academia he might
have conducted surveys and run regressions, but regardless of method the
methodology is the same. The psychology of moral judgement is then seen to
intertwine with views on philosophy. Thus, the principles included in Smith's
philosophy of deciding what is right and wrong are derived in part from his
reflections upon, and descriptions of, human social psychology.

In modern economics the interconnections are also evident. The
psychological model of the individual as primarily self interested restricts the
ability of economists to consider alternative philosophical perspectives. I
have argued elsewhere that this has affected the approach taken to long-term
environmental damages, intergenerational equity and discounting (Spash,
1993a). Economists tend to rely upon, an often implicit, utilitarianism. The
specific brand of utilitarianism linked to the psychological model describes
moral actions as those that increase happiness upon the basis of individual
preferences. Preference utilitarianism then excludes other models of the way
in which the world can be considered in a philosophical and ethical sense. For
example, rights based belief systems are rejected from this model of the self-
interested preference utilitarian and attempts to include altruism, equity and

justice are restricted by the extent to which a utilitarian interpretation can be supplied.

Interestingly Smith held utilitarianism in relatively low regard. He saw utility as a subordinate consideration in forming a moral judgement. Thus, a positive moral action would be ranked by the following set of codes. First, place yourself in the position of the impartial spectator to decide whether you have 'sympathy' with the motive of the agent. Second, place yourself in the position of the beneficiary of the action and consider whether you have 'sympathy' with their response for example, gratitude. Third, consider the action in terms of conforming with the general rules of morality. These general rules would be derived from the first two motives, that is sympathy with the motive of the agent and sympathy with the gratitude of the beneficiary. Finally, consider the pleasure from the thought of the utility. That is the link with utilitarianism comes in indirectly at the bottom of his list.

One aspect of the morality which this code brings forward is the evolution of social norms. That is, while the concept of 'sympathy' is seen to operate within an individual's current view of the impartial spectator, the code also requires reflection upon social rules derived from past reflections and developed through communication and exchange. Thus, individual behaviour is not only moderated by empathy with the position of others but also placed in the context of a social reference group. Loss of social context and alienation remove this reference group and an exclusive emphasis upon selfish motives to action excludes fellow feeling for others and diminishes the role of the impartial spectator.

Environmental Policy

If economic tools are developed within a model where 'sympathy' is excluded an important aspect of humanity is absent. Amongst other implications, this will mean the predictive power of economic models will be reduced. As a result, the ability of economists to inform policy decisions will be impaired and analysts will be surprised when their recommendations meet with moral protest.

Such situations have in fact been the experience of the British government in recent years. Arguments for greater efficiency in local government taxation led the central government to impose a poll tax in Scotland (and later England and Wales) during the 1980s. This met with widespread popular resistance over several years and was finally withdrawn. The resistance centred around the tax being unfair to those on low incomes and inequitable in terms of welfare. Similarly, the attempt to raise energy taxation as a supposedly ecologically driven measure failed because the impact on the poor was ignored (the suspicion was also strong that the tax was merely revenue raising rather than a serious attempt to change human behaviour as would be desired by an eco-tax). Another major cause of popular protest was the roads building programme. Road planning in the UK has for some time been based upon cost-benefit calculations which restrict attention to saving time and reducing congestion for the motorist (but has rejected the notion of environmental cost-benefit analysis). Public enquiries into the major developments have been conducted as part of the planning process, but have been seen as merely delaying the development process rather than allowing new options to be explored and policies to be reviewed. As a result the central government created a massive programme of road building which ignored public concerns. The financial case for new infrastructure to maintain private interests in car and lorry transportation systems confronted local concerns about loss of habitat, peace, quiet and seclusion, decay of social infrastructure and reductions in aesthetic quality. The extent of the popular protest lead to dramatic cuts in the road building programme after extensive and repeated civil protest began to raise the costs of the on-going road developments.

The issue of the social contest over decisions in the environmental area has been raised by the philosopher Mark Sagoff. One aspect of public policy which he strongly attacks is the use of economics to place monetary values upon the environment. He has devoted particular attention to the contingent valuation method under his title of The Wyoming Experiment (Sagoff, 1988). Contingent valuation has become extremely popular in recent years with hundreds of studies applied to environmental issues. Sagoff sees the contingent valuation method as economists taking on a political role, and applies this criticism more generally to any application of non-market valuation to the environment. He believes these decisions should be made in the political arena rather than in the economic arena. More than this he attributes a psychological model to the individual where political and economic decisions are separated. This allows the self-interested model of economic behaviour to continue because any considerations of an ethical nature are to be dealt with as political.

In effect the Sagoff critique asks us to consider the best approach for including individual members of the general public in the environmental decision process. This is a general problem which Sagoff narrows down to a confrontation between two supposedly separate realms of thought, that is, the political and the economic. Such a separation is familiar to those economists who argue in favour of positive economics as the correct area for scientific investigation, and tend to associate efficiency with markets unfettered by government intervention. Yet the need to involve a wider social ethic in any decision means even the simplest economic choice can become what Sagoff regards as political. Thus, while he regards buying a yo-yo as uncontroversial this would in fact depend upon the political situation in the country of origin (for example, democratic or dictatorship), the method of production (for example, child labour), the materials used in production (for example, toxic paints, tropical hard wood) and so on. In environmental terms there are few such decisions which can be regarded as politically neutral (that is, purely economic), which is why making choices in a modern economy and being environmentally aware can be so difficult to reconcile. In Smith's terms, the environmentalist appeals to the impartial spectator and asks is purchasing and consuming this item for my personal satisfaction harmful to others, and for many environmentalists those others may include non-humans. So the political and ethical decisions cannot be simply put to one side as separate from the economic.

However, this line of reasoning has taken others to the opposite extreme of regarding all social values as economic. That is, individuals are regarded as having their say in the market place and this is supposed to provide a democratic say in decisions. The problem with government policy can then be attributed to a failure to take these market votes into account. The current income distribution is assumed acceptable so that distributional issues can be given secondary attention or ignored. The emphasis is placed upon individuals' willingness to pay. Note, a willingness to pay is always matched by a willingness to accept in any market transaction so that trade can occur. These exchange values are then taken as indicative of a much broader conception of value, which has been termed 'total economic value.' This total economic value claims, at least implicitly, that all relevant values have been captured. Sagoff and others are rightly concerned about this extension of the economic value system, which readers should note is rejected by many neoclassical economists and accepted by some ecological economists.

In this context contingent valuation has been the essential tool because of the potential to include a greater range of value concepts than any other method of cost-benefit analysis. Contingent valuation has been used to give estimates of direct use values associated with a resource (for example, the value associated with fishing in a lake), but in addition has been the only method which gives estimates of the values associated with maintaining an option to enjoy that resource in the future and the value of passing on that option to future generations. Most controversially contingent valuation has been used to provide monetary values associated with the very existence of a resource. This has lead some economists to claim that they can now assess the intrinsic value of the environment; I have discussed this elsewhere, see Spash (1997). In relation to the earlier discussion in this chapter, what becomes evident here is how the required concept of value has extended well beyond the basis in utilitarian preference theory. Yet while the popular adoption of contingent valuation seems to recognise the need to extend the range of environmental values being taken into account by policy makers, the qualitative difference between types of values is neglected.

The type of difference being to referred to here is sometimes described as incommensurability. That is, objects of value can be regarded by their measurability and comparability. Degrees of measurability go from cardinal to ordinal, to being impossible to measure. Economics has moved from a belief in cardinal measures of utility to ordinal ones in this century, and generally rejects the notion of being unable to measure something, for example, infinite values. Comparability extends from strong through weak to zero. Thus, something which cannot be compared or measured is intrinsic value. Economists who have equated intrinsic value to existence values from contingent valuation are making a fundamental error, although the fact that these individuals' wish intrinsic values were measurable and comparable is interesting in itself. The claim that all objects are strongly comparable and ordinal is the realm of modern economics.

SOME IMPLICATIONS FOR ENVIRONMENTAL VALUATION

As a tool of modern economics contingent valuation fails to analyse fellow feeling as a motive for action; that is, the concept of this fellow feeling is excluded from the model. However, this does not prevent individuals' from trying to express their concern about various environmental values in a survey context. In fact surveys can be designed to either draw out or suppress the expression of different values.

In the case of biodiversity valuation, the expression of fellow feeling for plants and animals can be strong. The monetary value of forests' biodiversity has been of growing concern for the Forestry Commission in the UK as the Treasury has pressed the agency to justify its activities in terms of a 6 per cent financial rate of return. In Scotland a study was commissioned to investigate the value of biodiversity using contingent valuation (Spash and Hanley, 1995). The opportunity was taken to look at the concept of environmental lexicographic preferences, that is an individual's refusal to make a trade-off of money for the environment. Such refusals to trade are, as mentioned above, thought to be uncommon by economic theorists. However, the study showed that quite a large proportion of respondents were prepared to act in a manner consistent with rejecting any trade-off. More specifically, respondents who stated that animals, ecosystems or plants should be protected irrespective of the cost but who refused to give a willingness to pay an amount to achieve that protection were regarded as having lexicographic preferences; they also had to give a protest reason for their zero bid. That is, people might bid zero because they "don't care" for the particular forest to be preserved or they may have a low income and so be unable to bid. Others may refuse to bid because, for example, they reject the process of placing monetary values on the environment or believe there are better approaches to the problem at hand.

Interestingly, a sub-sample of individuals stated that animals, ecosystems or plants should be protected irrespective of the cost, but gave a positive willingness to pay. That is, from the economic perspective they implicitly gave an exchange value to the forest's biodiversity although they stated the forest was priceless. However, even if we exclude all these responses (as unexplained or irrational in some sense) we are still left with 23.2 per cent of individuals bidding zero for a protest reason and stating they believed animals, ecosystems or plants should be protected irrespective of the cost. More recent studies have started to try and push those individuals who claim rights based positions and reject trade-offs into realising the opportunity costs of their decision; this can reduce the numbers classified as lexicographic. However, the point here is that in a simple contingent valuation study, people can be found who express the wish to refuse to make trade-offs.

Another case where ethical values might be expected to arise strongly is in relationship to future generations. In order to probe this, a study was conducted of the enhanced greenhouse effect and the extent to which individuals believe that future generations have a right to be compensated for resulting damages (Spash, 1993b). Individuals can be categorised into four groups: (i) those who believe that future generations have a right to compensation, (ii) those who believe there is no such right, (iii) those who would only compensate relatively poor future generations, and (iv) those who would not compensate relatively rich future generations. Two categories of individuals can then be identified: deontologists or rights based individuals, and consequentialists or utilitarians. Those in categories (iii) and (iv) are prepared to trade-off the right to compensation with wealth; their position is fundamentally utilitarian in outlook. Category (i) consists of those who attribute an inviolable right to compensation for harm.

Several hypotheses might be put forward to investigate the role of ethics in the decision. First, that there is no difference between utilitarians and deontologists in terms of their willingness to participate in contingent valuation surveys. If there is a difference between the ethical groups in terms of their willingness to participate in contingent valuation studies we might expect that contingent valuation would be biased towards the utilitarians. This would be the case if rights based individuals either refuse to answer the survey (non-respondent, for which there is then no data) or refuse to answer the willingness to pay questions (item non-response). Second, there is no difference between utilitarians and deontologists in terms of their willingness to pay. If there is a difference between the utilitarians and the deontologists in terms of their willingness to pay we might expect deontologists to become 'outliers' by making extremely high bids or zero bids. They reject the process but wish to express this rejection. In this case their exclusion from the surveys as outliers would bias the sample in favour of the utilitarians. Third, there is no difference between utilitarians and deontologists in terms of their environmental attitude. If we find that environmentalists tend to be deontologists or rights based believers and that these people are more likely to participate in environmental questionnaires, we would expect to find that contingent valuation is biased in favour of the deontologists. There can also be a combined relevance of these three hypotheses. For example, if the deontolgoists refuse to bid or bid at the extremes or refuse to play the game (that is, fill in the questionnaires but leave out the willingness to pay questions), we will find that the deontologists, that are also environmentalists, are being excluded from this process of expressing their values. Their values, quite simply, fail to fit in with the economic model underlying the contingent valuation method.

The approach taken was to split the sample on the basis of ethical belief and also look at the responses in terms of the willingness-to-pay questions. The data are taken from a survey asking for willingness to pay to prevent five events occurring in the year 2100 due to the enhanced greenhouse effect. Three payment mechanisms were given providing fifteen willingness to pay responses. Thus, fifteen different correlation tables can be constructed to test for the importance of ethical beliefs. Six groups of willingness to pay are set up; namely zero bids, 0–£5, £5–£10, £10–£100, >£100, and no response. A non-respondent is an individual who answers the ethical and environmental questions but leaves the willingness-to-pay questions blank, that is, item non-response.

The sample was categorised into utilitarian, right to compensation and no right to compensation for comparison with the willingness to pay categories in chi-squared tables. Of the resulting 15 correlation tables only one result is insignificant at the 5 per cent level. Even at the 1 per cent level thirteen of the correlations remain significant. The strongest results specific to willingness to pay are found in the item non-response and in the 0–£5 categories. Both are consistent across events and payment mechanisms, and have high chi-squared results. Under item non-response a greater than expected number of rights based individuals is found. In the 0–£5 category there are fewer rights based individuals implying a tendency to bid high. While this trend in bidding high is also evidenced in the other categories the results are weaker and inconsistent across the fifteen tables. A lack of data seems to be hampering the results here, especially in the >£100 category. In general the rights affirming individuals were hypothesised to be over represented in the zero, item non-response and high bid categories. This hypothesis holds for the non-response categories and is supported for the high bid categories but fails to show in the zero bids. In fact, there are fewer than expected numbers of individuals in this category. The no rights group were hypothesised to refuse to bid or bid zero, and this hypothesis is strongly supported. There is also a tendency in the no rights group towards under representation in the positive bid ranges, especially strong for the 0–£5 category and consistent in the

£10–£100 category. The results for the sea level rise case with an R&D payment mechanism are shown in Table 9.1 (total chi-squared 29.294 with 10 degrees of freedom).

Additional evidence was found in support of the other hypothesis that ethical position is correlated to environmental attitude (Spash, 1997). More specifically those who believe in a rights based system tend to be at the extreme end of the environmental movement. Thus we find that the contingent valuation method might exclude those individuals from expressing their values, that is people can refuse to fall in with the contingent valuation method because of its implied philosophical position.

Table 9.1. Ethics and willingness-to-pay: sea level rise.

	Willingness-to-Pay (household, £ per annum)					
	0	0–5	5–10	10–100	>100	No Response
Rights						
Observed	24	17	15	23	6	17
Expected	30	21	14	21	5	10
Chi-squared	1.25	0.66	0.05	0.12	0.06	4.60
No Rights						
Observed	24	6	14	13	5	8
Expected	21	14	10	15	4	7
Chi-squared	0.53	4.74	1.89	0.20	0.43	0.15
Utilitarian						
Observed	35	34	10	23	4	3
Expected	32	22	15	23	6	11
Chi-squared	0.24	6.39	1.74	0.00	0.57	5.69
Total *N*	83	57	39	59	15	28

CONCLUSIONS

The argument put forward has been that a significant contribution was made by Adam Smith in terms of his moral philosophy and that this can have direct relevance to environmental policy today. The evidence from survey work linked to the contingent valuation method implies there are dangers in making the environment into a commodity. That is, the contingent valuation method tries to treat the environment as a group of goods and services which can be valued by individuals just as if they were consumer items. This trend to commodification was identified by Hirsch (1977) as one of the ways in which modern society fails to increase welfare and instead destroys values which have existed and been cherished throughout human history. Regarding the world in terms of commodities removes values that cannot be captured – such things as ethics, trust, romance and emotions.

Thus we are left with a legalistic definition of consumers' rights, citizens' charters and so on. While apparently trying to set up fair exchange this approach simultaneously squeezes all our conceptions of value and ethics into a very narrow commodity service space. As a result concepts of a wider social and ethical ethos are lost. Those expressing a concern that nature is betrayed by the cost-benefit approach have good cause when even existence becomes a monetary value, and intrinsic value is regarded as a utilitarian concept. However, the idea of this chapter was to show that this problem extends far beyond one method in cost-benefit analysis and has a long historical explanation. That is, that the rejection of Adam Smith's work on moral sentiments, as being relevant to economics, has given rise to a modern model of the individual which fails either as a description of human behaviour or as a predictor. The idea that ethics can be divorced from economics has resurged in the writings of Sagoff where political and economic decisions are split. Ironically Sagoff is reacting to the lack of social psychology in economics by recommending a vacuum in political economy. In practice, the political and economic are combined as are ethical and economic motives to action. Thus, when analysing environmental values ethical motives can be seen to have implications for economic decisions. As a result the economic model of human behaviour needs revision to allow for a wide range of value concepts. However, these concepts must be maintained as distinct rather than squeezed into a pre-existing preference utilitarian framework. How this can be achieved is a far more difficult task than merely pointing out the problem, although many still seem to be oblivious to either problem or task.

REFERENCES

Becker, G.S. 1976. 'Altruism, Egoism and Genetic Fitness: Economics and Sociobiology.' *Journal of Economic Literature* 14, 3, 817–826.

Elsner, W. 1989. 'Adam Smith's Model of the Origin's and Emergence of Institutions: The Modern Findings of the Classical Approach.' *Journal of Economic Issues* 23, 1, 189–213.

Friedman, M. 1953. 'The Methodology of Positive Economics.' In Friedman, M. (ed.) *Essays in Positive Economics*. Chicago: Chicago University Press.

Hirsch, F. 1977. *Social Limits to Growth*. London: Routledge and Kegan Paul Ltd.

Sagoff, M. 1988. 'The Economy of the Earth. ' MacLean, D. (ed.) *Cambridge Studies in Philosophy and Public Policy*. Cambridge: Cambridge University Press.

Sen, A. 1977. 'Rational Fools: A Critique of the Behavioral Foundations of Economic Theory.' *Philosophy and Public Affairs* 6, 317–344.

Sen, A. 1985. *Commodities and Capabilities*. Amsterdam: North-Holland Press.

Smith, A. 1759. *The Theory of Moral Sentiments*. Indianapolis: Liberty Fund.

Smith, A. 1776. *An Inquiry into the Nature and Causes of the Wealth of Nations*. Chicago: Chicago University Press.

Spash, C.L. 1993a. 'Economics, Ethics, and Long-term Environmental Damages.' *Environmental Ethics* 15, 2, 117–132.

Spash, C.L. 1993b. 'Estimating the Importance of Inviolable Rights: The Case of Long-Term Damages and Future Generations.' *Scottish Economic Society*.

Spash, C.L. 1997. 'Ethics and Environmental Attitudes with Implications for Economic Valuation.' *Journal of Environmental Management* 50, 4, 403–416.

Spash, C.L. 1998. 'Investigating Individual Motives for Environmental Action: Lexicographic Preferences, Beliefs and Attitudes.' In Lemons, J., Westra, L. and Goodland, R. (eds.) *Ecological Sustainability and Integrity: Concepts and Approaches*. Dordrecht: Kluwer Academic Publishers, 46–62.

Spash, C.L. and A. Clayton 1997. 'The Maintenance of Natural Capital: Motivations and Methods.' In Light, A. and Smith, J.M. (eds.) *Space, Place and Environmental Ethics*. Lanham: Rowman and Littlefield Publishers Inc., 143–173.

Spash, C.L. and N. Hanley 1995. 'Preferences, Information and Biodiversity preservation.' *Ecological Economics* 12, 3, 191–208.

PART III

Sustainable Production

10. Environmental and Economic Benefits of Sustainable Agriculture

David Pimentel

INTRODUCTION

Throughout the world, agriculture is suffering from many serious environmental problems. Soil is being lost from croplands 20 to 40 times faster than it can re-form (Pimentel *et al.*, 1993). Each year about 10 million hectares of agricultural land becomes unproductive and is abandoned (Pimentel *et al.*, 1995). Associated with this serious erosion is the rapid run-off of needed water and the loss of nutrients from agricultural lands that combine to further reduce land productivity (Lal and Stewart, 1990).

Degraded agricultural lands require more fertilisers and more irrigation in order to maintain production (Pimentel and Wen, 1990). This is costly in terms of energy and capital. In addition, abandonment of some technologies like crop rotations has resulted in increased insect pests, plant pathogens, and weeds, and these in turn have required the intensive use of pesticides (Pimentel *et al.*, 1991). As a result, the costs of agricultural production have escalated.

In addition to the direct effects of poor environmental resource management on agricultural production, the offsite environment has also been seriously damaged. Soil sediments and rapid water run-off from the land are estimated to cause about $10 billion in damages to the environment annually (Pimentel *et al.*, 1995). The offsite environmental damage caused by pesticides is estimated to cause at least $8 billion annually (Pimentel and Greiner, 1997).

In order to be able to remedy these serious problems and enable agricultural production to be more environmentally and economically sound in the future, the vital resources required by all agriculture must be identified and their damaging impact understood. In this chapter, I examine the diverse environmental problems associated with agriculture and how these problems increase the cost of crop and livestock production while at the same time cause serious offsite environmental problems. The environmental and economic benefits of sound ecological resource management are also assessed. Although the focus is primarily on U.S. agriculture, the findings can be extended to the environmental and economic problems that currently exist in other nations.

ENVIRONMENTAL PROBLEMS OF PRESENT DAY AGRICULTURE

Soil Erosion

World and U.S. food supplies depend on the availability of productive land. Currently, 99 per cent of the human food supply comes from the land rather than the oceans and other aquatic systems (FAO, 1991). Thus, the dimensions of land destruction in the United States and the world are of increasing concern. At present, soil erosion on U.S. cropland averages about 13 times faster than soil reformation. In Africa, Asia, and South America, erosion is 30 to 40 times faster than reformation (Khoshoo and Tejwani, 1993; Lal, 1993; McLaughlin, 1993; Wen, 1993; Pimentel *et al.*, 1993). Because of erosion and other land degradation practices now prevalent in agriculture, as mentioned, about 10 million hectares of agricultural land are abandoned each year (Pimentel *et al.*, 1995). This loss is occurring just at the time when more land is needed to grow food for the rapidly growing world population. Finding land and increasing food production to feed the nearly 400 million babies born each year is a sobering reality that we must face (PRB, 1995). In fact, an additional 4 million hectares per year of cropland has to be accessed and put into production in order to feed these new people. Adding these 4 million hectares to the 10 million hectares of degraded area means that about 14 million hectares of agricultural land has to be secured and put into crop production to maintain the basic food supplies for people. At present, valuable forestlands are being cleared to provide the 'new' agricultural land. As a result, deforestation has reached a crisis status (Pimentel *et al.*, 1986; Myers, 1993).

Erosion adversely affects crop productivity by reducing the availability of water, nutrients, soil biota, organic matter and soil depth (OTA, 1982). Reduction in the amount of water available to the crop is considered the most harmful effect of erosion (Follett and Stewart, 1985). After water, shortages of soil nutrients are the most important factors limiting crop productivity. One metric ton of rich agricultural topsoil contains a total of 4 kg of nitrogen as well as other nutrients essential for crop production (Alexander, 1977). Thus, associated with the tremendous amount of topsoil lost in the United States is a loss in fertiliser nutrients that totals $20 billion annually (Troeh *et al.*, 1991).

Erosion also rapidly removes organic matter from the soil because it is much lighter in weight than soil mineral elements. Organic matter is important to crop production because it helps retain water, improves soil structure, encourages soil biota, and is the source of a large portion of the nutrients needed by crops (Pimentel *et al.*, 1995).

The reason that crop yields have continued to grow during the past 40 years despite soil degradation is the 20-fold increase in the application of some fertiliser nutrients, increased irrigation, greater use of pesticides, and the introduction of new, high-yielding varieties (Pimentel, 1988). In general, farms have been substituting a non-renewable resource (oil) in the form of fertilisers, pesticides, and other input for the loss of a renewable resource (soil).

In addition to reducing the productivity of the land, erosion and water run-off cause offsite environmental effects. Estimates are that run-off in the United States delivers approximately 7 billion tons of sediment each year to waterways in the 48 contiguous states. The sediments have to be dredged from harbours, rivers, and reservoirs. Also, these sediments are detrimental to agriculture, burying young crop plants in the lowlands. The heavily sediment-loaded water is a hazard to industrial machinery. Several species of fish, including salmon and trout, are prevented from reproducing when streams and rivers contain heavy sediment deposits. Just the offsite environmental effects of erosion sediments cost an estimated $10 billion annually (Pimentel *et al.*, 1995).

These severe soil erosion and associated rapid water run-off problems are now seriously diminishing the food economy as well as the health of the environment. In total, soil erosion and associated offsite environmental impacts cost the U.S. an estimated $44 billion annually in direct and indirect effects (Pimentel *et al.*, 1995).

Wasting Water

Because all crops require and transpire massive amounts of water, losses in available water inhibit crop growth. Consider that a corn crop, which produces about 7500 kg/ha, takes up and transpires 4.5 million litres of water during the growing season (Leyton, 1983). Although sufficient rain usually falls upon eastern U.S. agricultural land, summer droughts limit yields. Elsewhere in the U.S., particularly in the Southwest, the land is arid and must be irrigated for agricultural production. On average, 10 million liters/ha of water are applied to irrigated land each year (Postel, 1989).

Although agriculture pumps about one-third of the total water from streams and aquifers, agriculture consumes 80 per cent of total U.S. water. The public, industrial, and rural sectors consume the remaining 20 per cent. The reason that agriculture consumes so much water is because of evaporation and transpiration. In contrast, the public and industry use the water but they return it to the stream or lake. It may be polluted, but they return the water they use.

Concern about water availability is growing both because of heavy pollution and excessive overdraft of aquifers (Postel, 1989). In the 48 contiguous United States, water overdraft exceeds replenishment by about 25 per cent, and in the Texas Gulf area, overdraft is as high as 77 per cent. This mining of aquifers is becoming a major environmental problem because the replacement of groundwater is slow at a rate less than 0.2 per cent each year provided that rainfall is adequate.

Special pollution problems are associated with irrigated agriculture, such as when river and stream water, as well as the land itself, degraded by the addition of salts. For example, as the Colorado River flows through Grand Valley and water is withdrawn for irrigation and later returned to the river, about 18 t/ha of salt are leached from the irrigated land and added to the detriment of river water (EPA, 1976). At times during the summer, the Red River in Texas and Oklahoma is more saline than the oceans (USWRC, 1979).

Unfortunately an enormous amount of irrigation water is wasted in the western states, primarily because the cost is subsidised and farmers essentially have free use of water. For instance, farmers in Utah pay only $44/ha for water from the Bonneville Water Project, while the U.S. government subsidises doing this at a cost of nearly $1500/ha. If farmers were paying the $1500/ha, they would be more careful in the use of this irrigation water. Growing low value forage crops to feed livestock as is done now would become uneconomical.

Pesticide Problems

Each year nearly 500,000 tons of pesticides are applied each year to U.S. agriculture at a cost of more than $8 billion; worldwide, about 2.5 million tons are used at a cost of about $18 billion (Pimentel, 1997). Despite this heavy use of pesticides, about 37 per cent and 40 per cent of all crops in the United States and the world, respectively, are lost to pests each year. The crop loss attributed to pests has been increasing slowly for many years in the United States. For example, the share of crops lost to insects has nearly doubled since 1945 even though the use of synthetic insecticides has increased 10-fold (Pimentel *et al.*, 1991). This rise in crop losses, despite increased insecticide use, can be accounted for by the many major changes that have taken place in agricultural technologies over the decades. Some of these changes include reduced crop rotations, greater use of crop monocultures, and the need to adhere to more stringent 'cosmetic standards' set by the Food and Drug Administration (FDA).

Of particular concern is that 99.9 per cent of the pesticide that is applied never reaches the target pests but instead disperses widely to contaminate the environment (Pimentel and Levitan, 1986). Furthermore, pesticides applied by aircraft are wasted because only 25–50 per cent of the pesticide ever reaches the target area under the most ideal spraying conditions (Mazariegos, 1985; Pimentel and Levitan, 1986). The remainder drifts offsite to contaminate the environment and sometimes threatens the health of people and animals.

For these reasons, the economic benefits of pesticides need to be balanced against waste, as well as the indirect environmental and public health costs, which are estimated to be about $8.3 billion each year (Pimentel and Greiner, 1997). Perhaps the most serious social cost is that of human pesticide poisonings. Each year in the United States about 100,000 accidental poisonings are reported. Worldwide, the estimate is 3 million human pesticide poisonings resulting in about 220,000 deaths (Pimentel and Greiner, 1997; WHO, 1992).

A recent study demonstrated that it would be possible to reduce pesticide use by one-half in the United States, provided a wide array of currently available non-chemical pest management practices were implemented (Pimentel *et al.*, 1991). If this were done, crop yields would remain the same or increase and production costs would increase about $1 billion per year. This would add only about 0.6 per cent to consumers' food costs. However, if the benefits accrued from reduced environmental and public health risks are subtracted, the actual cost to society of reducing pesticides might be zero. It may even show a return on the investment in non-chemical controls. Such plans to reduce pesticide use are already underway in Denmark, Sweden, the Netherlands, and the Canadian province of Ontario (Pimentel *et al.*, 1991).

Livestock Manure

Each year more than 7 billion livestock in the United States produce about 2 billion tons of manure. This amount of manure contains more than twice the total amount of nutrients than the commercial nitrogen fertiliser that is applied to U.S. crops annually. Half of this manure is deposited in pastures and rangeland and provides some fertilisation. Of the half that is collected, about 50 per cent is lost due to poor management practices. For example, approximately 50 per cent of the nitrogen is lost from the manure within 24 hours if it is not buried immediately or placed in a manure pond under anaerobic conditions (Exner *et al.*, 1989). As a result, only about 20 per cent of the nutrients in collected livestock manure is captured and available for crop production. Furthermore, a significant portion of the nutrients that are lost in run-off contaminates groundwater and adjacent rivers and lakes (Pimentel, 1989).

Fossil Energy

To produce a hectare of corn using hand tools requires about 1200 hours of labour (Lewis, 1951). In the U.S. today, a hectare of corn is produced with a farm labour input of about 10 hours (Pimentel and Wen, 1990). The reduction in labour input has been accomplished through farm mechanisation that uses enormous amounts of fossil fuel. For instance, to produce a hectare of corn requires about 700 litres of oil equivalents.

Furthermore, fertiliser inputs have increased as much as 20-fold just since 1945 (Pimentel and Wen, 1990). Also, pesticide inputs have risen 33-fold since 1945. Producing fertilisers and pesticides requires a large input of fossil fuels. The recent major changes in agricultural technology have occurred in a relatively short period of time and are consuming significant quantities of fossil energy.

Ethanol from Grain

Proponents of producing ethanol from U.S. corn and other grains claim that it reduces oil imports and saves the nation money (ERAB, 1981). Unfortunately, the opposite is true. Each gallon (3.8 litres) of ethanol requires 10.1 kg of corn and costs about $1.94 per gallon to produce (Pimentel, 1991). Assuming that distillers' dried grains were produced and utilised, this cost could be reduced by as much as $0.60 per gallon. However, most of this benefit is lost because of environmental pollution that costs at least $0.36 per gallon. In addition to this cost, federal and state subsidies average $0.79 per gallon (EPA, 1990). Thus, a gallon of ethanol costs the consumer $2.55 to produce compared with about $0.70 per gallon of gasoline (Pimentel, 1991).

Also, a gallon of ethanol has only about two-thirds as much energy as a gallon of gasoline. To produce a gallon of ethanol in a large 60 million gallon per year plant with all modern facilities requires an energy input of 35,046 kcal. A gallon of ethanol contains only 19,450 kcal. This means that it takes about 80 per cent more energy to produce a gallon of ethanol that can be obtained in net fuel. Therefore, not only does the nation have to import oil from the Middle East to fuel this corn–alcohol system but also ethanol production is costing taxpayers huge sums of tax money in the form of subsidies. Therefore, the nation has to import from the Middle East to fuel this corn–alcohol system, and ethanol production is costing taxpayers huge sums of money in the form of subsidies. Its production also adds to the environmental degradation of land, water, energy, and biological resources.

Assuming zero energy input for the fermentation and distillation processes of ethanol production and charging only for the fossil energy expenditure to culture the corn (essential to have corn–alcohol produce net energy), the amount of cropland required to fuel just one U.S. automobile is enormous. Based on these assumptions, more than 6 ha of cropland would be necessary to fuel one automobile for one year. In contrast, one person is fed using only 0.6 hectares of cropland (USDA, 1989). This emphasises the tremendous waste of agricultural resources when ethanol is produced from grains.

SUSTAINABLE MANAGEMENT OF NATURAL RESOURCES

The major difficulties associated with conventional, high-input agriculture are the following: high costs of production (Pimentel *et al.*, 1989); serious environmental resource degradation (Pimentel, 1990); and instability of crop yields (Brown, 1984). Numerous agricultural technologies already exist that can be implemented to make agriculture sustainable and ecologically sound. These technologies would reduce chemical inputs (including commercial fertilisers and pesticides), reduce soil erosion and rapid water run-off, and make better use of livestock manure (NAS, 1989; Paoletti *et al.*, 1989). The economic and environmentally sound agricultural practice of the ridge planting and rotation system is compared with the conventional system of producing corn (Table 10.1). Note the high level of inputs in the conventional corn system. The total costs of these inputs average $523/ha in the United States and do not include the average cost of irrigation water. The total energy input is 6.9 million kcal/ha, but this would increase to about 11 million kcal/ha if the average irrigation input were included (Pimentel and Wen, 1990). The present day yield is about 750 kg/ha/year which is excellent compared with corn yields obtained when 1/20th the fertiliser and 1/33rd the amount of pesticide were used. The yield in 1945 with very low inputs was about 1900 kg/ha/year.

The environmental costs attributed to both agriculture and society when corn is produced using conventional practices are listed in Table 10.2. The loss of fertiliser nutrients in total $113/ha/year is based on the calculation of Troeh *et al.* (1991) that $20 billion in nutrients are lost from agriculture via erosion and water run-off annually. The offsite environmental damage caused by sediments is estimated to be $10 billion annually. The loss of water caused by rapid run-off was estimated to be a conservative $50/ha (Pimentel *et al.*, 1987). Ground and surface water pollution costs associated with livestock manure were estimated to be a minimum of $5/ha/year. The yearly environmental costs of pesticides were calculated to be $25/ha based on an estimated $8 billion ecological impact each year from pesticides (Pimentel and Greiner, 1997). Taken together these environmental damages total at least \$281/ha/year for conventional corn production. If these environmental costs were added to the production costs, then the total cost of producing conventional corn rises to \$804/ha/year (Table 10.1).

Table 10.1. Energy and economic inputs per hectare for conventional and alternative corn production systems.

	Conventional			Ridge planting and rotations		
	Quan-tity	10^3 kcal	Econo-mics (\$)	Quantity	10^3 kcal	Econo-mics (\$)
Labour (hrs)	10 (a)	7 (f)	50 (r)	12 (cc)	9 (f)	60 (r)
Machinery (kg)	55 (b)	1485 (g)	91 (s)	45 (dd)	1215 (g)	75 (s)
Fuel (litres)	115 (b)	1255 (h)	38 (t)	70 (ee)	764 (h)	23 (t)
N (kg)	152 (b)	2280 (i)	81 (u)	27 (t)(ff)	5591 (l)	17 (mm)
P (kg)	75 (b)	450 (j)	53 (v)	34 (gg)	214 (j)	17 (v)
K (kg)	96 (b)	240 (k)	26 (w)	15 (hh)	38 (k)	4 (w)
Limestone (kg)	426 (b)	134 (l)	64 (x)	426 (ii)	134 (l)	64 (x)
Corn seeds (kg)	21 (b)	520 (m)	45 (y)	21 (b)	520 (m)	45 (y)
Cover crop seeds (kg)	–	–	–	10 (jj)	120 (jj)	10 (nn)
Insecticides (kg)	1.5 (c)	150 (n)	15 (z)	0	0	0
Herbicides (kg)	2 (c)	200 (n)	20 (z)	0 (kk)	0	0
Electricity (10^3 kcal)	100 (b)	100 (o)	8 (aa)	100 (b)	100 (o)	8 (aa)
Transport (kg)	322 (d)	89 (p)	32 (bb)	140 (d)	39 (p)	14 (bb)
TOTAL		6910	523		3712	337
Yield (kg)	7500 (e)	26,514 (q)		8100	29,160	
Output/ input ratio		3.84			7.86	

Sources for Table 10.1:
(a) Labour input was estimated to be 10 hours because of the extra time required for tillage and cultivation compared with no-till which required 7 hours (USDA, 1984a).
(b) Pimentel and Wen, 1990.
(c) Mueller *et al.*, 1985.
(d) Transport of machinery, fuel, and nitrogen fertiliser (Pimentel and Wen, 1990).
(e) Three-year running average yield.
(f) Food energy consumed per labourer per day was assumed to be 3500 kcal.
(g) The energy input per kilogram of steel in tools and other machinery was 18,500 kcal (Doering, 1980) plus 46 per cent added input (Fluck and Baird, 1980) for repairs.
(h) Fuel includes a combination of gasoline and diesel. A litre of gasoline and diesel fuel was calculated to contain 10,000 and 11,400 kcal, respectively (Cervinka, 1980). Weighted average value of 10,900 used in calculations. These values include the energy input for mining and refining.
(i) Nitrogen=15,000 kcal/kg.
(j) Phosphorous=6000 kcal/kg.
(k) Potassium=2500 kcal/kg (Dovring and McDowell, 1980).
(l) Limestone=315 kcal/kg (Terhune, 1980).
(m) Hybrid seed=24,750 kcal/kg (Heichel, 1980).
(n) Energy input for insecticides and herbicides was calculated to be 100,000 kcal/kg (Pimentel, 1980).
(o) Includes energy input required to produce the electricity.
(p) For the goods transported to the farm, an input of 275 kcal/kg was included (Pimentel, 1980).
(q) A kg of corn was calculated to have 4000 kcal.
(r) Labour=$5/hour.
(s) USDA, 1984a.
(t) Litre=$0.33.
(u) N=$0.53.
(v) P=$0.51.
(w) K=$0.27.
(x) Limestone=$0.15.
(y) USDA, 1984a.
(z) Insecticide and herbicide treatments = $10/kg for both the material and application costs.
(aa) kwh=7c.
(bb) Transport =10c/kg.
(cc) Five additional hours were necessary for collecting and spreading 27 tons of manure (Pimentel *et al.*, 1984).
(dd) 20 per cent smaller machinery was used because less power is needed in no-till and ridge planting (Colvin *et al.*, 1982; Muhtar and Rotz, 1982; Allen and Hollingsworth, 1983; Hamlet *et al.*, 1983; USDA, 1984b).

(ee) Nearly 40 per cent less fuel is required compared with conventional systems because the soil was not tilled, only lightly cultivated (Colvin *et al.*, 1983; Mueller *et al.*, 1985).

(ff) A total of 27 tons of cattle manure was applied to provide 152 kg of N.

(gg) A total of 41 kg of P was provided by the manure.

(hh) A total of 81 kg of K was provided by the manure.

(ii) Assumed that same amount of N, P, K, and Ca required in no-till.

(jj) About 10 kg of cover crop seeds were used (Heichel, 1980).

(kk) No herbicide used, weed control carried out by cultivation and cover crop.

(ll) About 1.9 litres of fuel were required to collect and apply 1 ton of manure (Pimentel *et al.*, 1984).

(mm)The value of manure was given for the fuel required to transport and spread.

(nn) kg of cover crop seed = $1.

The ridge planting and crop rotation system listed in Table 10.1 utilises readily available agricultural technologies that can make agriculture more productive, economic, sustainable, and environmentally sound than conventional corn production. In this system – which uses ridge planting, crop rotations, and a cover crop – soil erosion is reduced from approximately 20 t/ha/year for conventional and continuously grown corn to less than 1t/ha/year. Note the 1t/ha/year erosion rate equals the soil reformation rate under most agricultural conditions (Hudson, 1981; Lal, 1984a, 1984b; Elwell, 1985). Also, sound soil and water conservation technologies increase corn yields from 15 per cent to 30 per cent compared to corn grown under conventional systems that experience moderate to severe soil erosion (Follett and Stewart, 1985; ASAE, 1985). Note that for this analysis, I assumed a 15 per cent increase in yield over the conventional corn production system, which is at that minimum when sound soil and water conservation practices are employed (Table 10.1).

Table 10.2. Environmental costs both onsite and offsite from conventional agriculture per hectare annually (see text for details).

Item	Cost (U.S.$)
Loss of soil nutrients	113.00
Loss of water	50.00
Manure pollution	5.00
Offsite sediments impact	37.50
Pesticide impact	50.00
TOTAL	280.50

Selecting an appropriate crop, like soybeans, for rotation with corn reduces corn rootworm (Pimentel *et al.*, 1993), corn diseases (Pearson, 1967; Mora and Moreno, 1984), and weed problems (NAS, 1968, 1989; Mulvaney and Paul, 1984). Furthermore, a corn and soybean rotation system is more profitable than raising either crop alone (Helmers *et al.*, 1986). In part, this results when corn is grown in rotation because the corn rootworm problem is eliminated and there is no need for insecticide. Average corn loss to insects in conventional, continuous corn production is 12 per cent whereas corn loss to insects for corn grown in rotation is only 3.5 per cent (Pimentel *et al.*, 1991). Thus, corn yields increase more than 8 per cent if insecticides are withdrawn and corn is grown in rotation. For that reason, this 8 per cent was added to the yield in ridge planting and rotation system in this analysis (Table 10.1).

Several additional ecologically sound management practices were included in the ridge planting and rotation system (Table 10.1). These included recycling livestock manure and the use of a cover crop. Using farm manure reduces the pollution of groundwater and/or adjacent waterways, makes use of the valuable nutrients, adds organic matter to the soil, and reduces soil erosion (Pimentel *et al.*, 1987). Cover crops – especially legume cover crops like winter vetch – reduce soil erosion and water run-off, reduce weed problems and conserve soil nutrients. Soil nutrients are picked up and stored by the cover crop, which is subsequently ploughed under to contribute these nutrients once again to the soil.

Ridge planting, crop rotation, and the other techniques included in this particular analysis may not be appropriate for all types of soils, all crops, all pests, and all farming systems. However, these technologies were selected for this analysis to illustrate the potential that available technologies have to enhance the sustainability of agricultural production. Various combinations of these and other technologies have been developed for particular crops and farming systems (NAS, 1989; Paoletti *et al.*, 1989; Pimentel *et al.*, 1991).

The ridge planting and rotation system has the following advantages over the conventional corn system:

- soil erosion and rapid water runoff was reduced;
- smaller tractors were employed and less tractor fuel was used;
- mechanical cultivation substituted for the herbicides, but this was not essential;
- the rotation eliminated the need for all insecticides;
- on-farm livestock manure substituted for all the nitrogen and a large portion of the phosphorous and potassium nutrients; and
- a cover crop protected the soil and nutrients during the non-growing season.

The labour input was raised from 10 hours/ha to 12 hours/ha to include the time required to apply the livestock manure to the land.

All these modifications raised the corn yield from 7500 kg/ha in the conventional systems to 8100 kg/ha in the low-input ridge planting and rotation system (Table 10.1). The total energy input for the low-input system was only 3.7 million kcal or about half that of the conventional system. The total cost of production that included the added labour was $337 or 36 per cent lower than the conventional system. If, however, the environmental costs attributed to conventional production had been included, then production costs in the low-input system would be about one-half that of the conventional system.

Clearly, the substantially lower production costs of the low-input system, plus the 8 per cent higher yield of this system, generate greater profits for the farmer as well as for society. Specifically, soil and water conservation and reduced fertiliser and pesticide inputs result in major benefits now and in the future.

CONCLUSION

The careless use of soil, water supplies, non-renewable energy, and biological resources is contributing to the current high costs of agricultural production, as well as to the depletion of vital resources in both developing and developed nations. The analysis described in this paper indicates that the use of available, ecologically sound, cultural practices in the U.S. and other developed countries will not only maintain high yields but may, in some instances, actually increase yields while reducing production costs and protecting the quality of the environment.

In addition to ridge planting and rotations, a wide array of soil and water conservation technologies already exist and can be employed in corn and other major crop systems (Troeh *et al.*, 1991; Lockeretz, 1983; Pimentel *et al.*, 1987; NAS, 1989; Paoletti *et al.*, 1989; Pimentel, 1990). Also, the use of non-chemical alternative pest control technologies helps reduce costly pesticide inputs (PSAC, 1965; OTA, 1979; Pimentel *et al.*, 1991).

Selecting the particular combination of alternative practices depends not only on the conditions of soil, water, climate, and biota but also on the crop and/or livestock to be produced. Each agrarian ecosystem has to be designed and adapted for the particular biological and socio-economic environment in both developing and developed nations. In addition to conserving soil and water, the improved use of biological resources for biological control plus obtaining nutrients (nitrogen) from legumes and other technologies can help reduce agricultural production costs.

The proposed ecological approach for sustainable, productive, and environmentally sound agriculture calls for more knowledge and a better understanding of the interdependencies of natural resources, crops, livestock, and the environment than conventional agricultural production has provided (NAS, 1989; Paoletti *et al.*, 1989; Pimentel *et al.*, 1989). This ecological, sustainable approach needs to be implemented because of growing environmental concerns and economic problems plus the challenge of producing more food from the world resources that are available. Clearly, we have more sophisticated ecological knowledge and agricultural technologies than ever before. Future research findings will add to our arsenal of technologies to help agriculture become more productive and more sustainable while at the same time being more environmentally sound.

REFERENCES

Alexander, M. 1977. *Introduction to Soil Microbiology.* New York: John Wiley and Sons.

Allen, R.R. and Hollingsworth, L.D. 1983. 'Limited Tillage Sorghum on Wide Beds.' *ASAE Paper* 83, 1517.

ASAE (American Society of Agricultural Engineers) 1985. 'Erosion and Soil Productivity.' *American Society of Agricultural Engineering*, St. Joseph, Michigan. *ASAE Paper* 8, 85.

Brown, W.L. 1984. 'Some Observations on Changing Trends in Agricultural Production Systems.' Remarks delivered at the Agricultural Research Institute Conference, Changing Agricultural Production Systems and the Fate of Agricultural Chemicals, 21–23 February, Chevy Chase, Maryland.

Cervinka, V. 1980. 'Fuel and Energy Efficiency.' In Pimentel, D. (ed.) *Handbook of Energy Utilization in Agriculture.* Boca Raton: CRC Press, 15–24.

Colvin, T.S., Hamlett, C.A. and Rodriguez, A. 1982. 'Effect of Tillage System on Farm Machinery Selection.' *ASAE Paper* 82, 1029.

Colvin, T., Erbach, D., Marley, S. and Erickson, H. 1983. 'Large Scale Evaluation of a Till Plant System.' *ASAE Paper* 83, 1027.

Doering, O.C. 1980. 'Accounting for Energy in Farm Machinery and Buildings.' In Pimentel, D. (ed.) *Handbook of Energy Utilization in Agriculture.* Boca Raton: CRC Press, 9–14.

Dovring, F. and McDowell, D.R. 1980. 'Energy Use for Fertilizers.' Department of Agricultural Economics, Staff Paper 80 E-102, University of Illinois,

Urbana, Illinois.

Elwell, H.A. 1985. 'An Assessment of Soil Erosion in Zimbabwe.' *Zimbabwe Science News* 19, 3/4, 27–31.

EPA (Environmental Protection Agency) 1976. 'Evaluating Economic Impacts of Programmes for Control of Saline Irrigation Flows: A Case Study of the Grand Valley, Colorado.' U.S. Environmental Protection Agency, Denver, Colorado.

EPA (Environmental Protection Agency) 1990. 'Analysis of the Economic and Environmental Effects of Ethanol as an Automotive Fuel.' U.S. Environmental Protection Agency, Washington, D.C.

ERAB (Energy Research Advisory Board) 1981. 'Biomass Energy. Energy Research Advisory Board.' U.S. Dept. Of Energy, Washington, D.C.

Exner, D., Thompson, R. and Thompson, S. 1989. 'Case Study: A Resource Efficient Farm with Livestock.' In Francis, C.A., Flora, C.B. and King, A.D. (eds.) *Sustainable Agriculture in Temperate Zones*. New York: John Wiley, 263–280.

FAO 1991. 'Food Balance Sheets.' Rome: Food and Agriculture Organization of the United Nations.

Fluck, R.C. and Baird, C.D. 1980. *Agricultural Energetics*. Westport: AVI Publications.

Follett, R.F. and Stewart, B.A. 1985. 'Soil Erosion and Crop Productivity.' American Society of Agronomy, Crop Science Society of America, and Soil Science Society of America, Madison, Wisconsin.

Hamlet, C.A., Colvin, T.S. and Musselman, A. 1983. 'Economic potential of conservation tillage in Iowa.' *Trans. ASAE* 26, 719–722.

Heichel, G.H. 1980. 'Assessing the Fossil Energy Costs of Propagating Agricultural Crops.' In Pimentel, D. (ed.) *Handbook of Energy Utilization in Agriculture*. Boca Raton: CRC Press, 27–33.

Helmers, G.A., Langemeir, M.R. and Atwood, J. 1986. 'An Economic Analysis of Alternative Cropping Systems for East-central Nebraska.' *American Journal Alternative Agriculture* 4, 153.

Hudson, N.W. 1981. *Soil Conservation*. Ithaca: Cornell University Press.

Khoshoo, T.N. and Tejwani, K.J. 1993. 'Soil Erosion and Conservation in India.' In Pimentel, D. (ed.) *World Soil Erosion and Conservation*. Cambridge: Cambridge University Press, 109–145.

Lal, R. 1984a. 'Productivity Assessment of Tropical Soils and the Effects of Erosion.' In Rijsberman, F.J. and Wolman, M.G. (eds.) *Quantification of the Effect of Erosion on Soil Productivity in an International Context*. Delft: Delft Hydraulics Laboratory, 70–94.

Lal, R. 1984b. 'Soil Erosion from Tropical Arable Lands and Its Control.'

Advances in Agronomy 37, 183–248.

Lal, R. 1993. 'Soil Erosion and Conservation in West Africa.' In Pimentel, D. (ed.) *World Soil Erosion and Conservation*. Cambridge: Cambridge University Press, 7–25.

Lal, R. and Stewart, B.A. (eds.) 1990. *Soil Degradation*. New York: Springer.

Leyton, L. 1983. 'Crop Water Use: Principles and Some Considerations for Agroforestry.' In Huxley, P.A. (ed.) *Plant Research and Agroforestry*. Nairobi: International Council for Research in Agroforestry, 379–400.

Lewis, O. 1951. *Life in a Mexican village: Tepoztlan Restudied.* Urbana: University of Illinois Press.

Lockeretz, W. 1983. *Environmentally Sound Agriculture.* New York: Praeger.

Mazariegos, F. 1985. The Use of Pesticides in the Cultivation of Cotton in Central America. UNEP Industry and Environment. July/August/September 5.

McLaughlin, L. 1993. 'A Case Study in Dingxi County, Gansu Province, China.' In Pimentel, D. (ed.) *World Soil Erosion and Conservation*. Cambridge: Cambridge University Press, 87–107.

Mora, L.E. and Moreno, R.A. 1984. 'Cropping Pattern and Soil Management Influence on Plant Diseases: I. *Diplodia macrospora* Leaf Spot of Maize.' *Turrialbo* 341, 35–40.

Mueller, D.H., Klemme, R.M. and Daniel, T.C. 1985. 'Short- and Long-term Cost Comparisons of Conventional and Conservation Tillage Systems in Corn Production.' *Journal for Soil and Water Conservation* 40, 466–470.

Muhtar, H.A. and Rotz, C.A. 1982. 'A Multi-crop Machinery Selection Algorithm for Different Tillage Systems.' *ASAE Paper* 82, 1031.

Mulvaney, D.L. and Paul, L. 1984. 'Rotating Crops and Tillage: Both Sometimes Better Than Just One.' *Crop Soils* 367, 8–19.

Myers, N. 1993. *Gaia: An Atlas of Planet Management.* New York: Anchor Press/Doubleday.

NAS (National Academy of Sciences) 1968. *Principles of Plant and Animal Pest Control.* Weed Control Publication 1597. National Academy of Sciences, Washington, D.C.

NAS (National Academy of Sciences) 1989. *Alternative Agriculture*. National Academy of Sciences, Washington, D.C.

OTA (Office of Technology Assessment) 1979. *Pest Management Strategies in Crop Protection*. Office of Technology Assessment, U.S. Government Printing Office, Washington, D.C.

OTA (Office of Technology Assessment) 1982. *Impacts of Technology on U.S. Cropland and Rangeland Productivity*. U.S. Government Printing Office, Washington, D.C.

Paoletti, M.G., Stinner, B.R. and Lorenzoni, G.G. 1989. 'Agricultural Ecology and Environment.' *Agricultural Ecosystems and Environment* 27, 1–636.

Pearson, L.C. 1967. *Principles of Agronomy.* New York: Reinhold.

Pimentel, D. (ed.) 1980. *Handbook of Energy Utilization in Agriculture.* Boca Raton: CRC Press.

Pimentel, D. 1988. 'Industrialized Agriculture and Natural Resources.' In Ehrlich, P.R. and Holdren, J.P. (eds.) *The Cassandra Conference: Resources and the Human Predicament.* Texas A&M University Press, 53–73.

Pimentel, D. 1989. 'Impacts of Pesticides and Fertilizers on the Environment and Public Health.' In Summers, J.B. and Anderson, S.S. (eds.) *Toxic Substances in Agricultural Water Supply and Drainage.* Ottawa: U.S. Committee on Irrigation and Drainage, 95–108.

Pimentel, D. 1990. 'Environmental and Social Implications of Waste in U.S. Agriculture and Food Sectors.' *Journal of Agricultural and Environmental Ethics* 3, 5–20.

Pimentel, D. 1991. 'Ethanol Fuels: Energy Security, Economics, and the Environment.' *Journal of Agricultural and Environmental Ethics* 4, 1–13.

Pimentel, D. 1997. 'Pest Management in Agriculture.' In Pimentel, D. (ed.) *Techniques for Reducing Pesticide Use: Environmental and Economic Benefits.* Chichester: John Wiley and Sons, 1–11.

Pimentel, D. and Levitan, L. 1986. 'Pesticides: Amounts Applied and Amounts Reaching Pests.' *BioScience* 36, 86–91.

Pimentel, D. and Wen, D. 1990. 'Technological Changes in Energy Use in U.S. Agricultural Production.' In Carroll, C.R., Vandermeer, J.H. and Rosset, P.M. (eds.) *Agroecology.* New York: McGraw Hill, 147–164.

Pimentel, D. and Greiner, A. 1997. 'Environmental and Socio-economic Costs of Pesticide Use.' In Pimentel, D. (ed.) *Techniques for Reducing Pesticide Use: Environmental and Economic Benefits.* Chichester: John Wiley, 51–78.

Pimentel, D., Berardi, G. and Fast, S. 1984. 'Energy Efficiences of Farming Wheat, Corn, and Potatoes Organically.' *ASA Spec. Publications* 46, American Society of Agronomy, Madison, Wisconsin, 151–161.

Pimentel, D., Dazhong, W., Eigenbrode, S., Lang, H., Emerson, D. and Karasik, M. 1986. 'Deforestation: Interdependency of Fuelwood and Agriculture.' *Oikos* 46, 404–412.

Pimentel, D., Allen, J., Beers, A., Guinand, L., Linder, R., McLaughlin, P., Meer, B., Musonda, D., Perdue, D., Poisson, S., Siebert, S., Stoner, K., Salazar, R. and Hawkins, A. 1987. 'World Agriculture and Soil Erosion.' *BioScience* 37, 277–283.

Pimentel, D., Culliney, T.W., Buttler, I.W., Reinemann, D.J. and Beckman, K.B.

1989. 'Ecological Resource Management for A Productive, Sustainable Agriculture.' In Pimentel, D. and Hall, C.W. (eds.) *Food and Natural Resources.* San Diego: Academic Press, 301–323.

Pimentel, D., McLaughlin, L., Zepp, A., Lakitan, B., Kraus, T., Kleinman, P., Vancini, F., Roach, W.J., Graap, E., Keeton, W.S. and Selig, G. 1991. 'Environmental and Economic Impacts of Reducing U.S. Agricultural Pesticide Use.' In Pimentel, D. (ed.) *Handbook of Pest Management in Agriculture.* Boca Raton: CRC Press, 679–718.

Pimentel, D., Allen, J., Beers, A., Guinand, L., Hawkins, A., Linder, R., McLaughlin, P., Meer, B., Musonda, D., Perdue, D., Poisson, S., Salazar, R., Siebert, S. and Stoner, K. 1993. 'Soil Erosion and Agricultural Productivity.' In Pimentel, D. (ed.) *World Soil Erosion and Conservation.* Cambridge: Cambridge University Press, 277–292.

Pimentel, D., Harvey, C., Resosudarmo, P., Sinclair, K., Kurtz, D., McNair, M., Crist, S., Spritz, L., Fitton, L., Saffouri, R. and Blair, R. 1995. 'Environmental and Economic Costs of Soil Erosion and Conservation Benefits.' *Science* 267, 1117–1123.

Postel, S. 1989. 'Water for Agriculture: Facing the Limits.' *Worldwatch Paper* 93, Worldwatch Institute, Washington, D.C.

PRB (Population Reference Bureau) 1995. 'World Population Data Sheet.' Population Reference Bureau, Washington, D.C.

PSAC (President's Science Advisory Committee) 1965. 'Restoring the Quality of our Environment.' Report of the Environmental Pollution Panel, President's Science Advisory Committee, The White House, Washington, D.C.

Terhune, E.C. 1980. 'Energy Used in the United States for Agricultural Liming Materials.' In Pimentel, D. (ed.) *Handbook of Energy Utilization in Agriculture.* Bacon Raton: CRC Press, 25–26.

Troeh, F.R., Hobbs, J.A., and Donahue, R.L. 1991. *Soil and Water Conservation for Productivity and Environmental Protection.* Englewood Cliffs: Prentice-Hall.

USDA (United States' Department of Agriculture) 1984a. 'Economic Indicators of the Farm Sector. Costs of Production.' *USDA Econ. Res. Ser.,* ECIFS 4, 1.

USDA (United States' Department of Agriculture) 1984b. 'Returns to Corn and Soybean Tillage Practices.' *USDA Econ. Res. Ser.,* Agricultural Economics Report No. 508.

USDA (United States' Department of Agriculture) 1989. 'Agricultural Statistics.' U.S. Government Printing Office, Washington, D.C.

USWRC (United States' Water Resource Committee) 1979. 'The Nation's Water Resources. 1975–2000.' Second National Water Assessment. United States Water Resources Council. U.S. Government Printing Office, Washington, D.C.

Wen, D. 1993. 'Soil Erosion and Conservation in China.' In Pimentel, D. (ed.) *World Soil Erosion and Conservation.* Cambridge: Cambridge University Press, 63–85.

WHO 1992. *Our Planet, Our Health: Report of the WHO Commission on Health and Environment.* Geneva: World Health Organization.

11. Balancing Private Rights and Public Interests: Lessons from Pacific Salmon and Global Fishery Crises

R. Bruce Rettig

INTRODUCTION

Must we first fail to sustain environmental resources before we attain true sustainability over the long term? This paradox, that success may require failure, motivates this paper. Two observations drive it: (1) Major changes in fishery management regimes are associated with the near collapse of some prized fish populations. (2) Endangering valuable fish and wildlife species by destroying their habitat has triggered a wide public debate; that debate is clarifying the content of rights and responsibilities towards the critical habitat of those endangered species. But, even if crises are sometimes necessary, are they sufficient to find sustainable resource management approaches? Do we grasp fully the challenges we face?

What fundamental conflicts arise between people seeking to conserve environmental resources and those promoting economic development? Responding to concerns about the loss and degradation of environmental assets, governments have strengthened environmental protection. Protection measures help many people, but benefits are not highly visible and are small for each of the many people being protected. For example, limiting the development of wetlands may help all water consumers in a region, but only scientists may appreciate the gain. On the other hand, conservation and preservation prevent development opportunities that are expected as part of landowners' property rights. Although the total property value loss may be less than the total gain from conservation, the losses accrue to a few people who resent their loss of development rights. Intensifying the resentment is the perception of cavalier intrusion upon individual liberties.

Adopting new institutional arrangements can help resolve these conflicts, but only at a cost of new and more fundamental problems. Although all levels of government are targets for protests, expressions of resentment intensify for higher levels of government. In many countries, attempts to reduce conflict have included privatisation through harnessing market incentives to protect the environment and shifting more power and responsibility to lower levels of government. Privatisation and devolution of public rights and responsibilities to the community level reduce the intensity of some conflicts, but not others. In all circumstances, gains are offset by new problems.

In this chapter, two cases are treated: (1) shifts in ocean management regimes in response to continued declines in several valuable fisheries and competition for access to those fisheries and (2) changes in management of salmon and their habitat along the Pacific coast of North America. The chapter closes with a consideration of questions raised by John Gowdy in this volume. Are parties to these conflicts judging policies in different time and spatial scales? Does reconciliation of conflicts at one scale, for example, focusing on the immediate future and a local area, set the stage for a more fundamental conflict in the future and over a larger area?

THE GLOBAL FISHERY CRISIS

The current perception of crisis in global fisheries is similar to concerns that arose in the 1960s and early 1970s in response to the rapid growth and perceived abuse of marine fisheries by distant water fishing nations. At that time, the international community responded by establishing national responsibilities, and often rights, at the Third United Nations Conference on the Law of the Sea (UNCLOS III). More recently, when additional abuses were suspected in some international waters not clearly governed by UNCLOS III, the international response was the United Nations Conference on Straddling Stocks and Highly Migratory Stocks. In spite of positive contributions from evolving international marine law, many important fish stocks continue to be in trouble. Many argue that the solution is to further clarify property rights. The purpose of this section is to discuss the source of the global fishery crisis, the positive impact of property rights institutions and the mounting concerns about some of those developments.

Fishery Trends

Except for minor dips, global fish utilisation has increased steadily for many years. World commercial catch grew steadily from 33.3 million metric tons in 1958 to 66.1 million metric tons in 1971. After declining to 62 million metric tons in 1972, growth resumed and continued with minor year to year variation to 100.1 million metric tons in 1989. Following a dip to 97.4 million metric tons in 1990, growth resumed, reaching a record 109.6 million metric tons in 1994.

Lumping together all countries, all species, and all types of fisheries masks sharply differing trends. Some fisheries, such as freshwater aquaculture, which made China the leading fish producer in the world, have grown rapidly. Other fisheries have varied widely from year to year. For example, the Peruvian anchoveta fishery made Peru the leading fishing nation in the world (in weight of biomass landed) through most of the 1960s until landings in this fishery fell from 13.1 million metric tons in 1970 to 1.7 million metric tons in 1972. After recovering modestly in 1973-1976, Peruvian anchoveta landings hovered between 0.1 and 1.4 million metric tons between 1977 and 1985. Recently, this fishery appears to have recovered nearly to the peak levels attained three decades ago.

Trends in two other major fishing nations reveal other tendencies. Japan, which was the leading fishing nation throughout the peak days of distant water fishing operations in the 1960s and 1970s, has suffered declining harvest levels over the past decade. For example, Japan accounted for 16 per cent of all world fish landings in 1973, and 15 per cent in 1983, but only 8 per cent in 1993. On the other hand, Chile expanded its share of world harvest from 1 per cent in 1973 to more than 5 per cent in 1983, and continued to grow, now rivaling Japan. Chile's expansion is due to the recovery of anchoveta and some other stocks with wide year-to-year variability, development of previously under-utilised stocks off its southern coast, and successful aquaculture strategies.

In summary, continued growth in global fisheries masks the fact that, while some countries, especially China, have made good progress with aquaculture, the growth in the weight of capture fish landings may be approaching its peak and the net economic value of world fisheries may be declining. That is to say, increased capture fish landings are primarily from medium- to low-valued fish stocks, often used as fish meal and oil, whilst several valuable fish stocks such as cod have declined, triggering social unrest, economic hardships, and calls for institutional change. The conflicts now clearly evident in such developed areas as North America and Europe are likely to accelerate elsewhere. Why are these fisheries in such grave trouble?

Apparent Sources of Fishery Declines

Natural (climatic) variation
Lessons learned the hard way in Peru are relevant for many other fisheries. Namely, the carrying capacity of natural populations varies over time in ways that we understand incompletely and predict poorly, even when we understand causes. In the case of Peru (and neighbouring Chile and Ecuador), the enormous productivity of anchoveta is driven by coastal upwelling of nutrient rich water, which subsides and sometimes collapses during cycles

referred to as ENSO (El Nino/Southern Oscillation). In the middle of the 1970s, Peru was late to accept the consequences of a strong El Nino (drop in ocean productivity due to a cessation of coastal upwelling) and they heavily fished a declining biomass, extending the length and severity of the declining fortunes of their fishery. Declining salmon harvests in California, Oregon, Washington, and southern British Columbia are due, in part, to unfavourable ocean conditions, including periods of poor upwelling and some warm water conditions that are apparently not being caused by an El Nino event. That is to say, the unfavourable conditions are continuing on a time scale much longer than that associated with ENSO events. The precise role of ocean variability in the Atlantic cod decline is the subject of much speculation, but it appears to be playing a contributing role.

The central lesson to be drawn from fishery problems associated with natural variability is that sustainability cannot be equated to constancy in natural resource use. Rather, management must accommodate the rhythms of nature, whether the cycles and long term changes are understood or not. One of the central questions raised at the Second World Fishery Congress was why some fish stocks survive and some collapse (Sinclair, 1997). One possibility is that a preoccupation with maintaining full utilisation of valuable fish stocks at levels near their maximum sustainable yield creates a brittle structure that is vulnerable to dramatic and undesirable change when apparently small changes take place in the ocean environment. This parallels arguments of Holling (1986) who suggests that ecosystems are constantly changing and that self-renewing systems must be structured around and accommodate variability including 'surprise' (unexpected changes in the environment that alter the ecosystem).

Habitat degradation
Habitat loss and degradation present the greatest hazards for diadromous fish species (species that live part of their lives in the ocean and part in freshwater). This is also true for freshwater species, and the many other species that either spawn or spend other critical parts of their lives in coastal bays, estuaries, and nearshore waters. These waters are often polluted and weakly regulated. In rich and poor countries alike, whether near the equator or at high latitudes, human settlements concentrate near bays, estuaries, and riverbanks with accompanying waste products and disruption of natural systems. In low latitudes, the classic example is the loss of mangroves through coastal development; without the mangroves to filter wastes and anchor a complex ecological system, few islands can hope to retain important nearshore fisheries. Environmental degradation and loss of fish and wildlife habitat (for example, seagrass beds and coastal wetlands) has drawn much attention in the Mediterranean Basin. Mitigation efforts by the World Bank and the European Investment Bank have been substantial with much still

needing to be done (Pearce and Pearce, 1993). Major efforts are also under way in the Baltic, Black, Aral and Caspian Seas and in the Danube Basin. The loss of coastal wetlands in the name of flood protection and coastal development harms not only fish species that spend part of their lives in coastal marshes, but also rich wildlife and plant life. Shifting management responsibility from national governments to local governments or non-governmental organisations is both a partial solution to the habitat degradation and a new source of conflict between coastal residents.

Overfishing
When access to a fish stock is open to anybody, fish are harvested more heavily than when access is controlled. Fisheries are the standard illustration of what Hardin (1968) called the 'tragedy of the commons.' Since Hardin's classic metaphor captured the public imagination, marine fisheries have been termed 'common property' resources. However, anthropologists and other students of resource tenure regimes observe that the problem does not appear when social arrangements create a shared sense of responsibility. For this reason, they argue against use of the term common property and suggest preference for use of other terms such as 'open access.'[1]

Whatever term one uses, many valuable fish stocks were harvested heavily by competing and sometimes hostile nations in the 1960s and 1970s as distant water fishing fleets expanded the size and scope of their operations. Many of these stocks could be characterised as overfished in three senses: economically overfished, growth overfished, and recruitment overfished. Economic overfishing refers to the failure to consider stock externalities, the loss in future revenues or the increase in future costs caused by declining fish catchability. These losses are externalities because fishers affect each other but lack incentives to consider the consequences of smaller stock sizes. Economic overfishing is also associated with crowding externalities when congestion on the grounds increases costs imposed by fishers on each other. Growth overfishing refers to the reduced size and weight of the average catch; if fish were caught at later ages, the total weight of the catch could be higher. Recruitment overfishing refers to the possibility of reduced capability of the stock to reproduce itself because of insufficient numbers of adult fish; this is the equivalent of harvesting too much of a field crop and not providing enough seed to start the next crop.

---

[1] Feeny, Hanna, and McEvoy (1996) provide a critical review of the (mis)use of the metaphor of the tragedy of the commons. McCay (1996) points out that 'open access' is not quite right either since cultural norms may limit excessive exploitation. She prefers to fault a combination of failure to define property claims (open access) and the absence of any management regime (*laissez-faire*).

International Property Rights Assertions

Whether their motives were to provide stewardship over declining fish stocks or to seize more coastal waters for their territory, many nations unilaterally extended their fishery management jurisdictions from an average distance of 12 nautical miles to a wider exclusive economic zone, usually 200 nautical miles from the coast. Although this establishment of international law by widespread unilateral adoption and treaty negotiation was codified into UNCLOS III in the early 1980s, another decade would go by before enough signatures were gathered to ratify the treaty.

At first, the assertion of coastal national jurisdiction seemed to be enough to reverse the pressures resulting from the lack of property rights. However, coastal nations were eager to gain advantages by developing their own fisheries, collecting revenues from distant water fishing nations, or developing joint ventures with distant water fishing nations. The accompanying pressure to provide 'full utilisation' of managed stocks is a factor in the decline of several stocks including Atlantic cod stocks. Those declines were aggravated by the tendency of managers to encourage scientists to overestimate available stocks, and by the failure to allow for the variability of harvestable surpluses over time.

This worldwide tendency to overharvest was formally recognised by the United Nations in the UN Agreement on Straddling Fish Stocks and Highly Migratory Stocks (UN, 1995) through an explicit call for use of the precautionary principle. These concerns have been articulated in the FAO Code of Conduct for Responsible Fisheries (FAO, 1995), but as Garcia and Grainger (1997) observe, the real difficulty lies not in the recognition of the problem, but in the implementation of incentives (regulatory programmes and social customs) that will lead to new behaviours. International property rights are only as productive as their underlying intranational property rights.

Intranational Property Rights Assignments

Spurred on by the decline of valuable fish stocks, several nations are attempting to 'rationalise' their excess fishing capital.[2] In many fisheries, public policies aimed at reducing harvest rates continue to be strongly resisted, but in others wide-ranging discussion among varied interests creates hope for broad support for sustainable fishing strategies. Allocation of fishing rights takes many forms, and appears to be strongly path dependent.

Path dependency is the tendency for institutional change to be guided

---

[2] Global fishing fleets have massive excess capacity, perhaps at a scale of twice that needed to take sustainable capture fisheries (Mace, 1997). Among the boldest efforts to reduce capacity is that of the European Union (EU). As part of the European Union's Common Fisheries Policy, the EU is spending large sums to reduce the size of fishing fleets and develop alternative economic opportunities for displaced fishers (Laurec and Armstrong, 1997).

strongly by historical processes. North (1990) provides one clear view of this process. He notes that people make decisions in the face of both formal constraints (laws and regulations at many levels of government) and informal constraints (social constraints and accustomed practices that people follow even though not codified into law). Their decisions are influenced by the organisations that shape collective behaviour. For example, fishing fleets respond to fishing regulations and the social customs of the fishers. This response will depend on the form of labour organisations, marketing organisations, and other groups that shape the behaviour of their members, including religious affiliations. In turn, organisations evolve to reflect the formal and informal constraints people face. Consequently, changes in laws affect fishers, but the precise change depends on their social customs and organisations. Also, changes in these laws reshape both customs and organisations.[3]

For example, Japanese coastal fishing rights, although taking several forms, usually centre around assignment of an aquacultural area or fishing rights to a local community-based cooperative. These cooperatives, although shaped by decisions taken following World War II, derive from the cultural organisation found in feudal Japan. When the Japanese expanded their fishing farther offshore, decisions to grant licensing powers of company concessions derived from their history, but none of their practices proved as strong and durable as the community-based organisations rooted in their history.[4]

Intranational allocation of exclusive rights to a fishing area or a fish stock takes many forms. For example, allocations are sometimes made to a particular ethnic group; several examples involve aboriginal populations such as Maoris in New Zealand and Indians in the United States and Canada. Special treatment is sometimes made for companies operating under a franchise, such as the enterprise allocation system in Atlantic Canada and the offshore fishing quota system in New Zealand. Assignments are sometimes made for individual communities; a striking example of this is the community development quota programme along Alaska's Bering Sea coast, which is primarily an allocation to aboriginal villages. Of growing global interest are assignments of fishing privileges to individual fishers. This includes the

---

[3] Several authors are beginning to apply the new institutional economics to fishery concerns. See, for example, Rettig (1995) and Doeringer and Terkla (1996). One of the hallmarks of this tradition is the additional richness to economic analysis from drawing on contributions from other social sciences. An especially useful insight is to characterise human decisions as decisions embedded in communities and other social structures (Hanna and Jentoft, 1996).

[4] The influence of Western culture seems to be having an influence on Japanese fishing. One of these trends, which Liao (1997) discusses for Taiwan has long been evolving in the United States, Canada, Australia, and many other countries. This is the rising economic and political power of recreational fishing interests, which results in pressure to shift property rights from commercial fishing interests to a wider set of public uses.

famous individual transferable quota (ITQ) programmes, which carry many names depending on several factors including the nature of restrictions on transferability.

Because most ITQ programmes are relatively new,[5] their weaknesses and strengths are yet to be assessed fully. They do seem to address many of the concerns about open access. Fish are taken over a longer time of the year and the race for fish common to open access fisheries seems to be blunted. Those who qualify for quotas have increased wealth because quota ownership is a valuable asset. When asked whether they wish to end ITQ programmes fishers governed by such programmes strongly support continuance. On the other hand, some people are deeply opposed to and critical of ITQ programmes. Why?

What Are the Major Concerns about Individual Fishing Quotas?

Although quota programmes can have many flaws, the groups opposed to them emphasise two concerns: conservation and social justice. The concern for conservation is common from country to country, but social justice considerations vary with the culture of the people in the fishery and the adjustments made in response to their concerns about the quota programme.

The problem with discards
Many people are greatly concerned about the large amount of fishing mortality that is not converted into products used by anybody. Some fish are discarded because of a lack of a market or because the price in port is less than the cost of bringing the fish ashore. Discarding can also result from fishing regulations. When fishing regulations set a minimum size for retention, small fish are thrown overboard and many die. Another form of discards occurs when particular gear types can retain only certain species. For example, the groundfish trawl fishery in Alaska has had to discard salmon, halibut, and king crab because they can only be retained by other gear types (purse seine, gillnet, troll, longline, and pots). Responding to changes to the Magnuson-Stevens Fishery Conservation and Management Act, these and other fisheries will be required to make changes to provide for full retention and full utilisation of catches. Innovative programmes to reduce discards in other fishing nations including Norway serve as a valued model.

In a study done for FAO, Alverson *et al.* (1994) estimated that, for the

---

[5] Hannesson (1997) suggests that the modern debates over ITQs parallel earlier debates over use rights of terrestrial resources. Arguments published by Karl Marx in the newspaper *Rheinische Zeitung* in the early 1840s about the need for the state to protect common rights of the general public to wood gathered by tradition in the forest against legal assertions of private property rights reflect some of the concerns raised against ITQs today.

average catch of 77 million metric tons landed between 1988 and 1990, an estimated 27 million metric tons more were discarded at sea.[6] Although some of the species discarded may be as useful as nutrients when returned to the sea as they would be if brought to port, public sentiment to encourage more complete utilisation of marine fish brings sharp scrutiny to any policy that appears to encourage waste. In this environment, a programme that creates incentives to discard a portion of catch triggers sharp criticism.

Individual quota programmes may encourage a particular form of discarding called 'high grading.' Since only a limited weight of species controlled by a quota can be landed, fishers may throw some of the captured fish overboard to maximise the value of the catch brought back to port. Several quota programmes have struggled with incentive mechanisms to reduce high grading, such as the use of independent observers on board the fishing vessel. Nonetheless, the impact of individual quota programmes is more complex than simple intuitive reasoning would suggest. MacGillivray (1997) reports that "waste in the [British Columbia] halibut fishery, resulting from lost and abandoned gear and discarding undersized halibut, decreased by 50 per cent with the introduction of IVQs [individual vessel quotas]." Perhaps more to the point, this is not the strongest source of concern about using property rights-based approaches to fishery management. Whatever the gains (or losses) from economic efficiency, management effectiveness, and resource conservation, the social debate heats up enormously when social equity considerations are considered.

The shifting balance of power and wealth and the rise and fall of communities

The greater debate is related to how the initial allocation of the quota is made, and how either the initial allocation or terms of transfer affect communities. Shares of a fish quota can be allocated most easily to owners of vessel licences since their historical landing records are often documented through receipts of sales to first buyers. This leaves three groups vulnerable to economic losses: (1) Crewmembers. The adjustment from current fishing strategies to new arrangements decreases employment; some crewmembers either become unemployed or earn less money in the new arrangement. (2) Processors. The fact of holding quota shifts power from fish buyers (processors or other first buyers) to fish sellers (fish quota holders). Fishers will probably land their fish at different times and places, with losses to some processors. (3) Residents of coastal communities that experience reduced fishing activity. This last concern is especially strong in remote fishing communities with limited economic bases.

---

[6] Given the difficulties of estimation, the authors prefer to state a range of 17.9 to 39.5 million metric tons as the likely discard amount.

A recent study of the British Columbia halibut fishery since introduction of individual quotas is instructive on these three changes. Casey *et al.* (1995) found that the combination of a reduced number of boats and a slightly lower average crew on working boats led to about a one-third decline in crew employment. However, remaining crew members are working during a longer season and are gaining benefits from the higher value of catch (caused by the shift of product from the frozen market, required when seasons were kept short, to a fresh market which is earning a high price premium). Conclusion: some crew members gain, others lose, but even the gainers gain less than those who acquire the property right to a quota share which triggered a large windfall gain.

As in the case of crew members, some processors gained and some lost. Since the product shifted from frozen to fresh, much of the capital equipment associated with freezing and cold storage became stranded. More of the product was sold to small firms, and new entry into the processing sector was observed.

Like the firms, the British Columbia communities, associated with receipts of landings during the peak of the season and freezing, have lost economic activity and other regions have gained. In countries with longer experience, the shift in activity from community to community has created benefits as well as costs. Runolfsson (1997) observes that the regional share in demersal quotas showed a decline in the southwest region of Iceland including Reykjavik (29.7 per cent in 1984 to 26.1 per cent in 1995/6) and an increase in the north (21 per cent in 1984 to 27.3 per cent in 1995/6).

Reauthorization of the major fishing law in the United States the 'Magnuson-Stevens Fishery Conservation and Management Act' was complicated by perceptions of gains and losses from the introduction of individual transferable quota programmes in Alaska. Although the issues are complex, one view is that quick adoption of quota programmes would reward fishing interests based in the port of Seattle, Washington, which has long been a base of operations for seasonal operations in Alaska. The associated perception is that delays will lead to further expansion of fishing activity in Alaska and lay a stronger basis for quota shares being distributed to Alaskans. To the counterargument that those wishing early quota adoption are being paranoid, one might hear the old saying 'Just because I am paranoid does not mean that somebody is not out to get me.'

In summary, individual quota shares appear to improve net economic efficiency, but consequences for conservation and social justice are uncertain. To alleviate these tensions, many fishery management agencies, upon the instructions of their governments and upon their own initiatives, are sharing more rights and responsibilities with people in the fishing industries and residents of fishing communities.

The devolution of management: Hopes and fears

In many fisheries, management failures are associated with lack of communication between managers and those being managed. The reasons are complex, but they include mistakes made when national governments attempt to handle details of management without critical information about local fishing practices and other practical details. Also, enforcement is more difficult and compliance is weaker when regulated groups disagree with and do not feel fully consulted about regulations.

Experiences with a variety of consultation arrangements, often with some management tasks delegated to the groups being managed, are being reported, frequently with favourable reviews.[7] Everything being held equal, delegation of rights and responsibilities to resource users increases both economic efficiency and social equity. Problems arise because (1) incomplete property rights fail to allow resolution of competing claims and (2) myopic time preferences lead to the sacrifice of sustainable resource use to meet short-term interests. Under these circumstances either decision rules should ensure an appropriate amount of resource stewardship or local decisions should be constrained by an authority with a greater commitment to sustainability.[8] This is common to all world fisheries, but it is the essence of the struggle to preserve stocks of Pacific salmon in the face of past and continuing economic development in the United States and Canada.

THE ENDANGERED SPECIES CRISIS IN THE U.S. PACIFIC NORTHWEST

What Is Happening to Salmon and Why?

The second case comes from the shifting fortunes of endangered species protection, with emphasis on anadromous fish in the Pacific Northwest. Pacific salmon hatch from eggs in fresh water, live in fresh water for a period that varies from species to species, then migrate to sea to grow and mature before returning to their natal streams to spawn and die. For more than a century, their numbers, average weight, and genetic fitness have declined for

---

[7] Pinkerton (1989) assembled several experience papers and analyses in a widely cited volume. See Hanna (1995) for additional analyses and more current citations.

[8] Members of the European Union face a further layer of complexity as they balance the prerogatives of various decision-making bodies in the EU and decisions to be taken at national and sub-national levels. The important subsidiarity principle requires that decisions be made at the lowest possible level. On the other hand, the interdependence of decisions in different member nations requires deference to decisions by the Council of the EU acting on advice from their scientists (Laurec and Armstrong, 1997).

many reasons including overharvest and both loss and degradation of habitat. A recent report of the U.S. National Research Council (1996), drawing on data from the Wilderness Society, reported that 40 per cent of Pacific salmon stocks (chinook, coho, chum, sockeye, and pink salmon plus sea-run cutthroat trout and steelhead trout) in the Pacific Northwest were extinct. Another 13 per cent were endangered; 14 per cent were threatened; 17 per cent were of special concern; and only 16 per cent were not known to be declining.

Not only are salmon of concern to conservationists, many commercial fishers and fishing communities are suffering in economic terms. Prices of salmon in the marketplace are falling and are expected to fall further. Why? Because, although many wild salmon stocks returning to California, Oregon, Idaho, Washington, and British Columbia are in trouble, world availability of salmon continues to climb.

How can salmon abundance be rising while salmon stocks are in jeopardy? Salmon culture has been wildly successful. This is especially true for salmon farming (the culture of Atlantic salmon in cages), but also for salmon ranching (culture through hatchery release into the ocean with harvest when adult salmon return to the point at which they were released). Success has been worldwide with dominance by Norway, but significant production from Scotland, Canada, Chile, the United States, Japan, and several other countries (Anderson, 1997). Further, the salmon capture fisheries in Alaska continue to set record highs. On the other hand, the once powerful Sacramento River salmon runs, and many salmon stocks in coastal streams from central California to central British Columbia have been impaired by many factors. High on the list are logging, mining, water diversion for irrigation, livestock watering that degrades riparian corridors, dams that block fish passage or create hazards during assisted passage, urbanisation, and water pollutants that heat water above critical levels or add toxic substances.

Several laws passed in the 1970s, including the Magnuson Fishery Conservation and Management Act of 1976, the National Forest Management Act of 1976, and the Pacific Northwest Electric Power Planning and Conservation Act of 1980 promised to protect salmon. However, by the late 1980s, documentation of several stocks at risk compounded a parallel debate on the loss of habitat for the northern spotted owl, the marbled murrelet and other species. Resistance to the high costs of endangered species protection has opened a major debate over the meaning of sustainability of the region's natural environment and of the sustainability of its economic growth. Some argue that the cost of environmental protection is too high, especially when it reduces the value of private property rights. Others argue that the loss of natural values requires a fundamental reexamination of the structure of the economy and a greater sense of community in seeking new policies.

What Is the Response?

The United States
One species of salmon (winter-run chinook) is now listed as endangered under the U.S. Endangered Species Act in the Sacramento River system in California and pressure is building to list the summer run of chinook salmon in that system. Three stocks of salmon in the Columbia/Snake River Basin are also listed as endangered (sockeye salmon and two stocks of chinook salmon in the Snake River Basin). Recent listings include sea-run cutthroat trout in Oregon's Umpqua River basin and coho salmon in California and southern Oregon, and still more stocks will soon gain protection. Only a wide-ranging process to identify remedies for declining coho salmon stocks postponed the listing of that species along most of the Oregon coast. To protect coho salmon and steelhead trout, many millions of dollars are being spent by the government and by the private sector (especially the timber industry, which pledged $30 million to match an appropriation of $30 million from the Oregon legislature).

Listing a species as threatened or endangered immediately limits the activities that place it in jeopardy. 'Jeopardy rulings' have slashed fish harvest rates, stopped or altered timber harvests, reduced livestock grazing operations, halted mining, required major expenditures on stream protection, forced major retrofitting of hydroelectric dams and changed dam operations. In turn, the changes to dams reduce the availability of cheap electric power, increase the cost of irrigation water withdrawn from the river and reduce or eliminate much of the barge traffic on the Columbia/Snake system. Although a comprehensive benefit-cost estimate is not available, the cost of a half billion U.S. dollars per year for the next several years to help the Snake River stocks begins to give a feel for the large economic sacrifice planned to save the salmon.

Canada
To understand the Canadian response, one must first understand the years of frustration with policy towards the small-scale groundfish fishers of Atlantic Canada. In the recent 'turbot wars' between Canada and the European Union, Canada had to admit to her own role in the crisis in many fish stocks on the rich Grand Banks and Georges Banks. Those fish stocks had been declining in part because Canada refused to 'bite the bullet' and enforce serious harvest limits. Canada requested a restrictive harvest limit for European fleets that harvested fish stocks found outside the 200-mile extended economic zone. These fish stocks 'straddled' the 200-mile zone and lived much of their lives within that zone on the Grand Banks. To maintain credibility, Canada felt that it had to strictly limit domestic harvests and show commitment to a long run sustainability programme. At the same time, it had to admit that fishing

capacity far exceeded the sustainable harvest capacity. To assure Canadian voters that one more round of assistance to groundfishers in trouble made economic sense, individual transferable quotas based on strict harvest standards and a fleet reduction programme were selected.

Salmon do not fit well with individual quotas. Therefore, faced with major excess fishing capacity in the British Columbia salmon harvest sector, the national government selected a mixed policy of compensation for voluntarily surrendering licences and a reconfiguration of licences so that they applied only to a selected region within Canada. Unfortunately, this programme emerged in the midst of other disputes. After several years of developing what appeared to be a highly successful hatchery programme for chinook on the West coast of Vancouver Island, return rates of adults plunged for the second year in a row leading to sharp cutbacks for salmon trollers. As if this was not enough trouble, returns to some fisheries rose while others suggested stocks in peril. This led to much finger pointing. Alaskans were accused of catching too many fish that spawned in British Columbia waters, leading angry Canadian trollers to block an Alaskan ferry from landing in Prince Rupert, British Columbia. The federal government stands accused of inappropriately favouring aboriginal fishers. Both federal and provincial governments are accused of favouring recreational anglers over commercial fishers. The premiere of British Columbia is fighting for greater control of the Pacific salmon fishery, and the national government sees this as complicating already difficult international negotiations with the United States. Elsewhere in this chapter I refer to path dependence; I am in good company when I wonder what path Canadian salmon fishery policy will take.

What May Be Wrong with the Responses?

Public policy responses to date are not cost effective (alternate strategies with as sound chances of success may cost much less). Nor are they economically efficient (although placing a value on this cultural icon may be impossible). But, most importantly, some people believe they are bearing a disproportionate burden (Berry and Rettig, 1994). Landowners whose livestock and logging operations have lost economic value to facilitate recovery of endangered species bear much of the cost although the value is elusive and appears to be spread over much of society. Thus saving endangered species has been attacked on both economic efficiency and social equity grounds.

Some of the solutions that could improve economic efficiency have been identified in the theoretical literature and are being implemented in part in legislative arenas. Under current law in the United States, it is illegal for developers to take actions on private land that will take endangered species or to place these species in jeopardy.[9] Especially under circumstances of uncertainty and incomplete information, this leads to too much resource preservation when the benefits of development exceed the value of conservation. Species lack sufficient protection when the benefits of development fall short of the value of species protection, but transaction costs of monitoring and enforcement of species protection are high. Among the institutional improvements are holding property owners strictly liable with the burden of proof of no harm, but allowing development when development benefits exceed the value of species protection and developers compensate for lost species habitat. Alternatively, property owners with development rights could be induced by adequate compensation for forgoing development rights when species protection values exceed development benefits (Polasky *et al.*, 1997).

Although considerations for equity or other social objectives may supersede efficiency considerations, compensation for taking development rights increasingly is being urged by economists and environmental organisations and incorporated into legislation. Legal requirements to provide compensation appeared in most revisions to the U.S. Endangered Species Act, but the political heat of the 1996 election year pushed this and many other sensitive environmental policies aside. Because the political process appears to be poorly equipped to deal with profound environmental issues, local groups have sought to find their own solutions.

Seeking Common Ground at the Watershed Level

In the midst of the furor, the greatest promise has come from attempts to build a consensus on problems and needs for salmon protection at the watershed level. Groups of people in many watersheds are meeting to discuss concerns and seek low-cost solutions that are tailored to local circumstances. Although limited experience has been accumulated on these efforts, global experience with co-management solutions appears to apply here.

Scott (1993) reflects on co-management, praises it in circumstances in which results have been positive, and offers useful suggestions about some sources of difficulties. The three he identifies are deficient information, excessive numbers of fishers, and fisher heterogeneity. In the most successful co-management schemes, fishers can easily observe each others' behaviour and they have much accumulated knowledge about the fishery resources. This is most common with local, relatively immobile fish or shellfish stocks. In other cases in which fishers find it difficult to observe each others' behaviour or in which uncertainty about the status of the fish stock is held, fish stocks are often overfished, sometimes to a disastrous level.

---

[9] Both taking and jeopardy have specific legal meanings. See, for example, Rohlf (1989).

Excessive numbers of fishers create a problem for reasons understood by all scholars of transaction costs. Namely, the larger the size of the group, the greater the costs of reaching agreements and enforcing the agreements. Thus, the best experiments with self-governance come from small, isolated fishing communities and the most difficult challenges at reaching consensus come from areas with much excessive fishing effort such as the British Columbia salmon fishery and the large groundfish fishing fleets of eastern Canada and the United States.

And, the more heterogeneous the group of fishers, the more incomplete the information and the more costly the process of negotiating and enforcing agreements. We could also add, from North (1990), that the informal constraints of social customs are more likely to present problems than to reach solutions. This may be why the most successful early experiments with watershed coalitions appear to be in long-established communities with a shared sense of history.

How Fragile Are Local Efforts to Resolve Conflicts?

This question is still being investigated. Participants in consensus building are very supportive of these activities. However, agreement among people with divergent interests requires compromise. Those who carefully seek common ground may find that more extreme views held by people outside their group can unravel the whole process. In some ways this is reminiscent of sound community-based fishery management found in many less developed countries that unravelled when more advanced technology or infrastructure was introduced. There are many depressing stories of how the introduction of the outboard engine managed to decimate artisanal fisheries that had been sustained for very long periods.

What Dangers Lurk in Success?

Pacific salmon fisheries are one of several illustrations Holling (1986) uses to show how sustainability is often confused with stability. Holling's first phase, which he attributes to standard ecological reasoning, is one of exploitation in which plants and animals colonise recently disturbed habitat. This is followed by a conservation period featuring slow accumulation and storage of energy and material. To these conventional phases, Holling added a release or creative destruction phase in which biomass and nutrients become overconnected (fragile) until released by some agent such as forest fires, insect outbreaks, or intense pulses of grazing. If the structure of the ecosystem is healthy, this phase is followed by a period of reorganisation that sets the stage for another round of exploitation and conservation.

Holling criticises the widespread adoption of hatcheries and failure to protect wild salmon stocks, fire suppression, flood mitigation, and other human attempts to create stability in what is otherwise a highly variable ecosystem. He suggests that these errors laid the foundation for the drastic declines in many salmon stocks today. Proposals by the National Research Council (1996) and others now emphasise protection of habitat complexity, conservation of wild stocks, and greater care with the use of hatcheries. In the conclusion to this chapter, fundamental questions are posed about efforts to privatise resources and to devolve management responsibility to watershed or other local levels. Are these sound strategies to allow naturally varying ecosystem processes? Or, are they unhealthy conservation initiatives that create a fragile system and lead to a more fundamental collapse with worsened prospects for new rounds of release and reorganisation?

CONCLUSIONS

The hypothesis advanced in this chapter is that decisions about the sustainable use of fish and wildlife require resolution of conflicts. These are the tensions that arise when protection of the rights of the many for non-market attributes of wild resources diminishes the rights of traditional users to exploit those resources. Further, population growth increases the conflict by both increasing the development value of environmental resources and increasing the scarcity value of the diminishing supply of wild natural resources. In addition to providing examples of declining wild resources, fishery disputes have raised the level of the debate over the relevant roles of privatisation cautioned by regulated stewardship requirements and the devolution of resource regulations. In this closing section, some of the key trends in worldwide marine fishery management regimes and elements of changes in implementation of endangered species protection are reviewed, and their implications for sustainability are explored.

Responding to declining fish stocks, UNCLOS III expanded the rights and responsibilities of coastal nations to manage fish stocks within 200 nautical miles of their coasts. It also assigned to 'natal' nations the right to manage anadromous fish stocks that spawn inland and live much of their lives in the oceans before returning to fresh water. International negotiations stopped short of fully extending additional rights over straddling stocks (fish stocks that are found in areas partly inside 200-mile extended economic zones and partly outside those zones) and highly migratory stocks (especially the tuna and tuna-like species).[10] However, widely accepted language reflecting the precautionary principle and other statements about responsible fishing

---

[10] Burke (1997) provides an insightful review of trends in international law relating to high-seas fisheries management.

appears to be facilitating negotiations among nations in regional management organisations. One example is the Northwest Atlantic Fisheries Organisation, which is responding to recent conflicts over harvest by European nations of fish stocks of fish found on the Grand Banks just outside Canada's extended economic zone. However, the continued high level of fishing capacity in many nations with accompanying political pressure to overharvest stocks, especially shared stocks (stocks harvested by more than one nation) suggests a need for changing institutional arrangements within fishing nations.

The Multi-annual Guidance Programmes developed by the European Union as part of its still evolving Common Fisheries Policy illustrate both the need for changes and the difficulties encountered during changes (Laurec and Armstrong, 1997). Although the European fleets are clearly too large, restructuring processes must vary to recognise the major differences in fishing fleets and fisheries, especially between northern European countries where fleets often are specialised and southern countries. Not only do the fleets vary, but the target species differ substantially and the dependence of communities upon fishing for employment vary. Nonetheless, substantial funds are being expended to reduce the size of the fleet and channel displaced fishers into other useful occupations.

Fishers, managers, and academic observers agree that additional measures of responsibility for stock conservation are needed; many, but not all, support the extension of additional rights for fishers as a method to ensure greater stewardship over resources. In some nations, such as Australia and New Zealand, which have expanded the use of individual transferable quotas and related measures, those who fish for the resource also pay an increasing share of the cost of research and management. This is sometimes referred to as privatisation, but limits are placed on the assignment of rights to protect the broad public interest in the fish resources.[11]

Although individual transferable quota programmes and other management regimes assigning fishing rights to the industry are expanding in use and are stoutly defended for increasing the net profitability of the fisheries, they are also under attack. Many reasons are offered, but concern about the fairness of some reaping windfall profits while others lose livelihoods, the possibility of disruption of isolated, traditional fishing communities, and incidental wastage of fish as rights holders 'high grade' their fish catches, appear to be of highest concern. Some of these concerns are

---

[11] The value of collecting revenues from fishing enterprises (both recreational and commercial) has arisen not because of economists' call to 'collect the rent,' but because these nations face serious public financial difficulties. They must collect more revenue or face sharp budget reductions. These pressures are found in many nations and play an important role in recent Canadian initiatives to use fleet reduction to greatly reduce the size of Canadian fleets, while shifting more responsibility for resource management to local levels. That is to say, devolution of authority seems to accompany a call for more fiscal responsibility.

associated with a transition from one form of governance to another. Some may be an inevitable continuing consequence associated with the gains. Still others may be addressed through continuing refinements of today's institutions in response to changing information, evolving changes in organisational power, and changes in other social institutions.

The tension associated with institutional change may be blocking or distorting the most economically efficient and socially desirable changes. This may explain the delight expressed by many fishery managers with greater responsibilities being assigned to representatives of fishing organisations (co-management) and greater use of advisory panels with feedback to the panels indicating that their views are taken seriously and having an impact (consultative management). Transaction costs theory suggests that this result is emerging because the gains to all parties exceed the costs of negotiation and sacrifices needed. If so, case studies of these processes may provide insight into the long-term benefits and costs of these processes and their long-term viability as well as their value in insuring sustainability.

Changes in marine fishery management regimes and endangered species protection exemplify two trends: desire to maintain historic liberties to use property as it had been used in the past and a desire to protect the nonrival-goods attributes of undeveloped properties. These conflicting objectives create tension, and whether and how that tension is resolved will vary from area to area. Marine fishery management and endangered species protection also include policy initiatives to strengthen and create new forms of property-rights-based policy instruments and new ways to use community structures to develop consensus. The remaining question is whether these are simply battles along the road to an unsustainable level of natural resource use or new mechanisms to create sustainable resource use patterns.

Gowdy raises a fundamental question about mistaken strategies for sustainability in this volume. His argument reflects work by Holling and Sanderson (1996). The question is whether political pressure to seek sustainable strategies on a local scale, and to do it with payoffs in the near future, creates brittle ecological, social and economic systems. For sustainability to succeed we must hope that, as Hanna and Jentoft (1996) suggest, solutions will be selected in a culture that is aware that local decisions are nested in communities, which are nested in larger social groups. Further, designers of institutions must recognise that ecological systems vary on time scales of decadal and longer lengths with important processes of evolutionary change.

Political processes must allow the patience for the visions of complexity suggested by scientists and spokespersons for groups, such as many aboriginal people, who have successfully incorporated environmental variability into their philosophy of habitat protection and resource use. If not, then Holling's release phase can be called destruction, but not 'creative' destruction. For some natural resources, such as Pacific salmon, the complex, expensive, and disruptive nature of truly sustainable development seems a possibility (although even here this remains only that, a possibility). For other resources, what appears to be a resolution of conflicts between private property owners and conservation interests may actually be the groundwork for a more fundamental collapse. If, as the saying goes, for every complex question there is a simple, but wrong answer, much research and social attention must turn to the search for more complex, although less popular, answers.

REFERENCES

Alverson, D.L., Freeberg, M.H., Murawski, S.A. and Pope, J.G. 1994. 'A Global Assessment of Fisheries Bycatch and Discards.' *FAO Fisheries Technical Paper* 339.

Anderson, J. 1997. 'The Growth of Salmon Aquaculture and the Emerging New World Order of the Salmon Industry.' In Pikitch, E.L., Huppert, D.D. and Sissenwine, M.P. (eds.) *Global Trends: Fisheries Management.* Bethesda, Maryland, 175–184.

Berry, H. and Rettig, R.B. 1994. 'Who Should Pay for Salmon Recovery?' *Pacific Cooperative Extension Publication* PNW-470, Corvallis: Oregon State University.

Burke, W. 1997. 'Trends in International Law for High-Seas Fisheries Management.' In Pikitch, E.L., Huppert, D.D. and Sissenwine, M.P. (eds.) *Global Trends: Fisheries Management.* Bethesda, Maryland, 50–60

Casey, K.E., DeWees, C.M., Turris, B.R. and Wilen, J.E. 1995. 'IVQs in the B.C. Halibut Fishery.' *Marine Resource Economics* 10, 3, 211–230.

Doeringer, P.B. and Terkla, D.G. 1996. *Troubled Waters: Economic Structure, Regulatory Reform and Fisheries Trade.* Toronto: Toronto University Press.

Feeny, D., Hanna, S. and McEvoy, A.F. 1996. 'Questioning the "Tragedy of the Commons" Model of Fisheries.' *Land Economics* 72, 2, 187–205.

Food and Agriculture Organization of the United Nations (FAO) 1995. 'Code of Conduct for Responsible Fisheries.' Rome: FAO.

Garcia, S.M. and Grainger, R.J.R. 1997. 'Fisheries management and sustainability: a new perspective on an old problem?' In *Developing and Sustaining World Fisheries Resources: The State of the Science and Management: 2nd Word Fisheries Congress Proceedings.* Collingwood: CSIRO Publishing, 631–654.

Hanna, S. 1995. 'Efficiencies of User Participation in Natural Resource

Management.' In Hanna, S. and Munasinge, M. (eds.) *Rights and the Environment: Social and Ecological Issues.* Washington, D.C.: The World Bank.

Hanna, S. and Jentoft, S. 1996. 'Human Use of the Environment: An Overview of Social and Economic Dimensions.' In Hanna, S., Folke, C. and Mäler, K.-G. (eds.) *Rights to Nature.* Washington, D.C.: Island Press.

Hardin, G. 1968. 'The Tragedy of the Commons.' Science 162,1243–1248.

Holling, C.S. 1986. 'The Resilience of Terrestrial Ecosystems: Local Surprise and Global Change.' In Clark, W.C. and Munn, R.E. (eds.) *Sustainable Development of the Biosphere.* Cambridge: Cambridge University Press.

Holling, C.S. and Sanderson, S. 1996. 'Dynamics of (Dis)harmony in Ecological and Social Systems.' In Hanna, S., Folke, C. and Mäler, K.-G. (eds.) *Rights to Nature.* Washington, D.C.: Island Press.

Laurec, A. and Armstrong, D. 1997. 'The European Common Fisheries Policy and its Evolution.' In Pikitch, E.L., Huppert, D.D. and Sissenwine, M.P. (eds.) *Global Trends: Fisheries Management.* Bethesda, Maryland, 60–71.

Liao, D. 1997. 'Demand for Recreational Fishing and Stock Enhancement Programmes in the Northeast Region of Taiwan.' In *Developing and Sustaining World Fisheries Resources: The State of the Science and Management: 2nd Word Fisheries Congress Proceedings.* Collingwood: CSIRO Publishing, 504–508.

Mace, P. 1997. 'Fisheries at a Critical Juncture: Understanding the Cause, Correcting the Course.' In *Developing and Sustaining World Fisheries Resources: The State of the Science and Management: 2nd Word Fisheries Congress Proceedings.* Collingwood: CSIRO Publishing, 779–782.

MacGillivray, P. 1997. 'Individual Vessel Quotas in the Halibut Fishery of British Columbia.' In Jones, L. and Walker, M. (eds.) *Fish or Cut Bait: The Case for Individual Transferable Quotas in the Salmon Fishery of British Columbia.* Vancouver: The Fraser Institute, 107–112.

McCay, B. 1996. 'Common and Private Concerns.' In Hanna, S., Folke, C. and Mäler, K.-G. (eds.) *Rights to Nature.* Washington, D.C.: Island Press.

National Research Council 1996. 'Upstream: Salmon and Society in the Pacific Northwest.' *Report of the Committee on Protection and Management of Pacific Northwest Anadromous Salmonids. Board on Environmental Studies and Toxicology, Commission on Life Sciences.* Washington, D.C.: National Academy Press.

North, D.C. 1990. 'Institutions, Institutional Change and Economic Performance.' Cambridge: Cambridge University Press.

Pearce, D.W. and Pearce, L.L. 1993. *World without End: Economics, Environment, and Sustainable Development.* New York, Oxford University Press.

Pinkerton, E. (ed.) 1989. *Co-operative Management of Local Fisheries.* Vancouver: UBC Press.

Polasky, S., Doremus, H. and Rettig, R.B. 1997. 'Endangered Species Conservation on Private Land.' *Contemporary Economic Policy* 15, 66–76.

Rettig, R.B. 1995. 'Management Regimes in Ocean Fisheries.' In Bromley, D. (ed.) *Handbook of Environmental Economics.* London: Blackwell.

Rohlf, D.J. 1989. *The Endangered Species Act: A Guide to Its Protections and Implementation.* Stanford: Stanford Environmental Law Society.

Runolfsson, B. 1997. 'Regional Impact of the ITQ System in Iceland.' In Jones, L. and Walker, M. (eds.) *Fish or Cut Bait: The Case for Individual Transferable Quotas in the Salmon Fishery of British Columbia.* Vancouver: The Fraser Institute, 65–89.

Scott, A.D. 1993. 'Obstacles to Fishery Self-Government.' *Marine Resource Economics* 8, 3, 187–199.

Sinclair, M. 1997. 'Why Do Some Fisheries Survive While Others Collapse?' In *Developing and Sustaining World Fisheries Resources: The State of the Science and Management: 2nd Word Fisheries Congress Proceedings.* Collingwood: CSIRO Publishing, 169–176.

United Nations (UN) 1995. Agreement for the Implementation of the Provisions of the United Nations Convention on Law of the Sea of 10 December 1982 Relating to the Conservation and Management of Straddling Fish Stocks and Highly Migratory Stocks. UN A/CONF.164/37.

12. Firms and Dematerialisation

Julia Haake, Michael Kuhndt, Christa Liedtke, Thomas Orbach and Holger Rohn

INTRODUCTION

The best-selling book, *Limits to Growth*, told us that the usage rate (in 1972) of earth's finite material and energy resources could not continue indefinitely (Meadows *et al.*, 1972). Today, the sequel, *Beyond the Limits*, tells the same story, but with increased urgency; raw materials are being used at a faster rate than they are being replaced or that alternatives are being found (Meadows *et al.*, 1992). As a result of these and other alarming reports, it is becoming more and more clear that the future of the planet depends on a modification of current human activities.

According to a metabolic world view based on material resource flows as adopted by quite a number of researchers, an economic system is environmentally sustainable only as long as it is physically in a (dynamic) steady-state, that is, the amount of resources used to generate welfare is permanently restricted to a size and a quality that does not overexploit the sources or overburden the sinks provided by the ecosphere. Every time coal, steel, gravel or sand is used in industrial processes, and each time soil, water or overburden is moved or re-directed by technical means, ecological changes are caused. While natural cycles (of water, carbon, nitrogen, and so on) are closed, industrial cycles (of energy, steel, chemicals, and so on) are basically still open, that is, they involve losses into the biosphere like wastes, emissions, and so on. In particular, the industrial system uses high quality materials (like fossil fuels and metal ores) as inputs and then returns them to nature in degraded form. Therefore we consider industry to be one of the main relevant actors for sustainable development, and in particular the industrial firm as microeconomic actor.

In this chapter, we present some relevant factors that need to be taken into account in order to integrate traditional business goals with the idea of sustainable development. We build our arguments on a concept developed in the course of the last 20 years in Europe and in the United States:

dematerialisation (or resource efficiency) is an approach that considers material throughput of the economy to be at the roots of environmental destruction. Material flows should thus be reduced in order to contribute to sustainable development. This basic idea can be applied at all levels of the economy – from the national (meta) level, over sector (meso) levels, and on to the single firm and the consumer (micro level). We propose a framework for a dematerialised, resource efficient firm performance. In the first section, we introduce in a more detailed way the concept of dematerialisation and how it can, on the basis of material flow analyses, be realised. In the second section, we propose a typology of firm strategies and instruments adapted to dematerialisation, and demonstrate how quantitative targets can be derived and used to define performance indicators. We illustrate our arguments by presenting a German furniture-producing firm, which has modified its performance in a dematerialising way.

SUSTAINABLE DEVELOPMENT THROUGH DEMATERIALISATION

The standard definition of sustainable development demands that the satisfaction of the needs of current generations should not negatively influence the opportunities of future generations. A various number of suggestions have been made for an operationalisation of this basic concept. These proposals usually lead to so-called management rules for sustainable development. One of the most prominent of these rules was suggested by the group around David Pearce, who differentiates between weak and strong sustainability (Turner *et al.*, 1994). While claiming that only strong sustainability is a sufficient criterion, Herman Daly (1992) provides similar macro-economic management rules for sustaining the ecosphere and thus a safe human development. Other forms of operationalising sustainability lead to concepts such as environmental space (Weterings and Opschoor, 1992) and ecological footprints (Rees and Wackernagel, 1995).

These concepts are based on various views of economic, social and ecological systems. They are connected to different economic and ecological theories, and they correspond to different viewpoints concerning the two concepts of weak and strong sustainability dealing with natural capital. For an economist these rules are immediately convincing as long as they do not ask what natural capital really is and how it can be measured. If we take into account the high degree of uncertainty with regard to (potential) future ecological impacts of human interference with complex natural systems, such a measurement becomes highly questionable. Only if we had sufficient knowledge of natural reactions to anthropogenic impairments, could we estimate the (potential) loss of natural capital, which is related to certain economic activities. In this respect, environmental space and ecological footprints are certainly better concepts, since they are more explicit as to what they regard as environmentally harmful.

Even if a conceptualisation of sustainability leads to the 'right' results on a macro-economic scale, and might therefore give a device for measures of environmental policy on the national level, many of them cannot be applied to the decisions of individual economic agents. From a socio-economic point of view, economic agents need principles by which individual decisions can be guided towards patterns of sustainable production and consumption. It is a necessary condition for the sustainability of macroeconomic development that individual economic agents possess appropriate information on how to produce and consume in an environmentally sound way.

One such way to provide information about the environmental relevance of different economic activities is the application of the concept of dematerialisation. This concept is based on the idea that traditional ways of environmental policy making have not been able to efficiently manage the growing environmental deterioration our societies are facing. The resolution of existing and known ecological problems like emissions, wastes, and other forms of pollution has proven to be unmanageable in the long run because the increasing discovery of new to-be-treated problems does not allow the rather inert policy making processes to keep track. In addition, we are dealing with uncertainty – knowledge we have today on environmental problems might be reversed in the future. The problem of environmental policies *vis-à-vis* the growing number of urgent problems will thus only become more serious in the coming years.

These difficulties suggest that instead of focusing on existing and known environmental problems, caused by the economic activity of Mankind, a concentration on their sources might be a solution. Instead of looking at the output side of the economy, the input side should be the starting point of a sustainable development. The industrial system can be seen as a metabolic system of material inflows, throughflows, and outflows: in order to produce goods and to keep up the functioning of the economy, materials are extracted from the natural system, transformed in industrial processes, and finally 'given back' to nature in the form of wastes, waste water, air emissions, or just as unused and displaced material like erosion or translocations. Both the extraction process and the output into the natural system are harmful to the environment: ecosystems are degraded, health problems arise, and ecological problems such as acid rain, climate change or the depletion of the ozone layer are caused. Besides, ecological problems may arise in the future, which are still unknown today. It is thus suggested to reduce the material input into the economy in order to decrease the overall negative impact on the environment of economic activity. This goal is called dematerialisation, as proposed by quite a number of authors and research groups.

Dematerialisation comprises two steps – a positive one and a normative one. Since the main goal is the reduction of material flows in the economy, methods of measurement are needed that enable researchers to assess material flows. This can be called the positive step in implementing dematerialisation and we will discuss in the following section, in some detail, one method of material flow analysis. The normative step then consists of the definition of reduction goals and of instruments that can lead to an ecological structural change. These goals and instruments can be applied to all levels of an economy – from the national level to microeconomic agents like firms and consumers. In the second part of our contribution we deal with material flow reduction at the firm level.

Knowledge Needed for Dematerialisation: The Measurement of Material Flows

Valid and comparable physical data about material and energy flows is the prior condition for successful dematerialisation. In order to provide such information, material and energy flows can be accounted for at the national or supranational level, at regional and community levels and at a microeconomic level. Material flow accounting (MFA) provides information that goes beyond single indicators by monitoring the interlinkage of different flows and their interdependencies with human activities. Through the combinations of regional and national MFA on the one hand, and product and process oriented MFA on the other hand, it is possible to detect life-cycle wide improvement opportunities for increasing resource productivity by minimising inputs and losses of materials. The goal is to harmonise the local planning of processes and products with priorities for materials management on the (supra-) national and regional level. In economic terms, MFA should be further developed to close the gap between the micro and the macro level (the firm and the national level), thus providing a micro–macro link.

For this purpose, the concept of Material Input Analysis (MAIA) and the resource-efficiency measure MIPS (material input per unit of service) were introduced at the Wuppertal Institut in Germany (Schmidt-Bleek, 1994).[1] MIPS is a methodology to measure material input (MI) at all levels (product, company, region, national economy) including all their 'ecological rucksacks,' that is, the total mass of material flows activated by an item of

---

[1] Besides the Wuppertal Institute in Germany, there are0 several expert groups working on and applying material flow analyses all over the world, for example the IFF in Vienna, Austria, the World Resources Institute in Washington, USA, and the National Institute for Environmental Studies in Tsukuba, Japan. For further information see Adriaanse *et al.* (1997) or Hüttler *et al.* (1997).

consumption in the course of its life cycle. This MI is then referred to the end user service (S) derived from the product in question.

In this manner, the environmental quality (associated with the resource effort) of all functionally equivalent goods or production sites can be directly compared. Whatever knowledge available about the toxicity of materials involved is to be included in all decision-making processes – which is generally already required by law.

The material input (including energy and transport intensities) thus reflects all the material displaced in nature with the help of technology measured either in kilograms or in tons, and with reference to a service provided. An example would be the sum total of all resources which were afforded on a life-cycle wide basis for one person-kilometre in an automobile. Waste flows *per se* are not accounted for in this approach, since they are outputs, not inputs. As for material flows of secondary materials, only the natural materials used for the secondary processing are taken into account. By doing so, double-counting is avoided.

The material input is summarised in five different statistical categories:

- Abiotic (non-renewable) raw material,
- Biotic (renewable) raw material,
- Shifted soil (in agriculture and forestry),
- Water (any volume removed from natural water ways or reservoirs),
- Air (if it is chemically or physically transformed).

The material intensity in each respective category contains the material or resource input per ton of material or specific product weight. Seven tons of abiotic raw materials are for instance used for the production of one ton of sheet steel, or 88 tons abiotic raw materials per 110 kV reinforced concrete power pole (Merten *et al.*, 1995). The ecological rucksack, then, represents the resource consumption without the tare weight of the material or product in question. In the case of sheet steel ($MI_{abiotic\ raw\ materials} = 7t/t$), the ecological rucksack of abiotic raw materials makes up six tons (seven tons of abiotic resource consumption minus one ton tare weight of abiotic raw materials).

The MIPS concept can be used to analyse both durable and less durable goods, and in principle it can also be used to examine complex facilities and infrastructures. With the help of the indicator MIPS (which is equivalent to 'resource productivity'), it is possible to identify sustainable market niches for materials and products. In this context, the term 'sustainable' is used to denote a marriage between what is economically feasible and ecologically necessary.

The main advantage of the MIPS concept is the fact that a variety of microeconomic strategies can be identified that can lead to a reduction of material inputs 'from cradle to grave' in the life cycle of a product so that the macroeconomic result can be effectively achieved. These strategies comprise all kinds of economic activities from production to consumption.

A Quantitative Goal for Dematerialisation: Resource Productivity Times Ten

Resource productivity is fundamental for dematerialisation. So far, however, we have not dealt with the question of how much, on a global level, resource efficiency should be increased in order to reach sustainable development. One proposal is that of a factor of two on the global level, which, if combined with North–South equity considerations (a kind of 'human right' to resource use),[2] can be translated into a factor ten improvement in resource productivity for the industrialised countries (Factor Ten Club, 1994).

This factor of ten refers to the entire life cycle of economic services. For the industrial production of goods and services, this does not mean that the resource productivity of every single process or every individual phase of the life-cycle must be drastically increased, but rather that the resource consumption in societies should be reduced as much as possible. In the big picture, it may turn out to be ecologically preferable to 'invest' more resources at particular stages in the life of a product, in order to increase the resource productivity across the entire life-cycle. This is most often the case with durable goods such as office furniture made out of stainless steel or wood, furniture in general, pipes, bridges or large architectural constructions. Besides exhausting the technical potential for efficiency increases, a fundamental revisioning of our patterns of consumption might additionally be necessary, even if not as easily implementable as technological solutions.

Whatever the final reduction goal chosen, it is even more important to develop possible implementation measures and instruments and to prove their viability and efficiency. We will, in the following, present one such possibility, which focuses on the firm as the relevant actor.

DEMATERIALISATION AND FIRM STRATEGIES

... From a Theoretical Point of View

When discussing firm strategies in relation to the environment, a distinction among different types of strategies has in the last few years become pertinent,

---

[2] The rich countries with 20 per cent of the world's population and with their present levels of consumption and investment are responsible for 80 per cent of the world's natural resource use.

distinguishing different kinds of firm performance according to the importance granted to the environment. One thus speaks of pro-active environmental strategies when a firm regards the environment as a strategic option, permitting a 'win-win' situation. On the one hand, the firm contributes to sustainable industrial development ('win' on the environmental side); on the other hand, strategic advantages in economic terms are achieved through the protection of the environment ('win' on the economic side) by reducing costs, by occupying market niches, and so on. In contrast to such pro-active strategies, a firm can adapt a defensive strategy, which corresponds to a respect for the environment, only when legislation demands to do so. In between these two opposite strategies, the one probably most adopted today is the 'follower' strategy. In this case, a firm will see the environment as strategically important, but only if this has already been shown by other (pro-active) firms.[3]

This distinction shows us that an environmentally advantageous firm performance can also be economically beneficial. This depends essentially on the economic situation of a firm and the market in which it performs. Cost savings as well as competitive advantages are the strongest arguments for a firm to adapt environmental strategies. We will show in the following that an adaptation of the described concept of dematerialisation at the firm level can lead to such advantages.

Since in many cases, current technologies, products and processes can be considered as inefficient from a resource perspective, some kind of innovation will be essential for the implementation of dematerialisation at the firm level. We consider not only technological innovation but also modifications in other areas to be important for sustainable development, and we have established the following distinction of innovation for dematerialisation (Table 12.1).

These forms of innovation concern different spheres (material or immaterial) as well as different actors (firms, governments, consumers ...). We will in the following concentrate only on technological and 'immaterial' innovation that can be realised by a firm.

---

[3] On the distinction of different firm strategies concerning the environment see for example Porter and van der Linde (1995) or Faucheux *et al.* (1997).

Table 12.1. Innovative strategies of the dematerialisation process.

Technological Innovation	Strategic Innovation	Innovative Use Forms	Institutional Innovations
• Products • Processes	• Focus on the needs of consumers	• Alternative forms of sale • Alternative forms of property	• Measures of well-being • Behaviour patterns • Policy reforms

Source: Haake (1998)

As for (technological) product innovation, the following attributes of products contribute to the improvement of resource productivity:[4]

- Durability,
- Decomposability,
- Recyclability,
- Reduced weight and size,
- Combined functions in one product,
- Reparability,
- Upgradability.

A large number of examples show that this dematerialising kind of product innovation is possible:[5] Dell Computer Corporation has realised a series of recyclable and upgradable PCs based on simplified and less costly production processes. Weizsäcker *et al.* (1995) add CD ROMs to the list of dematerialised products, replacing encyclopaedia, dictionaries, and so on. Finally, an even more extreme miniaturisation of products could in the near future lead to a reduction of whole libraries to the size of microprocessors based on silicium (Gabriel, 1996).

One of the most important of the named product attributes, for an increase in resource productivity, is durability (see Haake and Hinterberger, 1998; Haake, 1996). With an increase of the life spans of products, the total number

---

[4] See for example Haake and Hinterberger (1998), Garud and Kumaraswamy (1996) or Schmidtheini (1992).

[5] Dematerialisation is today more and more accepted in industry as an important contribution to sustainable industrial performance, as witnessed by several examples. The NRTEE (National Round Table on Environment and the Economy) in Canada is holding a series of workshops with some industrial firms on their experiences with eco-efficiency and the improvement of resource productivity. An important part of these experiences is based on material flow measurement instruments. Another example is a trade fair (Faktor 4 and Messe) took place in June 1998 in Klagenfurt, Austria, where firms exhibited examples of dematerialised products.

of existing products could ideally be decreased and with it the environmental effects of mass consumption. In addition, durability does not necessarily imply a technological redesign of the product in question. Of course, more robust materials or a more careful production can lead to a longer life of a product. But many products today are already durable, but are being thrown away before the actual end of their life span. This shows that besides technological means, consumption patterns are of considerable importance, as already mentioned in the above.

The second technological kind of innovation necessary for dematerialisation concerns production processes. These should be characterised by low material and energy input or by a simplification of the number of steps involved. With the help of an analysis of the material use of a firm's processes, reduction potential can be determined and realised. For example, recycling within the production processes of a firm or an industrial site may lead to dematerialisation: Volkswagen Germany has reduced its use of fresh water by 40 percent since 1973 by means of water recycling. It is however worth mentioning that recycling processes also necessitate material and energy inputs and cause 'downcycling,' that is, a deterioration of the quality of materials. Recycling can thus not be judged as thoroughly positive from a materials perspective and analysis of specific processes are necessary to decide if recycling is worth being applied or not.

The second group of innovation for dematerialisation is of an 'immaterial' and non-technological kind, including strategic innovation as well as innovation of use forms. Strategic innovation for dematerialisation is characterised by a change in the strategies of a firm concerning the needs of its customers. This means that the product offered by a firm can change its character (but not its form) according to what the consumer actually demands. An example illustrating this is energy supply: a firm offering electricity can modify its offer from simple units of electricity to, say, heated apartments or lighted rooms. Then, the object can be changed from a simple transaction to the supply of energy in the most environmentally efficient way.

Innovations of use forms, concern what we have already stated above on product durability. Often, products are technologically durable and resource efficient, but they are used in a way that does not take advantage of these environmental attributes. A firm can contribute to an improvement in the use of products with the help of a change in the way it offers its products. The simple sale of products can be harmful from an environmental point of view: many environmentally friendly products are too expensive in comparison to their more inefficient substitutes, which can keep people from buying them. Or, as is the case for cars, some people tend to buy the largest (and less resource efficient) version that they will need only sometimes, even if they need a smaller or less powerful version in everyday life. Alternatives such as leasing or sharing can thus contribute to an improvement in resource efficiency.

... From a Practical Point of View: The Example of the German Firm Kambium

Based on the MIPS concept presented above, the Wuppertal Institute has developed a resource management program that combines an input–output analysis for a firm and a product life wide analysis of resource use with the firm's cost accounting procedures. The case study 'Eco-Audit and Resource Management' (Liedtke *et al.*, 1994) in co-operation with the Kambium Furniture Workshop tested this resource management program 'in real life,' and analysed the question whether it satisfies the requirements of the European Eco Audit system. A further goal was to specify a resource management strategy for Kambium that permits the determination of methods for firm specific material flow management, product management and ecological product design, incorporating the discussed alternative modes of product use, as well as of firm specific environmental management. The results of the material flow analysis for the whole firm, that is from 'gate to gate,' as well as for Kambium's products – from 'cradle to grave' – is presented below.

The Kambium Furniture Workshop is a small to medium sized business with about 40 employees and a fairly horizontal organisational structure, typical for a German company of this size. In 1996, about 120 kitchens, as well as some other kinds of furniture were produced, yielding a turnover of 6.5 million DM. The kitchens are made of solid wood from European sources and marketed directly (local markets within a radius of about 100km). The use of paint is entirely avoided – the furniture surfaces are impregnated with natural oils.

The enterprise: material flow analysis from 'gate to gate'
In this part of the material flow analysis, all relevant material and energy flows were recorded. Alongside the basic objective of tabulating all relevant in-house material and energy flows, the system of mass accounts had the additional task of ensuring a parallel sequence of cost and mass accounting (Preimesberger, 1994) as well as facilitating a direct link of the firm to a product life-cycle wide material flow analysis. The expressed objective was thus to standardise all accounts to mass units (kg or t). The conceptual and methodological delineations are based on the MIPS concept and its tabulation criteria.

Table 12.2. The structure of analysis.

I.		Input	O		Output
I.	1.	Raw materials	O.	1.	Products
I.	2	Energy	O.	2.	Energy
I.	3.	Water	O.	3.	Waste water
I.	4.	Air	O.	4.	Vitiated air
I.	5.	Products	O.	5.	Waste
I.	6.	Merchandise	O.	6.	Merchandise
I.	7.	Communication	O.	7.	Communication
I.	8.	Services	O.	8.	Services
I.	9.	Transport	O.	9.	Noise

S.		Store	A.		Assets
S.	1.	Raw materials	A.	1.	Land areas
S.	2.	Energy	A.	2.	Structures
S.	3.	Water	A.	3.	Plant and equipment
S.	4.	Products	A.	4.	Vehicle fleet
S.	5.	Merchandise			
S.	6.	Communication			

The basic structure, shown in Table 12.2, reflects a hierarchical tabulation framework, organised according to useful categories. By analogy to management accounting, the basic structure includes input (I) and output (O), as well as asset accounts (A). In addition, a category inventory or store (S) was created.

The various areas were divided into accounts and subsidiary accounts, all of which are assigned a specific index. With the continual tabulation of all environmentally relevant data, it becomes possible to regularly verify the results, providing a basis for assessing the firm's environmental performance and its development. On the basis of the multi-level interconnections between product life-cycle and firm specific analyses, improvements and the cost saving potential at all important levels and in all areas can be shown. Additionally, the system of mass accounts can serve as an important environmental information system in the firm's external environmental communication. Table 12.3 summarises selected material flows of Kambium for 1994.

The depicted input and output accounts convey a classification of the material flows while simultaneously pointing to some operational realms of particular environmental relevance – such as unused resources (wood scrap), waste heat or packaging – as well as to some potential improvement areas.

Table 12.3. The material flows of Kambium in 1994.

Input		Output	
Energy		**Energy**	
Fossil energy carriers	49 t	Heat, unused	92.216 kWh
Electricity from public		Electricity input to	
net	79.480 kWh	public net	27.855 kWh
Products		**Products**	
Stainless steel	0,3 t	Kitchens	113 pieces
Cloth	0,5 t	Other furniture	76 pieces
Linoleum	0,6 t	Wood	19 t
Vegetable oils	0,7 t		
Sand paper	1,2 t		
Glue	1,9 t		
Glass	0,7 t		
Interior trim, fittings	> 0,8 t		
Granite	20,5 t		
Wood	331 t		
Water	178 t	**Wastewater**	293 t
Air		**Exhaust air**	
Combustion air (oxygen	139 t	Exhaust gas	538 t
demand)		Emissions	83 t
		Waste	
		Production waste	122 t
		Household waste	12 t
		Packages	9 t

A case study carried out in 1996 by the same research group of the Wuppertal Institute analysed the resource management in 11 companies (who passed the EMAS requirements) in the wood-processing industry. The results of this study show that most of the firms were successfully conducting an 'in-house' material flow management. However, only two of them indicated a deeper knowledge and information about the material flows from 'cradle to grave' (for example, in the form of a life-cycle analysis or material intensity analysis). This suggests that companies are still lacking a comprehensive understanding of the full life cycle concerning a reduction of environmental impacts and costs.

The product: material flow analysis from 'cradle to grave'
In the framework of the extensive ecological assessment at Kambium, the environmental effects associated with the product life-cycle 'solid wood kitchens' were tabulated. These include all material flows attributable to production, which were determined and evaluated using the MIPS concept. The material intensity analysis covers the entire life cycle of the kitchen, that is, from raw material procurement and extraction, over the production of lumber, the assembly of the boards and assorted other parts, to the finished

kitchen, in the use phase and the recycling or disposal of the kitchen. This was compared to an equivalent kitchen constructed of formica-covered particleboard. Table 12.4 presents the results of the analysis.

Table 12.4. A comparison of material flows in two alternative goods.

	Solid wood kitchen	Formica/particle board kitchen
Net weight	421 kg	520 kg
Production energy	Electricity from own production	Electricity from public net
Primary construction material	Solid wood	OSB, particle board and plywood laminated with formica
Lifetime	50 years	20 years

For the construction of the solid wood kitchen, high quality lumber is used, whereas the particleboard kitchen is made of low grade industrial and scrap wood. The high quality wood is the primary product of forest management; industrial wood by contrast is a secondary product. Scrap wood is, as the name implies, a waste product, added to the primary products in the analysis. Secondary products have a material input consisting of the specific resource flows associated with their production (for example, transport, specific machining or specific fuels or auxiliary materials that yield secondary products in the desired quality that can be reused).

The solid wood kitchen is identified as a significant resource saving product. Looking at the life cycle wide resource consumption, the input of biotic materials for the solid wood kitchen is thirteen times higher than in the case of the particle board kitchen. The input of abiotic materials, water and air on the other hand is about four times higher for the particle board kitchen than for the solid wood kitchen. This has to do primarily with the difference in material inputs for the various energy transforming systems, and with the difference in lifetime.

CONCLUSION

In this chapter we proposed a possible way to encourage ecological structural change from the starting point of the firm as microeconomic actor. We based our reasoning on the idea of dematerialisation, a concept more and more accepted in research, politics, and everyday life.

We introduced the concept of dematerialisation and in particular the tool of material flow analysis, and we further developed a general framework of dematerialising firm performance. The case study of the German firm Kambium demonstrated that an application of our theoretically developed ideas is possible in industrial practice.

We can thus conclude that dematerialisation represents a concept, which harmonises with the goal of 'win-win' industrial practice. While respecting and protecting the natural environment, an adequately adapted firm performance sustains the competitive situation of a firm via reduced costs, consumer friendliness, long-living and valuable products and a positive environmental image of the firm.

REFERENCES

Adriaanse, A., Bringezu, S., Hammond, A., Moriguchi, Y., Rodenburg, E., Rogich, D. and Schütz, H. 1997. *Resource Flows: The Material Basis of Industrial Economies*. Washington D.C.: World Resources Institute.

Factor Ten Club 1994. *The Carnoules Declaration.* Wuppertal: Wuppertal Institut für Klima, Umwelt und Energie.

Faucheux, S., Haake, J. and Nicolaï, I. 1997. *Implications de la Mondialisation Economique sur la Rélation Environnement-Entreprises.* Research Report to the French Ministry of the Environment, Rapport C3ED/DGAD/SRAE No: 95285, Paris.

Gabriel, K.J. 1996. 'Mikroskopische Maschinen' *Spektrum der Wissenschaft*, Special edition 4, 98–102.

Garud, R. and Kumaraswamy, A. 1996. Technological Designs for Retention and Reuse. *International Journal of Technology Management,* Special Publication on Unlearning and Learning 11, 7/8, 883–891.

Haake, J. 1996. 'Langlebige Produkte für eine zukunftsfähige Entwicklung. Eine ökonomische Analyse.' *Wuppertal Papers* 62, Wuppertal: Wuppertal Institut für Klima, Umwelt und Energie.

Haake, J. 1998. *Corporate Environmental Strategies, Organization and Cooperation for a Dematerialised Sustainable Development.* Paper presented at the Second International Conference of the European Society of Ecological Economics, March 4th–7th 1998, Geneva, Switzerland.

Haake, J. and Hinterberger, F. 1998. 'Product Durability: Economic and Ecological Aspects.' In Dwyer, S., O'Connor, M. and Ganslasser, U. (eds.) *Ecology, Society, Economy: Life Sciences Dimensions*, Aldershot: Edward Elgar.

Hüttler, W., Payer, H. and Schandl, H. 1997. 'National Material Flow Analysis for Austria 1992. Society's Metabolism and Sustainable Development.' *Schriftenreihe Soziale Ökologie* 45, Institut für

Interdisziplinäre Forschung und Fortbildung der Universitäten Innsbruck, Klagenfurt und Wien, Abteilung Soziale Ökologie.

Liedtke, C., Manstein, C. and Merten, T. 1994. 'MIPS, Resource Management and Sustainable Development.' *Proceedings of the International ASM Conference*, The Recycling of Metals, Amsterdam.

Meadows, D.H., Meadows, D.L., Randers, J. and Behrens, W.W. 1972. *The Limits of Growth*. New York: Universe Books.

Meadows, D. Meadows, D.L. and Randers, J. 1992. *Beyond the Limits*. London: Earthscan.

Merten, T., Liedtke, C. and Schmidt-Bleek, F. 1995. 'Materialintensitäts-analysen von Grund-, Werk- und Baustoffen (1). Die Werkstoffe Beton und Stahl. Materialintensitäten von Freileitungsmasten.' *Wuppertal Papers* 27, Wuppertal: Wuppertal Institut für Klima, Umwelt und Energie.

Porter, M. and van der Linde, C. 1995. 'Toward a New Conception of the Environment – Competitiveness Relationship.' *Journal of Economic Perspectives* 9, 4, 97–118.

Preimesberger, C. 1994. *Die Materialintensität pro Dienstleistungseinheit als ökologische Schadschöpfungseinheit der betrieblichen Stoffflußwirtschaft*. Master Thesis at the Institut für Gesellschaftspolitik, Abteilung für Ökologie und Politik, Johannes Kepler Universität, Linz.

Rees, W. and Wackernagel, M. 1995. *Our Ecological Footprint*. London: Gabriola.

Schmidt-Bleek, F. 1994. *Wieviel Umwelt braucht der Mensch? Faktor 10 – Das Maß für Ökologisches Wirtschaften*. München: DTV.

Schmidtheini, S. 1992. *Kurswechsel. Globale unternehmerische Perspektiven für Entwicklung und Umwelt*. München: Artemis and Winkler.

Turner, R.K., Doktor, P. and Adger, N. 1994. 'Sea-level Rise and Coastal Wetlands in the U.K.: Mitigation Strategies for Sustainable Management.' In Folke, C., Hammer, M., Costanza, R. and Jansson, A.M. (eds.) *Investing in Natural Capital. The Ecological Economics Approach to Sustainability*. Washington D.C.: Island Press, 266–290.

Weizsäcker, E.U.v., Lovins, A.B. and Lovins, L.H. 1995. *Faktor Vier. Doppelter Wohlstand – halbierter Naturverbrauch. Der neue Bericht an den Club of Rome*. München: Droemer Knaur.

Weterings, R.A.P.M. and Opschoor, J.B. 1992. *The Ecocapacity as a Challenge to Technological Development*. RMNO 74a, Rijswijk.

13. Sustainability and Joint Abatement Strategies under Multiple Pollutants and Multiple Targets: The Case of Tropospheric Ozone and Acidification in Europe

Ekko C. van Ierland and Erik C. Schmieman[1]

INTRODUCTION

In the protocols to the 1979 convention on transboundary air pollution (UN, 1984), on sulphur (UN, 1985 and UN, 1994), nitrogen oxides (NO_x) (UN, 1988) and volatile organic compounds (VOCs) (UN, 1991), a number of European countries agreed to reduce their emissions of the various pollutants in the coming decades.

Various studies show that results, conclusions and policy recommendations change, depending on whether pollutants are jointly or separately incorporated into the model employed.[2] Hahn (1989) states that it is useful for purposes of analysis to break down a complex problem into separate parts. The disadvantage of this approach, however, is that problems are studied in isolation, potentially leading to undesired consequences. The challenge is to incorporate more information into the problem and to formulate multiple objectives in such a way that better decisions can be made. Michaelis (1992), in a study on global warming and the case of multiple

[1] We would like to thank Paul Mensink for his very helpful suggestions during the formulation of the optimisation model as used in the GAMS-MINOS software package. A part of this chapter was written during a visit to the Institute for Environmental Studies, University of Illinois, Urbana Champaign, under an exchange program funded by the U.S. Information Agency (agreement No. IA-ASPS-G1190234). An earlier version of this chapter was presented as a paper at the Eighth Annual Conference Of The European Association Of Environmental And Resource Economists held in Tilburg, the Netherlands at 26–28 September 1997.
[2] See for example Beavis and Walker (1979), Michaelis (1992), Grenfelt et al. (1993), Olsthoorn (1994) and Amann et al. (1995).

pollutants, concludes that 'the greenhouse problem is more than a CO_2 problem' and that policy measures should also account for emissions of methane, nitrogen oxides, chlorofluorcarbons and their interactions. Amann *et al.* (1995) write that "the interrelation of several environmental effects (acidification, eutrophication, tropospheric ozone[3], human health and so forth) constitute a *multi-effect, multi-pollutant* problem." The same holds for combating acidification and tropospheric ozone. Because of the connections among the sources of emissions and the central role of NO_x in both problems these two should be analysed in conjunction.

The search for cost efficient abatement strategies is an important task in studying sustainability. This chapter combines the pollution reduction targets set in different, more or less isolated UN protocols in a framework of *multiple targets*, for example, reduce simultaneously acidification and tropospheric ozone and *multiple pollution*, for example, SO_2, NO_x and VOCs.

The structure of this chapter is as follows. The first section briefly describes the connection between acidification and the problem of tropospheric ozone. The second section presents the model and its assumptions. Next the data used in the analysis are discussed followed by the optimisation results based on single and joint abatement scenarios. In the last section conclusions are drawn and recommendations for further research are formulated.

BACKGROUND OF THE RELATION BETWEEN ACIDIFICATION AND TROPOSPHERIC OZONE

The problems of acidification and tropospheric ozone are connected at the sources of emissions and in complex chemical atmospheric processes (see Figure 13.1 for the main sources, interactions between various pollutants and different environmental effects). NO_x has a central position in this figure. If measures are taken to reduce NO_x emission, both acidification and tropospheric ozone (hereafter mentioned as ozone) are affected. However, the environmental effects of NO_x reduction are fairly complicated. NO_x not only affects eutrophication and acidification,[4] it also affects ozone formation.

The formation of ozone is mainly determined by the concentration of NO_x and VOC in the air and by the level of solar energy.[5] To make things more

---

[3] Stratospheric ozone relates to the problem of ozone-layer depletion due to CFKs. Tropospheric ozone refers to smog periods either in summer or winter.

[4] NO_x and NH_3 also cause eutrophication. In this study this aspect is omitted. The acidifying capacity of NH_3, which is mainly produced by the agricultural sector as a result of production, storage and distribution of manure is not taken into account.

[5] Ozone formation involves very complex chemical reactions. Kelly and Gunst (1990) and Heyes *et al.* (1995) give the most important features and relations between the major particles.

complicated, there is a non-linear relation between the concentration of ozone and its precursors NO_x and VOCs. In some countries a reduction in the NO_x concentration will lead to an increase in the ozone concentration. Reduction of NO_x emissions may increase ozone levels, especially in the UK, Germany, the Netherlands, Belgium and Luxembourg (EMEP[6], 1996a). These countries, having relatively high NO_x densities, can be located in the upper left part of the diagram in Figure 13.2. VOC abatement seems to be most effective for reducing ozone concentrations in these countries. Countries with relatively low NO_x concentrations such as Russia, the Ukraine, France, Italy and Spain (EMEP, 1996a), can be located in the lower right part of Figure 13.2. In these countries the reduction of NO_x seems to be most effective for reducing ozone concentrations.

To employ some measure of damage for ozone, the concept of accumulated ozone above threshold (AOT) values for ozone is applied. This is in accordance with the assumptions and the results presented in recent EMEP MSC W studies. For details or definitions and possible applications of the AOT concept see EMEP (1996a); in particular part one chapter 6 and the references therein. For the application here the most important features of AOT values are summarised.

An AOT value is defined as an integral over maximum hourly ozone values above a concentration of 60 parts per billion (ppb) over daylight hours and over the relevant growing season. The AOT60 value is given in equation (1). If the maximum O_3 value is smaller than 60 ppb the maximum is set to zero.

$$(1)$$

It is clear that AOT values for ozone will play an important role in optimisation calculations. WHO recommends a maximum of 120 μgm^{-3} ozone (60 ppb) in its guidelines. Lower levels of ozone are assumed to have no negative health effects (EMEP, 1996a). At this moment it is not clear how these AOT values can be translated into measures for health effects. However, on a UN-ECE workshop on health effects of ozone (Eastbourne, UK, 10–12 June, 1996) it is agreed that a simple statistic as the AOT60 value can be used as a preliminary indication of the existence of ozone levels above the WHO health guidelines in assessment modelling purposes (EMEP, 1996a), above the WHO health guidelines in assessment modelling purposes (EMEP, 1996a).

---

[6] EMEP stands for Co-operative Programme for Monitoring and Evaluation of the Long-range Transmission of Air Pollutants in Europe

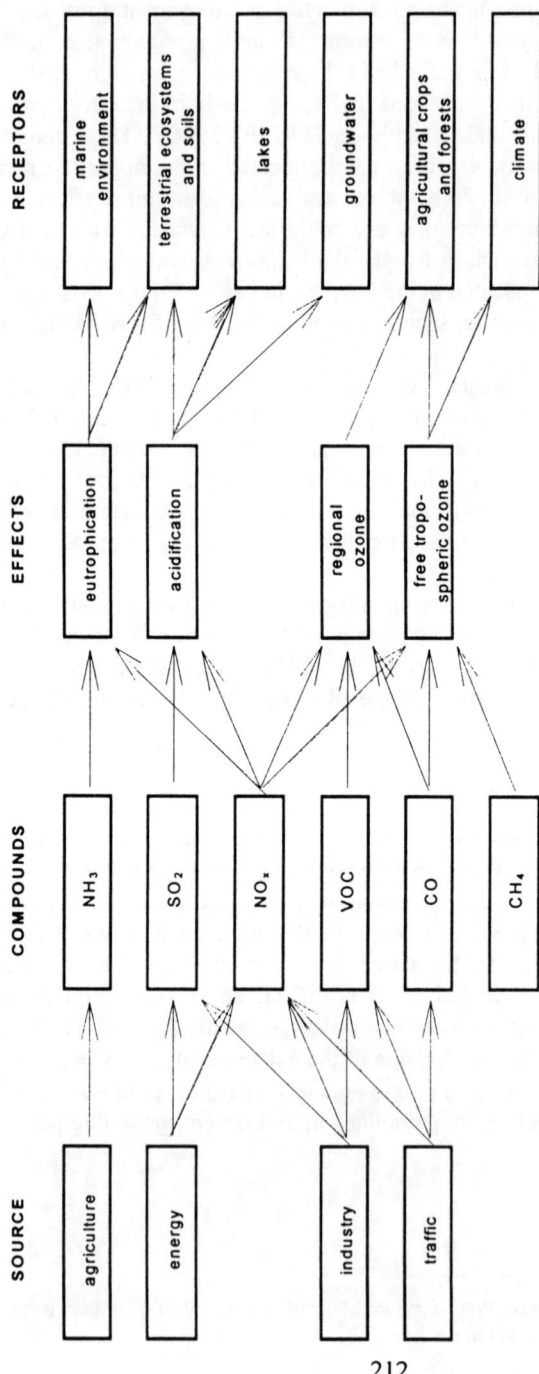

Figure 13.1   The regional air pollution problem. Main relations between dominant sources, emitted compounds and their various receptors (Based on Grennfelt et al., 1993).[1]

[1] For sake of simplicity only the most important aspects of acidification and tropospheric ozone are incorporated. This implies that for example CO_2 and its effects are omitted.

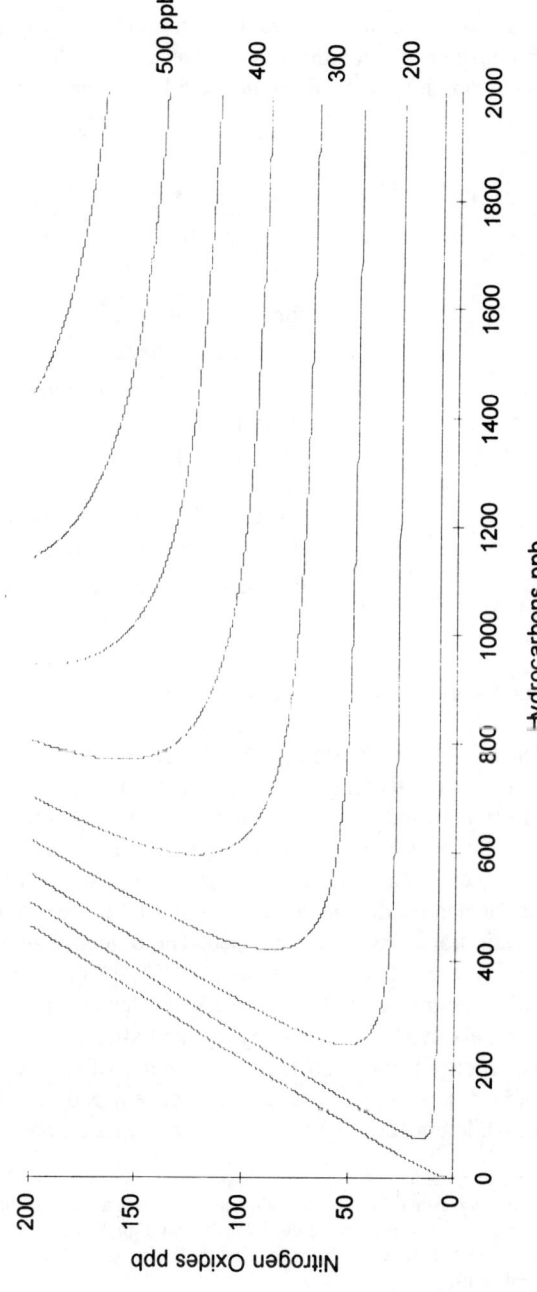

Figure 13.2.   The relation between VOC, NO_x and ozone under certain conditions in an ozone isopleths diagram based on Kelly and Gunst (1990).

Sustainability in Question

THE MODEL

Let us assume that I European countries are incorporated in the model. Emitting countries are indexed i; if a country is a receiver of air pollution it is indexed j.[7] The pollutants that are involved are denoted by k. The model can be summarised as follows:

$$(2) \quad Min \sum_i^I \sum_k^K CA_{i,k}(A_{i,k}) + \sum_i^I CF_i(F_i) + \sum_i^I CR_i(R_i) + \sum_i^I CE_i(E_i)$$

Subject to:

$$(3)\ ED_i^c = ED_i - E_i \qquad \text{for every country } i$$

$$(4)\ ED_i^c \le F_i + R_i \qquad \text{for every country } I$$

$$(5)\ EM_{i,k}^a = EM_{i,k}(F_i, R_i) - A_{i,k} \qquad \text{for each emitting country } i, \text{ for every pollutant } k$$

$$(6)\ A_{i,k} \le EM_{i,k}(F_i, R_i) \qquad \text{for every pollutant } k \text{ and for every country } i$$

$$(7) \sum_{k=1}^2 \alpha_k \sum_{i=1}^I a_{ij,k} * EM_{ij,k}^a \le D_j \qquad \text{for each receptor country } j \text{ and for pollutant } k, \text{ for } k=1, 2$$

$$(8) \overline{OI}_j - \sum_{k=2}^3 \sum_{i=1}^I b_{ij,k} * \Delta EM_{j,k}^a \le O_j \qquad \text{for each receptor country } j \text{ and for pollutant } k, \text{ for } k=2, 3$$

Variables used in the model are explained in Table 13.1.

The object function in equation (2) states that the sum of the abatement costs $(CA_{i,k})$, plus the cost of satisfying the energy demand $(CF_i(F_i)$ plus $CR_i(R_i)$ plus $CE_i(E_i))$ are minimised over all emitting countries. Formulating the objective function in this way implies that the system will minimise the sum of energy costs, conservation costs and emission reduction costs. If energy conservation (a demand side factor) turns out to be the cheapest energy 'source' in a certain trajectory it will be used. The objective function is subject to a number of constraints given in equations (3) to (8). Equations (3) and (4) deal with the energy demand. Actual energy demand is energy demand minus energy conservation. Actual energy demand after conservation is satisfied by the use of energy from fossil fuels and the use of energy from renewables. Equation (5) describes the relation between emissions, energy sources and abatement, while equation (6) ascertains that emission reduction

---

[7] A country usually is both a receiver and emitter of pollutants. To make a clear distinction between source and receptor countries, two indices are used, i for an emitting country and j for a receiving country. Moreover, if in the source receptor matrix $i = j$ then an emitting country receives (a part of) its own emissions.

never exceeds emission levels. Constraints are imposed on acid deposition and ozone levels in equations (7) and (8). Equation (7) determines the acid deposition in a receiving country using data on emission and the source receptor relations for SO_2 and NO_x. Equation (8) determines the ozone level as an AOT60 value in a receptor country j. This level depends on the base year ozone concentration in country (j) minus a change induced by a change in the NO_x emissions, minus a change induced by a change in the VOC emissions, both in emitting country i. These changes in NO_x and VOC emissions are relative to a reference year. [8]

DATA USED IN THE ANALYSIS

For the stylised facts of the model we have taken data for the Netherlands and western Germany in order to provide parameters for the model that *grosso modo* reflect some real world proportions. Of course, different studies that can be found in the literature provide different estimates for the costs of energy conservation or the cost of renewables. The purpose of this chapter is not to provide an in-depth analysis of these data, but just to select the parameters in such a way that at least some approximation of actual figures is obtained.

First some details on energy use and energy prices. [9] Initial energy use is approximately 3100 PJ and 14000 PJ for the Netherlands and the Federal Republic of Germany respectively (UNEP, 1992). [10] Energy demand in 2010 before energy conservation is estimated respectively 3410 PJ and 15290 PJ for Netherlands and Germany, assuming a yearly increase of about 0.5 per cent. Average fuel costs have been estimated on the basis of the expenditure on fuel in the Netherlands. The average price of fossil fuel is estimated at 17 million per PJ NLG (1990) for both 1990 and 2010. The costs of renewables are reflected by a cost function starting from 1.5 times the price of fossil fuel for low levels with costs per unit energy increasing more than proportionally. [11] The price for renewables in 2010 decreases by 20 per cent relative to the price in 1990. The costs of energy conservation start at 1.2 times the price of fossil fuels for low levels and are assumed to increase in the same way as the cost for renewables see footnote 11. It is expected that

---

[8] For more details on these relations see the EMEP MSC W report 1/96 and its references.

[9] If no other sources are cited, data are taken from Ministry of Economic Affairs, Third Energy Report, 1995 (in Dutch: 'Ministerie van Economische Zaken, Derde energie nota').

[10] In the model, calculations are made by use of Exa Joules (EJ). Exa stands for $* 10^{18}$, peta (P) for $* 10^{15}$, giga (G) for $* 10^9$, mega (M) for $* 10^6$ and kilo (K) for $* 10^3$.

[11] Cost function used for renewables and energy conservation are of the form $C = px + bx^2$ with C representing cost, p and x representing price and quantity, and a and b being coefficients. For both conservation and renewables $a=1.1$ and $b=0.9$.

energy conservation increases with about 1 per cent per year without any incentives.[12]

To establish a relation between energy use and emissions of various pollutants, emission coefficients are calculated. Coefficients for SO_2, NO_x, and VOC are determined as the annual SO_2, NO_x, and VOC emissions divided by national energy use. Data are taken from UNEP (1992) for energy use, emission date of SO_2, NO_x and VOC for both countries are borrowed from EMEP MSC W 1/96 (1996a). The abatement costs 'functions' for SO_2 and NO_x are based on calculations using the Official Energy Pathway of the ECE as developed and regularly updated by IIASA (Amann and Kornai, 1987; Amann, 1989; Alcamo *et al.*, 1990) and are estimated by van Egmond and Rasenberg (1990).[13] The costs of VOC reduction in the Netherlands are approximately 2000 NLG per tonne VOC (calculated on the basis of data given in RIVM, 1993) and are assumed to increase quadratically for both countries.

Source receptor matrices have been taken from EMEP (1996a), but they have been adjusted for the two countries case in a rather arbitrary way. Of the Dutch SO_2 emissions, 81 per cent is assumed to stay in the Netherlands, while 19 per cent is exported to the Federal Republic of Germany. The German SO_2 emissions are assumed to stay in Germany for 74 per cent in Germany, 26 per cent is transported to the Netherlands (based on EMEP MSC-W, 1/1996a). Of the Dutch NO_x emissions 74 per cent remains in the country, while the other 26 per cent is exported to the Federal Republic of Germany. Of the German NO_x emissions 71 per cent remains, while 29 per cent is exported to the Netherlands. (based on EMEP MSC-W, 1/1996a).[14] For ozone a source receptor matrix has been developed by EMEP (1996a, b),[15] that calculates

---

[12] This figure results in about 20 per cent energy conservation in 2010. Data from Energy Research Center (ECN), 1997.

[13] The abatement cost functions as employed in the RAINS model are stepwise linear functions. In our model we used smooth approximations. The functions that are estimated are of the form $c = a \cdot x^b$, with c costs of abatement, x emission reduction and a and b estimated coefficients. The values of the coefficients a and b are given in the GAMS/ MINOS model code in appendix I.

[14] Because both Netherlands and Germany are net exporters of SO_2 and NO_x the abstraction to a two countries world will result in relatively high values of acid deposition compared to real world values.

[15] As stated above there exist non-linear relations between NO_x, VOC and ozone. In the EMEP (1996) different linearity issues are evaluated. It is concluded that 'source receptor relationships can play a valuable role in predicting the likely effects of emission reductions from European countries.' (EMEP MSC W 1996, p. 141). For the countries with relatively high NO_x concentrations the linear relationships hold for at least 30 per cent reductions in NO_x and 50 per cent reductions in VOC. For other countries it seems to be that the source receptor relationships are valid for a range up to 50 per cent reduction in both NO_x and VOC.

changes in ozone levels due to changes in emission levels of NO_x and VOCs.[16]

Table 13.1. Explanation of the variables used in the model.

$CA_{I,k}(A_{i,k})$	Emission abatement costs in country i of pollutant k are a function of emission abatement ($A_{i,k}$), for all k in NLG prices of 1990
$CR_I(R_i)$	Cost of renewables in country i are a function of the use of renewables (R_i)
$CF_I(F_i)$	Cost of fossil fuel in country i are a function of the use of fossil fuel (F_i)
$CE_I(E_i)$	Costs of energy conservation in country i are a function of the use of energy conservation (E_i)
F_I	Use of fossil fuel in country i in PJ
R_I	Use of renewables in country i in PJ
E_I	Use of energy conservation in country i in PJ
ED_I	Energy demand in country i before energy conservation in PJ
$A_{i,k}$	Abatement of emissions in country i of pollutant k, for all k
$EM_{i,k}(F_i, R_i, E_i)$	Emission in country i of pollutant k are a function of the use of fossil fuel, renewables and energy conservation, for all k
$EM_{i,k}^a$	Emission in country i of pollutant k after abatement, for all k
D_j	Maximum (policy) target deposition in acid equivalents in receptor country j
ED_i^c	Energy demand in country i after energy conservation in PJ
$\overline{OI}_j$	Initial (1990) ozone concentration in receptor country j
O_j	Maximum (policy) target ozone concentration in receptor country j
$a_{ij,k}$	Source receptor matrix from country i to j for pollutant k, k=1, 2 and $a_{ij} \geq 0$
α_k	Coefficient to calculate acid equivalents for pollutant k, k=1, 2
$b_{Ij,k}$	Source receptor matrix for ozone (AOT60) from country i to country j for pollutant k, k=2, 3
K	Number of pollutants, k=1 for SO_2, k=2 for NO_x, k=3 for VOC.
I	Emitting country i=1 to I
J	Receptor country j=1 to J

[16] For more details, see appendix I: the model as employed in the GAMS MINOS software package.

MODEL RESULTS AND ANALYSIS

The model has been used to analyse a number of cases successively (1-5).

Case 1   The reference case for the reference year 1990.
Case 2   The base case for 2010, this case includes no emission or deposition restrictions. Energy demand (before conservation) has increased with about 10 per cent compared to 1990.
Case 3   An 80 per cent acid deposition reduction is imposed for both countries.
Case 4   A 30 per cent ozone AOT60 value reduction is imposed for both countries.
Case 5   A combined constraint of 80 per cent acid deposition and 30 per cent AOT60 value for ozone reduction is imposed for both countries.

Case 1 refers to the reference case for the year 1990, showing the levels of emissions, acidification, tropospheric ozone and energy supply and demand for the base year. The total costs of the energy system in both countries amount to 289 billion NLG (1990).

Case 2 shows the base case for the year 2010 as calculated on the basis of the assumptions specified for energy demand and the cost function for emission reduction and energy supply. Emissions of SO_2 and NO_x are reduced as compared to 1990 in both countries, as are emissions of VOC. This results in less deposition of acidifying compound and lower AOT60 value for ozone. Energy demand increases before conservation in both countries, because of economic growth. Renewables are not introduced as they are expensive according to the cost functions used. However, energy conservation amounts to about 18 per cent in The Netherlands and 25 per cent in Germany. The total costs of the energy system equals 317 billion NLG (1990).

Case 3 illustrates that 80 per cent reduction of acid deposition can be reached by a combination of energy conservation, end of pipe emission reduction and introduction of a modest quantity of renewables in Germany (116 PJ). The costs increase considerably by about 14 billion NLG (1990), and the cost increase falls mainly in Germany. An interesting result is that the AOT60 value for the Netherlands increases, while in Germany the AOT60 value decreases. VOC reduction induces a decrease in AOT60 ozone levels in both countries, but for the Netherlands this decrease is more than compensated by an increase in the AOT60 value due to NO_x emission reduction in both countries.

Case 4 focuses on 30 per cent reduction of AOT60 values for ozone in both countries. The calculation shows that this can be reached by technical reductions of VOC in both countries, combined with energy conservation in

Germany and the Netherlands. The costs are slightly higher than in case 2. Additional energy conservation leads to an improvement for acidification as a side effect.

Case 5 combines the restriction for acidification (-80 per cent) and ozone (-30 per cent) for both countries. This leads to a combination of end of pipe technology for SO_2 and NO_x, but NO_x emissions in Germany are reduced less than in case 3. VOC emissions are also reduced, but less than in case 4 in the Netherlands. Additional energy conservation and introduction of renewables in Germany make it possible to meet the specified constraints. The costs of the system increase from 317.4 billion NLG (1990) in case 2 to 334.2 billion NLG (1990) in case 5.

The resulting changes in a percentage of 1990 levels for depositions of acidifying compounds and changes in AOT60 values for ozone are given in Table 13.3 for all cases 2 to 5.

As shown in Table 13.3, acid deposition will decrease for the Netherlands and Germany respectively with 17 per cent and 19 per cent. For ozone these figures are different. Only a 4 per cent reduction in ozone levels is realised by means of energy conservation for the Netherlands. This is remarkably lower than the decrease in ozone levels in Germany. For case 3, the 80 per cent acid deposition reduction scenario there is an even more peculiar result. For Germany a reduction of 43 per cent in ozone levels will be realised if the acid deposition targets are reached. But for the Netherlands the ozone level will increase with 2 per cent implying that without extra measures the ozone problem will be worse in the Netherlands.

The other way around, a reduction of ozone levels (as implied in case 4) will reduce acid deposition levels for both countries by respectively 32 per cent and 34 per cent. This reduction of acid deposition is due to a reduction of NO_x emissions (see Table 13.2 for more details). But to reach the 30 per cent ozone reduction target in the Netherlands a reduction of 50 per cent will be reached in Germany.

Case 5 shows that the continued reduction of acidification and ozone implies a reduction of 70 per cent for AOT60 levels for ozone in Germany, as a combined result of NO_x and VOC emission reduction.

Additionally, the calculations show that in a combined emission reduction approach, energy conservation and renewables play a more important role. At the same time, it is illustrated in case 5 that more NO_x reduction takes place in the Netherlands (as compared to case 3), while less end of pipe NO_x reduction occurs in Germany. This is possible because of a higher level of renewables in Germany, which reduces the need for end of pipe technologies because of lowered emissions.

Table 13.2. *Results for total cost^a and various combinations of compounds for the reference case 1990, and for 2010 respectively the no abatement base case, 80 per cent acid deposition reduction, 30 per cent ozone AOT60 value reduction and a combined 80 per cent acid and 30 per cent ozone AOT60 value reduction.*

Year Description	Case 1 1990 Reference case	Case 2 2010 base^b case	Case 3 2010 80% acid deposition reduction		Case 4 2010 30% ozone AOT60 value reduction		Case 5 2010 80% acid deposition and 30% ozone AOT60 reduction	
	level	level	level^c	reduc-tion^d	level^c	reduc-tion^d	level^c	reduction^d
SO$_2$ (Kt)								
Netherlands	205	186	14	122	161	0	14	122
Germany	5331	4312	754	2720	3518	0	665	2584
NO$_x$ (Kt)								
Netherlands	575	521	131	249	451	0	122	257
Germany	3071	2484	1096	905	2027	0	1235	636
VOC (Kt)								
Netherlands	444	403	293	0	35	313	29	262
Germany	2986	2415	1964	0	1349	622	725	1094
Acid (acid equivalents/hectare)^e								
Netherlands	21730	17970	4346	–	14843	–	4346	–
Germany	4920	3990	983	–	3261	–	983	–

	–	–	–	–	–
	–	–	–	–	–
Ozone (AOT60)[f]					
Netherlands	6000	5731	6121	4200	4200
Germany	5000	4083	2826	2482	1455
Energy demand before conservation (PJ)					
Netherlands	3100	3410	3410	3410	3410
Germany	13900	15290	15290	15290	15290
Fuel (PJ)[g]					
Netherlands	3100	2811	2046	2430	2046
Germany	13900	11245	9058	9174	8470
Renewables (PJ)[g]					
Netherlands	0	0	0	0	0
Germany	0	0	116	0	704
Conservation (PJ)					
Netherlands	–	599	1364	980	1364
Germany	–	4045	6116	6116	6116
cost (Billion 1990 NLG)[a]					
Total cost	289	317.4	331.1	318.5	334.2
Netherlands	52.4	57.9	58.3	58.1	58.5
Germany	236.6	259.5	272.8	260.3	275.7

221

[a] *cost are total cost for both energy use and conservation and emission abatement costs.*

[b] *the lower emission levels in the no abatement base case for 2010 compared to emissions in 1990 are due to energy conservation.*

[c] *for the time being a maximum for emission reduction is set at 90 per cent of the actual emission level for all emitted pollutants.*

[d] *Reduction only includes reduction by end of pipe technologies.*

[e] *The Netherlands and Germany are both net exporters of the pollutants under consideration. Therefore, the simplification to a two country world can lead to high values compared to real world measured values.*

[f] *We apply the source receptor relations for ozone to changes in emissions of NO_x and VOC that are larger than 50 per cent keeping in mind the limitations stated in footnote 15.*

[g] *after energy conservation.*

Table 13.3. Reduction of acid deposition and ozone AOT60 levels as a percentage of 1990 values for the various cases.

	Case 2	Case 3	Case 4	Case 5
Year	2010	2010	2010	2010
Description	Base case	80% acid deposition reduction	30% ozone AOT60 value reduction	80% acid deposition and 30% ozone AOT60 reduction
Acid deposition				
Netherlands	0.17	0.80	0.32	0.80
Germany	0.19	0.80	0.34	0.80
Ozone AOT60				
Netherlands	0.04	-0.02	0.30	0.30
Germany	0.18	0.43	0.50	0.71

Another interesting result is the fact that the additional costs of reaching combined environmental targets for acidification and ozone are in our example more than the sum of the additional costs for reaching the targets for acidification and ozone separately. Reducing NO_x emissions for realising the targets for acidification, requires additional reductions of VOC in either Germany or the Netherlands for realising ozone targets. This is a result of the non-linearities in the function for ozone formation. This result is surprising because in normal circumstances a multiple pollutant/multiple target approach will result in considerable cost savings, because of positive side effects of energy conservation and renewables, and optimal emission reduction for the relevant compounds by end of pipe technologies.

CONCLUSIONS AND RECOMMENDATIONS FOR FURTHER RESEARCH

Although this study is preliminary and a large number of simplifying assumptions have been made, the following conclusions can be drawn.

The reduction of acidification requires large reductions of both SO_2 and NO_x emissions, that only can be reached by a combination of end of pipe technologies, energy conservation and introduction of renewables. For this particular case, reduction of NO_x may lead to increased ozone concentrations due to the non-linearities in ozone formation

The study shows that in the situation analysed in this chapter, multiple reduction targets on acidification and tropospheric ozone will not lead to cost savings as compared to single pollutant/single target policies. This is explained by the fact that a reduction of emissions for acidification can leads to higher ozone concentrations. In these circumstances further reduction of ozone concentrations should be reached by substantial reduction of VOC emissions.

The calculations also show that renewable energy will only be used in modest quantities by the year 2010. This is explained by the relatively high price of renewable energy sources as compared to the price of fossil fuels, and the fact the renewables are expensive as compared to end of pipe technologies for emission reduction. The study shows that the interactions of emissions at the source and the interactions of pollutants in the atmosphere have major impacts on the reduction policies to be pursued. The study confirms that a simultaneous analysis of the various pollutants and their effects contributes to a better understanding of the various policy options.

The non-linear relations between the formation of ozone and its precursors NO_x and VOCs. are typically found in a number of central European countries. This non-linearities explain the results emerging from the case study employed (the Netherlands and Germany) to a large extent. Further research is necessary to investigate whether the mechanisms described in this chapter also hold at the European level. Regions with a much lower NO_x/VOC ratio than those in the Netherlands and Germany should be included. Using a more detailed model can give better insights, and may give new directions to cost effective abatement strategies, if a larger number of countries are included in the analysis, and if the cost functions are specified in more detail. Also the impact of energy conservation on the cost functions for end of pipe technologies should be analysed in more detail. A further refinement of the energy module, for example by including various categories of energy carriers, would contribute to improving scenario studies for sustainability in transboundary air pollution.

REFERENCES

Alcamo, J., Shaw, R.W. and Hordijk, L. 1990. *The RAINS Model of Acidification Science and Strategies in Europe.* Dordrecht: Kluwer Academic Publishers.

Amann, M. 1989. *Potential and Costs for Control of NO_x Emissions in Europe.* Status Report (SR–89–1), Laxenburg: International Institute for Applied Systems Analysis.

Amann, M., Baldi, M., Heyes, C., Klimont, Z. and Schöpp, W. 1995. *Integrated Assessment of Emission Control Scenarios Including the Impact of Tropospheric Ozone.* Laxenburg: International Institute for Applied Systems Analysis.

Amann, M. and Kornai, G. 1987. *Cost Functions for Controlling SO_2 Emissions in Europe.* Laxenburg: International Institute for Applied Systems Analysis.

Beavis, B. and Walker, M. 1979. 'Interactive Pollutants and Joint Abatement Costs: Achieving Water Quality Standards with Effluent Charges.' *Journal of Environmental Economics and Management* 6, 275–286.

ECN (Energy Research Center), 1997. Personal Communication of O. van Hilten.

Egmond, P. and Rasenberg, S. 1990. *Een Optimalisatiemodel voor de Bestrijding van Grensoverschrijdende Verzurende Componenten in Europe.* Wageningen: Agricultural University Wageningen.

EMEP MSC W, 1996a. *Estimated Dispersion of Acidifying Agents and Near Surface Ozone.* Oslo: The Norwegian Meteorological Institute.

EMEP MSC W, 1996b. *Numerical Addendum to Estimated Dispersion of Acidifying Agents and Near Surface Ozone.* Oslo: The Norwegian Meteorological Institute.

Grennfelt, P., Hov, Ø. and Derwent, R.G. 1993. *Second Generation Abatement Strategies for NO_x, SO_2 and VOC.* IVL Report, B1098, Stockholm: Swedish Environmental Research Institute.

Hahn, C.W. 1989. 'A New Approach to the Design of Regulation in the Presence of Multiple Objectives.' *Journal of Environmental Economics and Management* 17, 195–211.

Heyes, C. and Schöpp, W. 1995. *Towards a Simplified Model to Describe Ozone Formation in Europe.* Laxenburg: International Institute for Applied Systems Analysis.

Heyes C., Schöpp, W. and Amann, M. 1995. *A Simplified Model to Predict Long-term Ozone Concentrations in Europe.* Laxenburg: International Institute for Applied Systems Analysis.

Kelly, N.A. and Gunst, R. 1990. 'Response of Ozone to Changes in Hydrocarbon and Nitrogen Oxide Concentrations in Outdoor Smog

Chambers Filled with Los Angeles Air.' *Atmospheric Environment* 24A, 12, 2991–3005.

Michaelis, P. 1992. 'Global Warming: Efficient Policies in the Case of Multiple Pollutants.' *Environmental and Resource Economics* 2, 61–77.

Ministry of Economic Affairs 1995. *Third Energy Report.* Den Haag: Sdu Uitgevers.

Olsthoorn, X. 1994. *Towards an Integrated Assessment Model for Tropospheric Ozone. Emission Inventories, Scenarios and Emission Control Options.* Laxenburg: International Institute for Applied Systems Analysis.

Rijksinstitut voor Volksgezondheid en Milieuhygiene 1993. *Nationale Milieuverkenning.* Tjeenk Willink: Samson.

UNEP (United Nations Environmental Programme) 1992. *United Nations Environment Programme Environmental Data Report.* Oxford: Basil Blackwell.

United Nations 1984. *Protocol to the 1979 Convention on Long-range Transboundary Air Pollution on Long-term Financing of the Co-operative Programme for Monitoring and Evaluation of the Long-range Transmission of Air Pollutants in Europe (EMEP).* ECE/EB.AIR/11.

United Nations 1985. *Protocol to the 1979 Convention on Long-range Transboundary Air Pollution on the Reduction of Sulphur or their Transboundary Fluxes by at least 30 per cent.* ECE/EB.AIR/12.

United Nations 1988. *Protocol to the 1979 Convention on Long-range Transboundary Air Pollution Concerning the Control of Emissions of Nitrogen Oxides and their Transboundary Fluxes.* ECE/EB.AIR/21.

United Nations 1991. *Protocol to the 1979 Convention on Long-range Transboundary Air Pollution Concerning the Control of Emissions of Volatile Organic Compounds or their Transboundary Fluxes.* ECE/EB.AIR/30.

United Nations 1994. *Protocol to the 1979 Convention on Long-range Transboundary Air Pollution on Further Reduction of Sulphur Emissions and Decision on the Structure and Function of Implementation Committee, as well as Procedures for its Review of Compliance.* ECE/EB.AIR/40.

PART IV

Sustainable Consumption

14. Consumer Behaviour, A Modelling Perspective in the Context of Integrated Assessment of Global Change

Wander Jager, Marjolein van Asselt, Jan Rotmans and Charles Vlek

INTRODUCTION

Past and present civilisations have been more or less successful in combating human poverty, ignorance, discomfort and diseases. However, several ancient cultures collapsed, because population growth and increase of affluence implied an over-exploitation of the natural environment (Ponting, 1993). Examples are the Mesopotamians (2000 BC), the Mayas (800 AD) and the Polynesians on Easter Island (16th century). At present, the socio-economic system of Western industrialised countries might be overshooting its natural resource basis. During the last decades awareness has emerged that the environmental impacts of our economic system not only affect the regional or national level, but also have an impact on the world as a whole. These global changes, such as global warming, the thinning of the stratospheric ozone layer and large-scale deforestation, seriously jeopardise the basic conditions for existence. People are not only causing and exacerbating these various processes of global change, but they also have a (limited) control over them. As such, to prevent people from degrading their environment and thereby indirectly victimising themselves, and in order to develop effective policy strategies for changing environmentally destructive behaviour, it is necessary to identify the socio-behavioural processes underlying global change.

To fully understand the causes and mechanisms of global change, the natural sciences and the social sciences must co-operate in order to develop a common language and methodological tools. So-called integrated assessment addresses the interdisciplinary process of combining, interpreting and communicating knowledge from diverse scientific disciplines such that the whole cause–effect chain of global change can be evaluated from a synoptic perspective (Rotmans *et al.*, 1996). Given the complexity and the dynamic nature of the mutual interdependencies, integrated assessment can help to foster understanding of the causal and mutual relationships between processes within the human and the environmental systems. Within integrated assessment, computer models are used as a framework to integrate knowledge of a wide variety of disciplines. This integration requires the simplification of single-discipline expert models into meta-models, and the subsequential linking of these meta-models, for example, for energy or water consumption and population dynamics. Integrated assessment models can be used as tools to project specific future processes of global change, and to indicate the effectiveness of different management strategies (policies). As such, integrated assessment models are opposed to single-discipline oriented assessment models, and they thereby provide useful information to decision-makers.

This chapter aims to provide a conceptual model on human consumption behaviour that will guide the development of a behaviour-simulation model. Because such a simulation model will be computer-programmed, it should provide means to include behavioural dynamics in integrated assessment modelling, thus building a bridge between the applied natural and social sciences.

In the following sections of this chapter we will first address the principles of integrated assessment. Following that, we will discuss the modelling of behaviour in integrated assessment modelling, introducing the conceptual model. A subsequent section discusses the computer programming of the conceptual model. In the final section some conclusions and remaining questions are discussed.

INTEGRATED ASSESSMENT

In 1992 the National Institute of Public Health and Environmental Protection (RIVM) in The Netherlands launched the research programme 'Global Dynamics and Sustainable Development.' The main objective of this programme is to operationalise, and to render applicable, the concept of sustainable development from a global perspective (Rotmans *et al.*, 1994). Furthermore, this research project aims to improve communication processes among scientists from various disciplines, and between scientists and policy-makers. In order to achieve this, an integrated assessment model entitled TARGETS (Tool to Assess Regional and Global Environmental and health Targets for Sustainability) is being developed (Rotmans and De Vries, 1997). The global issues covered in TARGETS are human health and population dynamics, energy resources, global cycles (transformation and movements of chemical substances in the global environment), land-use, and water resources.

In the TARGETS research project, a systems approach is advocated. This concentrates on the interactions and feedback mechanisms between the different subsystems of cause–effect chains of global change, rather than focusing on each subsystem in isolation. Using a systems approach, the anthropogenic disturbances of the global processes can be represented by a set of interrelated cause–effect chains. Together, these cause–effect chains provide a conceptual framework that considers the Earth as a system of human and environmental reservoirs and of natural and societal processes connecting these reservoirs. A general division of any cause–effect chain into subsystems on a global scale is denoted in Figure 14.1.

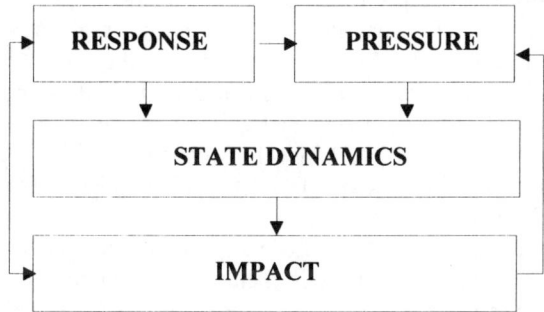

Figure 14.1. Systems diagram of the general Pressure-State-Impact-Response (P-S-I-R) system of global change (Source: Rotmans et al., 1994).

The PRESSURE subsystems describe the continuously changing pressures on the human and environmental system, as well as their driving forces. The pressures act upon the state dynamics subsystem. The STATE DYNAMICS subsystems describe changes in the physical, chemical and biological state of environmental systems as well as changes in human population, human behaviour patterns and environmental resources and capital. This system acts upon the impact system. The IMPACT subsystems describe anthropogenic impacts on aquatic and land ecosystems, the consequences for human health, and socio-economic effects for various sectors of society. Impacts act upon the pressures, but also responses can be elicited by impacts. The RESPONSE systems describe users' possibilities to influence either human activities or environmental states, which also includes human responses to societal and ecological impacts. Responses can be aimed at all other three subsystems. All of these subsystems have their own characteristics, which may change as a result of anthropogenic or evolutionary processes.

Within the TARGETS framework the major issues at a global scale are translated in terms of Pressure, State, Impact and Response (P-S-I-R). For the various subsystems of the global system a series of highly aggregated modules have been built, interlinked and integrated within the overall TARGETS framework, namely, a population/health module (Niessen and Hilderink, 1997), an energy module (De Vries and Janssen, 1997), biochemical cycles module (Den Elzen *et al.*, 1997), a land and food module (Strengers *et al.*, 1997) and a water module (Hoekstra, 1997). These submodels are all built according the P-S-I-R systems approach as depicted in Figure 14.1. The complexity of the TARGETS model arises from the many relationships and feedback loops between these submodels. The TARGETS model serves to explore the long-term dynamics of global change, using a time horizon that spans about two centuries, starting at the year 1900 until the year 2100. As TARGETS adopts a generic approach, it is applicable irrespective of the level of analysis. This implies that the submodels can be applied on a global as well as on a regional scale. It is evident that the input data should be compatible with the level of analysis. Following the top-down approach, analysis starts at the highest aggregation level, that is, a global level, considering the Earth as a whole. In the next phase TARGETS will be disaggregated to the level of economic world regions, river basins and ecosystems, using regional data sets. This implies that reasonably specific case studies will be carried out.

From an evaluation of TARGETS 1.0 it appears that the model does not explicitly address consumption behaviour. Inclusion of behavioural modelling, which would allow for a more comprehensive assessment of the effectiveness of policy strategies aimed at behavioural change, and it would therefore significantly improve the TARGETS model and integrated assessment modelling in general. A behavioural model should address behavioural processes in a generic manner, that is, irrespective of regional and temporal differences. This implies that some kind of 'meta-consumer' will be constituted that will represent a group of people corresponding to the level of modelling. For example, if a modelling exercise contrasts the northern hemisphere with the southern hemisphere, two meta-consumers will be constituted, representing the consumers in the north and the south respectively. Depending on the aims one has with the modelling and the level of analysis, more of these 'meta-consumers' can be included in a model.

MODELLING CONSUMPTION BEHAVIOUR WITHIN AN INTEGRATED ASSESSMENT OF GLOBAL CHANGE

The growing concern about the environment has stimulated the social sciences to develop conceptual multi-theoretical models describing various environmentally detrimental behaviours. 'Multi-theoretical' indicates here that various theories on specific types of behaviour are combined. These conceptual models are useful for the post-hoc explanation of environmentally relevant behaviour, and they indicate policy strategies that might be effective in changing such behaviour. However, because these conceptual models generally involve a poor specification of the relations among relevant variables and lack a system-dynamic approach, they do not allow for the translation into mathematical models, which would fit in the framework of integrated assessment models. A useful behavioural model within the framework of integrated assessment should enable us to develop projections of future behaviour, thus providing a tool for the simulation of behaviour. Such a generic behaviour model provides means to generate possible answers to the following central questions:

- How do various kinds of consumption behaviour interact with projected developments in various domains, for example, population dynamics, water, food and energy resources?
- Which response strategies provide effective means to change particular kinds of environmentally detrimental consumption behaviour in the context of the search for a sustainable future?

In order to be able to address these questions, the dynamics of the behavioural process have to be modelled in a formal quantitative way. In line with the TARGETS philosophy, the P-S-I-R approach will be adopted. Consequently, the following questions need to be answered:

- What are the main pressures on certain kinds of consumption behaviour?
- Which mechanisms and processes characterise the behaviour of consumers?
- What are the impacts of various types of consumption behaviour on human and environmental systems?
- What is the influence of different policy response strategies on consumption behaviour?

This implies that the behavioural model will include a Pressure system, describing the driving forces behind consumption behaviour, a State dynamics system, describing the behavioural process itself, an Impact system, describing the quantities or volumes of consumer goods used and outcomes with respect to the satisfaction of needs, opportunities and abilities, and a Response system, describing the policy strategies aimed at changing behaviour (Jager *et al.*, 1997; see also Figure 14.1). Because of the feedback in the model, the possibility arises to let the simulated consumers learn and adapt to changing circumstances (pressures) and thus processes of self-organisation may be simulated.

The simulated use of consumer goods (as Impacts in the conceptual behaviour model) can itself be included as part of the Pressure system within other submodels of TARGETS. For example, an increase of meat consumption would serve as a pressure variable for the land-use model TERRA. Within the range of this chapter, however, the concepts of Pressure, State, Impact and Response are used within the context of the conceptual behaviour model, and they are exclusively referring to human consumption behaviour. The next sections will conceptualise the Pressure, State dynamics, Impact and Response systems of the behaviour model, respectively.

The Pressure System

The Pressure system is dealing with the various driving forces underlying consumption behaviour. In research on consumption behaviour, three pressure variables are recognised, labelled as Motivation, Opportunity and Ability, respectively (the so-called MOA-model, see, for example, Batra and Ray, 1986; Robben and Poiesz, 1992; Ölander and Thøgerson, 1994; Gatersleben and Vlek, 1997). As the conjunction of motivations, opportunities and abilities determines the behavioural process and the resulting consumption behaviour, this section delineates these three pressure variables.

The concept of *Motivation* is concerned with the satisfaction of human needs by means of 'opportunity consumption.' The more one perceives an opportunity, as a possibility to satisfy certain needs, the higher one's motivation to use this opportunity will be. In line with Max-Neef (1992), we assume the existence of nine fundamental human needs. They are, respectively, the needs for Subsistence, Protection, Affection, Understanding, Participation, Creation, Leisure, Identity and Freedom. These needs are conceived as being independent of culture. However, culture may determine to a large extent the preferred types of opportunities used to satisfy one's needs. As such, Cultural Theory (Douglas and Wildavsky, 1982; Thompson *et al.*, 1990; Schwarz and Thompson, 1990; Rayner, 1991; O'Riordan and Rayner, 1991) provides an organising framework which claims that distinctive sets of values, beliefs, perceptions and habits are reducible to only a few basic cultural attitudes and preferences. Cultural Theory generally distinguishes four different perspectives from which people perceive the world and behave in it, namely the *Hierarchist*, the *Egalitarian*, the *Individualist* and the *Fatalist* perspectives. Notwithstanding the (empirical) limitations of Cultural Theory, the associated typology of cultural perspectives enables us to characterise different culture-biased motivations. The relationship between one's perspective and one's preferred types of consumer opportunities (seen as needs satisfiers) involve the concept of lifestyle. The actual degree of (multiple) need-fulfilment might be conceived as directly underlying one's quality of life.

Within the MOA-model, the concept of *Opportunity* is concerned with the availability of the various products and services one might consume. The use of an opportunity may satisfy certain consumer needs. The various need-satisfying capacities that one unit of a certain opportunity has may be understood as the service units provided by that opportunity. For example, the service units provided by owning and driving a car can be understood in terms of need-satisfying capacities with respect to freedom (to move), identity (status) and subsistence (transportation to one's job). Moreover, (groups of) consumers differ with regard to their level of need satisfaction. Consequently, the consumption of an opportunity will provide differing amounts of service units to different consumers. For example, an old car that is 'out of fashion' will provide more service units to a farmer in a relatively poor country than to a successful businessman in a relatively rich country. Linking fundamental human needs to the concept of service units thus provides a behavioural perspective on the concept of Material Inputs Per Service unit (MIPS) (Schmidt-Bleek, 1994). The use of an opportunity also requires certain human investments. As such, opportunities may be characterised in terms of the physical means, money, authorisation, knowledge, and the social and organisational support that are needed to utilise them. These required investments are referred to as resource demands imposed upon an individual by an opportunity to consume. The combined use of different opportunities (that is, a certain consumption pattern) is denoted as the opportunity distribution.

The concept of *Ability* as the third MOA-model factor is concerned with the skills and capacities one may utilise to perform a certain consumption behaviour. These skills and capacities are conceived as one's physical means financial means, permits and privileges, knowledge, and social and organisational support. These skills and capacities are referred to as one's available resources. The degree to which a consumer has sufficient resources available to utilise an opportunity with specific resource demands tackles the concept of behavioural control. If a consumer has plenty of resources available to utilise a specific opportunity, one's behavioural control is high. If a consumer lacks sufficient resources, one's behavioural control is low.

It is supposed that background variables, such as population-size and gross national product (GNP), partly determine consumers' motivations, opportunities and abilities. Projected data on such (global) developments will eventually be imported from other modules within TARGETS.

The State Dynamics System

The State dynamics system describes the behavioural process of how motivations, opportunities and abilities (Pressures on behaviour) lead towards a certain consumption of goods (Impact). Depending on the level of motivation, opportunities and abilities, this behavioural process may include more or less deliberation or cognitive processing. This varying degree of cognitive processing provides a major perspective for distinguishing among different behavioural processes. These processes range from a deliberate consideration of all behavioural possibilities (consumer options) on the one hand, to habitual or automatic performance of behaviour on the other, involving only minor cognitive activity, if any at all. In behavioural theories this perspective has led to the emergence of two important paradigms, namely, the cognitive and the behavioural approach towards behaviour and behaviour change. Each paradigm involves several theories addressing the dynamics of different types of consumption behaviour. A second classification can be made with respect to the processing of individual versus social information. A combination of these two dimensions yields the four-fold categorisation of Table 14.1, which simultaneously classifies eight major theories of human behaviour.

Table 14.1. A classification of eight major theories of human behaviour.

	Individual behaviour	Social behaviour
Reasoned behaviour	• Decision and choice theory (for example, Janis and Mann, 1977; Hogarth, 1987; Yates, 1990) • Theory of reasoned and planned behaviour (Fishbein and Ajzen, 1975; Ajzen, 1985, 1988; Ajzen and Madden, 1985)	• Social comparison theory (Festinger, 1954) • Relative deprivation theory (for example, Masters and Smith, 1987)
Automatic behaviour	• Classical conditioning theory (Pavlov, 1927) • Operant conditioning theory (Skinner, 1938, 1953)	• Social learning theory (Bandura, 1977) • Theory of normative conduct (Cialdini, Kallgren and Reno, 1991)

The degree of cognitive processing before using or rejecting any opportunity depends on the strength of a consumer's motivation to use this opportunity and on his or her behavioural control. If motivation is low, because the opportunity is perceived as not contributing to the satisfaction of needs, one will not engage in extensive cognitive processing. That is, one has a low motivation to elaborate. It is most probable that the opportunity will be rejected and not considered any further. If, however, the motivation to use the opportunity is high, the behavioural control one has is also taken into account. The higher behavioural control, the easier it is to use the preferred opportunity, and thus the less a consumer is motivated to elaborate on the use of other opportunities for satisfying the same needs. The lower the consumer's behavioural control, the more difficult it is to use a preferred opportunity, and the more one may be motivated to elaborate on strategies to increase behavioural control and/or to elaborate on alternative opportunities.

Depending on the types of needs that are satisfied by using an opportunity, individual or social processes of behaviour will prevail. Although most human needs as described by Max-Neef (1992) include both individual and social aspects, it is asserted that the needs for Subsistence, Protection, Understanding and Creation primarily are individually relevant needs, whilst the needs for Affection, Participation, Leisure, Identity and Freedom rather are socially relevant needs. It is assumed that individual needs will stimulate individual behaviour (see Table 14.1), and that socially oriented needs will stimulate social behaviour. Because most opportunities may satisfy different needs, often individual and social processes of behaviour are combined.

To give an example of such behavioural processes, suppose a consumer has a strong need for Identity and perceives ('cultural perspective-ridden') the ownership of an expensive car as an excellent opportunity to satisfy this need. However, the opportunity 'expensive car' may require more financial resources than the financial abilities of the consumer allow for. This would result in a low behavioural control over acquiring the car. According to the above-postulated mechanism, this would yield a high motivation to elaborate on strategies to increase behavioural control and/or to elaborate on alternative opportunities (which is 'reasoned behaviour'). Because the need for Identity is a social need, the behavioural process will be socially oriented, and it may be modelled under the theories indicated in the upper right cell of Table 14.1. The consumer may start to look at 'expensive-car owners' to learn how to realise this opportunity, thus learning how his or her abilities may be sufficiently increased to use this opportunity (for example, by not going on a holiday, to save money). If this social comparison process does not yield adequate means to rearrange one's resources so as to buy an expensive car, the consumer may start elaborating on other opportunities to satisfy her or his need for Identity. The process of rearranging one's resources is referred to as a substitution process.

When a certain opportunity is repeatedly used to satisfaction, the behavioural process may be automated to a certain degree, resulting in a consumption *habit*. However, the origins of a habit often lie in reasoned behaviour or in social imitation. Much consumption behaviour is repetitive in character, for example, buying of food, using of appliances (cars, showers, and so on) and disposing of garbage.

The Impact System

The *Impact system* addresses the observable human consumption pattern. This implies that given an opportunity distribution, as determined in the State system, the corresponding amount of product use has to be estimated. At this stage, information about the physical (environmentally relevant) outcomes of the behaviour is needed. For example, given that a certain opportunity distribution denotes the frequencies and volumes which a consumer drinks, showers, cleans, irrigates and so on, the resulting amount of water use can be estimated. The Impact system will display the amount of human consumption in terms of litres of water, miles of transportation, kWh electricity or cubic metres of natural gas. Depending on the level of consumption and the type of opportunity (for example, exhaustible, renewable, recyclable), these impacts may cause a societal scarcity or even a depletion of opportunities. Especially in the case of renewable resources, an overconsumption can be understood as the overshooting of the carrying capacity of a certain environmental system (see Köhn, chapter 6 in this volume).

Naturally, these environmentally relevant impacts cover only part of the outcomes that a consumer may experience. Primary impacts (for him or her) involve the level of need satisfaction (which indicates quality of life), the availability of opportunities (for example, the emergence of scarcity) and the development of abilities (for example, learning). As such, these impacts, as feedback, subsequently may evoke changes in motivation and/or behavioural control. These processes of feedback reflect the autonomous or self-regulating processes of behaviour change.

The Response System

The joint behaviour of people can be conceived as a self-regulative system. As such, the Pressure system, State system and Impact system can be used to describe the self-regulating process of behaviour. The Response system is added to explicitly address the policy-making aimed at influencing these social behavioural processes. As such the Response system describes the actions that governments, industries, non-governmental organisations (NGOs), consumer organisations, and so on, take to deliberately change consumer behaviour. Policy measures are directed at the pressures underlying behaviour, thus they involve change of consumer motivations, opportunities and abilities. Several researchers present a taxonomy of strategies for behaviour change (see for example Sheth and Frazier, 1982; Cook and Berrenberg, 1981; Vlek and Michon, 1991; De Young, 1993). Building on these contributions, we adopt a categorisation in four general types of strategies, as follows:

1. *Provision of physical alternatives and (re)arrangements* refers to the shaping of new opportunities and the changing or dismissing of existing opportunities through changing technology and infrastructure. This would also change the consumers' motivation to use opportunities, because the need-satisfying attributes of opportunities are changed. The basic assumption is that changing the physical environment, in which it takes place, can shape behaviour. Some exemplary types of physical alternatives and (re)arrangements are:
   - Optimisation of existing technology (improving efficiency and so on);
   - Innovation and development of new technologies;
   - Infrastructure changes.

2. *Regulation-and-enforcement* serves to restrict or enlarge the opportunities one has to behave in a certain way, and thus relates to consumers' freedom of choice. This strategy is based on the enforcement of laws, rules, regulations and standards adopted by the government. Violations of them 'if detected' are met with some kind of punishment, fine or disapproval. This requires an adequate organisation for supervision, monitoring and enforcement. The basic assumption is that regulations can be internalised, thereby leading towards a motivational change. In the long run, even a cultural change may occur, for example, with respect to waste disposal. Some exemplary types of regulation-and-enforcement are:
   - Civil law, determining the rules which apply to interactions between citizens;
   - Constitutional law, determining the rules which the state imposes on its citizens;
   - International law, determining the rules which apply to the interaction between states.

3. *Financial-economic stimulation* refers to the financial rewarding of preferred behaviour, using subsidies, discounts, and so on, and to the financial charging of unpreferred behaviour, using taxes, fines, and so on. The basic assumption is that the behaviour in question is susceptible to the price-mechanism and that the demand-price elasticities involved are reasonably high. Besides affecting the motivation of people and the demands of the opportunities they can choose from, drastic financial-economic measurements may also change the financial abilities people have. Some exemplary types of financial-economic stimulation are:
   - Microeconomic measures, employing the price-mechanism. As such,

they are directed at the change of opportunities, especially the financial abilities they require.

- Macroeconomic measures, addressing the financial abilities of consumers in a state.

4. *Social and cognitive stimulation* aims to increase consumers' problem awareness, to alter problem perception and to motivate people towards preferred behaviours. This strategy involves giving information, education, arguments, social rewards, behavioural examples (role-models), prompts, advice and appeals to morality. Changes of attitudes and values, seeing role-models being rewarded and changes in people's perceptions of quality-of-life may increase the motivation to change existing behaviour. Also, offering knowledge and advice can increase the ability to change one's behaviour. The basic assumption here is that lifestyles and specific behaviours are determined by cognitions, social factors such as social norms and customs, and by cultural perspective-ridden values and morality. Some exemplary types of social and cognitive stimulation are:

- Information, education and communication, aiming to increase consumers' abilities;
- Social modeling and support, aiming to change consumers' motivation;
- Appeals to morality, aiming to change consumers' motivation.

The four general strategies delineated above may be directed at individual consumers (the micro-level of society), but also at organisations (the meso-level) such as industries, special interest groups, public services and so forth, and at the level of states (countries) and interstate-organisations such as the World Bank and the OESO (the macro-level).

A well-designed combination of two or more of these response strategies may yield a set of specific policy measures that induce changes in the relevant pressures – motivations, opportunities and abilities – underlying consumption behaviour. At the same time, the strategies should be fine-tuned towards the four basic behaviour mechanisms: reasoned versus automatic, and individual versus social behaviour, so as to be optimally effective. Altogether, application of appropriate policy measures is designed to yield a reduction of environmentally harmful volumes or quantities of energy, materials and products consumed.

The conceptual operationalisation of the Pressure, State, Impact and Response systems, as originally depicted in Figure 14.1, yields the schematic behavioural model as presented in Figure 14.2.

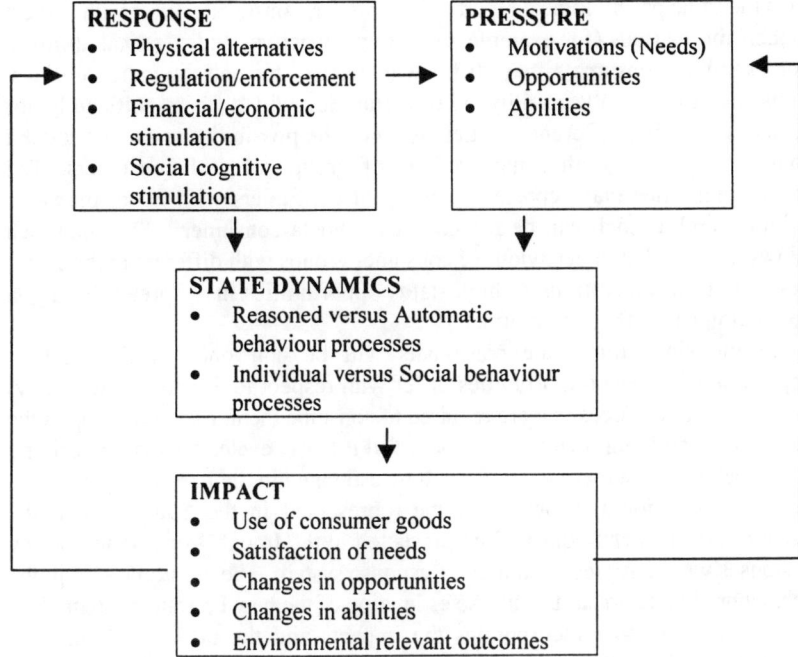

Figure 14.2. Schematic representation of the conceptual behavioural model.

TOWARDS COMPUTER SIMULATION OF CONSUMER BEHAVIOUR

The next stage of research is directed at the translation of the conceptual behavioural model into a behaviour simulation model that can actually be run on a computer. Such a model would provide the means to study the dynamics of consumption behaviour, and it would be a tool to experiment with different policy-measures in a dynamic environment. As such, simulations of consumption behaviour should also provide information on the stability of social systems (see also Gowdy, chapter 5 in this volume), and on the possibilities to (fundamentally) change consumption patterns whilst avoiding chaotic developments.

To represent different types of consumers in the simulation programme, we propose to model consumers as computerised agents, which we call 'consumats.' The basic design of every consumat comprises a set of rules, which are derived from the conceptual behavioural model of Figure 14.2. As such, all consumats have the same psychological repertoire. However, consumats differ with respect to their motivations (for example, cultural perspective) and personal abilities. For example, consumats may differ with respect to their financial abilities. Consequently, the attainability of opportunities will differ significantly for consumats having different abilities. As such the possibility arises to model a consumat's abilities after the abilities of groups of real consumers. The consummate thus may represent a group of consumers with about the same abilities, and as such can be regarded as a 'meta-consumer.' This approach allows us to study the behaviour of consumer groups with different abilities, for example, how innovations or high status opportunities may spread through a population ('trickling down effect').

In the simulations, the consumats will be confronted with a set of opportunities. These opportunities differ with respect to the needs they (may) fulfil, and the resources that are required to consume them. Each time step in the behaviour simulation would comprise a full P-S-I-R cycle. That is, the driving forces behind consumer behaviour will be estimated in the Pressure system, the resulting behavioural process will be represented in the State system, the outcomes of the behaviour will be presented in the Impact system, and policy responses will be represented in the Response system. The next time step in the behaviour simulation starts with the estimation of the new Pressure system. This new Pressure system incorporates the impacts and the policy responses as designated in the previous time step. As such, these impacts and policy responses will feed back to the driving forces behind the simulated consumer behaviour. As a modelling tool, we use a multi-agent simulation approach. Within the social sciences, a growing number of scientists that are working with computer simulations adhere to this approach (see for instance Brehmer and Dörner, 1993; Gilbert and Doran, 1994; Conte *et al.*, 1997). This approach allows consumers to interact with each other, so that processes of social comparison may also be simulated.

Currently, we are developing a series of simple simulations to test various behavioural rules. Subsequently we will study the behaviour of more complex consumats in a microworld. This microworld contains a lake with fish (a replenishable resource) and a goldmine (a finite resource) which pollutes the lake. This microworld offers a tool to experiment with the consumats in an environment with well-defined dynamics. In a subsequent report (Jager *et al.*, in preparation) we will discuss the methodology and present simulation results. The experiments we intend to conduct with the behaviour simulations serve to test and calibrate the behaviour model. In a subsequent research phase we aim to model consumer behaviour in a realistic domain using empirical data.

CONCLUSIONS AND REMAINING RESEARCH QUESTIONS

Currently, a conceptual behavioural model (Figure 14.2) is available which has several important features. First, it describes the pressures on consumer behaviour in terms of people's motivation, opportunities and abilities (MOA). Second, the relation between the MOA variables and behavioural processing is described, with eight main theories on behaviour being taken into account. Third, the conceptual model describes the impacts of behaviour in terms of consumption, need-satisfaction, opportunity change and ability change. Fourth, the conceptual model incorporates four general strategies for behaviour change that allow for the specification of specific policy-measures. And finally, the conceptual model comprises a system-dynamical structure, thus providing a framework for modelling feedback loops.

Furthermore, the first simulations have been computer programmed, offering a platform for the further computer programming of the conceptual behavioural model. In these simulations we operationalise several consumats which may interact directly (by means of comparison processes) and indirectly (by means of opportunity or environmental changes). Such a multi-agent modelling approach is adopted to study the micro–macro dynamics of human behaviour. Successful operationalisation and implementation of the conceptual behaviour model in this modelling context would allow us to experiment with some basic behavioural dynamics of environmental degradation. Experimenting with the consumats in a microworld allows us to study the interactions between human behaviour and the physical environment. As this requires linking the behavioural model to an environmental model, such experiments fall in the young tradition of integrated assessment modelling.

Further research involves experimenting with the consumats to test and develop behavioural rules. These simulations will be of an artificial nature; that is, the processes simulated cannot be directly related to a specific empirical situation. In subsequent stages of the research the relation between the simulations and empirical data will be given more attention. This requires an adequate diagnosis of a particular domain, for which a further specification of major kinds of motivations, opportunities and abilities towards selected kinds of consumer behaviour will be required. Such simulations may reveal several factors that influence the relative effectiveness of policy response strategies for changing consumption behaviour. Both the importance of specific behaviour determinants and the effectiveness of particular response strategies are likely to depend upon the cultural perspective or the general lifestyle of the relevant consumer groups. Possible domains of consumption behaviour that are nominated for modelling are household energy consumption, the use of private motor-cars, and air travelling for purposes of recreation and tourism.

REFERENCES

Ajzen, I. 1985. 'From Intentions to Actions: A Theory of Planned Behaviour.' In Kuhl, J. and Beckmann, J. (eds.) *Action-Control: From Cognition to Behaviour.* Heidelberg: Springer, 11–39.

Ajzen, I. and Madden, T.J. 1985. 'Prediction of Goal-Directed Behaviour: Attitudes, Intentions, and Perceived Behavioral Control.' *Journal of Experimental Social Psychology* 22, 453–474.

Bandura, A. 1977. *Social Learning Theory.* Englewood Cliffs: Prentice Hall.

Batra, R. and Ray, M.L. 1986. 'Situational Effects of Advertising Repetition: The Moderating Influence of Motivation, Ability and Opportunity to Respond.' *Journal of Consumer Research* 12, 4, 432–445.

Brehmer, B. and Dörner, D. 1993. 'Experiments with Computer-Simulated Microworlds: Escaping Both the Narrow Straits of the Laboratory and the Deep Blue Sea of the Field Study.' *Computers in Human Behavior* 9, 171–184.

Cialdini, R.B., Kallgren, C.A. and Reno, R.R. 1991. 'A Focus Theory of Normative Conduct: A Theoretical Refinement and Reevaluation of the Role of Norms in Human Behavior.' *Advances in Experimental Social Psychology* 24, 201–234.

Conte, R., Hegselmann, R. and Terna, P. (eds.) 1997. *Simulating Social Phenomena.* Berlin: Springer.

Cook, S.W. and Berrenberg, J.L. 1981. 'Approaches to Encouraging Conservation Behavior: A Review and Conceptual Framework.' *Journal of Social Issues* 37, 2, 73–107.

Den Elzen, M.G.J., Beusen, A., Rotmans, J. and Köster, H.W. 1997. 'The Biochemical Submodel: CYCLES.' In Rotmans, J. and De Vries, H.J.M. (eds.) *Perspectives on Global Change. The Targets Approach.* Cambridge: Cambridge University Press.

De Vries, H.J.M. and Janssen, M.A. 1997. 'The Energy Submodel: TIME.' In Rotmans, J. and De Vries, H.J.M. (eds.) *Perspectives on Global Change, The Targets Approach.* Cambridge: Cambridge University Press.

De Young, R. 1993. 'Changing Behaviour and Making It Stick: The Conceptualisation and Management of Conservation Behaviour.' *Environment and Behaviour* 25, 4, 485–505.

Douglas, M. and Wildavsky, A. 1982. *Risk and Culture: An Essay on the Selection of Technical and Environmental Dangers.* Berkeley: University of California Press.

Festinger, L. 1954. 'A Theory of Social Comparison Processes.' *Human Relations* 7, 117–140.

Fishbein, M. and Ajzen, I. 1975. *Belief, Attitude, Intention, and Behaviour: An Introduction to Theory and Research.* Reading: Addison-Wesley.

Gatersleben, B. and Vlek, C. 1997. 'Understanding Household Metabolism in View of Environmental Quality and Sustainable Development.' In Antonides, G., Maital, S. and van Raay, W.F. (eds.) *Advances in Economic Psychology*. Dordrecht: Kluwer.

Gilbert, N. and Doran, J. (eds.) 1994. *Simulating Societies: The Computer Simulation of Social Phenomena*. London: UCL Press.

Hoekstra, A. 1997. 'The Water Submodel: AQUA.' In Rotmans, J. and De Vries, H.J.M. (eds.) *Perspectives on Global Change. The Targets Approach*. Cambridge: Cambridge University Press.

Hogarth, R.M. 1987. *Judgement and Choice*. Chichester: John Wiley and Sons.

Jager, W., van Asselt, M.B.A., Rotmans, J., Vlek, C.A.J. and Costerman Boodt, P. 1997. 'Consumer Behaviour: A Modelling Perspective in the Context of Integrated Assessment of Global Change.' *Globo Report Series* 17, RIVM, Bilthoven, The Netherlands.

Jager, W., Janssen, M.A., De Greef, J., De Vries, H.J.M. and Vlek, C.A.J. forthcoming. *Simulating Human Behaviour within an Integrated Assessment Model*. Bilthoven: RIVM Report.

Janis, I.L. and Mann, L. 1977. *Decision Making: A Psychological Study of Conflict, Choice and Commitment*. New York: The Free Press.

Masters, J.C. and Smith, W.P. (eds.) 1987. *Social Comparison, Social Justice and Relative Deprivation: Theoretical and Policy Perspectives*. Hillsdale: Erlbaum.

Max-Neef, M. (1992). 'Development and Human Needs.' In Ekins, P. and Max-Neef, M. (eds.) *Real-life Economics: Understanding Wealth Creation*. London: Routledge.

Niessen, L.W. and Hilderink, H.B.M 1997. 'The Population and Health submodel.' In Rotmans, J. and De Vries, H.J.M. (eds.) *Perspectives on Global Change, The Targets Approach*. Cambridge: Cambridge University Press.

Ölander, F. and Thøgerson, J. 1994. *Understanding Consumer Behaviour as a Prerequisite for Environmental Protection*. Keynote Address presented at the 23rd International Congress of Applied Psychology. Aarhus: Aarhus School of Business.

O'Riordan, T. and Rayner, S. 1991. 'Risk Management for Global Environmental Change.' *Global Environmental Change* 1, 2, 91–108.

Pavlov, I.P. 1927. *Conditioned Reflexes*. New York: Oxford University Press.

Ponting, C. 1993. *A Green History of the Earth*. London: Penguin.

Rayner, S. 1991. 'A Cultural Perspective on the Structure and Implementation of Global Environmental Agreements.' *Evaluation Review* 15, 1, 75–102.

Robben, H.S.J. and Poiesz, T.B.C. 1992. 'The Operationalisation of Motivation, Capacity, and Opportunity to Process an Advertising Message.' In van Raaij, W.F. and Bamossy, G.G. (eds.) *Advances in Consumer Research*. Amsterdam: Association for Consumer Research, 160–168.

Rotmans, J. and De Vries, H.J.M. (eds.) 1997. *Perspectives on Global Change, The Targets Approach.* Cambridge: Cambridge University Press.

Rotmans, J., Dowlatabadi, H. and Parson, E.A. 1996. 'Integrated Assessment of Climate Change: Evaluation of Methods and Strategies.' In Rayner, S. and Malone, E. (eds.) *Human Choice and Climate Change: An International Social Science Assessment.* New York: Cambridge University Press.

Rotmans, J., van Asselt, M.B.A., De Bruin, A.J., Den Elzen, M.G.J., De Greef, J., Hilderink, H., Hoekstra, A.Y., Janssen, M.A., Koster, H.W., Martens, W.J.M., Niessen, L.W. and De Vries, H.J.M. 1994. 'Global Change and Sustainable Development: A Modelling Perspective for the Next Decade.' *Globo Report Series* 4, Bilthoven: The Netherlands.

Schmidt-Bleek, F. 1994. *Wieviel Umwelt braucht der Mensch? MIPS – Das Maß für Ökologisches Wirtschaften.* Basel: Birkhäuser.

Schwarz, M. and Thompson, M. 1990. *Divided We Stand – Redfining Politics, Technology and Social Choice.* New York: Harvester Wheatsheaf.

Sheth, J.N. and Frazier, G.L. 1982. 'A Model of Strategy Mix Choice for Planned Social Change.' *Journal of Marketing* 46, 1, 15–26.

Skinner, B.F. 1938. *The Behavior of Organisms: An Experimental Analysis.* Englewood Cliffs: Prentice-Hall.

Skinner, B.F. 1953. *The Behavior of Organisms.* New York: Appleton-Century-Crofts.

Strengers, B.J., Den Elzen, M.G.J. and Köster, H.W. 1997. 'The Land and Food Submodel: TERRA.' In Rotmans, J. and De Vries, H.J.M. (eds.) *Perspectives on Global Change, The Targets Approach.* Cambridge: Cambridge University Press.

Thompson, M., Ellis, R. and Wildavsky, A. 1990. *Cultural Theory.* Boulder: Westview Press.

Vlek, C.A.J. and Michon, J.A. 1991. 'Why He Should and How We Could Decrease the Use of Motor Vehicles in the Near Future.' *Journal of International Association of Traffic and Safety Sciences* 15, 82–93.

Yates, J.F. 1990. *Risk-taking Behavior.* Chichester: John Wiley and Sons.

15. Some Themes in the Discussion of the Quality of Life

Inge Røpke

INTRODUCTION

This chapter is motivated by the need to discuss the quality of life as a part of the background for devising environmental strategies.[1] When environmental strategies are devised, it is often more or less tacitly assumed that we should try to avoid measures that imply a decrease in the level of consumption, and sometimes it is even assumed that the continued growth of consumption in the affluent societies must not be threatened. The underlying idea is that consumption is the most important determinant of welfare. This chapter intends to provide a critical perspective on this underlying idea. I have developed the critical perspective by dealing with welfare or the quality of life: what does it mean to have a good life? On the basis of this discussion, the relationship between consumption and welfare can then be assessed. The approach to the discussion of the quality of life in this chapter is first of all abstract and theoretical, as a number of different theoretical themes are dealt with. It is not a concrete analysis of present life patterns, but at the end of the chapter there are a few suggestions as to how the themes can inspire a concrete debate.

The chapter has three main sections. First, some background considerations are outlined regarding the reasons for considering growing consumption as a problem, the need to form political strategies, and the problems related to the establishment of points of reference for the necessary political discussion. The second main section of the chapter deals with the different themes in the discussion of the quality of life. The point of departure is taken in some critical considerations relating to the traditional conceptualisation of welfare. After that,

---

[1] A previous version of this paper was first presented at the conference in Versailles of the European Society for Ecological Economics in 1996 and later at the conference on sustainability in Rostock in July 1997. The comments at these conferences have been helpful in restructuring and clarifying the ideas in this chapter. Finally, I am grateful to the editors of this volume for their more detailed comments and suggestions.

some inspiration from the debate on basic needs is outlined and supplemented with some reflections on the dual character of needs. Finally, the collective dimension is included as a part of the conceptualisation of a good life. In the third main section, the themes are summarised as a critical perspective on the traditional idea of consumption and welfare, and suggestions are made about how the themes can inspire a more concrete discussion.

BACKGROUND

The Need to Reduce Consumption

The discussion in this chapter only makes sense if it is accepted that material consumption in the North should be reduced. This view is based on three statements: First, global biophysical limits constrain human economic activity, so the standard of living now common in the North cannot be attained in the South as well (except for the privileged few). Second, an ethical obligation exists to contribute to the fulfilment of basic human needs all over the world. Our knowledge about the real poverty of the South (and of parts of the population in the North as well) implies an obligation to share. Third, the dominant economic and political mechanisms imply transfers of resources in the wrong direction from South to North. If we choose to change these mechanisms we will have to face a fall in material consumption. The concept of material consumption suggests that some consumption can be called immaterial. However, a really immaterial form of consumption is a rare thing, but, of course, there are great differences in the quantity of material inputs needed for different forms of consumption. It is often claimed that the problem of consumption in the rich countries can be solved, partly by changing the composition of consumption, that is, goods and services with a relatively low materials- and energy-intensity increase their share, and partly by reducing the materials- and energy-intensity of each type of consumption goods. Efforts in these directions are certainly admirable, but so far little has indicated that they will be sufficient, as long as the total quantity of consumption still increases. Thus the point of departure here is that we also have to deal with the problem of the total quantity, and this is expressed in a simplified way by saying that material consumption has to be reduced.

Obviously, the statement that material consumption in the North should be reduced is normative, and it can apply at both individual and collective levels. At the individual level, it can imply suggestions to buy products that are more expensive because of ecological and social considerations, to reduce one's income by working less in the formal economy and/or to reduce one's consumption and spend the remaining income on charity or on investments in resource-savings. Some people actually pioneer the development of all kinds of consumption-reducing measures, including organisational arrangements to share household capital goods, the establishment of ecological villages, the strengthening of the civil society, and so on. However, the huge task of reducing consumption should not be left solely to the efforts of a few pioneering individuals and small groups. Consumption-reducing measures must also be taken at the collective level to have pervasive effects. Several options are open, which can be illustrated with a few examples:

- a green tax reform changing relative prices so that material consumption becomes more expensive (an hour of labour would 'buy' less material products),
- trade agreements ensuring higher prices for products from poor producers in developing countries,
- restrictions on advertising and consumer credit,
- planning for local shops in order to reduce the need for car transport,
- progressive taxes to reduce the incentive to earn a high income.

Such measures would narrow the possibilities or reduce the incentives to consume material goods, so they would constitute a collective 'cold turkey' with regard to our addiction to consumption (an expression inspired by Claxton, 1994).

In many cases, consumption-reducing measures would run counter to many of the dominant economic and political mechanisms, the vested interests of privileged groups, established power relations, etc. It would be a great challenge in a democratic society to implement 'cold turkey solutions' in opposition to the traditional trends. There is always an abundant supply of legitimising theories questioning the necessity to reduce consumption – for example, technological change will overcome any biophysical limits; people in developing countries are poor because of their own faults; growth in the South depends upon growth in the North. The political conflict about these issues is an important part of paving the way for democratic decisions on 'cold turkey solutions,' but here it is just assumed that it is necessary to reduce consumption.

Making Strategies

The focus is now directed to another aspect of establishing the conditions for making difficult collective decisions regarding consumption. To discuss strategies in this field, inputs regarding at least three aspects are needed, see Figure 15.1.

1. Assessments of the environmental effects of consumption (see for example,
    Biesiot and Moll, 1995; Christensen, 1995): Which aspects of consumption
    are more problematic than other ones?
2. Knowledge about the dynamics underlying growth (see for example,
    Røpke, 1997): What are the driving forces behind the ever-increasing level
    of consumption in the North? How do economic, political and cultural
    aspects interact?
3. Discussions about the relationship between consumption and the quality of
    life: Will decreasing consumption entail a fall in quality of life, or does our
    way of life have inherent costs so that a reduction of consumption could
    give a 'double dividend?'

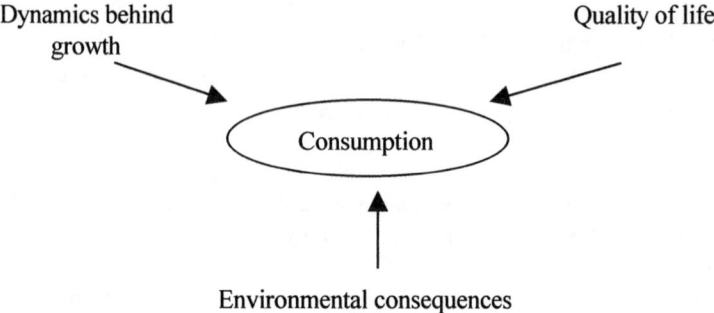

Figure 15.1.   Aspects of strategic considerations.

The three aspects are interrelated. For instance, our conceptions of quality of
life influence the dynamics underlying growth of consumption, but for analytical
purposes the aspects can be separated. Together the three aspects form the
background for democratic discussions about strategies to reduce consumption.
If we gain more insight into the nature of the problems and the dynamics
underlying them and combine this with a more conscious and broader
conception of priorities and values, it may be easier to take steps towards new
strategies.

   This chapter deals only with the third question. A serious obstacle to
consumption-reducing measures seems to be the widespread assumption of a
close relationship between consumption and welfare. An important part of
forming strategies is thus to reconsider this assumption. Immediately, several
critical questions arise:

*   Do we use material means to fulfil needs which could just as well be
    fulfilled with fewer resources?

- Do the socio-economic processes create needs that we would prefer not to have?
- Does our way of living entail an outright deterioration of the quality of life?
- Are some important needs only scantily fulfilled in our society?

The discussion includes both positive and normative aspects. It is a positive analytical task to uncover the prevailing conceptions of a good life and the roots of these conceptions, while it is normative to assess the conceptions critically. However, the two aspects are intertwined, as on the one hand the critical assessments are inputs to a discussion that can influence the prevailing conceptions. Social changes presuppose ideas, and ideas are formed by changes (a dialectical relationship), which gives the theoretical work meaning as part of a political process. On the other hand, the normative assessments are based on positive analysis and axioms regarding human needs, relations between individuals and society, and so on. In this chapter the major issue is the normative aspect.

The Problem of Endogenous Preferences

Immediately, two difficulties arise for the discussion of welfare or the quality of life. The first one is related to the phenomenon that values and preferences are endogenous to the social system. Take, for instance, the historical change of relative prices that has resulted in a dramatic increase in the opportunity cost of repair services measured in industrial products. A parallel shift has taken place in our priorities and values making it much more socially acceptable to throw things away. With a green tax reform this trend in relative prices could be reversed, and gradually we would get used to the changes and adapt our values – and probably be quite satisfied with a lower level of material consumption. However, the decision to initiate a green tax reform has to be taken in a situation where consumer values are dominant. This is very different from the historical situation, where the change in relative prices came about as a result of economic processes and not as a result of conscious political decisions. Social changes co-develop with changes in values and priorities, but we have to take decisions regarding social changes on the basis of the values now dominant and not on the basis of the values that the social changes could give rise to. If this is not going to place us in a situation of complete stalemate, the normative questions can be helpful. Should the present values be dominant, are we in fact doing the best for ourselves, or would it be better to revise our priorities? The questions cannot be left only to individuals, because collective decisions are necessary to change the social structures and conditions of life. We have to have priorities in society, and discussions of the normative questions can help us to assess critically the dominant aims and what is usually accepted as valid. In this collective decision-making process, points of reference are needed (Keat, 1994). The discussion of the normative questions should give us points of reference outside the dominant values at a given point of time so that we can escape from the stalemate situation. Collective decisions must be based on rationales or shared values that can be referred to in the discussions. It will often be considered a strong argument, if something can be said to improve quality of life.

Valuing with Subjective or Objective Criteria

A second problem arises: is the assessment of the quality of life a completely individual issue or can we agree on common points of reference about what constitutes a good life? An important issue in the theoretical discussion of welfare has always been whether the quality of a person's life can be assessed only by the person her-/himself or whether more objective criteria can be used. Different versions of utilitarian theories adhere to the idea that only the individual can judge, but many objections are recognised. Sometimes people want to fulfil needs that they would be better off not to have (for example, persons addicted to drugs or alcohol). Another example is that people's assessments of their own lives are socially constructed, and the human ability to adapt means that sometimes people even internalise their own repression (Sumner, 1992). Some theorists suggest solving the problem by assuming that the subjects are fully informed and rational so that a person's own assessment can be considered reliable. However, to make this assumption is really to introduce the objective criteria by the back door, as this is the only way to judge whether someone is rational and sensible. This is also the case in an example given by Sandøe (1992) where he compares two persons. One is Ambitious Rita who is very successful in relation to family, job, and so on, but who does not feel completely satisfied, because she would like to achieve even more. The other is Satisfied Ole who is doing quite well, but not as well as Rita. However, Ole has a lower level of expectations, so he is very satisfied. Sandøe is convinced that Rita has the highest quality of life, and he tries to resolve the paradox by letting the level of ambition be only one of the desires in a vector of desires, and then the (weighted) sum of the degrees of desire-fulfilment will be higher for Rita. But this is an unsatisfactory device that cannot explain away the fact that he substitutes objective criteria for the subjective valuation.

Fundamentally, the individual experience of the quality of life has much to do with a person's psychological constitution, not least the ability to come to terms with the conditions of her/his life (Deurzen-Smith, 1995). A person's assessment of her or his own situation is a function of the social and individual conditions of life, the personal priorities as well as the person's psychological constitution. Some people can cope with very hard conditions, while others find it difficult to meet a little adversity. Therefore, there will always be individual differences with regard to the assessment of lives that seem to be very much alike, but the question is whether it makes sense to discuss common points of reference regarding what a good life is in spite of these differences. I think that it does make sense. It is not acceptable to say that if people can just cope with their conditions, anything goes. At an abstract level there are some common human elements in having a good life, even if these elements are shaped by culture and appear in different forms. The criteria that can be used as points of reference will obviously include objective conditions of life. However, they can also extend further: the perceived quality of life can be low under ostensibly good conditions, if people's ability to come to terms with life is weakly developed; and this ability is not only a personal characteristic, but can characterise people living in a specific society. Thus, it is a strong critique of Western societies that this ability seems to be rather poor, because the level of expectations has been raised to such heights.

THEMES IN THE DISCUSSION OF THE QUALITY OF LIFE

Means-ends Rationality

In the discussion of the quality of life, as well as many other discussions, our thinking is confined by customary conceptions. One of the most constraining conceptions seems to be that we often think in a means-ends rationality. Preferably, one ultimate end is identified and this end is achieved through a process by some ultimate means. It is a conception from a production process where an output is produced by the use of some input. In some cases, the end can be divided into several intermediate ends, and the process can contain several steps where some means are means to other means in a chain. Of course, we all know that things are more complicated, for instance, work will often be considered to be both a means and an end in itself. Nevertheless, much effort is aimed at fitting the understanding of social processes into this scheme of thought. Usually, these efforts are motivated by the necessity to make priorities, and this requires distinguishing means from ends.

An example of such efforts is the attempt to develop welfare indicators by adjusting GDP. In a Danish project of this kind (Zeuthen and Jensen, 1995), the intentions and the limitations of the exercise have been stated very clearly. The intention was to examine the change in real consumption over a period of twenty years by developing a so-called material indicator of welfare. It was emphasised that this indicator could not say anything about how good we feel or how much we profit from consumption. It can only shed light on the changes in material consumption, but not on whether these changes made us happier. Welfare is subjective, and it is very difficult to assess individual welfare and even more difficult to assess the welfare of the population as a whole, the report states. The project thus intends to analyse the economic activities that are the foundation of welfare and not welfare itself. It was also made perfectly clear that the project did not intend to assess sustainability; it was not a 'greening of GDP' exercise, so environmental effects were only included in so far as they had consequences for present consumption possibilities.

Even though the limitations of the project are emphasised, I find it rather problematic. The rationale of the project must obviously be that there is a clear positive correlation between material consumption and welfare – otherwise the exercise would be meaningless. But exactly the same economic activities that are the basis of increasing consumption simultaneously have many other effects that are important for other dimensions of welfare: the nature of labour processes, social networks, distribution nationally and internationally, social cohesion, risks, health, expectations regarding future environmental problems, and so on. These effects are co-produced with increasing consumption. The project does not analyse the economic activities behind consumption, but rather chooses only one aspect from which to look at some activities that have a wide range of welfare effects. Stating that consumption is the ultimate aim of economic activities motivates the perspective. However, it cannot be concluded from this statement that consumption is the most important aspect of welfare. Of course, some consumption is a precondition for life, but it is not obvious that more consumption is very important for welfare when a high level has been reached. This has to be assumed if a welfare indicator based on consumption is to be meaningful. Unfortunately, the construction of such an indicator tends to become a self-fulfilling prophecy, because it contributes to the focus on consumption as promoting welfare, while all the other dimensions are ignored.

The project illustrates how difficult it is to carry through means-ends rationality, even when the end is so narrowly defined. It is acknowledged that it is difficult to distinguish between what should be considered as costs and what should be considered as really contributing to welfare. Parts of the final consumption in GDP are really inputs to production as they are intended to maintain, for instance, the quality of the workforce. Thus a part of the investments in education as well as some health services are subtracted from consumption. It could be argued that this logic could apply to food as well: would it not be a logical consequence to subtract the calories necessary to maintain the workforce and let only the rest of the food be welfare-improving? Especially when it is noted that the time used for eating is not leisure time. Another example of the difficulties with sticking to the logic is the handling of leisure. Leisure is treated as a good to be consumed, given an attributed value and included in the indicator. But what is the logic of including leisure in an indicator measuring material possibilities of consumption, when so many other dimensions of welfare are left out? It seems to be so logical to regard economic activities in a means-ends perspective, but the strategy is permeated with dead ends and absurdities.

What is the alternative then? Economic activities are intertwined with the totality of social structures and processes, so they are 'responsible' for much more than the goods and services for consumption. Inseparable social processes generate simultaneously the nature of labour processes, social networks, the relationship with nature, distribution, the degree of freedom and democracy, participation, and so on. Instead of regarding social processes as chains linking ends with means, they could be seen as a complex whole, which can be assessed from the perspective of different rationales. Do these complex processes provide us with appropriate material means for living? Do they result in satisfying labour processes, social cohesion or ecological sustainability? The suggestion is not to introduce a kind of multi-criteria analysis, although this would obviously be much better than the traditional narrow focus on consumption. Multi-criteria analysis would still stick to the means-ends rationality and to the idea of optimisation, while the suggestion here is to accept that means and ends are intertwined. The different rationales, from which the social processes can be assessed, cross over each other, and there is no easy way of balancing them against each other.

Quality of Life as a Quantity

When a process is regarded in a means-ends perspective, it is natural to aim at the best possible achievement of the end, maximisation or optimisation. The ultimate goal is typically conceived as either welfare or a high quality of life, and the various intermediate ends are seen as contributing to the ultimate one. The quality of life can only be maximised if it can somehow be conceived as a quantity, of which we can have more or less. The idea must necessarily include some form of unit or common denominator, but it is not necessary to assume that the quantity of life-quality can be measured in practice.

In simple hedonistic theory it is assumed that all experiences have a common denominator in the sense that they give rise to more or less pleasure or more or less pain. Thus pleasure/pain is the common quality that theoretically can be measured in units. It has rightly been criticised as a false psychological assumption that all experiences have such a direct common quality. As an alternative it has been suggested that what all experiences have in common is that they are related to our desires. The more a person gets the things or experiences that she/he prefers or desires, the better off is the person. According to this theory it is not a quality inherent in the experience that determines its contribution to the quality of life, but rather the degree to which this experience was desired or preferred by the person in question. The common denominator is thus desire-fulfilment, and the quality of life increases the more of all one's desires that are fulfilled and the higher the degree to which they are fulfilled. The idea seems to be that a person has a vector of desires and that the quality of life is the (weighed) sum of the degrees of desire-fulfilment. It seems to me to be an unsuccessful device to substitute desire-fulfilment for simple hedonism. It is just as much an absurd postulate that all experiences have in common that they are more or less desired or preferred. Many of our experiences are related to habits and routines, and many experiences occur without a preceding desire or fear. The theory has to assume a kind of unconscious mapping of desires so that all habitual or unexpected experiences can be assessed according to their degree of desire-fulfilment. But when we introduce such a strange construction to get the assessment, how can desire-fulfilment then be the common denominator for the quality of life? Another objection is that sometimes an event can make everything else unimportant: if my child is hurt in a traffic accident, it would not make me at all happy to win a fortune in the lottery. It has been suggested (Parfit, 1984, p. 498) that the summation theories of desire-fulfilment could be replaced by a global version of the theory in the sense that the desires should regard life as a whole or the whole life. The question is, however, whether it is then meaningful to talk about desires or preferences. It would be very difficult to specify desires and to assess whether they were fulfilled. The quality of a person's life is a complex whole with many interdependencies among the different constituents, so it cannot reasonably be conceived in terms of desire-fulfilment or any other common denominator. This means that the quality of life cannot be conceived as a quantity that can be maximised. However, we do not have to give up completely a discussion about whether we are better or worse off in different situations. Instead of framing the assessment in a quantitative perspective, the quality of life can be discussed in terms of states (or situations). Some states are attractive, while others are very unpleasant, but the states cannot be compared with each other on a scale; they are discrete situations.

Basic Conditions for an Individual Person

Usually, the debate about the quality of life relates to the individual level. This perspective dates from the Renaissance, where the idea of the individual as an independent entity took root. In another cultural context it would not make sense to separate the individual from society and to look at the quality of life only from the perspective of the individual. The culturally specific perspective is taken as the point of departure here, while a later section discusses how to reintegrate individual and collective perspectives. Much of the debate about the quality of life in economics relates to developing countries and concerns basic human needs, etc. (Sen, 1987; Max-Neef, 1992 a, b; Doyal and Gough, 1991; Gasper, 1993). These discussions have been sources of inspiration, even though the context here is different.

Basically, a good life for the individual requires the fulfilment of two conditions. First, it must be possible to live, that is, to get the necessary calories and protection. Second, the willingness to live is just as crucial; a life must have a meaning. In different terms the conditions can be expressed as good physical and mental health. However, this formulation implies that it is possible to specify what it means to be physically and mentally healthy and what the opposite means, that is, when are our minds distorted or frustrated? This problem is evaded here by focusing on conditions, but, of course, this is a device. Basically, it makes sense to use the concept of health, but I do not define it. While it is obvious that food, drink and some kind of shelter or protection against the weather are fundamental for a good life, it is less obvious how meaning in life is established. Partly, it depends on the life story of the individual, because mental health depends on having had the basic material and emotional needs reasonably fulfilled as a baby. Partly, it depends on the present situation of the individual, which has at least three aspects. First, meaning in life depends on having close emotional relationships with others. Second, it is vital to have social functions, to do things that are important to others. Third, a good life depends on having some security regarding the future, that is, that it can reasonably be expected that the person will have a full life. Expressed visually, a person, to have a good life, must stand on a platform that rests on various pillars: food/drink/protection, social functions, emotional relationships and security. If one of the pillars breaks down, the quality of life is seriously threatened, for example, if a person loses a close personal relationship, gets a serious disease, loses her/his job, or if some kind of external threat (social disorder, war, environmental disruption) comes close.

This account of the basic pillars of the platform is culturally specific in the sense that it takes an individual perspective, but it captures some conditions that are essentially human across time and culture. One more condition could be included, if the account can be a little more culturally specific. This can be called autonomy, as Doyal and Gough (1991) suggest, or freedom, in the terms of Max-Neef (1992a, b). Max-Neef argues that fundamental human needs change with the rate of evolution, that is, very slowly. Freedom arose as a need late in human history, but it has penetrated most cultures and can now be considered a universal human need. Autonomy or freedom relates to the discussion of human rights, which is a specific social construction of Western societies. To avoid the risk of 'over-reach' (Gasper, 1993), the condition freedom or autonomy is here conceived in very general and vague terms as freedom from outright oppression and as having influence on one's own living conditions.

The discussion of basic needs takes us part of the way in finding points of reference for discussing the quality of life. It is important in the perspective of distribution, as it emphasises some necessary conditions for having a good life –

a good life is not just a matter of individual preferences. The ethical obligation emanates from the idea that we all have legitimate claims, so the concept of needs is important to go beyond the neoclassical concept of preferences.

Dualities of Needs

Even though the concept of basic needs takes us part of the way, it does not take us far enough in the discussion of points of reference for assessing the quality of life. The concept of needs easily leads to a focus that is too narrow, as needs are often conceived in a narrow sense, modelled on the need for food. The need expresses itself as a growing sense of hunger that can be satisfied with food for a while and then builds up again. Some of the conditions for a good life do not resemble this kind of need very much. Max-Neef chooses to use the concept of need, but he gives the term a very broad interpretation. He emphasises that needs have a double character as both deprivation – which is the dominant perspective in traditional economic theory – and potential, resources for change. Human beings do not only want to be passive receivers of satisfaction – they also get satisfaction by being the active organisers of the process. A related interpretation is suggested by Scitovsky who distinguishes between two different forms of satisfaction (Gasper, 1993). One relates to the achievement of an optimal level of arousal and can be called 'comfort.' The other form has to do with change and variation or challenges, where the satisfaction is derived from 'stimulation.' The search for comfort can entail stimulation, and if a person just gets comfort immediately, without having to do anything, it can cause frustration because of the lack of stimulation.

The mental aspect of a good life often makes it clear that the traditional concept of needs is too narrow. In many cases we need both sides of a duality, as can be seen from the examples in Figure 15.2 (inspired by Christensen and Nørgård, 1976).

We need both

To be alone	To be together with others
To be different from others	To belong to a group
To decide for oneself	To have social role
Freedom	Responsibility
To be well-balanced	To be appreciated
Excitement, challenges	Security, safety
Experiences	Contemplation
Activity	Rest

Figure 15.2. Dualities of needs.

The dualities also illustrate the dynamic potential related to needs. In Western societies social changes have resulted in a strong emphasis upon the left side of the list: we have good possibilities to fulfil our needs for individualisation, freedom, adventure and so on, while the needs on the right in practice get a lower priority. As social values co-develop with social changes, we also emphasise individual freedom and independence as very important values. Nevertheless, the other part of the dualities, the right side of the list, reveals itself in a widespread feeling that something is missing: affection, community, and contemplation. Ambivalence thus characterises our assessment of society and the quality of life. Empirical evidence of such ambivalence can be found, as in the Harwood report (1995) where the values of Americans are studied. The Harwood Group notes that ambivalence can help to explain the paralysis of action, because initiatives to improve the quality of life relating to family, responsibility and community can entail costs relating to individual freedom – and this is a value with a very high priority. However, people still have some values which they do not follow in practice, and this implies a potential for changes. A deeper discussion of the psychological aspects of a good life related to the environmental debate can be found in Læssøe (1997).

Ambivalence also illustrates the fact that a good life will never be a life without problems. A good life is not something absolute, static and exclusively good. It is impossible to feel good all the time, so it is important to be able to cope with adversity. However, it still makes sense to discuss whether the conditions for a good life can be reasonably fulfilled.

A Good Life in the Perspective of the Collective

Debates on the quality of life are usually framed in terms of the individual. The perspective is built into the concepts, as only individuals can feel that their lives have quality, and as needs can only be ascribed to individuals. Even when needs are conceived very broadly, the focus is still on elucidating what will make the individual feel good. At the time of Aristotle, the discussion of the constitution of a good life was framed differently, as virtues were at the centre. The present trend towards an Aristotelian revival is promising for a broader perspective on the quality of life.

Basically, human beings are social; apart from rare exceptions, we live our lives in collectives. Therefore, a good life has to be conceptualised in a way that encompasses a good society. The intention is to replace methodological individualism at the normative level with a broader alternative. This corresponds to what I tend to do at the analytical level: explaining social phenomena I not only refer to individual behaviour, but also to the social and cultural motivations and indirect influences underlying this behaviour (Røpke, 1998). The broader framework for a normative assessment of the quality of life is illustrated in Figure 15.3.

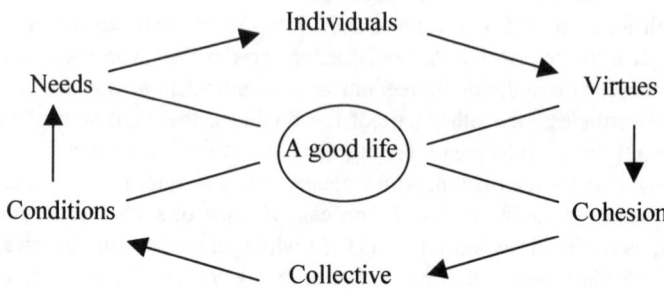

Figure 15.3. A framework for assessment of the quality of life.

The framework differs in two respects from the traditional way of conceiving a high quality of life in economics. First, the individual is not only seen as a being with needs, but simultaneously as an ethical being. Second, society is not only seen as an instrument providing goods for individuals, but simultaneously as being an end in itself. The individual and the collective levels are thus seen in an analogous way, as they are both conceptualised as having a double character.

Take first the conceptualisation of human beings. In mainstream economics the individual is conceived only as a being with needs, and the acts of taking care of others are interpreted as the fulfilment of a special kind of need. It is a need alongside other needs to do something good, for example, because it is satisfying to get acknowledgement from others and to keep up one's own self-esteem. No doubt, such psychological interpretations of human behaviour are relevant, but it is too constricting to reduce altruistic acts to acts fundamentally motivated by selfishness – that we do something good, because we feel better doing so. Rather I would adhere to the opinion that ethics is concerned with acts that are basically motivated outside us. Human beings have an ethical instinct that can be awakened, an ability to understand that something must be taken care of and a willingness to take responsibility also beyond their own interest.

Ethical behaviour primarily emanates from perception: when we perceive the child with all our senses, we feel the urge to take care of it, even if we have to set ourselves aside. It is not a rational calculation that awakens our ethical instinct. However, ethics is not bound to the close relationships, the direct meeting with the neighbour. In modern societies, our behaviour has effects far away from ourselves. We have to combine our ethical instinct with knowledge about the relationships to argue, for instance, we ought to pay much higher prices for the goods we buy from developing countries. Ethical behaviour or, in other words, the virtues of human beings, which arise between individuals in social life, are important for the proper functioning of the collective. However, even though the collective depends upon the virtues, these are not motivated by the collective necessity. The virtues can be rationalised subsequently in the discourse on the common good, but the rational discussion is not the source of the virtues. What then can be said about the virtues? They are socially constructed, just as needs are, but analogous to the discussion of needs it can be argued that a core of virtues holds true across time and culture. Nussbaum (1993) explains how Aristotle tried to deduce this core from the so-called grounding experiences of human beings. I find this attempt very interesting, but as in the case of needs it is difficult to judge whether the result is well defined and exhaustive. The discussion about the specification of the virtues is beyond the scope of this chapter.

Because of the dominance of the individual perspective in the discussion of the quality of life, it seems natural to introduce the collective level by first discussing the idea that it provides conditions for individuals. What conditions should be provided to contribute to a good life? The traditional focus on consumption as something that increases welfare points to economic growth as an important condition. This focus has been questioned by economists such as Fred Hirsch (1976), who emphasises that we will not necessarily become more satisfied by an increase in consumption, because the transformation from micro to macro has counter-productive aspects – there is an 'adding-up' problem. The individual will be better off with increased consumption, and in affluent societies this is particularly the case if the consumer can get ahead of others, because much satisfaction is derived from being better off relative to others. However, if everybody increases consumption proportionately, nobody gains by the higher level of consumption. This result is further aggravated, if the more widespread use of a good entails congestion that reduces the utility of the good: the individual profits from getting a car, until everybody has a car and nobody moves. Therefore, even if it is accepted that individuals in affluent societies are better off with increasing consumption, society does not necessarily provide the best conditions for individual welfare by increasing the level of consumption. By the way, if we are, in fact, as single-minded about our relative position as the theories on relative needs suggest, we have an interesting case of the social construction of needs that cannot be satisfied within the society that has formed them.

The comments above concern goods that are consumed individually, but where the related pleasure is dependent on the consumption of others. Another part of the conditions provided by the collective concerns the more general conditions of life. Relating to the pillars of the platform for the individual quality of life, good social conditions include:

- the existence of a well-functioning social order (even if some people obviously profit from social disorder, as is being demonstrated in Russia at present),
- a social structure that does not expel anyone,
- a social life that promotes the establishment of close human relations,
- the absence of serious social tensions, and
- the absence of environmental hazards.

These conditions are concerned with the present life of the members of society. In Figure 15.3, another perspective on the collective level is introduced as well: the collective as an end in itself. This implies the postulate that a collective has a value over and above the value it has for its members. One argument is that the individual and the collective are fundamentally inseparable, two sides of the same coin, and therefore, their well-being cannot be separated. Another argument is that the existence of the collective is important as such; it matters whether a family, a neighbourhood, a society or a culture dies out. If for instance the 50,000 people from Greenland could be integrated without any problems in Danish society, it would still matter that the society and culture of Greenlanders will die out. This means that a good life must also include criteria relating to the collective level as such. Sustainability is an example of a criterion that only makes sense at the collective level, because it relates to the future, extending beyond the life of now living individuals. However, the criteria will typically have much in common with the criteria regarding the provision of good conditions – only the perspective is different. The life of society depends on social cohesion, the absence of serious social tensions, an economy that does not abuse its natural environment, and a political system that does not create serious conflicts with other societies.

CONCLUSION

The point of departure here is the traditional idea of consumption as a very important determinant of welfare. What can be said about this idea on the basis of the different themes outlined above? The main conclusion is that the idea does not make much sense because it is based on a much too simplistic notion of a good life. The discussion can be summarised as follows:

- Social processes cannot be conceptualised in a means-ends perspective. When we discuss the quality of life in a specific society, numerous criteria can and should be applied. No one measure can be used.
- Therefore, it is not possible to talk about the quality of life in terms of quantity. Even if a person's situation improves for one criterion, he is not

necessarily better off, because the appreciation depends on his situation in other respects. One can be sad, even if much is good – as well as the opposite. There are so many ways to feel that they cannot be compared on a scale.

- It makes good sense to say that some fundamental conditions have to be fulfilled to make sure that most individuals in a society can have a good life. The discussion of basic needs singles out food/drink/protection, social functions, emotional relationships, security and autonomy. But fulfilling the basic needs is only a foundation, a point of departure, as they are necessary but not sufficient conditions.
- The discussion of basic needs does not take us far enough. A further step can be taken by realising the dual character of many needs. This opens up a deeper discussion of life patterns. Again the complexity of a good life is emphasised, as well as the unreasonable simplification expressed in the idea of the importance of consumption for welfare.
- Finally, a good life has a collective dimension that is grossly underestimated in the traditional conception of welfare. One aspect of this dimension is that a good life for the individual also includes ethical behaviour that cannot be reduced to utility. Another aspect emphasises that the collective is crucial both for the conditions of the lives of individuals and, simultaneously has an intrinsic value which also constitutes a good life.

The discussion of the quality of life is very complex and it is a very dubious idea that welfare increases with increasing consumption. However, neither does it make sense to say the opposite – that welfare is reduced with increasing consumption. In discussions of the quality of life, consumption is often seen as a separate source of welfare separated from other qualities in life such as family life, friendships, to have a good job, and so on. This way of separating consumption from other qualities is typically related to the statement that many other things in life are more important than consumption. This sounds reasonable, but again it is far too simplistic. The problem with this reasoning is that consumption is completely integrated with all the activities of everyday life – it is not a separate activity that can be placed beside a number of other activities. Caring for the family, meeting friends, having experiences and so on, all imply consumption. The relationship between consumption and welfare thus has to be conceptualised in a different way. Instead of asking whether consumption increases welfare inside the framework of a given society, it should rather be asked whether life is good inside the framework of a society where growth in material consumption is part of the 'package.' Consequently, it is society as such that has to be discussed, when the question of consumption and welfare is raised.

This discussion would take us too far away from the framework of this chapter, but a few suggestions can be made to illustrate how the question of the quality of life in a society like the Danish one could be dealt with, using the themes as points of reference. Obviously, much is good for many people in this society:

- the favourable economic conditions,
- the great scope for the individual,
- the freedom to think and speak,
- the relatively good conditions of health,
- the fact that more people than ever have the experience of forming couples and having children,
- the social safety net,
- the stability of the social order.

Thus it is very understandable that most people express a high degree of satisfying their needs if they are asked for their views, as demonstrated by different studies. However, the discussion of the themes can point to reasons for a more critical assessment:

- The risk of being affected as an individual by the inconveniences and elements of danger that are characteristic of this type of society: partly the widespread inconveniences like noise and the common health problems, partly the more seldom, but still relatively frequent, lifestyle diseases and traffic accidents.
- The more long-term risks related to, for instance, the chemical universe we live in, to the greenhouse effect and to other serious environmental problems.
- The risk of not being able to keep up with the pace of society and the demands for education and normality, with the effect that one is marginalised as a social loser, isolated and lonely.
- The widespread costs of the rapid tempo of life, the individualisation and the level of ambitions in the form of stress and difficult conditions for family life.
- The undermining of communities based on necessity and, consequently, a weakening of the basis for solidarity and ethically motivated behaviour. The undermining of democracy and the related expectations that it is possible to change something by joint efforts. The very limited time used for serving the common good.
- The ethical problems related to achieving goods and benefits at the expense of others and at the expense of animal welfare.

As these points suggest, the present way of life also has serious flaws from a welfare point of view. The basic mechanisms that provide us with great possibilities for consumption in relation to our everyday life activities are, at the same time, the mechanisms that give rise to the central problems. Therefore, it might turn out to have a positive impact on the quality of life, if the environmental challenge prompts us to take steps towards reduction of consumption, at least in a long-term perspective when social changes and changes in norms and values have made their mark.

REFERENCES

Biesiot, W. and Moll, H.C. (eds.) 1995. 'Reduction of CO$_2$ Emissions by Lifestyle Changes.' Groningen-Utrecht: Center for Energy and Environmental Studies IVEM.

Christensen, P. 1995. 'Impact of Different Lifestyles on the Environment.' Paper for the International Sustainable Development Research Conference, Manchester, March 27–28.

Christensen, B.L. and Nørgård, J.S. 1976. 'Social Values and the Limits to Growth.' *Technological Forecasting and Social Change* 9, 411–423.

Claxton, G. 1994. 'Involuntary Simplicity: Changing Dysfunctional Habits of Consumption.' *Environmental Values* 3, 71–78.

Deurzen-Smith, E. van 1995. *Eksistentiel Samtale og Terapi.* Copenhagen: Hans Reitzels Forlag.

Doyal, L. and Gough, I. 1991. *A Theory of Human Need.* London: Macmillan.

Gasper, D. 1993. 'Re-theorizing Human Needs.' Paper for the 1993 Conference of the European Association for Evolutionary Political Economy, Barcelona, October 28–30.

Harwood Group, The 1995. *Yearning for Balance.* Maryland: Bethesda.

Hirsch, F. 1976. *Social Limits to Growth.* Cambridge: Harvard University Press.

Jacobs, M. 1996. 'Environmental Valuation, Deliberative Democracy and Public Decision-making Institutions.' In Foster, J. (ed.) *Valuing nature.* London: Routledge.

Keat, R. 1994. 'Citizens, Consumers and the Environment: Reflections on 'The Economy of the Earth'.' *Environmental Values* 2, 333–349.

Læssøe, J. 1997. 'Quality of Life as an Eco-political Argument – A few Psychological Reflections.' Paper for the workshop: Consumption, Everyday Life and Sustainability, Lancaster April 6–8.

Max-Neef, M. 1992a. *Human Scale Development: Conceptions, Applications and Further Reflections.* London: Zed Books.

Max-Neef, M. 1992b. 'Development and Human Needs.' In Ekins, P. and Max-Neef, M. (eds.) *Real-life Economics. Understanding Wealth Creation.*

London: Routledge.

Nussbaum, M.C. 1993. 'Non-Relative Virtues: An Aristotelian Approach.' In Nussbaum, M.C. and Sen, A. (eds.) *The Quality of Life*. Oxford: Oxford University Press.

Parfit, D. 1984. *Reasons and Persons*. Oxford: Oxford University Press.

Røpke, I. 1997. 'The Dynamics of Consumption Growth.' Paper for a workshop on consumption, Lancaster, April 4–5.

Røpke, I. 1998. 'Sustainability and Structural Change.' In Faucheux, S., O'Connor, M. and van der Straaten, J. (eds.) *Sustainable Development: Concepts, Rationalities and Strategies*. Dordrecht: Kluwer.

Sandøe, P. (ed.) 1992. *Livskvalitet og Etisk Prioritering*. Copenhagen: Nyt Nordisk Forlag.

Sen, A. 1987. *The Standard of Living*. Cambridge: Cambridge University Press.

Sumner, L.W. 1992. 'Two Theories of the Good.' In Frankel Paul, E., Miller, F.D. and Paul, J. (eds.) *The Good Life and the Human Good*. Cambridge: Cambridge University Press.

Zeuthen, H.E. and Jensen, B. 1995. *Hvad fik vi ud af den økonomiske vækst? Forbrugsudviklingen i miljøpolitisk belysning*. Copenhagen: Spektrum.

16. Sustainable Consumption: A Research Agenda

Friedrich Hinterberger, Aldo Femia, Maria-Elisabeth Fischer, Fred Luks and Nese Yavuz

INTRODUCTION: KEY QUESTIONS OF SUSTAINABLE CONSUMPTION

Today's environmental pressure is largely the result of our patterns of consumption (in terms of structure, quality and amount), which along with other factors determine the intensity of exploitation of natural resources. On the other hand consumption is a potential driving force in a process of transformation of the industrialised economies towards sustainability. These two observations show the importance of a sustainable pattern of consumption in the context of sustainable development. From this follows the need for more research in this area. One should keep in mind, however, that if the production sector manages to increase resource productivity while consumption demand still rises, then any efficiency strategy to reduce the anthropogenic environmental impact potential must be accompanied by a complementary strategy to ensure that the necessary efficiency gains are not 'eaten up' by increasing consumption (Sachs, 1993; Spangenberg, 1995).

The report of the Oslo Ministerial Roundtable uses the following working definition of sustainable consumption (SC): "the use of goods and services that respond to basic needs and bring a better quality of life, while minimizing the use of natural resources, toxic materials and emissions of waste and pollutants over the life cycle, so as not to jeopardize the needs of the future generations" and states that SC is an "umbrella term that brings together a number of key issues, such as meeting needs, enhancing the quality of life, improving resource efficiency, increasing the use of renewable energy resources, minimizing waste, taking life cycle perspective and taking into account the equity dimension." (Miljøverndepartementet Norway, 1995) In this paper we will specify the concept of SC. We understand consumption as the end-use of products and services by households.

Environmentally aware consumer behaviour may influence other determinants of the pressure exerted on the environment such as the choice of production techniques. As of today, however, consumers lack relevant information in order to decide how to behave in an environmentally friendly way, for instance when choosing between different products (Schmidt-Bleek, 1994; Hinterberger *et al.*, 1996).

In fact, the issue of sustainable consumption patterns is not new. Governments, companies and NGOs have indeed focused their strategic goals on this crucial element of the broader sustainable development agenda. The North–South tensions that marked the negotiations of Agenda 21, chapter 4, on 'Changing Consumption Patterns' have given way to a more pragmatic debate. The OECD governments and many companies now recognise that changes of consumption patterns towards a sustainable lifestyle can be induced without reducing competitiveness and economic welfare. Nevertheless, there are many open questions which have to be dealt with in a satisfactory way.

Three types of questions have to be answered in the context of sustainable consumption: positive, normative, and policy oriented.

1.   Positive: a comprehensive description of the consumption-environment relationship as of today (how unsustainable is consumption today?)
2.   Normative: what is sustainable consumption as a general goal?
3.   Policy-oriented: how do we achieve SC? Which instruments are best suited?

To answer these three questions we need information about the underlying models of consumers' behaviour as well as of the consumption – environment interaction (societal metabolism). Societal, economic, political, and geographical dimensions need to be specified. Another differentiation can be made according to the quantity and qualities of basic consumption.

Up to now we had only a very broad definition of SC. For the normative aspects of the discussion it is important to develop a more concrete definition. This definition can be derived from the factor 10 concept (Factor 10 Club, 1994). This means that a per capita reduction of the life cycle wide material flows by factor 10 is seen as necessary in the industrialised countries. The reduction is to be understood in absolute terms and implies an annual reduction of about four to five per cent over a 50-year-period. Since we are talking about industrial countries we do not need to be concerned with population growth (if, as some prognosis say, the U.S. population will double until the year 2050, the need for change would be even higher). We call a society's consumption pattern which yields this reduction sustainable consumption.

CONSUMER BEHAVIOUR

If policy is to be effective it is necessary to understand the underlying models of the consumption environment interaction (societal metabolism).

Approaches to describe consumer behaviour can be found in the economic, psychological, sociological, and biological literature. Consumption is an umbrella issue also from a scientific point of view: to understand consumption issues, economic, psychological, sociological *and* biological knowledge is important. Households decide between material and non-material goods, they buy products produced in the economic sphere, but they also produce goods in their own sphere (using again products bought outside); household members work inside and outside the household and both spheres underlie completely different principles.

Unfortunately most of the literature capturing consumption and the consumption–environment interrelation to date is mutually exclusive:

* In economics, microeconomic theory of individual behaviour deals mainly with (rational) choice in a given (and highly abstract) economic environment. Determinants considered are mainly market oriented. Reference can be made to any microeconomic text book (for example, Luckenbach, 1982, 1986; see also Yavuz, 1995).
* In psychology, authors stress behavioural aspects, such as imitative behaviour, motivation, empathy or education (see Fietkau, 1984; Kapp, 1988; Scherhorn, 1993, 1997).
* Sociological literature focuses on societal determinants such as social position, family size and composition, habits and social rules (see Aumann, 1996; Winterfeld, 1996; Scherhorn, 1993).
* Biology stresses physiological needs, inherited behaviour and reproductive traits (see Köhn, 1996).
* Consumer research and marketing studies investigate empirically and theoretically the demand behaviour of individuals and households in formal markets.
* Finally, anthropologists see the behaviour of individuals and groups as depending on their geographical and cultural environment (see from an evolutionary perspective Durham, 1991).

All this disciplinary work has not delivered sufficient answers to the key questions stated above. Nevertheless, a number of attempts have been made to transcend the boundaries of disciplinary work:

* A 'New Microeconomic Theory' attempts to integrate a broader range of factors determining demand not only for products but for functions (see, for example, Lancaster, 1971, 1991; Becker, 1982).

- Consumer economists such as Gerhard Scherhorn (1993, 1997) look at the impact of values, addiction and institutional regimes.
- Studies such as 'Sustainable Europe' (see Spangenberg, 1995), and 'Greening the North' (see Sachs *et al.*, 1998) look at the development of new paradigms for consumption (in terms of well-being instead of well-having).
- Evolutionary economists look at preference formation, the mutual interdependence of preferences and market results (see Hinterberger, 1992) and the socio-biological roots of consumption patterns (see Penz, 1991).
- Structural economists (such as Duchin, 1996; Røpke, 1994a) investigate consumption in the framework of work and spend cycles.
- From a feminist economic perspective (see Ferber and Nelson, 1993) the gender-specific division of labour must be considered in this context.
- Researchers who are interested in the organisation of every day life look at non-market relations; (see, for example Biesecker, 1997; Schor, 1995a, b).
- Any study that investigates the interrelation of market-oriented and intra household activities (work, production *and* consumption; see Winterfeld, 1996; Aumann, 1996) needs to integrate economic, sociological and anthropological thought.

A model of SC integrating these interdisciplinary attempts is beyond the scope of this chapter. A combination of these approaches should help to get a more comprehensive view when evaluating consumption's impacts on the environment. Further research is needed regarding the influence of production on consumer behaviour and vice versa.

THE ENVIRONMENTAL IMPACT OF CONSUMPTION PATTERNS

A large number of factors is involved in the impact of the environment on consumers' behaviour. Furthermore, a change in the behaviour of consumers in the choice and use of products can be a driving force in the process of industrial transformation. We need a comprehensive understanding of how environmental change can be attributed to specific household/consumption activities (see Behrensmeier and Bringezu, 1995; Strassert, 1996). In this section we briefly discuss some conceptual issues of the consumer–environment relationship before we discuss the relation role of consumption in comparison with other factors. Following that, we deal with the development of indicators to measure the impact of consumption on the environment.

Direct and Indirect Impacts of Consumption

A distinction can be drawn between the *direct* and *indirect* burdens imposed by consumption on the environment:

- as far as the *direct* impact is concerned, the main component is the emissions arising from the act of consuming. Direct emissions include dissipative losses of substances and heat to water, ground and air, the direct disposal of wastes into the environment, the water flowing into ground water from irrigation of gardens and similar phenomena. In addition, the use of space and the aesthetic aspects of changes of landscape have to be taken into consideration as well. The direct intake of resources from the environment by consumers should also be considered, though they clearly constitute a minor phenomenon, as the inputs to consumption are mostly produced items: their environmental cost is only indirectly ascribable to consumption.
- as for *indirect* impacts, in principle all the inputs and outputs to the environment caused by the production processes that are necessary in order to supply the final goods and services to the consumers can be considered as an environmental cost of consumption activities. The main waste flows from households can also be considered as indirect flows since they go through further processing stages during or before disposal (preparation for land filling, incineration, separation for recycling, and so on). Indirect impacts are clearly quantitatively much more relevant than direct ones.

Consumers Are Not The Only Actors Relevant For Sustainable Consumption

The direct or indirect distinction is useful for analytical purposes, but it can only to a very limited extent be considered as the basis for a distinction between different *actors* involved in their determination:

- relating to the *direct* emissions, it must be noted that their main determinant is the 'use technology' which is built into the products or the services. Quantity and kind of emissions per unit of service depend only partly on consumers' behaviour, although correct use and appropriate servicing of owned durables can be important. Relevant actors are all those who take part in the design and development process of consumer goods and services;
- as for the *indirect* environmental burden, the same consideration applies with respect to the production technology on one side and to the 'disposal technology' on the other side. Apart from use, consumers are not directly involved in these two moments of the life cycle of products.

However, it would be incorrect to say that they do not have any role to play in the change of these technologies. Consumers can choose between different goods and/or purchase services with different input and emission efficiencies, or choose to substitute the purchase/use of goods with more eco-efficient services. An example is the alternative between private and public transport. In some cases, consumers can refrain from consuming at all.

Thus, consumers' choices crucially contribute to the determination of the overall inputs and outputs of production, use and disposal processes. However, they are not always in a position to really choose, because they do not have access either to the alternatives themselves or to the knowledge necessary in order to rank the available alternatives according to environmental efficiency. Furthermore, imagine the consumers had the possibility to rank the alternatives according to their environmental impacts: it is not clear that they will act according to this and always choose the environmentally best alternative. This relates to the structure of the preferences and income.

Clearly, some needs and wants can only be satisfied by one certain type of goods or services, and in those cases there is only a very narrow scope for substitution; but considering needs as given is not always appropriate: changes in historically determined needs did certainly play a major role in the evolution of the economy, and will continue to do so in the future – the question is how we allow environmental concern to influence this change.

Measuring the Environmental Burden of Consumption Alternatives

As stated above, in order to enable consumers to make environmentally aware purchases, they should be provided with a clear and easy-to-understand assessment of the burden imposed on the environment by their consumption choices. In order to measure the environmental impact potential of products, we must strive to establish reliable, internationally harmonisable, as well as time- and cost-efficient ecological assessment procedures for millions of presently available products on the world market. Therefore, we have to take into consideration information having to do with the input side (the resources energy, materials, and surface use), as well as with the output side (emissions, effluents, and solid waste). This means that we must trace back the effects of different consumption choices on the environment to the environment-technosphere border.

On the input side, as well as for the emissions connected to the production phase of goods and services, a 'vertical integration' of the production processes can be performed by use of input–output tables (Leontief, 1970; Victor, 1973; Duchin and Lange, 1994; Behrensmeier and Bringezu, 1995; Femia, 1996). This gives a broad idea, on a sector level, of what 'lies behind' the delivery of final products and services to households. To a certain extent, it allows decomposing the effects of changes in final demand composition from the effects of the production technology. This method is best suited for modeling and model testing, because such models are compatible with the available data.

Much more accurate, but also more limited in scope is the Life Cycle Analysis (LCA) of specific products, that is, a study of their entire story of matter flows connected to their production, use, and disposal, from the environmental cradle of the materials (and energy) to the environmental grave of the wastes. Highly sophisticated approaches of LCA depending on 10 to 100 specific environmental impacts and their harmonised evaluation will probably not be applied to the millions of products which today are offered on the market. The necessary information for this kind of assessment is substantially reduced if the analysis is restricted to all the *inputs* to the production system (with the possible integration to the direct inputs from the environment to households). With this background, material intensity analysis (MAIA), developed at the Wuppertal Institute, as a part of basic resource intensity analysis can serve as a screening tool that provides a first approximation of the order of magnitude of the environmental impact potential of goods and services. So we obtain direction-safe indicators of the global environmental disruption potential of human activities (Schmidt-Bleek, 1994; Liedtke, 1997). When we juxtapose this material intensity against the sum of the service units yielded we obtain the MIPS indicator (Material Input per Unit Service). MIPS meets the above requirements of a practicable indicator as well as the prerequisites for a screening procedure. Also, and more important, such an indicator has the advantage that it can be easily communicated to consumers.

FROM MICRO TO MACRO: DELINKING AND REBOUND EFFECTS

It is often suggested that increasing resource productivity is a sufficient goal of ecological policies. This is certainly crucial. Ultimately, however, consumption changes will be crucial for achieving sustainability, which implies the need for reducing overall consumption of 'natural capital,' not only the specific use of natural capital for a given production.

Improving the ratio between any measure of consumption and material use is necessary, but in the context of aiming at sustainable development, it cannot serve as a goal in its own right. We define delinking as the decoupling of economic growth from growth in material input. To use the terminology developed in the study 'Sustainable Europe' (Spangenberg, 1995, chapter 9): while 'relative delinking' (that is, decreasing the relation of material and resource consumption to GDP) can save time, what is needed for a sustainable development is 'absolute delinking' (that is, the goal is to reduce the absolute amount of energy consumption). As long as the material intensity of output improves without leading to an absolute reduction of material consumption, only time has been gained without reducing the anthropogenic burden on the environment.

The core question here is whether efficiency gains can contribute to an 'eternal delinking,' that is, an economy with constantly shrinking use of energy and materials with growing GNP at the same time. From a 'prudently sceptic perspective,'[1] one cannot assume this to be possible. There are at least three factors which indicate that there are limits to (the effects of) delinking. First, there are limits to the delinking since one cannot produce 'something with nothing.' Secondly, a decoupling can reduce the environmental pressure in a certain period of time (for example, a year), that is, the flow. What counts in the long run, however, is the absolute burden put on the environment, which means that the cumulative effects have to be taken into account. Thirdly, efficiency gains can be compensated by the growth of the economic product (Spangenberg, 1995, chapter 9). Hence, one cannot expect a constantly rising consumption when we reduce and finally stabilise resource use. The upshot here is that when 'absolute delinking' is the goal, technological improvements must not be 'eaten up' by growth effects.

Rebound effects can be defined in general terms as counter productive effects on the macro, meso and micro level due to adaptive behaviour on the demand side when new resource saving technologies and/or behavioural options are introduced, for, if new technological options of energy and material utilisation open up, the resulting behavioural changes can lead to a growth effect. "The increasing service component in the economy is doubtless one of the reasons why energy consumption per unit of economic output has steadily fallen but (...) this has not stopped total energy consumption from rising." (Brooks, 1990, p. 187; see also Nørgard, 1995) Therefore, in the context of the delinking-rebound-problematic, the issue of changed *behaviour* is key. In the case of energy and material use, the hope for technological improvements is in vain as long as this is not accompanied by behaviour that is potentially resource saving. Hence, sustainable consumption will be key also from this perspective.

When energy saving or dematerialisation programmes are introduced all the barriers to reaching a well-defined purpose should be identified. As new technologies determine neither the organisation of a sector (or a firm) nor the organisation of processes, there are always different opportunities for their use. This represents a source of uncertainty about the assessment of the results.

---

[1] Such a perspective assumes that "[g]iven our high level of uncertainty about this issue, it is irrational to *bank on* technology's ability to remove resource constraints. If we guess wrong then the result is disastrous − irreversible destruction of our resource base and civilization itself. We should, at least for the time being, assume that technology will *not* be able to remove resource contraints. If it does, we can be pleasantly surprised. If it does not, we are still left with a sustainable system." (Costanza *et al.*, 1991, p. 7; emphases supplied).

The freedom to use flexible technologies leads to ecological, economic and sociological side effects that modify the original resources-saving purpose. Therefore the expected effect of a measure can be influenced in a way that the degree of saving is lower (relative rebound) or that the use of energy/materials even increases in total (absolute rebound). The main obstacle for the identification and modeling of the scope for delinking and possible rebound effects comes from the uncertainty of the behaviour variables (human behaviour and especially the emergence of new demand are partly 'unforeseeable'), which always induce repercussions on economic decisions and consequently on energy saving or on dematerialisation. Here we have a large field for further research, an interdisciplinary approach to explain consumer behaviour as demanded above is needed.

Technological options will 'translate' into different behaviour, resulting in actions on the side of households and firms (and, more general, socio-economic systems) which will have, for better or worse, some ecological effect. Secondly, the behavioural aspects are, as a consequence, crucial for the effect that technology has on general patterns (how do people use their leisure time, and so on) and in the economy, namely, spending behaviour.

INSTRUMENTS FOR SUSTAINABLE CONSUMPTION

Consumption patterns cannot be changed by politicians or benevolent dictators. But a variety of instruments and measures can support activities in a society in which steps towards sustainability are being part of the individuals' norms and preferences. The underlying concept here is based on influencing the decisions that are taken along the life cycle of a particular good or service by households in order to reduce progressively the environmental damage. The aim for policy instruments is to empower and educate end-use consumers to enable them to act sustainably. Therefore effective incentives, accessible facilities, and cultural norms that reward sustainable consumption practices are needed.

A difference should be made between technical progress or efficiency improvements which occur as a 'natural by-product' of economic development on the one hand and deliberate attempts to reduce energy and material consumption on the other. In the first case, energy/materials efficiency is a means to improve overall economic performance, while in the latter (our case), it is an end in itself. Grubb (1990) points out that this difference is crucial for the macroeconomic implications of efficiency measures. Kinderman and Schumacher (1990, p. 389) state that energy conservation "is a natural consequence of technological development and economic competition among the many suppliers of goods and services to the marketplace." Even if one accepts this idea, the distinction drawn above holds: for then the goal of energy efficiency programmes is to increase efficiency even further than it would 'naturally' occur. Another difference is that improvements occurring 'naturally' do not face the problem of steering socio-economic processes (which is a central problem for environmental policy, Hinterberger *et al.*, 1996), while deliberate policy measures face this problem.

The distinction made here between consumers' behaviour on one side and its effects on the environment on the other side may prove to be useful in the choice of instruments for sustainable consumption. This does not imply that the use of an instrument will only affect one side of the problem. The correctness and transparency of information about what consumers buy is a critical issue: the growing use of ecolabels shows that selling 'ecological' products is already a good business, as the majority of consumers prefer, ceteris paribus, a product which has such a claim on the label rather than one that does not. Ecolabels are intended to bring significant environmental benefits through their positive influence on consumers' purchasing decisions. The problem is that there is no way for the consumer to tell what really is the cost to nature of what he buys. Surely, we cannot expect anyone to perform a life-cycle analysis of what he intends to buy. A simple hypothesis consists in tagging goods (and services) not just with prices but also with an indicator of their environmental efficiency, as for instance MIPS (see above).

A further environment-saving (and money-saving) option for consumers is the sharing of durable goods, such as cars, washing machines, houses and so on, or the purchase of corresponding services available on the market (for example, public transport or laundry service) rather than of goods. In this respect, both the promotion of a more favourable social and institutional environment and monetary incentives can be suited to pursue the goal of sustainable consumption. Since sustainable consumption operates in a dynamic economy it generates new product-service combinations. The qualities of these combinations largely determine the progress towards sustainable consumption (see Berndt 1998).

As for direct emissions and operation inputs of durable goods, the theme of eco-design comes into question. In this case, substantial innovation is required, and the willingness of consumers to adopt novelty is a crucial point. Since price signals remain one of the most effective incentives to industry and consumers to produce and consume more sustainably, an environmentally sound pricing is an absolute necessity in the process towards sustainable consumption. A strategy of attempting to internalise costs as far as possible must be pursued by changing the existing tax system. Economic activities must become more labour intensive and less material intensive. Governments are supposed to set an example in sustainable consumption through environmentally sound public procurement and administration. Since in democratic societies political reality is such that it is much easier to change consumption patterns instead of consumption volumes, the most pressing issue now is the extent to which necessary improvements in environmental quality can be achieved through substitution of more efficient and less polluting goods and services rather than through reductions in the volumes of goods and services consumed. Materials taxes and/or tradable materials permits (see Stewen, 1996; Lemmer, 1996) could help to direct relative consumer prices in a more sustainable direction. In the medium and long run however, the volume of consumption will have to be addressed.

The Oslo Symposium on sustainable consumption identified some of the critical themes for further action, including improving analysis and raising of public awareness, providing incentives for sustainable consumption, making the use of energy more sustainable and efficient, implementing new strategies for transportation and cities as well as accelerating the use of more efficient and cleaner technologies. Beyond this, one must not forget that the absolute reduction of the impacts on the environment is the crucial goal of sustainability. Therefore, all political actions must focus on this topic.

CONCLUSIONS: A PRELIMINARY MAP FOR A RESEARCH AGENDA ON SUSTAINABLE CONSUMPTION

A comprehensive study of the impact of consumption patterns and lifestyle on the environment and how these could be changed is still out of sight. In the following we sketch some key issues to be addressed in order to develop such a comprehensive research agenda.

In the framework of the industrial transformation research agenda, the following questions are of central importance:

- What is the material/energy consumption that can be attributed to specific consumption activities of households?
- Seeing consumption as an activity mirroring production, what is the interrelation of both – beyond mere price adaptation (the role of endogenous preferences, institutions, life-styles, marketing, and so on)?
- Based on a proper conceptual understanding of needs, welfare, motivation, and services provided by industrial activity, what are the tendencies towards dematerialisation and what are the main drivers against this tendency?
- What is the role of values, ethics, collective activities and consumer sovereignty in both consumers' decisions and policies aimed at stimulating sustainable consumption?
- How are (formal or informal) work, employment, leisure activities and (private or public) consumption interrelated (including an investigation of work-and-spend-cycles)?
- What is the role of (sustainable or unsustainable) consumption on the macro level, including an investigation of multiplier effects, the dynamics of the well created in an economy, rebound effects?

- How can economic instruments help to steer consumption towards a more sustainable development?

We will continue to analyse these questions and hope that other scientists will find it worthwhile to address the questions which are crucial for the sustainability of economic development.

REFERENCES

Aumann, R. 1996. 'Anforderungen zur Überwindung der vorhandenen geschlechtlichen Arbeitsteilung in ökologischer Perspektive.' Wuppertal: Wuppertal Institut für Klima, Umwelt, Energie. Manuskript.

Becker, G.S. 1982. *Der ökonomische Ansatz zur Erklärung menschlichen Verhaltens.* Tübingen: Mohr.

Behrensmeier, R. and Bringezu, S. 1995. 'Zur Methodik der volkswirtschaftlichen Material-Intensitäts-Analyse: Der bundesdeutsche Umweltverbrauch nach Bedarfsfeldern.' Wuppetal: *Wuppertal Papers* 46.

Berndt, A. 1998. 'Die Erhöhung der Ressourcenproduktivität durch die gemeinsame Nutzung von Gütern. Eine ökonomische Analyse.' Wuppertal: *Wuppertal Papers* 82.

Biesecker, A. 1997. 'The Market as an Instituted Realm of Social Action.' *Journal of Socio-Economics* 26, 3, 215–241.

Brooks, L.G. 1990. 'The Greenhouse Effect: The Fallacies in the Energy Efficiency Solution.' *Energy Policy* 199–201.

Costanza, R., Daly, H.E. and Bartholomew, J.A. 1991. 'Goals, Agenda, and Policy Recommendations for Ecological Economics.' In Costanza, R. (ed.) *Ecological Economics. The Science and Management of Sustainability.* New York: Columbia University Press, 1–21.

Duchin, F. 1996. *Household Lifestyles: The Social Dimension of Structural Economics.* Tokyo: United Nations University.

Duchin, F. and Lange, G.-M. 1994. *The Future of the Environment.* Oxford: Oxford University Press.

Durham, W.H. 1991. *Coevolution. Genes, Culture, and Human Diversity.* Stanford: Stanford University Press.

Factor 10 Club 1994. *Carnoules Declaration.* Wuppertal: Wuppertal Institute.

Femia, A. 1996. *Input-Output Analysis of Material Flows: an Application to the German economic system.* Ancona: University di Ancona.

Ferber, M.A. and Nelson, J.A. 1993. *Beyond Economics Man. Feminist Theory in Economics.* Chicago: Chicago University Press.

Fietkau, H.J. 1984. *Bedingungen ökologischen Handelns – Gesellschaftliche Aufgaben der Umweltpsychologie.* Weinheim: Beltz.

Gershuny, J. 1981. *Die Ökonomie der nachindustriellen Gesellschaft. Produktion und Verbrauch von Dienstleistungen.* Frankfurt a.M.: Campus.

Giarini, O. 1994. 'Notes on the Concepts of Risk Management, Service Quality, Productivity and Economic Value.' In Carraro, C., Haurie, A. and Zaccour, G. (eds.) *Environmental Management in a Transition to Market Economy. A Challenge to Governments and Business.* Paris: Éditions Technip, 105–118.

Grönemeyer, M. 1988. *Die Macht der Bedürfnisse: Reflexionen über ein Phantom.* Reinbek bei Hamburg: Rowohlt.

Grubb, H. 1990. 'Energy Efficiency and Economic Fallacies.' *Energy Policy* 783–785.

Hinterberger, F. 1992. 'From Preference Theoretic 'Paradoxes' to Market Failure?' Paper presented at the University of Firenze.

Hinterberger, F., Luks, F. and Stewen, M. 1996. *Ökologische Wirtschaftspolitik. Zwischen Ökodiktatur und Umweltkatastrophe.* Berlin: Birkhäuser.

Kapp, K.W. 1988. *Soziale Kosten der Marktwirtschaft.* Frankfurt a.M.: Fischer-Taschenbuch-Verlag.

Kinderman, E.M. and Schumacher, W.J. 1990. 'Keepin and Kats – A Comment.' *Energy Policy* 389–394.

Köhn, J. 1996. 'Thinking in Terms of System Hierarchies and Velocites. What Makes a Development Sustainable?' *Thünen-Series of Applied Economic Theory* 4, Rostock: Rostock University Press.

Lancaster, K.J. 1971. *Consumer Demand: A New Approach.* New York: Columbia University Press.

Lancaster, K.J. 1991. *Moderne Mikroökonomie.* Frankfurt a.M.: Campus.

Lemmer, A. 1996. 'Material-Input-Zertifikate als Instrument zur Reduktion des Materialverbrauchs einer Volkswirtschaft.' Wuppertal: *Wuppertal Papers* 58.

Leontief, W. 1970. 'Environmental Repercussions and the Economic Structure: An Input-output Approach.' *The Review of Economic and Statistics* 52, 3

Liedtke, C. 1997. 'Ökologische Rucksäcke von Produkten – Neue Wege in der Produktgestaltung.' UWF 1, 97.

Luckenbach, H. 1982. 'Nachfrage des Haushalts.' In Beckmann, M.J. (ed.) *Handwörterbuch der Wirtschaftswissenschaften.* Wiesbaden: Gabler, 300–314.

Luckenbach, H. 1986. *Theoretische Grundlagen der Wirtschaftspolitik.* München: Vahlen.

Miljøverndepartementet Norway 1995. *Elements for an International Work Programme on Sustainable Production and Consumption.* Conference on Sustainable Production and Consumption, February 6th–10th, 1995, Oslo.

280

Nørgard, J.S. 1995. 'Declining Efficiency in the Economy.' *Gaia* 4, 5–6, 277–281.

Offe, C. 1991. 'Selbstbeschränkung als Methode und als Resultat.' In Beck, U. (ed.) *Politik der Risikogesellschaft.* Frankfurt a.M.: Suhrkamp Taschenbuch, 225–231.

Penz, R. 1991. *Ökonomie und Soziobiologie – ein methodischer Vergleich.* Hamburg: University of Hamburg.

Røpke, I. 1994a. 'Sustainability and Structural Change.' Paper presented at the Symposium Models of Sustainable Development – Exclusive or Complementary Approaches of Sustainability? Paris, March 16th–18th 1994.

Røpke, I. 1994b. 'Technology Optimism in the Perspective of Distribution.' Paper presented at the 3rd Biennial Meeting of the International Society for Ecological Economics, San José.

Sachs, W. 1993. 'Die vier E's. Merkposten für einen maßvollen Wirtschaftsstil.' Politische Ökologie, Special, 69–72.

Sachs, W. *et al.* 1998. *Greening the North. A Post-Industrial Blueprint for Ecology and Equity.* London, New York: Zed Books.

Scherhorn, G. 1993. 'Die Notwendigkeit der Selbstbestimmung.' Politische Ökologie, Special, 6–9.

Scherhorn, G. 1997. 'Das Ganze der Güter.' Manuskript.

Schmidt-Bleek, F. 1994. *Wieviel Umwelt braucht der Mensch? MIPS-Das Maß für ökologisches Wirtschaften.* Basel: Birkhäuser.

Schor, J. 1995a. 'Can the North Stop Consumption Growth? Escaping the Cycle of Work and Spend.' In Bhaskar, V. and Glyn, A. (eds.) *The North, the South and the environment. Ecological Constraints and the global economy.* London: United Nations University Press, 68–84.

Schor, J. 1995b. 'A New Analytic Basis For: An Economic Critique of Consumer Society.' *The Newsletter of the Committee on the Political Economy of the Good Society* 5, 1; 1–15.

Spangenberg, J. 1995. *Towards Sustainable Europe. The Study.* Luton: FoE Publications.

Stewen, M. 1996. 'Eine Materialinputsteuer zur Reduzierung anthropogener Stoffströme? – Erste Überlegungen.' In Köhn, J. and Welfens, M.J. (eds.) *Neue Ansätze in der Umweltökonomie.* Marburg: Metropolis, 173–202.

Strassert, G. 1996. 'System-Metabolismus und Haushaltsproduktion-konzeptionelle Überlegungen zur physischen Umweltgesamtrechnung.' Überarbeitete Fassung eines Vortrages im Rahmen des Kolloquiums Bioökonomie und Haushaltsmetabolismus. Bonn: University of Bonn.

Winterfeld, U. von 1996. 'Zwischen Rationalisierungsdruck und ökologischem Imperativ? Zur Bedeutung eines anderen Umgangs mit Natur für die Arbeit in der Landwirtschaft.' Wuppertal: *Wuppertal Papers* 59.

Yavuz, N. 1995. 'Umweltbewußter Konsum und zukunftsfähiger Wohlstand.' Wuppertal: University of Wuppertal.

PART V

Sustainability and Political Economy

17. Politics and Economics in Relation to Environment and Development: On Participation and Responsibility in the Conceptual Framework of Economics

Peter Söderbaum

INTRODUCTION

Although environmental issues have been high on the political agenda in many countries for many years, we are still far from a situation where one can speak of a successful environmental policy. The state of the environment or the natural resource base is still deteriorating in many ways. In other areas, improvements can be reported and there are signs of changes in attitudes among citizens more generally and in some influential professional groups.

There are countries where the Rio conference in 1992 and its Agenda 21 has led to a co-operative learning process at the local and regional levels with many actor categories involved. Representatives from business, municipalities and universities refer increasingly to their social responsibility, engage in voluntary agreements or partnerships and try to improve monitoring and accounting practices to learn more about the environmental performance of their organisations. Environmental Management Systems, such as the ISO 14 000 and EMAS are increasingly applied in business and other organisations. Approaches to Environmental Impact Assessment are institutionalised in EU countries and elsewhere. In addition to making environmental impacts more visible, these approaches often contain recommendations concerning procedure, where steps can be taken to allow for an open, participatory process. Actors in the market place are becoming sensitive to the environmental implications of their decisions. Not only purchasing decisions can be changed in the direction of bringing in Green considerations but also, for instance, hiring and saving decisions. We hear about Greening of business, environmental marketing, Green labelling, and so on. In addition, education at various levels and research activities increasingly reflect a concern for the environment.

Present understanding of environmental problems raises issues of value orientations of individuals and even their life-styles. Institutional arrangements in our societies are similarly challenged. As an example, interest in the environmental performance of business as part of the mentioned EMAS approach, means that our understanding of business corporations or firms gradually changes. In addition to monetary ideas of efficiency, non-monetary efficiency indicators of various kinds are gaining ground.

Some of the above phenomena may certainly be interpreted as part of the now dominant paradigm in economics that is neoclassical economics. An increased role for Green consumerism, for instance, may be reflected in a shift (or gradual change) in demand curves. But my overall judgement is that neoclassical economics is not very helpful in understanding these phenomena. Reducing man to the role of being a consumer who maximises utility will not raise any issues about ethics and environmental responsibility. Assumptions about perfect knowledge or information are far from the reality of political debate concerning environment and development. Focusing on man as a consumer, who is endowed with perfect knowledge, tends to make participation in political processes a non-issue as part of the neoclassical perspective. Assuming that institutional arrangements are given, with firms as the almost exclusive organisational form, does not help us in attempts to perceive gradual changes in institutions and institutional arrangements. Assuming that firms maximise profits does not make environmental impacts more visible, and so on.

In this situation, the dominance of neoclassical economics as a conceptual ground for interpretation of the mentioned phenomena and for environmental policy becomes questionable, if not dangerous. A more pluralistic strategy is suggested where additional sources of knowledge are considered. Within economics there are alternative paradigms or theoretical perspectives, such as institutional economics. Social sciences, other than economics, such as sociology, political science and business management can also contribute as part of a more transdisciplinary approach. As an example, attempts have been made to reconsider economics on the basis of knowledge from sociology or social psychology by reference to 'social economics' or 'socio-economics.' In relation to environmental issues, some ecologists interact with economists as part of an 'ecological economics.'

Finally, listening to and participating in public debate about current development and environmental issues in our societies is, as I see it, of no less importance as a source of knowledge than learning from science. In fact social science knowledge should also be tested with respect to relevance in relation to the perception of problems and value orientations of various actors and stakeholders in society.

A EUROPEAN TRADITION IN ENVIRONMENTAL AND DEVELOPMENT ECONOMICS

Of the above mentioned approaches, many overlap in important respects. I will here somewhat arbitrarily refer to an 'institutional version of ecological economics' and try to elaborate it for present purposes of dealing with environmental problems and environmental policy. I will furthermore contend that there is a European version of institutionalism, which is particularly relevant when dealing with development and the environment. However, neither 'institutionalism,' nor 'ecological economics' has a clear-cut meaning. One of the ideas behind these currents is that they build on some degree of pluralism. It is also possible to find scholars in other social sciences who refer to a similar institutionalism, for instance in sociology and business administration (Powell and DiMaggio, 1991). There are even neoclassical economists, who refer to themselves as institutionalists, Oliver Williamson being an example. Williamson (1988) refers to his transaction cost approach as a 'new institutionalism.' Similarly, there are neoclassical economists who provide their usual message under the label of 'ecological economics.'

But let us now focus on the evolution of institutionalism as a competitor to neoclassical economics. Institutionalism goes back to the German Historical School in the middle of the nineteenth century with scholars such as Wilhelm Rocher, Bruno Hildebrand, Karl Knies and later Gustav Schmoller and Werner Sombart (see Gill 1967, p. 34). These economists were interested in historical patterns of events and argued that theory has to build on a richness of empirical facts, rather than on assumptions that are far from reality and chosen mainly to fit into a specific mathematical language. This German school was succeeded by the American institutionalism of Thorstein Veblen and followers. Veblen was active between 1870 and 1930. Sharing the interest of the German Historical School in patterns of events in historical time (as compared with emphasis on equilibrium in neoclassical analysis), Veblen referred to an 'evolutionary' theory and argued that economists can learn more from biology than from physics. His transdisciplinary orientation is another feature that deserves attention. In 'The Theory of the Leisure Class,' Veblen emphasised socio-psychological aspects of consumption and coined terms such as 'conspicuous consumption' and 'conspicuous leisure.' In this part, Veblen was not far from the more recent literature about 'status seekers.'

As the naming of the school suggests, a readiness to problematise institutions, power relationships and organisational issues is another characteristic of Veblen's writings and also of institutionalism. He referred to 'vested interests' and identified various conflicts of interest in society such as an emerging conflict in industrial corporations between shareholders, who were perceived as 'conservative', and engineers, who were 'innovative.' John R. Commons is a second prominent American institutionalist. He took an interest in work conditions, power relationships and the emerging labour unions. On the basis of contemporary ideas about fairness in social and economics affairs, Commons suggested a number of institutional reforms, that is, changes in formal rules that regulate relationships between interested bodies or parties.

Returning to Europe, we will add to the features of the present 'institutional version of ecological economics.' K. William Kapp was a Swiss economist at Basel University who spent part of his working life at universities in the USA (Columbia, Cornell, Wesleyan and the City University of New York). He can be described as the first 'modern' environmental economist with his pioneering book originating from 1950 'The Social Cost of Private Enterprise.'[1] In his book Kapp (1971, p. 11) pointed to the tendency in business to "shift part of the costs of production to third persons and to the community as a whole" and argued that "the original presumption against governmental intervention and the bias against planning which still pervades much of neo-classical value theory must be abandoned."

In some cases, the social costs of production are felt immediately; in other instances the ill effects of private production remains hidden for considerable periods of time, so that the injured persons do not become immediately aware of their losses. Furthermore, certain social losses affect only a limited group, whereas other losses may be felt by all members of society. Indeed, the actual damages caused by private productive activities may be distributed over so many persons that any one of them will individually sustain a relatively small loss. Although aware of the losses, the individual may not consider it worthwhile to take defensive action against the particular industrial concern responsible for his losses. In short, the term social cost refers to all those harmful consequences and damages which third persons or the community sustain as a result of the productive process, and for which private entrepreneurs are not easily held accountable. (Kapp, 1971, pp. 13f)

Kapp regarded environmental charges as a possible way of making some corrections for 'social costs' but was sceptical to ideas that non-monetary impacts can be reduced to some monetary equivalent from a societal point of

---

[1] In a later edition the title of the book was changed to 'The Social Costs of Business Enterprise', since Kapp realised that also publicly controlled organisations and activities may negatively affect the environment.

view as in neoclassical cost-benefit analysis. His ideas about decision making and environmental policy are published in a number of articles. Some of these articles are published in the books of Ullman and Preiswerk (1985) and Leipert and Steppacher (1987).

Kapp referred repeatedly to another European economist, Gunnar Myrdal. The career of the latter as an economist began in the neoclassical school. He wrote about price theory and became a prominent figure in the Stockholm School of Economics of the 1930s. While the mainstream of economists in Sweden remained neoclassical, Myrdal's transdisciplinary orientation (in the study of racial discrimination in the USA, or development in India) and his sensitivity to value issues made him declare himself an institutionalist. Transdisciplinary approaches are needed because of the impossibility of meaningfully demarcating some problems from others as being 'economic.' "In reality, there are no 'economic,' 'sociological,' or 'psychological' problems, but just problems, and they are all complex." (Myrdal, 1975, p. 142)

When speaking of a European institutionalist tradition with Kapp and Myrdal as the leading names, Myrdal's emphasis on value issues is of special interest. Myrdal argued that the idea of value neutrality is an illusion, especially for the social sciences.

Valuations are always with us. Disinterested research there has never been and can never be. Prior to answers there must be questions. There can be no view except from a viewpoint. In the questions raised and the viewpoint chosen, valuations are implied.

Our valuations determine our approaches to a problem, the definition of our concepts, the choice of models, the selection of observations, the presentation of our conclusions – in fact the whole pursuit of a study from beginning to end. .... In this context I have argued for, and in my own research from an American Dilemma onward have tried to observe, the necessity in any scientific undertaking of stating, clearly and explicitly, the value principles which are instrumental. They are needed not only for establishing relevant facts but also for drawing policy conclusions. (Myrdal, 1978, pp. 778f)

Rather than speaking about values and valuation, I will here refer to 'ideology' and 'ideological orientation.' Ideology is defined in rather broad terms and refers to 'ideas about means-ends relationships.' Douglas North (1990, p. 23) is among those who use 'ideology' in a similar broad way. Liberalism, socialism, ecologism qualify as 'ideologies' in the present sense, but also specific 'health-care ideologies,' 'environmental ideologies' and 'educational ideologies' refer to ideas about good care in connection with specific activities, and the resources or means to achieve it, that is management practices. We will furthermore argue that each individual is lead by an 'ideological orientation,' a set of motives and interests that is more or less coherent or fragmentary. This concept is part of our Political Economic Person assumptions and can be compared to the utility concept connected with neoclassical Economic Man.

According to this line of reasoning, neoclassical economics is not only science, but also ideology, and the same argument applies for any other school of thought, such as the kind of institutionalism advocated here. This means that a scholar's preference for one school of thought, as opposed to another, is as much a matter of her/his ideology and value orientation. If neoclassical economics unavoidably represents ideology, then the next question to ask is what kind of ideology or 'ideas about means and ends?' In my judgement textbooks in neoclassical microeconomics, international trade theory, and so on are based on and promote an ideology of 'market liberalism.' Neoclassical economics is very much associated with our present political economic system that is a kind of 'capitalism.' Freedom in trading commodities (goods and services), moving money capital (and real capital when locating industry or service outlets) and in searching employment anywhere are at the heart of market liberalism. With respect to responsibility, the market actor is free to act in a responsible manner in relation to the environment, or people and their cultures, but that is mainly regarded as his/her own business. The now dominant form of market liberalism (backed up by neoclassical theory) also legitimises a transfer of power in society from citizens to national and transnational corporations with limited responsibility. Even persons who have benefited significantly in money terms from this market liberalism now appear among the critics of the system. Edward Goldsmith (1997) is one, who with his analysis of how 'corporate colonialism' can be seen as a follower of previous kinds of colonialism. This discussion leads to the conclusion that a shift in dominant paradigm in economics is not merely a matter of good science. Powerful interest agglomerations outside universities may prefer a status quo with respect to paradigm, implying a continued dominance of neoclassical economics.

Focusing now on research and education in economics (and largely also business management literature), a pessimistic view holds that these activities have been carried out in a way which minimises responsibility for the scholars themselves and for other actors in society. Reference to 'objectivity' and 'value-neutrality' is the rule. Individuals are seen as maximisers of utility, whatever that means in ethical terms. The neo-classical theory of the firm legitimises a focus limited to monetary profits, and so on. The alleged value-neutrality therefore has a specific ideological and value content. In this case, science has been a rather kind business in relation to what happens outside the universities and as scholars, we tend to see ourselves as rather innocent people. Today, actors in the business community or politicians sometimes feel that they have to remind representatives of the universities of their historical role as critical examiners of what goes on in society.

In sociology and other social sciences, the issue of 'social constructivism' is increasingly discussed, and attempts to reason along these lines exist even for environmental problems (Hannigan, 1995). As I see it, social constructivism can be made an issue also in relation to research in economics. Concepts and theories in mainstream economics are perhaps not there only as a result of 'disinterested' research, but have been constructed to legitimise certain thought patterns and interests in our societies. Since current development trends become increasingly problematic according to many, one may ask whether some other micro- and macroeconomics could be 'constructed' to better serve the ideological purpose of sustainable local and national societies, and thereby also a sustainable global society.

OUTLINES OF A CONCEPTUAL FRAMEWORK FOR ENVIRONMENTAL AND OTHER POLICY

The theory of the consumer (emphasising maximisation of utility) and the theory of the firm (emphasising profit maximisation) are essential building blocks in the neoclassical approach to environmental policy. The market, understood in terms of supply and demand for commodities, is at the heart of this analysis. Manipulating the market through governmental intervention (changes in laws regulating activities that are permitted or prohibited and laws about environmental charges and taxes) is the main recipe for environmental policy. While direct intervention in the form of prohibitions is part of the formula, manipulation of the price mechanism is seen as the main instrument in influencing the behaviour of firms and consumers.[2]

Environmental charges and the tax system certainly represent powerful tools in attempts to move the economy in an environmentally more friendly direction. Some attempts in this direction have been made and there are certainly good reasons to continue on this path. As long as the main ideology among market actors and politicians is one of market liberalism, however, only minor changes in environmental charges will be accepted by powerful interest groups. A broader approach to environmental policy is therefore needed:

If our interest is in environmental and development policy, it appears 'natural' to start with a view of man as a political being. The 'Economic Man' of neoclassical economics will therefore be replaced by 'Political Economic Person' (PEP).

According to PEP assumptions, man is seen as an actor with many roles rather than exclusively that of being a consumer (and wage-earner). Each

---

[2] For a critical examination of the more common neoclassical textbooks in environmental economics, see Söderbaum, 1993.

individual is assumed to refer to a world-view and conceptual framework. Our Political Economic Person is furthermore led by a political or 'ideological orientation.'

Human beings are related to each other and since it is assumed that each individual is led by a political orientation, also relationships of a market and non-market nature have a potential ideological dimension. We will therefore refer to Political-Economic Relationships (PER). Each individual is part of many relationships and a number of individuals who share a similar ideological orientation may be linked to each other in networks. In this case one may speak of Political Economic Networks.

Actors also relate to each other in organisations. Just as the individual who relates to the organisation refers to an ideological orientation, the organisation as a collective is also interpreted as having an ideological and political dimension. In addition to Political Economic Woman/Man and Political Economic Relationships, we therefore have Political Economic Organisations (PEO). Organisations are of many different kinds from churches and universities through voluntary organisations dealing with social and environmental issues, to business corporations. Within each organisation, for instance a business corporation, reference can be made to a 'business concept,' which can be interpreted in political terms. The organisation (corporation) may articulate an 'environmental policy,' and try to implement this policy.

The mainly co-operative character of an organisation, however, does not exclude tensions between individuals as actors or stakeholders (interested parties) connected with the organisation. Reference will therefore be made to organisations as 'polycentric' units, each individual being a centre or an actor who can initiate activities or influence the agenda in relation to environmental issues. As an example, a business corporation or a university department that is changing in a Green direction will experience many kinds of inertia. Actors (employees and other stakeholders) do not change their minds at the same time and in the same way. Some tensions exist not only within individuals (often referred to as dissonance) but also between individuals in the same organisation or in different organisations and these tensions may be beneficial (as a source of creativity, for instance) or harmful in relation to a specific value standpoint.

While neoclassical economics with its liberal market ideology emphasises individualism and tends to ridicule all kinds of social considerations, man will here be seen not only as a political being, but at the same time a social being. In this context, Amitai Etzioni (1988) refers to an 'I and We Paradigm.' The existence of a strong ego in the healthy individual does not exclude a concern for others. Rather, the stronger the ego, the greater the potential to consider interests outside oneself. An individual is normally a member or part of a number of 'we-categories' from the small group (for instance a family) through larger groups such as neighbours living in a certain area and organisations to the local, regional, national and even global community. At each level, there are institutions and institutional arrangements that influence the interaction of individuals. And this interaction is not exclusively an interaction of egoists thinking in simplistic market terms, but as much an interaction of individuals who feel sympathy for each other and who reason in terms of shared interests. In his writings about 'communitarians,' Etzioni (1993) furthermore argues that, no society can exist without some bonds, shared meanings and interests. Mary Clark (1991) emphasises the social and community aspect of human life, reminds us that co-operation is also a characteristic in the world of animals and therefore questions the often repeated simplistic idea that animals as well as human beings essentially compete with each other.

While the presence of a social as well as political dimension is assumed, the social orientation as well as the ideological (political) orientation may differ considerably between individuals. Each individual is 'embedded' in a specific socio-cultural and institutional context, which together with previous socialisation, education and indoctrination processes will help us understand the individual's particular social and ideological orientation. In fact, this essay is based on a belief that education and indoctrination processes are of importance in relation to environmental and development issues. Debate about ideology and paradigms in economics is seen as being of importance in gradually influencing the social and ideological orientation of individuals.

MORE ABOUT POLITICAL ECONOMIC PERSON

Some of the features of our Political Economic Person will now be elaborated. Each individual or person can be characterised by his/her:

- roles
- relationships
- activities and
- motives/interests.

At a more integrated level, reference can be made to the person's:

- identity
- ideological orientation
- life-style.

Our person is furthermore 'embedded' in a context where different aspects can be emphasised:

- political
- socio-cultural
- institutional
- physical, man-made
- ecological.

Rather than exclusively focusing on man as a market actor, it is here emphasised that man is an actor in a much broader sense, engaged in many kinds of roles, many kinds of relationships and many activities. The individual is furthermore led by many kinds of motives or interests. In relation to environmental issues, the role as consumer is certainly important, but the same can be said about the roles as professional, parent or citizen. Similarly, there are market relationships as well as non-market relationships and market related activities as well as non-market activities. Motives and interests could also focus on other things than commodities, markets and money.

These motives, roles, relationships and activities are interrelated in various ways. All motives and interests come together in the 'ideological orientation' of the individual. 'Identity' of the individual and all activities are behind the different roles and relationships and can be summarised in an activity pattern or 'life-style' of the individual (Söderbaum, 1993). The individual furthermore interacts with her/his environment and this environment or context will facilitate certain actions, activities and patterns of behaviour, while disencouraging other activities and behaviour. There is a political aspect of this context, as well as a socio-cultural and institutional aspect. The latter refer to market and non-market rules, organisations, and power relationships. In addition a physical, man-made aspect of the context (physical infrastructure, for example, in the form of roads, telecommunications, and so on) and an ecological aspect are here suggested as being relevant to our present inquiry into environmental and development issues.

Our present model of a person allows for some complexity. The identity of an individual, his or her ideological orientation or life-style, involve tensions of various kinds. Dissonance theory, learning theories and other parts of social psychology are seen as relevant and useful in understanding behaviour. The individual strives for some degree of congruence and balance between roles, relationships, activities and interests, and may at times experience such congruence, but incongruence and tensions are equally characteristics of the human existence. Egoistic versus 'other-related' or 'community oriented' motives is an example of such possible tensions.

While neoclassicists, in their models, tend to see individuals as robot-like instant optimisers, institutionalists and many representatives of other social sciences tend to point to the important role of habits in human behaviour. The individual is largely 'locked into' specific habits of thought and specific habitual activities that together form a pattern, here referred to as a life-style. Herbert Simon's (1945) early arguments about selective perception, limited cognitive capacity and search costs are relevant here. As humans we tend to stick to familiar environments and use various rules of thumb to deal with complexity. Emphasis on habitual behaviour does not exclude the possibility of 'problemistic search' and conscious decision making. At times the individual perceives a problem and alternative courses of action. Habits are reconsidered and behaviour may change. Such decision situations can be discussed in conventional terms of maximising an objective function, subject to various constraints. However, as part of the present approach, a more holistic idea of rationality related to the ideological orientation of the individual, will be emphasised. Decision-making is seen as a 'matching' process, where the ideological orientation of specific decision-makers is related to the impact profile of specific alternatives considered. 'Pattern-recognition' is a key concept in understanding this idea of asking whether or not a specific alternative with its pattern of impacts 'fits' well into the value or ideological pattern of the decision-maker or other interested party.

THE IMPERATIVES OF DEMOCRACY

The institutional framework in a local community, nation or group of nations, such as the European Union, is subject to some change over time. To some extent these gradual (or more sudden) changes may be influenced by different actors and in this connection reference to dominant ideas about democracy might be a good idea. Democracy is very much connected with the rights of citizens to participate in public affairs and with majority voting, where the 'one man – one vote' idea applies. While being important, majority voting is not enough as a characterisation of democracy. According to a more offensive interpretation, individuals do not merely have the right to vote. They have additional rights to participate in public affairs and they are also encouraged to do so. It is furthermore believed that not only the people but also politicians and administrators will learn a lot through public debate.

In addition, there are some basic rights and freedom, which are regarded as essential to a functioning democracy. Among these rights are freedom of speech, freedom of religion, freedom to organise for political purposes, rules about public availability of information, and so on. Such rules sometimes represent a protection of minority groups and some limits to the rights of a majority in relation to various minorities are recognised.

Democracy as a concept can also be defined in relation to its opposite, dictatorship. Democracy then stands for some degree of 'pluralism' in public affairs, where many voices should be heard, while political dictatorship, as when only one political party is permitted, is a monistic governing regime. Let us once more take a look at the ideology of neoclassical economics and relate it to our previous attempt to clarify the meaning of democracy. For the mainstream economist, the neoclassical paradigm is a given, that is something which is not subject to debate. In this sense, neoclassicism represents a kind of fundamentalism or monism within science and in relation to society. There is not much 'freedom of speech' concerning these broader issues in the economics departments of most 'Western' universities and this lack of freedom tends to spread to other parts of the world.

Neoclassical economics also embraces an ideology in relation to public decision making, which has been made operational in the form of cost-benefit analysis (CBA). Neoclassical economists, as other citizens, have understood that democracy is a kind of 'meta ideology' in our societies that cannot easily be disposed of. But for them, science stands above democracy and faithfulness to the neoclassical paradigm is the first consideration. The task then becomes one of looking for a kind of democracy, which may differ a bit from normal ideas of democracy, but which has the advantage of essentially being compatible with the neoclassical paradigm. The result of this effort is a specific 'market democracy,' which is connected with the specific valuation rules of CBA. Each citizen is seen as a consumer voting with her/his purchasing power in a world of commodities. Contingent valuation methods, that is, attempts to estimate 'willingness to pay,' and other 'modern' features of CBA represent a continued deviation from original ideas about democracy in terms of one man, one vote. As we all know, also business corporations and other organisations have monetary voting power as part of the CBA idea of democracy.

The CBA philosophy represents a departure from pluralism. Applying CBA in specific areas such as transportation, energy systems or housing projects means that a specific set of valuation rules are being used. These rules of valuation aim at a specific conclusion about the 'allocative efficiency' of one option (course of action) in relation to another. Rules of valuation, which makes it possible to rank a set of options represent a specific ideology. There could be no 'value-neutral valuation.'

Concerning this subject – the ideology of CBA – some observers argue that the CBA ideology, with its emphasis on 'net-value-added' or present value as a result of a specific project is part of the GNP-growth ideology (see for instance Johansen, 1977). GNP-growth at the macro level is generally seen as an indicator of welfare, although neoclassical economists themselves admit some of the pitfalls of this view. But their attitude is somewhat divided and also involves arguments about politicians who need a one-dimensional indicator or 'common yard-stick.' And to fill this gap nothing is better than GNP in money terms.

In relation to environmental issues, the attempt to connect GNP per capita and welfare becomes particularly suspect. As part of normal neo-classical thinking, proposals have been made to construct a 'Green GNP' by subtracting certain parts of the conventional GNP and adding others. According to the present author, these efforts are futile. A wiser strategy is instead one of moving away from one-dimensional thinking to a multidimensional set of indicators. Thinking in terms of multidimensional profiles or patterns when considering impacts of individual projects or the development of the economy as a whole is a much more fruitful strategy.

It should be added here first that CBA is perhaps the weakest part of neo-classical economics and that other parts of the paradigm are less exposed to the present criticism. Secondly, at least some authors of textbooks and manuals in CBA appear to know what they are doing (Mishan, 1971).[3] Mishan was also one of the scholars behind 'A Blueprint for Survival,' a special issue of the Ecologist (1972) which appeared at the time of the United Nations conference on the Human Environment in Stockholm 1972. Especially with reference to environmental problems of an accumulating and often irreversible character, the whole idea of correct rules of valuation from a societal point of view becomes absurd (Mishan, 1980; see also Söderbaum, 1983). Science cannot dictate correct rules for resource allocation in society. Only if there is a consensus about the valuation rules of CBA in a particular society can these rules be used for decision-making purposes. In the present situation no such consensus appears to be realistic (Mishan, 1980). The best one can do is therefore to put the CBA manuals on a shelf to await some future time when such a consensus may possibly emerge.

One can therefore safely conclude that CBA is not compatible with dominant ideas about democracy in our societies. As part of CBA the analyst becomes an expert in a social engineering sense, which tends to make politics and politicians superfluous. 'Technocracy' (Fisher, 1990) and 'econocracy' (Self, 1975) are labels that have been used to warn against these threats to democracy. A more modest role of illuminating an issue, rather than claiming ability to 'solve' it, seems more appropriate for the analyst.

---

[3] In other writings, Mishan (1967) has demonstrated a concern for the emerging environmental crisis as exemplified by the book 'The Costs of Economic Growth.'

AN AGENDA FOR ENVIRONMENTAL AND DEVELOPMENT POLICY

Our emphasis on a political dimension in understanding actors, relationships and organisations leads to an agenda for environmental policy that differs in important respects from the neoclassical perspective. Issues of worldview, ideology and science can no longer be assumed to be given or excluded from analysis. 'Internalising externalities' and otherwise correcting for 'market failure' and 'government failure' represents a rather limited view. In addition, one has to account for an additional number of possible failures, such as 'failure of worldview,' 'failure of ideology,' 'failure of science,' 'failure of organisations' and more generally, 'failure of institutional arrangements.' Individuals may furthermore fail, for instance in their professional roles or in their life-styles as a whole. The present development in Sweden or the European Union with continued degradation of the environment and high levels of unemployment has to be met with an open mind. But any reference to failure or success refers to some ethical or valuation standards, and as we all know, values are a matter of judgement and ideology.

In the present chapter, I will not repeat the mistake of the neoclassical economists by claiming that I know the 'correct solutions' to specific societal problems. Correctness in the form of specific priorities is, as we have seen, not only a matter of science but also of ideology. With reference to democracy as a meta-ideology (that is an ideology that almost all citizens share), however, some broad recommendations can be made.

Studies about the evolution of world views in Western societies appear extremely important to increase our consciousness about the present situation and options for the future. Stephen Toulmin's study of 'modernism' (1990) is one example. Among other things, the role of science as part of these world-views should be discussed and illuminated. Any idea that science always contributes positively to development appears ideologically biased, to use an understatement.

It has sometimes been argued that ideology is dead and a non-issue (Fukuyama, 1989). Such statements are based on the judgement that there exists a global consensus about the superiority of market liberalism in the present form (with a minimum of government intervention for social security purposes, and so on). Considering various environmental and social problems in our societies, my judgement is that there perhaps are more reasons than before to continue ideological debate and to try to articulate ideologies that appear appropriate and fruitful for present times. Or to put it differently, the Fukuyama thesis can be seen as being socially and ideologically constructed by groups or power agglomerations, which prefer a status quo with respect to ideology.

The theoretical framework and language of neoclassical economics has for a long time played a dominant role in public discourse. In relation to other social sciences, neoclassical economists have claimed self-sufficiency, while at the same time assuming a role of 'the' social science. It seems therefore important to strengthen the role of other social sciences in relation to environmental and development issues. As an example, organisation theory and theories of organisational change as part of business administration and sociology literature have a lot to offer as a way of understanding and facilitating change towards improved environmental performance. Within economics, an increased degree of pluralism is a necessity. More recent organisations bringing together heterodox scholars as well as co-operative efforts in the International Confederation of Associations for the Reform of Economics (ICARE) are of importance, but not enough. Intervention by actors in other disciplines and from society at large seems necessary to change the present monistic situation. Since ideology is involved, departments of economics cannot claim autonomy in this respect.

To be more explicit, economics has to be reconsidered in relation to democracy. The attractiveness of CBA to economists who wish to achieve power in society and to some politicians who may prefer to hide behind one-dimensional present values is certainly understandable. But as has been shown, CBA with its ideologically specific monetary reductionism has to be abandoned since it is not compatible with dominant ideas about democracy. Multidimensional approaches which make non-monetary impacts visible and which build on a holistic idea of economics and resource management seem necessary. Environmental Impact Assessment (EIA) represents a step in the right direction. The idea of solving problems should be replaced by one of illuminating problems and conflict management (Söderbaum, 1987; Leskinen, 1994). An approach that is compatible with democracy should also open up for participation of those affected and others concerned and therefore contain procedural recommendations. Participation and public discourse is seen as a learning process for all involved and the result of this interaction process will more often than not improve the decisions taken in terms of results and acceptance or legitimacy.

Our frame of reference also suggests that policy is not something reserved uniquely for national governments. Also individuals, voluntary organisations and business corporations may refer to an environmental policy and environmental strategies. Changes in attitudes, values and behaviour may take place at the level of individuals and organisations and this can be the case also within the scope of an unchanged national environmental policy. A business corporation may choose a proactive strategy rather than a reactive one of compliance and such changes at the levels of individuals and organisations will influence the possibilities to gain acceptance for the implementation of a more stringent national environmental policy.

It may be argued, finally, that an environmental policy should influence the context of individuals and organisations in a way that facilitates environmentally friendly behaviour. In this respect the socio-cultural context may be as important as the context in terms of infrastructure (roads, telecommunications, and so on). I will here only point to one aspect of the 'institutional infrastructure' since it is often forgotten in neoclassical environmental economics. Our emphasis on democracy in the sense of democracy for citizens suggests that the tendencies of increasing the power of organisations through lobbying activities and otherwise may represent a danger. Sometimes one meets attitudes that the market is such a democratic instrument that a democracy for corporations is as good as democracy at the level of individuals. Again the market ideology is seen as being superior to other considerations. My argument here is that institutional options should be considered within individual countries, the European Union and internationally, that will reduce the power of transnational corporations and increase that of citizens. I am furthermore naive to believe that an increasing number of individuals as leaders or employees in such corporations and even a considerable part of the shareholders in many corporations will welcome such a change in power relationships. Part of the hope lies in the fact that a shareholder is not only a shareholder and a business leader not only a business leader. We are then back to our Political Economic Person assumptions, implying that individuals may be influenced by motives connected with all their roles.

ACKNOWLEDGEMENTS

The emphasis and description of a Myrdal-Kapp school of thought in environmental economics has been much influenced by the work of Markku Turtiainen and his student Anja Kiviluoto, Helsinki University, Department of Environmental Economics. Mary E. Clark has given valuable comments on an earlier draft of this essay.

REFERENCES

Clark, M.E. 1991. 'Rethinking Ecological and Economic Education: A Gestalt Shift.' In Costanza, R. (ed) *Ecological Economics. The Science and Management of Sustainability*. New York: Columbia University Press.

Ecologist, The 1972. *Blueprint for a New Economy*. London: Ecosystems Ltd.

Etzioni, A. 1988. *The Moral Dimension. Toward A New Economics.* New York: The Free Press.

Etzioni, A. 1993. *The Spirit of Community. Rights, Responsibilities and the Communitarian Agenda.* New York: Crown Publishers.

Fisher, F. 1990. *Technocracy and the Politics of Expertise.* London: Sage.

Fukuyama, F. 1989. 'The End of History?' *The National Interest* 16, 3–18.

Gill, R.T. 1967. *Foundation of Modern Economics.* New York: Englewood Cliffs.

Goldsmith, E. 1997. 'Development as Colonialism.' *The Ecologist* 27, 2, 69–76.

Hannigan, J.A. 1995. *Environmental Sociology. A Social Constructionist Perspective.* London: Routledge.

Johansen, L. 1977. 'Samfunnsökonomisk Lönnsomhet. En dröfting av begrepets bakgrunn og innhold (Efficient resource allocation with CBA. Assumptions and conceptual background).' Industriökonomisk Institutt, Report No. 1, Tanum, Oslo.

Kapp, K.W. 1971 (1950) *The Social Cost of Private Enterprise.* New York: Shocken.

Leipert, C. and Steppacher, R. (eds.) 1987. *K. William Kapp. Für eine ökologische Ökonomie. Entwürfe und ideen – Ausgewählte Aufsätze.* Frankfurt am Main: Fischer Verlag.

Leskinen, A. 1994. 'Environmental Planning as Learning: The Principles of Negotiation, Disaggregative Decision-making Method and Parallel Organization in Developing the Road Administration.' University of Helsinki, Department of Economics and Management (Environmental Economics), Publication No. 5, Helsinki.

Mishan, E.J. 1967. *The Costs of Economic Growth.* Harmondsworth: Penguin Books.

Mishan, E.J. 1971. *Cost-benefit Analysis.* London: George Allen and Unwin.

Mishan, E.J. 1980. 'How Valid are Economic Evaluations of Allocative Changes?' *Journal of Economic Issues* 14, 143–161.

Myrdal, G. 1975 (1972). *Against the Stream. Critical Essays on Economics.* New York: Random House.

Myrdal, G. 1978. 'Institutional Economics.' *Journal of Economic Issues* 12, 4, 771–783.

North, D.C. 1990. *Institutions, Institutional Change and Economic Performance. Political Economy of Institutions and Decisions.* Cambridge: Cambridge University Press.

Powell, W.W. and DiMaggio, P.J. (eds.) 1991. *The New Institutionalism in Organizational Analysis.* Chicago: Chicago University Press.

Self, P. 1975. *Econocrats and the Policy Process. The Politics and Philosophy of Cost-benefit Analysis.* London: Macmillan.

Simon, H.E. 1945. *Administrative Behavior.* New York: The Free Press.

Söderbaum, P. 1983. 'Ezra Mishan on Economic Evaluation. A Comment.' *Journal of Economic Issues* 17, 206–213.

Söderbaum, P. 1987. 'Environmental Management. A Non-Traditional Approach.' *Journal of Economic Issues* 21, 1, 139–165.

Söderbaum, P. 1993. 'Values, Markets, and Environmental Policy: An Actor-Network Approach.' *Journal of Economic Issues* 27, 2, 387–408.

Söderbaum, P. 1994. 'Actors, Ideology, Markets. Neoclassical and Institutional Perspectives on Environmental Policy.' *Ecological Economics* 10, 47–60.

Toulmin, S. 1990. *Cosmopolis. The Hidden Agenda of Modernity.* Chicago: Chicago University Press.

Ullman, J.E. and Preiswerk, R. (eds.) 1985. *The Humanization of the Social Sciences. K William Kapp.* Lanham: University Press of America.

Williamson, O.E. 1988. 'Transaction Cost Economics. The Comparative Contracting Perspective.' *Journal of Economic Behavior and Organization* 8, 617–625.

18. A Distributional Barrier to Ecological Modernisation

Frank J. Dietz and Jan van der Straaten

INTRODUCTION

Economic policies need to have a relationship with economic theory. If this were not the case, the goals, measures and results of a particular policy could not be evaluated on the basis of some coherent theoretical framework. Owing to fundamental theoretical obstacles, this relationship is weak in the case of environmental policies. In particular, it appears to be almost impossible to base the goals of environmental policies on individual preferences, as is the customary approach in mainstream economic theory. This obstacle to the development of environmental policies will be discussed briefly in section 2.

As an alternative, sustainability has been introduced as a policy goal. Although this concept was warmly welcomed by most governments, problems have arisen with respect to operationalisation. Two of these problems, that is, the flawed knowledge of the effects of human actions on ecosystems and the social dimensions of the sustainability concept, will be discussed in section 3.

If we know, or more probably, if we decide which actions are sustainable (and which of them are not!), the issue then is who may use the limited possibilities for sustainable actions, or, in other words, who may use which elements of the ecological utilisation space?[1] In environmental policies attention is focused on reducing the obvious overexploitation of nature. Getting back within the biophysical constraints, that is, reducing emissions and stopping the deterioration of nature and landscapes until sustainable levels are attained, absorbs all attention. As a result, the distribution of natural assets which could be used and applied sustainably, has been ignored so far. Usually, environmental policies lack criteria or even some reflections on the distribution of shares in the ecological utilisation space. To put it differently, attention lacks on who gets which entitlements to use the natural resources available. The ignorance of this

---

[1] For elaborations on the concept of ecological utilisation space, see Siebert (1982) and Opschoor (1987; 1995).

distributional matter has adverse effects on the effectiveness and efficiency of environmental policies, as will be illustrated in section 4 for the case of the abatement of acidification in the Netherlands. To reduce this distributional barrier to ecological modernisation, we need an institutional framework to allocate entitlements to the ecological utilisation space in a civilised way, that is, by avoiding the huge costs of social conflicts on environmental issues. In section 5, we start the search for such a framework. At first sight, the resemblance between the social question that accompanied the industrialisation of society and the current ecological question is striking. For this reason we are looking for an institutional framework to facilitate the settlement of environmental issues like the institutional framework that has developed to settle social conflicts in the area of industrial relations. A provisional conclusion is presented in section 6.

ENVIRONMENTAL POLICY GOALS IN MAINSTREAM ECONOMIC THEORY

In the literature environmental problems are traditionally described as negative externalities. Internalisation of these externalities is in line with the optimisation philosophy of mainstream economic theory. This is briefly illustrated in Figure 18.1 for the simple case in which pollution varies exclusively with production.

The emissions of an unspecified production process generate damage by environmental degradation which is assumed to rise exponentially with the amount of production (depicted as the rising linear curve for marginal environmental costs MEC). The polluting producer is only concerned with the marginal net benefits of his production (MNB), which is, also by assumption, linearly depicted in Figure 18.1. To maximise profit, the producer increases production until the level is reached at which the marginal net benefits are zero (q_0 in Figure 18.1). Regarding the damage a third party suffers from production, a decrease of production is socially desirable. Standard economic reasoning produces the socially optimal level of production q_1. Until q_1, the marginal net benefits more than outweigh the marginal environmental costs, offering socially beneficial possibilities for production increase. Beyond q_1, the marginal environmental costs are higher than the marginal net benefits, requiring a decrease of production from a social point of view. Hence, the social optimum, that is, the incorporation of adverse environmental effects into economic decisions, implies, in this case, a production decrease from q_0 to q_1 corresponding to the intersection S of the MNB-curve and the MEC-curve.

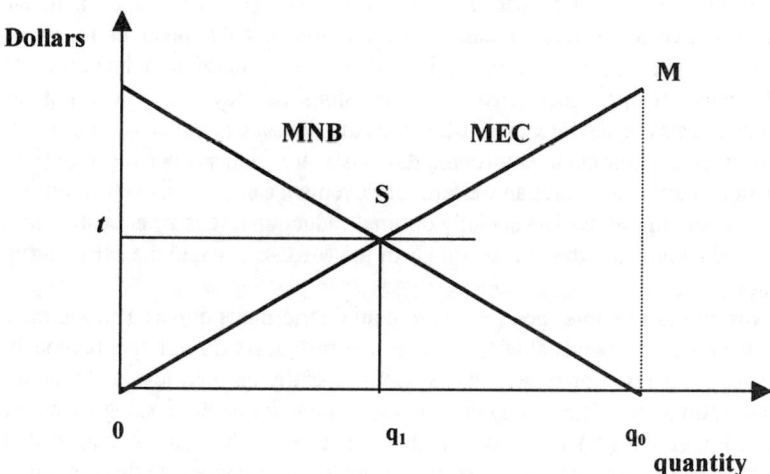

Figure 18.1. The individual and social optimum level of production.

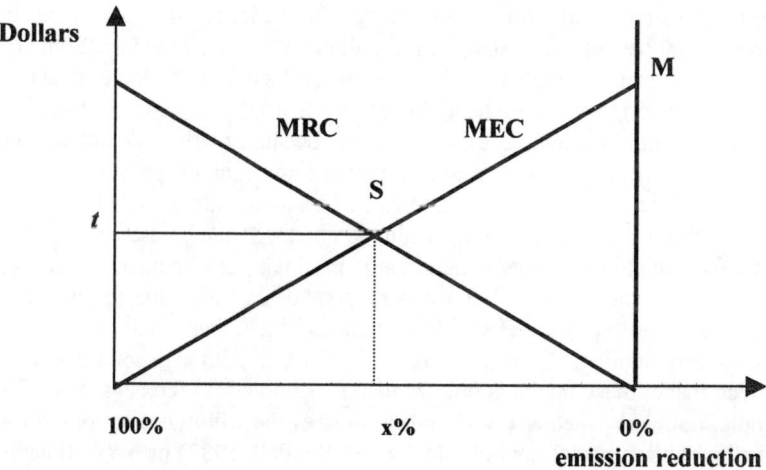

Figure 18.2. The individual and social optimum level of emission reduction.

A similar line of reasoning applies if the polluting emissions can be reduced by adapting the production process or by purifying process water or filtering waste gasses. Instead of diminishing net proceeds due to a production decrease, the producer faces extra costs for emission reduction. We assume a linear relation between the rate of emission reduction and the level of marginal reduction costs. As shown in Figure 18.2, there are no marginal reduction costs MRC when the producer leaves the emissions as they are. The marginal reduction costs are at a maximum when the emissions are completely eliminated. So long as the marginal environmental costs are higher than the marginal reduction costs, a neo-Paretian welfare improvement can be realised by a further reduction of emissions. The socially optimal reduction rate is x per cent, which is located underneath the intersection S of the MRC-curve and the MEC-curve in Figure 18.2.

This analysis enables economists to explain the status quo as a *suboptimal state* because it is reasonable to assume that producers do not spontaneously decrease production or reduce emissions to socially optimal levels. To attain Pareto-optimality a (emission) tax t is recommended or the issuing of either production quotas (q_1) or emission rights (x per cent) which are recommended to be tradable. In practice, however, it appears to be hard to locate this optimum, because the shape and position of the MNB-curve and especially the MEC-curve are hard to determine. Estimates meet with the *evaluation problem*. Problems arise especially with respect to the estimation of the damage from an increase in pollution, which is the mirror image of the benefits of a decrease in environmental damage, for example, if a polluted river is cleaned up. Some of these benefits can be derived from market prices, such as the lower costs of producing drinking water and the higher proceeds from fishing. Other benefits, however, are more difficult to estimate simply because markets do not always exist, for instance, markets for public goods like valuable ecosystems and landscapes. What is, for example, the price of a square mile of wetlands?

In the absence of markets, other evaluation methods can be used to estimate the benefits economic agents experience if particular environmental damage decreases or is avoided. In the last decades a great deal of economic research has been done on alternative evaluation methods, including 'hedonic pricing methods' and 'contingent valuation methods' (CVM).[2] Although some progress has been made, these methods only *indicate* individual preferences. It is, for example, not clear whether CVM underestimates the willingness to pay for a particular environmental quality (Hoehn and Randall, 1987) or overestimates this willingness to pay (Crocker and Shogren, 1991). In addition, the crucial problem of how to aggregate individual preferences into a collective statement on the value of specific natural resources is still very difficult to solve. Attempts

---

[2] Surveys of these methods can be found in Mäler (1985), Anderson and Bishop (1986), Cropper and Oates (1992), and Freeman (1993).

to aggregate are thwarted by the problems of the money metric measurement of utility and of interpersonal comparisons of utility. Hence, the precise shape and position of MEC-curves is often hidden. The MNB- and MRC-curves can usually be derived from marginal reduction costs curves, which seem to be less difficult to obtain empirically. However, cost observations are not always available or reliable. To put it differently, the determination of the optimal policy intervention may imply high agency costs linked with collecting and processing the necessary information and may even be impossible due to lack of information.

We conclude that using the optimisation approach as the basis for setting the goals of policy interventions is extremely difficult. Individuals have to reveal what a particular item, good or bad, is worth to them. Usually economists take these valuations as their most important source of information, but in this case, they are not available or are at best incomplete.

BARRIERS TO THE OPERATIONALISATION OF THE SUSTAINABILITY CONCEPT

Due to the difficulties with deducing environmental policy goals on the basis of the optimisation approach, policy-makers in most Western-European countries welcomed the concept of sustainable development (World Commission on Environment and Development, 1987) as an alternative basis for establishing environmental policy goals. For instance, in its *1989 National Environmental Policy Plan* (NEPP), the Dutch government officially accepted this concept as a goal for all its policies, including policies on traditional socio-economic areas, such as agriculture, transport, and industrial production. Despite its wide approval, the concept of sustainability in the formulation of the World Commission is rather vague. If it is wanted as a basis for environmental policies, it needs operationalisation.

Operationalisation of the sustainability concept implies a search for the concrete biophysical constraints on human actions. These biophysical constraints are sometimes referred to as the environmental utilisation space. However, biophysical constraints appear to be difficult to determine for both scientific and social reasons. To begin with the *scientific difficulties*, the dose-effect relations are often obscure. The knowledge of the effects emissions and interventions in landscapes have on natural processes are flawed and incomplete. In general, processes in nature and, hence, human interventions in these processes, appear difficult to predict for at least three reasons. Firstly, synergetic effects increase the impact on the environment of separate emissions. For example, laboratory experiments have demonstrated that the combined impact of the acidifying substances SO_2, NO_x, NH_3 and O_3 on plant growth is substantially more severe than the (linear) addition of the impacts of each of these substances alone would be. Secondly, thresholds are very common in ecosystems. Again, acidification serves as an excellent example. The sudden acceleration of the deterioration of forests and subsequent dying-off of large parts of European forests at the beginning of the 1980s came out of the blue for most people – many scientists among them. It appeared that the buffering capacity of the soil had for decades protected trees from serious damage. Once this capacity had been reached, acidifying substances could do considerable damage to trees and 'kill' them within a couple of years. Thirdly, many emissions have a delayed effect on the environment. It takes decades, for example, before nitrogen from manure and chemical fertilisers is washed from the top layer into deeper layers of the soil, causing severe nitrate pollution of the ground water, which in most countries serves as drinking water. Even if nitrogen leakages to the ground water could be stopped immediately, nitrate pollution of ground water will increase considerably for decades into the next century.

The flawed and incomplete knowledge of dose-effect relations frustrates attempts to determine biophysical constraints on human actions. The controversial relation between the increasing CO_2 emissions and the greenhouse-effect illustrates this difficulty. It is a scientific fact that the concentrations of CO_2 in the atmosphere have increased for many decades because of the increased use of fossil fuels. Great uncertainty exists, however, about the effects increasing CO_2 concentrations will have on the global climate. Some scientists argue that dramatic climatic changes with severe effects on ecosystems and economies will occur. Other scientists state, however, that such predictions are speculations which cannot be confirmed or rejected scientifically (see for instance Beckerman, 1991). But even if climatic changes result from the increasing CO_2 concentrations, it is not certain that they will have severe effects on ecosystems and economies. If, under these circumstances, authorities wish to reduce the use of fossil fuels in order to reduce the greenhouse effect, fierce resistance from diverse societal groups (energy-intensive industries, car owners, transportation companies) can be expected. This implies that in the case of the use of fossil fuels, it is difficult to define and to implement a scientifically based environmental utilisation space which could be called sustainable.

But even if all the gaps in our knowledge of both the effects of particular emissions on nature and the non-linear relations between emissions and environmental degradation could be filled in, the biophysical constraints on human actions which are necessary to define the environmental utilisation space cannot yet be easily deduced. Biophysical constraints appear to have a *social dimension,* which means another complication for the operationalisation of the environmental utilisation space concept. The abatement policy on acidifying depositions in the Netherlands serves as an illustration. In 1984, the Dutch Minister for Environmental Affairs announced as a long-term policy goal a deposition limit of 1,800 acid equivalents per hectare per year.[3] This deposition level is seen as a critical load. If depositions are reduced to that level, no significant damage to forests will occur. The level was based on scientific research on forestrial ecosystems in Scandinavia. However, this critical load would not protect nutrition-poor ecosystems, such as heather vegetations, which are more vulnerable to acid precipitation. This implies that the critical load for acidifying depositions was based on scientific information on the one hand, and on political decisions on the other hand. In other words, the Dutch government could have chosen a much lower maximum deposition level, say 400 acid equivalents per hectare per year, in order to conserve all existing ecosystems, including heather vegetations. Hence, both ethical considerations and socio-economic valuations influence the levels of sustainability that are to be distinguished, implying different levels of biophysical constraints.

From the previous discussion, it can be concluded that the operationalisation of the environmental utilisation space concept is hindered by obscure dose-effect relations. Synergetic effects, threshold and delays imply non-linear relations between emissions and environmental degradation, preventing the formulation of clear criteria for sustainable behaviour. Furthermore, several levels of sustainability must be distinguished, depending on the social valuation of ecosystems, biodiversity, the stocks of non-renewable natural resources, etc. This social dimension of sustainability is illustrated by the critical loads for acidifying substances in the Netherlands, which was determined with the aim of conserving forests, leaving aside more vulnerable types of ecosystems.

DISTRIBUTIONAL EFFECTS IN THE PROCESS OF GOAL SETTING FOR ENVIRONMENTAL POLICIES

Confronted with critical loads, emission standards, and subsequent environmental measures, polluting economic sectors become aware of the fact that the environmental utilisation space is limited and that they have to reduce

---

[3] By using acid equivalents, it is possible to combine all the effects of acidifying substances regardless of the type of emissions.

their claims on nature and the environment. At the same time, however, there is another problem. How should the limited possibilities to use ecosystems be distributed? To support their interests, polluting industries usually argue that ecological knowledge is incomplete, being an insufficient basis for a strict environmental policy. If a strict environmental policy is nevertheless implemented, polluting industries stress their considerable contribution to GNP, employment, and the balance of payments, referring, in other words, to the short-term but vested and hence traditional economic interests. If the government does not recognise, or is not able to deal with, these complications adequately, environmental policies could easily be frustrated. Such a neglect of distributional effects has been the case for the abatement policies of acid rain in the Netherlands. This section is devoted to this issue.

In short, acid rain is caused by the emissions of SO_2, NO_x, and NH_3. Sulphur dioxide is emitted when fossil fuels containing sulphur are burned, in particular in oil refineries and power plants. High temperatures in combustion processes in oil refineries, power plants, and motor cars result in the emission of nitrogen oxides. Ammonia emissions originate mainly from manure which is a by-product of the dairy sector and the intensive livestock sector (pigs and chickens).

As we have seen in the previous section, the Dutch Minister of Environmental Affairs defined a critical load of 1800 acid equivalents per hectare per year in 1984. The total level of emissions in that period was approximately 5500 acid equivalents per hectare per year, and the emissions amounted to 7000 per hectare per year acid equivalents. The difference between emission and deposition levels indicates that the Netherlands is a net exporter of acidifying substances. Owing to the great distances SO_2 and NO_x emissions are dispersed, the national acid deposition originates partly from foreign emittants.

The transboundary character of the acidification problem complicates Dutch abatement policy considerably, since some of the benefits of Dutch efforts to reduce acidifying emission will go abroad, while foreign emission reductions cannot be enforced. Despite this complication, it was very clear that all Dutch sources would have to decrease their emissions substantially to reduce the huge gap between the deposition level of 5500 acid equivalents per hectare per year in 1984 and the goal of 1800 acid equivalents per hectare per year. In 1989, the Minister of Environmental Affairs introduced in the *National Environmental Policy Plan* a timetable for the reduction of the total acid deposition. A critical load of 2400 acid equivalents per hectare per year was set for the year 2000. For the year 2010, the aim is a maximum of 1400 acid equivalents per hectare per year. If depositions can be brought down to those levels, most forests would be protected against the damaging effects of acid rain.

As can be seen in Figure 18.3, the share of each acidifying sector in the total amount of acid deposition has not been stable over the last 40 years. In the eighties, the total acid deposition decreased to approximately 4500 acid equivalents per hectare per year due to reductions of especially SO_2 emissions. Hence, the share of ammonia (agriculture) and NO_x (traffic) emitting sectors in total acidification increased. At the moment the government announced the critical loads as abatement policy goals, the question was asked to what extent each sector must reduce their emissions. This implicitly introduced the issue of the distribution of the available (but scarce) acidifying rights. Which sector would be allowed to use which percentage of the critical load? However, this issue has never been recognised, as the documents of the Minister of Environmental Affairs demonstrate. This implies that there is not the slightest idea of an ex ante distribution of the acidifying rights in the end-state situation, nor have criteria been developed (even a debate has never been initiated) which could underpin an ex ante distribution. Such a distribution of acidifying rights is an indispensable reference point in negotiations with particular sectors on emission reductions.

Owing to the corporate character of Dutch society, the emission reduction target of each acidifying sector is the result of consultations and negotiations between the Minister of Environmental Affairs and a particular sector. Each sector has several possibilities to resist the attempts of the Minister of Environmental Affairs to reduce the acidifying emissions. First, the sector will point at the incomplete knowledge of dose-effect relations, which enables the sector to trivialise its contribution to acidification. Second, each sector will emphasise its importance for the Dutch economy, mentioning its contribution to the balance of payments, to employment, to GNP, and so on. Third, the lack of an ex ante distribution of the acidifying rights offers the most powerful sectors the opportunity to shift some emission reductions to other sectors, that is, to claim a more than proportional share of the acidifying rights. The agricultural sector and the transportation sector in particular have proved to be clever negotiators, increasing their shares in acidifying emissions in the last decade. Their success must partly be ascribed to their close relations with other members of the Cabinet, namely, the Minister of Agriculture and the Minister of Transport and Public Works.

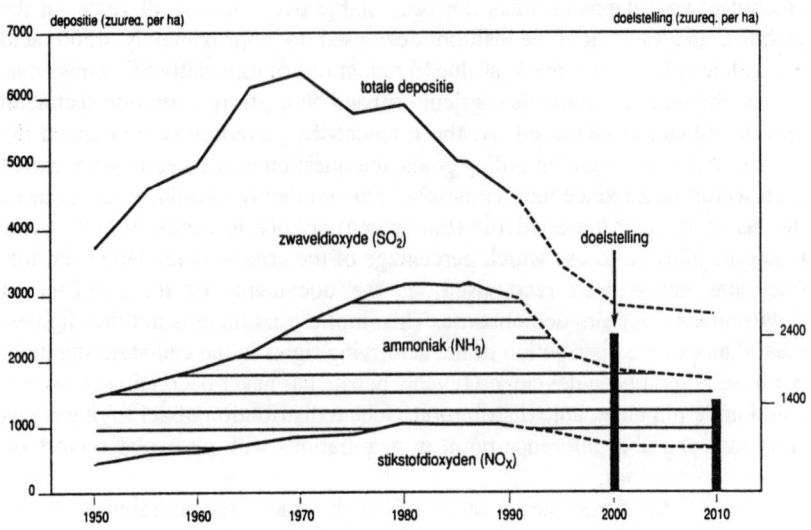

Note: Deposition is measured in acid equivalents per ha per year. The policy aims in the year 2000 and 2010 are indicated with a black line.

Source: Rijksinstituut voor Volksgezondheid en Milieuhygiëne (1991: 203).

Figure 18.3. Depositions of potential acid precipitation in the Netherlands for the period 1950–2010.

IN SEARCH FOR AN INSTITUTIONAL FRAMEWORK

If different polluters use the same environmental utilisation space, it goes without saying that, one way or another, this limited space has to be distributed among polluters. In other words, each environmental policy includes, implicitly or explicitly, ex ante or ex post, the distribution of entitlements to the environmental utilisation space. The issue of this section is formulated in the phrase 'one way or another.' More precisely, we are in search of an institutional framework for distributing entitlements to the environmental utilisation space which enhances rather than erodes the effectiveness and efficiency of environmental policies. In this section, we present our view, which could be called the contours of such a framework, including the reasons for searching in this direction.

To economists, the distribution of entitlements to the environmental utilisation space is usually thought to be a consequence of allocative processes once the environmental utilisation space has been determined. After operationalising the ecological constraints into concrete policy targets (such as specified emission standards), a set of appropriate economic or market-based instruments (levies, marketable pollution rights) could achieve these (exogenous) targets in a cost-effective way (Baumol and Oates, 1988, 159–176). Unlike the command-and-control instruments usually used in environmental policy, market-based instruments permit flexibility in the amount of pollution reduction achieved by each source, allowing polluters with low abatement costs per emitted unit to reduce emissions to a greater degree than polluters with high abatement costs per emitted unit.

This approach only takes effect if the particular environmental policy targets are fixed, are transparent to the economic agents, and are largely shared in society because there is a sufficient scientific basis and/or social understanding (environmental protection as a social priority). However, environmental policy targets that fulfil these conditions cannot be deduced from the preferences of individual economic agents (due to both the valuation problem and the aggregation problem). In terms of section 2, both the shape and the position of the MRC-curves and, in particular, the MEC-curves (see Figures 18.1 and 18.2) are rather uncertain, if not unknown. Also, it often appears to be impossible to deduce the policy targets from the available scientific knowledge (due to synergy, delays and thresholds; see section 3). Consequently, the environmental utilisation space cannot be precisely demarcated. Hence, policy targets (that is, emission levels) will be forcefully attacked on their uncertain, and thus deniable, scientific basis. The result has been demonstrated in section 4 for the case of acidification in the Netherlands: Instead of efficiently allocating the entitlements to the environmental utilisation space, the leaders of polluting sectors question the targets for emission reduction, and succeed in playing down the reduction targets or even declaring the targets as untenable and therefore impossible to achieve.

From an administrative point of view, the circumstances described above make us suggest what is, at first sight, a suboptimal solution. We propose assigning a particular set of pollution rights or imposing particular emission reduction levels per economic sector by the regulating agency. Typical of this approach is the public admission that the allocation of pollution rights is highly politically determined, using, of course, the available but incomplete economic and ecological insights as much as possible. The reason for dealing with environmental issues this way is the perspective of a change of orientation of the economic agents by creating, step by step, an environmental zero-sum game: the gain of one, that is, an increase in the entitlements to the environmental utilisation space, means a loss to the other(s), that is, a decrease in the entitlements to the utilisation space. Interest groups, their leaders, and captains of industry become aware, more than is the case now, of the zero-sum character of the game. Consequently, they cannot focus exclusively on contesting the emission levels ('nature can carry or process much more emissions'), but must keep an eye on their share in the environmental utilisation space, implying increasing competition concerning the available pollution rights. The better the regulating agency (in co-operation with NGOs such as the environmental movement, consumer organisations, and so on) succeeds in embedding the idea of environmental utilisation space or ecological constraints in society, the more the attention of economic agents is shifted to their *share* in the environmental utilisation space and less to demarcating issues of the environmental utilisation space itself.

Structured and regarded this way, the ecological question shows a remarkable similarity with the social question of (approximately) a century ago:

- The physical capabilities of the workforce was exceeded with a workday of 14–16 hours, child labour, dangerous work, no social security, and so on.
- The government started by curtailing the freedom of employers to use their workforce as they wish (laws on child labour, on working conditions, and so on), despite the fierce protests that these laws deteriorate international competitiveness.
- Within the politically determined social and legal framework (which was improved and developed in the course of decades), employers and employees played a zero-sum game concerning the distribution of the operating results (wages, pensions and other claims versus profits and safeguarding the future of the company).
- Since the Keynesian Revolution, the understanding that employers and employees need each other has grown. Employees are no longer seen as pure production costs; they are also seen as a spending category that absorbs sales which benefits employer interests too. We now talk about negotiations between social partners instead of the class struggle between capital and labour.
- This development could not have been realised without an appropriate institutional framework channelling fierce labour conflicts into professional negotiations. For instance, it is common practice in the Netherlands for representatives of employees and employers to negotiate on working

conditions, pensions, the wage level, and so on, in an almost continuous process. Representing their members has become a fulltime job, allowing for professional negotiations with some distance to the shop floor and the boardroom. Although the interests represented often conflict, it is in the interest of the professional negotiators to remain on speaking terms with the other side. The distance from everyday life within firms combined with the interest of the negotiators to keep their jobs (implying that the representatives of the negotiating parties need each other) allows them to keep an open mind about long-term issues, such as the future of the sector, and to broadly interpret of the interests they represent, such as job creation and social security. This explains why the Dutch labour union federations are so interested in macroeconomic developments, keeping their wage claims modest and oriented on employment in general rather than negotiating for as much money as possible for their own members.

Unfortunately, a similar framework to channel fierce environmental conflicts in society into well-organised debates on goals and instruments of environmental policy is lacking. We need such a framework to generate and carry on debates and to reflect on the issues. The focus would then be long-term interests and consistent strategy (aiming at sustainability) instead of short-term (polluting) interests and ad hoc solutions to environmental calamities. Such a framework would require the conflicting parties (environmental movement, industry, agriculture, consumer organisations, and so on) to understand that they need each other in the search for a sustainable society. But, conversely, such a framework could also increase this mutual understanding, avoiding battles such as the one between Shell and Greenpeace concerning the Brent Spar.

Such an institutional framework for dealing with environmental questions has not yet been developed in society. However, promising examples of co-operation between stakeholders in the field of environmental policy are emerging in some parts of society. For instance, whenever the government has to decide on new emission levels of acidifying substances, these new standards are not only discussed with the polluting sectors, but the environmental movement, recognised as a relevant stakeholder by the government, also plays a role in the bargaining process with regard to these levels of emissions. The influence of the environmental movement can also be recognised in the issue of collecting and separating household waste. It was the environmental movement in particular which dramatically influenced the Dutch population's awareness of the waste problem. This has resulted in a very high separation percentage of household waste in the Netherlands. The Dutch government co-operated with the environmental movement to influence public opinion about these issues. More examples of co-operation between the government and the environmental movement could be mentioned, such as the local implementation of the Rio Agenda 21, environmental education at primary schools, the monitoring of birds, butterflies, and plants by nature groups, seats for the environmental movement in official commissions, and so on. In all these cases, it is understood by the environmental groups as well as by the government that they will realise better results when they co-operate with each other.

Despite these promising initiatives, only tiny steps have been taken in an institutionalising process. Regular consultation of other stakeholders, in particular the polluters, is needed. Furthermore, we should not underestimate the social position of the polluting sectors. In these sectors, capital and labour 'resolved' their differences by expanding the level of production without paying attention to the damages to nature and the environment. It goes without saying that they are still inclined to marginalise the environmental argument if it could weaken their privileged position in society.

The question that arises is under what conditions could an environmental policy lead to any results. Is it possible to change the ideas and attitudes of relevant stakeholders? Obviously, a successful environmental policy will place the polluting sectors in a less favourable position. A significant point is who has to pay for the effects of stricter environmental standards? The agricultural sector in the Netherlands is a good example of this problem. For many decades, the Dutch government supported the agricultural sector significantly. This sector created a high surplus on the balance of trade which made this sector powerful. In the course of time, however, Dutch agriculture became a top polluter in the world. This resulted in a general feeling that measures had to be taken. But the agricultural sector has been able to establish a very strong position in the state machinery. Now that they are being confronted with a different attitude from the Dutch government with regard to pollution caused by the agricultural sector, they are not able to understand why this position has changed. There is a general belief among farmers that the strict environmental standards, which were recently passed in Parliament are not the result of a normal democratic process, but the result of the exaggerated demands of environmental groups. Additionally, there is a general feeling that the social effects of this policy are being ignored. The resistance in the sector against environmental policies is so high that recently Dutch farmers blocked Parliament with manure carts during the debate about these standards.

The same can be said about the position of the labour unions. Given the high unemployment figures, they are not in a position to support strict environmental standards. If strict environmental standards will lower the level of production and, subsequently the level of employment, labour unions are of the opinion that the costs of these measures will be paid by the workers. To get the support of relevant interest groups in society, in environmental policies attention has to be paid to the problem of the distribution of costs and to the position of those groups which have to pay more than others. Generally speaking, this problem is not being given sufficient attention by either policy makers nor environmental economists. The question of *why* economic instruments are seldom introduced in Western economies hardly ever comes up; nor is the question of *why* environmental policies in Western countries are not so successful analysed.

It is not a given that the interests of labour and capital will forever obstruct the implementation of strict environmental measures. Polluting sectors are becoming increasingly aware of the negative influences of their attitude and behaviour upon their market position. Dutch farmers are losing markets in the Netherlands and elsewhere in Europe because of their negative environmental image. The task of the environmental movement and the government is to make it clear that production and consumption are only possible if a sufficient quantity and quality of nature and the environment are available in the coming decades. In a situation in which the environmental movement is supported by the majority of the population, polluting sectors are forced to change their position if they do not want to lose their market share. However, we have to be aware that it took nearly a century to solve the social question, which implies that the ecological question cannot be solved in a few decades. In both situations, the real issue is the distribution of power in society. We cannot expect polluting sectors to give up their privileged position without struggle.

To civilise this struggle and to advance the transition to an ecologically sustainable society, we proposed in this section a search for a new institutional framework. We suggest to look for a framework which has great resemblance to the way the corporate Dutch industrial relations are organised. In this respect essential elements are a growing awareness of the need to share the limited ecological utilisation space (zero-sum game), and continuously ongoing negotiations between professionals. Regulating agencies have to initiate and facilitate such negotiations on diverse environmental issues, but cannot impose them. It has to be taken care of that institutionalising sustainability this way must be a bottom-up process of, and not a top-down diktat for sustainable behaviour.

IN CONCLUSION

It is not economic theories which create environmental problems. Even when one comes to the conclusion that traditional economic theory is not adequate for analysing and solving environmental problems, it is too easy to blame the theories for the shortcomings in the implementation of environmental policies. Furthermore, it can be argued that strict environmental standards can be supported by theoretical economic arguments, as the costs of environmental disruption are, in most cases, much higher than the costs of protection and abatement policies. In addition, many studies have made it clear that the implementation of strict standards will not lead to economic disasters. A significant problem of environmental policies is found in the ignorance of the distributional effects resulting from environmental policies.

The environmental utilisation space has been decreased for many decades. The distribution of this limited space among polluting sectors and among different countries is one of the great challenges of the next decades. A solution is possible only when conflicting interest groups become aware of the necessity to come to an agreement.

It took a long time to 'solve' the social question, as this was strongly related to the distribution of power in society. Who can decide on what? The same can be said about the 'ecological' question. Again the problem is related to the issue of whose interests count in society. The case study on the effects of the Dutch acid rain policy clearly demonstrates the importance of trade-off relations instead of the win-win relations on which most of the literature on ecological modernisation is based. This especially holds when the 'easy' emission reductions (for example, sulpherdioxide emissions from stationary sources) are already accomplished. Then, the costly emission reductions are left, such as ammonia emissions from the dairy and intensive livestock sector, imposing the issue who may use which part of the environmental utilisation space. If society and their representatives in Parliament neglects this distributional issue, it will remain a barrier to ecological modernisation.

REFERENCES

Anderson, G.D. and Bishop, R.C. 1986. 'The Valuation Problem.' In Bromley, D.W. (ed.) *Natural Resource Economics; Policy Problems and Contemporary Analysis.* Amsterdam: North-Holland, 89–137.

Baumol, W.J. and Oates, W.E. 1988. *The Theory of Environmental Policy.* Cambridge: Cambridge University Press.

Beckerman, W. 1991. 'Global Warming; A Sceptical Economic Assessment.' In Helm, D. (ed.) *Economic Policy towards the Environment.* London: Blackwell, 52–85.

Crocker, T.D. and Shogren, J.F. 1991. 'Preference Learning and Contingent Valuation Methods.' In Dietz, F.J., van der Ploeg, F. and van der Straaten, J. (eds.) *Environmental Policy and the Economy*. Amsterdam: North-Holland, 77–93.

Cropper, M.L. and Oates, W.E. 1992. Environmental Economics: A Survey. *Journal of Economic Literature* 30, 675–740.

Freeman III, A.M. 1993. *The Measurement of Environmental and Resource Values. Theory and Method.* Washington D.C.: Resources for the Future.

Hoehn, J.P. and Randall, A. 1987. 'A Satisfactory Benefit Cost Indicator for Contingent Valuation.' *Journal of Environmental Economics and Management* 14, 226–247.

Mäler, K.G. 1985. 'Welfare Economics and the Environment.' In Kneese, A.V. and Sweeney, F.L. (eds.) *Handbook of Natural Resource and Energy Economics,* Volume 1, Amsterdam: North-Holland, 3–60.

Opschoor, J.B. 1987. *Duurzaamheid en Verandering* (Sustainability and Change), Amsterdam: Free University Publishers.

Opschoor, J.B. 1995. 'Ecospace and the Fall and Rise of Throughput Intensity.' *Ecological Economics* 15, 137–140.

Rijksinstituut voor Volksgezondheid en Milieuhygiëne (State Institute for Public Health and Environmental Policy). *Nationale Milieuverkenningen-2 1990–2010.* (National Environmental Outlook-2 1990–2010). Samsom H.D. Tjeenk Willink, Alphen aan den Rijn, 1991.

Siebert, H. 1982. 'Nature as a Life Support System. Renewable Resources and Environmental Disruption.' *Journal of Economics* 42, 2, 133–142.

World Commission on Environment and Development 1987. *Our Common Future.* Oxford: Oxford University Press.

19. Some Methodological Reflections A Plea for a Constitutional Ecological Economics

Andreas Renner

INTRODUCTION

Which policy recommendations make sustainable development more likely? – To answer this question we may recollect the following argument: sustainability implies the co-evolution of nature and society, of ecological and socio-economic systems (Hinterberger, 1994; Norgaard, 1994).[1] A wide consensus exists among scientists that a society's development path can be sustainable only if both our socio-economic system *and* the ecological system are well functioning and stable. Within both natural and social sciences a long tradition – related to persons such as Alexander von Humboldt or Adam Smith respectively – explores the working properties of complex ecological systems and the complexity of the social world. Both natural and social scientists have found that complex systems are to a large degree self-organising and hence cannot be 'managed' in a technical sense. Complex ecological systems abruptly loose their balance if human interventions exceed their carrying capacity. The same reasoning applies to socio-economic systems. They too are self-organising – or as Hayek (1967) puts it: their spontaneous order is the "result of human action but not of human design." Until recently little effort has been made in order to integrate the two disciplines – natural and social science. This may surprise, because ecological and socio-economic systems are necessarily interdependent. A stable and well functioning development of society implies a stable and well functioning ecological system within which society is embedded. The conditions for a

---

[1] Many publications refer to the 'triad of sustainability,' that is, the three dimensions of sustainability – the ecological, the social and the economic dimension – rather than the two named in this chapter.

sustainable co-evolution of natural and socio-economic systems represent a wide and fruitful field of research for Ecological Economists.

Many Ecological Economists seem to be unaware of the necessity of coping with two types of complex systems. Based on the works of Herman E. Daly, one of the 'founding fathers' of Ecological Economics, it is argued that, particularly during the early stage of this new science, Ecological Economists tended to follow an ecology-centred – and this means, a single-sided – approach. They developed policy proposals for the protection of natural ecosystems without considering how to implement their policy proposals within society. However, the most sophisticated arguments why politicians should set up an ambitious environmental regulation or why people should change their personal life-styles will not have any impact if the addressees – politicians, consumers – have no incentives to act accordingly. For implementing a strategy for sustainable development it is important to consider the structure of incentives – the institutional setting.

Ecological Economics today is addressing this challenge. The science is undergoing a phase of re-orientation; currently several different, – often incompatible, – approaches to an Ecological Economics coexist and it is not clear whether Ecological Economists will find a common basis for a new paradigm (Hinterberger, 1997). On the one side there is what we might call the *traditional* approach deriving policy recommendations directly from ecological criteria for sustainability. On the other side more and more Ecological Economists are building *new* bridges to social theory; they link Ecological Economics for example to 'Socio-Economics' or to 'Evolutionary Economics.' Within such a wider concept Ecological Economics is a science of 'social change' dealing with the question of how to design an institutional framework for evolving sustainable production and consumption patterns.

The struggle between the traditional ecology-centred and a social-science based approach is illustrated by the study *'Sustainable Germany.'*[2] In this study, which is intensely discussed in Germany, researchers from the *Wuppertal Institute for Climate, Environment, and Energy* develop several scenarios for development paths towards a 'Sustainable Germany.' The study is structured as follows:

- The first part of the study (chapters 2 and 3) is based on a traditional Ecological Economics methodology. Specific environmental objectives – in this case: maximum material flows within the socio-economic system (based on Opschoor's 'environmental space' enriched by certain distributional criteria for inter- and intragenerational justice) – are defined

---

[2] 'Zukunftsfähiges Deutschland' (BUND and Misereor, 1996); the study was translated into English and published under the title 'Greening the North' (Sachs and Loske, 1996).

based on arguments from natural science. These *ecological targets* are defined ex ante by natural scientists. That is, by a scientific elite. They are considered as externally given, they are not subject to discussion.

- The other parts of the study (chapters 4 to 6) focus on 'social change.' It is argued that sustainable development can only be achieved if new patterns of social interactions – so called 'social innovations' – take place. The study suggests searching for socially attractive 'social innovations' for ecologically sustainable life styles such as car sharing (and other forms of shared use of goods), the use of resource-efficient, long-lasting and easily repairable goods or the formation of markets for local goods. That is, the *implementation* of the given targets is seen as a creative process of social change.

As the policy proposals given in the study are very vague,[3] it may not be clear at first glance that the two parts of the study, the natural-scientific based first part and the social-science-based second part, do not fit together. They are incompatible. Ex-ante defined objectives cannot be 'implemented' via an open process of social evolution driven by technological and social innovations.

It is this choice among two major lines of interpretation that lead (and still leads) to quite some confusion and controversial discussions.[4] We have to decide whether to interpret the study in a 'direct' way taking the pre-defined targets as externally given or whether to interpret it in an 'indirect' way recommending changes in the structure of incentives so that new forms of resource-efficient production and consumption patterns will be discovered. The ecological targets then no longer would be seen as given; their definition would be part of a scientific, public and political discourse.

This ambiguity of the study has lead to criticism as it may suggest a destructive interpretation. Following common sense, we may be tempted to interpret the study as suggesting that in order to reach sustainability, we simply have to change our personal life styles according to the appeals which are brought forward in the study. But as long as the structure of incentives are unchanged, our life styles will not change (much) either. And once moral suasion is proven to have little effect, another 'direct' policy to 'implement'

---

[3] The policy conclusions remind of a 'brain storming.' The authors name various policy options including an ecological tax reform, a more stringent liability law, political reforms for a better citizens' participation and others without specifying their proposals (BUND and Misereor, 1996).

[4] The controversy tends to be that both social and natural scientists criticise the seeming domination of the other discipline's arguments. Economists then point out that the natural-scientifically defined targets cannot be reached within a democratic, market-oriented social order, whereas ecologists highlight the social-science foundations of the study arguing that the targets are to be met within a democratic process of social change.

the targets may be called for a based on command-and-control strategy. In other words, the study suggests an interpretation which presumably was not intended by the authors, because it is not based sufficiently on a theory which links individual behaviour to the, – politically designed, – institutional framework (Suchanek, 1997, 56ff; Renner, 1998).

This paper intends to fill this gap in part. It develops some thoughts on how Ecological Economists could derive policy recommendations to alter a society's evolution towards sustainable development. It is argued that powerful policy recommendations could be derived if Ecological Economists based their arguments on the methodology of Constitutional Economics. The question is: how can an institutional framework be designed to render the sustainable development decision making process responsive to what we may call 'informed' citizens' preferences? In other words: how can institutions be designed so that arguments of both natural and social scientists will be reflected in a society's development path?

The chapter proceeds as follows: In section 2, I show that we cannot derive powerful policy recommendations from an ecology-centred approach and that we would better integrate the natural scientific knowledge into an approach that is based on social science. I develop in section 3 a new approach – '*Constitutional Ecological Economics*.' I conclude with some methodological reflections.

FROM ECOLOGICAL ECONOMICS TOWARDS 'SOCIO-ECOLOGICAL ECONOMICS'

The origin of Ecological Economics may be seen in the perception that socio-economic systems are embedded in a larger ecological system. Ecological Economists point out that a 'desirable social order'[5] cannot be maintained if the natural ecosystems are not well-functioning and stable, too. From this starting point Ecological Economists began to derive ecological criteria for sustainability. Human societies should recognise that natural ecosystems have a limited 'carrying capacity' which means that the amount of use of resources and the amount of emissions that could constantly be absorbed by the natural ecosystems cannot be expanded beyond a certain limit.

Ecological Economists usually derive their policy recommendations from this knowledge of a limited carrying capacity of the planet earth. However,

---

[5] For Ecological Economists this tends to be a 'sustainable' social order, for liberal social philosophers a 'human and well functioning' (*menschenwürdig und funktionsfähig*; Eucken, 1952/90) or a 'just and stable' (Rawls, 1993) social order. Communitarians speak of a 'good society' (see Bellah *et al.*, 1991, referring to a book from Walter Lippmann, 1937).

their methodology on how to derive policy recommendations differs widely. For analytical purposes we may distinguish between two major methodologies:

- the traditional 'direct' approach, and
- a new 'indirect' (institutional) approach.

The first is related to a basically natural-science based concept of Ecological Economics whereas the latter focuses on institution building, that is on social science.

The 'Direct' Approach

During the early stage of this new science Ecological Economists tended to base their policy recommendations *directly* on natural scientific evidence. They pleaded for the definition of strict limits on the use of resources and on emissions. The argument is that the 'scale' of the socio-economic system has to be adapted to the carrying capacity of the ecological system. Daly (1992) compares these limits on the throughput of the economy to Plimsoll lines on a boat that define the maximum load. Obviously the definition of a Plimsoll line is a technical problem. We may also say that it has little to do with individual preferences. We may assume that there exists a preference for preventing our planet from ecological collapse in the same way as we assume that nobody wants to let his or her boat sink. Therefore experts should define Plimsoll lines for ecological systems.

Daly points out that the question of an adequate scale of the economy (in terms of resource use and emissions) has to be addressed separately from the question of an efficient resource allocation. If the load exceeds the maximum, the boat is likely to sink – no matter how smartly we balance the load in the boat. For the sustainable development policies to be recommended this implies let first the natural scientists define the maximum scale, that is, the maximum resource use of the socio-economic system. In a second step we may then introduce certain distribution criteria.[6] The question of economic efficiency is to be resolved last: "Only in third place, after having made social decisions regarding an ecologically sustainable scale and an ethically just distribution, are we in a position to allow reallocation among individuals through markets in the interests of efficiency." (Daly 1992, 188)

---

[6] Daly pleads for "minimum and maximum limits on income and the maximum limit on wealth." (Daly, 1977, p. 53).

Daly's three-step approach is best met by tradable emission permits (1992).[7] A policy based on tradable emission permits rather than on command and control finds wide acceptance among economists (see for instance Maier-Rigaud, 1994). Daly's hierarchy of giving the ecological objective of an 'optimal scale' priority over distribution and allocation though does not (Stewen, 1998). Environmental objectives cannot be discussed independently from distribution and allocation issues, that is, from social and economic objectives. Daly's proposal may be enough to maintain ecological stability; however, it ignores socio-economic stability. The selection of an 'efficient' instrument (in the neoclassical sense) such as tradable emission permits alone is not sufficient to maintain the capacity of evolution of the economic system (that is, the instrument may not be efficient in an evolutionary sense). Tradable emission permits could be implemented in such a restrictive way that the economic actors could not adapt to the new institutional environment by developing environmental sound innovations except by exiting the market (Wegner, 1994). This implies defining an 'optimal' scale independently from distribution and allocation deliberations would most likely fail the ends of a co-evolution of nature *and* society – the social order would be destabilised.

Daly ignores potential trade-offs with other – social and economic – objectives. Like many ecologists Daly shares the understanding that the state of environment is so critical (the level of emissions so close to the carrying capacity limit) that environmental objectives must be given priority over other objectives. He implicitly assumes that a consensus on how to define the pollution limits (the Plimsoll line) could be reached. This assumption may be true for shipbuilding, it definitely is not true for defining an 'optimal' scale of environmental pollution. Eco-systems are too complex for precise capacity limits to be defined. In a way, Daly seems to accept this fact when he proposes to keep resource use and emissions below the assumed limit[8] (even though he does not refer to the argument of uncertain knowledge) – in order to keep the boat from sinking in case that it is not well balanced. But he does not draw the conclusion that we should take into account the potential trade-offs between ecological and socio-economic issues when we decide on a desirable level of environmental protection.

---

[7] In his book 'Steady-State Economics' Daly proposes other forms of tradable permits, too: depletion quotas auctioned by the government (1977, pp. 61–68) and transferable birth licences to control population growth (1977, pp. 56–61).

[8] Daly here follows the natural scientists' viewpoint that we would have to 'minimise' human intervention into the ecological system in order to raise the chance to keep natural ecosystems in balance. From a social scientist's viewpoint a 'minimum' option does not exist – emission cannot be reduced to zero. Ecologically informed social scientists therefore tend to plead for an 'Ecological Economic Policy' based on the precautionary principle (Hinterberger et al., 1998; Hinterberger and Wegner, 1996).

Daly's concept is too single-sided to provide a basis for an acceptable policy recommendation. By categorically giving ecological criteria priority over other criteria of human well-being Daly copies a structure of argument which he strongly opposes when applied within neoclassical economics. Whereas neoclassical economists take 'economic efficiency' (narrowly defined) as the only relevant criterion, Daly takes the 'optimal scale.' The economy-centred neoclassical approach is simply substituted by an ecology-centred approach. We may go as far as to say that there exist certain parallels between Daly's definition of an 'optimal scale' and Nordhaus' 'economics of the greenhouse effect' (Nordhaus, 1991). Both the Ecological Economics approach (Daly) and the Neoclassical approach (Nordhaus) assume the knowledge of an optimum level of emissions and therefore of the critical point – the Plimsoll line. It is assumed that at this point global ecosystems will abruptly destabilise. In economic terms the point where damage costs (the benefits of emission abatement) abruptly rise to the unlimited. Both Daly and Nordhaus pretend to know how best to weigh ecological against socio-economic objectives.

The Indirect Approach

The indirect, or institutional, approach is based on the argument that sustainability cannot be 'managed' in the way suggested by the direct approach. The notion of 'managing sustainability' (Costanza *et al.*, 1991) is understood as 'management of social change.' Policy recommendations focus on the institutional setting of the political and economic order, that is, the set of rules defining the possible forms of interactions of the various actors within society. They reflect not only the complexity of ecosystems but also the complexity of the social world. Society is seen as a complex, to a high degree self-organising system. Its evolution depends on the interaction of citizens in their roles as, among others, consumers, entrepreneurs, environmental activists, journalists, scientists or politicians. Citizen preferences, the role of the media, of environmental movements, of research institutes for the formation of 'informed' preferences, the attractiveness of a policy of sustainable development within the political process and the competition among alternative theories about the working properties of ecological systems, are all elements which can be analysed within a social-science based indirect approach focusing on institution building.[9] Within this perspective Ecological Economics is understood as *'Socio-Ecological Economics.'*[10]

---

[9] Various case studies illustrate the interdependency of institutional and social change (Gunderson *et al.*, 1995; Glasbergen, 1995).

[10] The term was suggested at a workshop organised in 1994 at the Wuppertal Institute.

The indirect approach is 'process-oriented', it focuses on rules as problem-solving mechanisms, whereas the traditional Ecological Economics approach is 'end-state-oriented', it is based on the assumption that we could define sustainability in quantitative terms. But how can we define precise ecological targets – Plimsoll lines – if we cannot anticipate which challenges may have to be tackled in the future in order to reach and stay on a sustainable development path? Today we know that certain patterns are non-sustainable. But we do not know which environmental risks will occur, or be recognised, in the future.[11] Within the traditional direct concept, the policies have to be redesigned whenever new information is generated. The indirect approach, however, can cope with a changing environment. The institutional framework may be designed in a way that allows for adaptation to future challenges. For example, setting up a sophisticated liability law or creating a transparent ecological advisory council for government are options that insure that new knowledge about ecosystems and possible environmental hazards is permanently generated and immediately taken into account.

Natural science based Ecological Economists may argue that today we already know the limits to carrying capacity which must be respected if ecological sustainability is to be maintained. How can we transform natural scientific evidence into policy recommendations if not straightforwardly, the direct way, by defining environmental objectives directly from natural science? Besides, it may be asked how a 'socio-ecological economics' could cope with the idea of interdisciplinary science. These questions are important. Still, interdisciplinary science cannot mean that natural scientists define ecological targets and that social scientists propose policy instruments. To me it seems a better understanding of interdisciplinary work that social scientists deal with processes of environmental change which are defined within society. Coping with environmental change caused by social processes may support policy proposals restructuring political decision-making. This might be done so that natural scientific knowledge on the limits to carrying capacity will be taken into account.

Such a research programme would focus on the rules of the political order. Public choice theory tells us that often a policy recommendation for sustainable development is inattractive to political leaders. It lacks the short-term results which are essential to win elections. We therefore would have to ask how natural scientific knowledge is transformed 'into the society' and processed within the political discourse. And we must ask how best to weigh ecological, economic and social criteria for a 'desirable' social order. Policy

---

[11] As permanently new substances are developed (maybe even as a reaction to environmental policy, Wegner 1994, p. 15), the uncertainty about ecological stability does not decrease in the course of time. Increasing knowledge may even lead to the opposite: more awareness of potential environmental risks.

recommendations that derive from this research programme would give us an answer as to how we should frame the political decision-making process by a set of (constitutional) rules. Such a process can make sure that politicians reflect the citizens' long-term interests in a sustainable development – that is, the arguments of both social and natural scientists are reflected within the public and political discourse.

Within Ecological Economics such a research programme is not well-established yet. Ecological Economists have made an important contribution by showing that complex ecological systems cannot be treated adequately within the scheme of mainstream neoclassical welfare economics. However, within social sciences exist several ideas about how to form a new paradigm by linking ecology with other (non-neoclassical) economic theories. Among these are evolutionary economics (Norgaard, 1994; Hinterberger and Wegner, 1996), socio-economics (Etzioni, 1988) and constitutional economics, the normative strand of public choice theory.

FROM SOCIO-ECOLOGICAL ECONOMICS TO A 'CONSTITUTIONAL ECOLOGICAL ECONOMICS'

It has been argued so far that Ecological Economists should focus on institutional questions asking how to influence a society's development path towards sustainability. How can an institutional framework be designed so that the spontaneous interaction of the members of the society leads to a 'desirable' – more precisely a 'sustainable' – social order? Constitutional Economics, the normative strand of public choice theory, may provide a methodology which could be applied fruitfully to the question of sustainable development.

Constitutional economists point out that the desirability of the outcome of social interaction depends on the given set of rules, that is, the institutional setting. The idea that the spontaneous interaction of individuals could, under specific conditions, produce socially desirable outcomes was first developed systematically by the classical liberal social philosopher Adam Smith. There are two major schools of thought which have further developed Adam Smith's constitutionalist approach:

- the German ordoliberal *Freiburg School* (Franz Böhm, Walter Eucken, Friedrich August von Hayek) and
- the American constitutional economic *Virginia School* (James Buchanan, Gordon Tullock, Viktor Vanberg).

The Freiburg School

The social scientists of the Freiburg School conclude that the principal role of government is to design a coherent set of long-lasting rules rather than to pursue a policy of short sighted interventions into the market process. In other words, government should pursue what ordoliberal economists call *Ordnungspolitik* – a policy of institutional design (Eucken, 1952/90).[12]

Friedrich August von Hayek highlights that *Ordnungspolitik* should be based on *general and abstract rules* 'independent of purpose' (Hayek, 1973/93, p. 50) and "applicable to an unknown and indeterminable number of persons and instances." Hayek further explains that such "rules are almost all negative in the sense that they prohibit rather than enjoin particular kinds of actions, that they do so in order to protect ascertainable domains within which each individual is free to act as he chooses" (Hayek 1976/93, p. 36). This way, the search for innovative ideas is not blocked through regulation (no direct interventions occur)[13] and expectations are mutually stabilised (by rule setting).

The central idea of the Freiburg School is that citizens (consumers) profit from market competition as a 'socially productive' process – in a modern term we could say: as a positive sum game. The set of rules should be specified in such a way that constructive forms of competition (*Leistungswettbewerb)* are promoted and destructive forms (*Behinderungswettbewerb*) are hindered. As competition is not self-sustaining – firms have an interest in gaining monopolistic power and in seeking protection from government – an external institution has to keep guard on competition. The government therefore should pursue what Eucken calls a 'policy of competition order' (*Politik der Wettbewerbsordnung*; Eucken 1952/90) and stick to certain principles.[14]

Applied to the question of sustainable development, the message of the Freiburg School is to make use of competitive processes in order to find new sustainable consumption and production patterns. Eucken and Böhm (1948) point out that the set of rules should be designed in such a way that the social interactions lead to a social order that meets economic *and social* criteria for a 'desirable' social order alike. Today we would add the third element of the

---

[12] For English translations of various original contributions of the Freiburg School see Peacock and Willgerodt (1989).

[13] A negatively defined general rule such as the prohibition of the use of a specific substance reduces the set of opportunities of the concerned economic actors *by* one whereas a mandatory product standard reduces the set of opportunities *to* one single option.

[14] Walter Eucken lists the following elements constituting a 'desirable' economic order: a functioning price mechanism, a stable currency, open markets, private property, liberty of contract, liability rules and continuity of economic policy (Eucken, 1952/90, pp. 254–289).

sustainability-triad and insist that this set of rules meet economic, social *and ecological* criteria.

Gerken and Renner (1996, pp. 46–91) evaluate eight different policy instruments in a 1996 study and conclude that four of them go along with the criteria established by the Freiburg School: liability rules, non-discriminating administrative regulations, consumer information and tradable emission permits.[15] Adding the 'property rights solution' (Renner, 1997) we get five policy recommendations, which either refer directly to Eucken's basic principles of *Ordnungspolitik* (proposals 1 and 2), or are judged as compatible with the ordoliberal criteria of the Freiburg School (proposals 2 to 5).

Recommendations of the Freiburg School
(1) Individual Property Rights: Specifying property rights with respect to the environment is *Ordnungspolitik* as the role of government is limited to setting-up general and abstract rules. This holds true for the privatisation of the environment as a public good (for example, a public fish pond) as well as for the regulation of its use (for example, 'for fishing only'). Whereas privatisation may lead to a sustainable management of economicly valuable natural resources (for example, fish), it does not present a solution for complex ecological systems (such as biodiversity or climate stability); in that case property rights have to be further specified.
(2) Environmental Liability Rules: Environmental Liability rules limit the role of government to a minimum and strengthen the self-organising capacity of society. They give incentives to individuals to anticipate potential future environmental risks in order to reduce them. No further political decisions will have to be taken not even when new information about environmental risks is available. It corresponds, therefore, to the ordoliberal criteria 'par excellence' (Gerken and Renner, 1996; p. 86). However, its environmental effectiveness is limited. The application of liability law requires that a *polluter* can be identified. But within a mere *preventive* strategy for protecting complex ecological systems (providing public goods such as biodiversity or a favourable climate), there are few identifiable polluters.
(3) Non-discriminating Administrative Regulations: Administrative regulations can be defined positively (mandatory standard) or negatively (prohibition). They can be defined either in a general way being "applicable to an unkown and indeterminable number of persons and instances" (Hayek, 1973/93, p. 50, see fn 10) or case-by-case. Only

---

[15] The other four instruments are mandatory standards, subventions, voluntary agreements and environmental taxes.

negatively defined general and abstract rules (such as a general prohibition of CFCs) do not discriminate against some economic actors and therefore correspond to the ordoliberal criteria.

(4) Tradable Emission Permits: Tradable emission permits are the most market-oriented instrument to implement a *given* environmental objective such as a reduction of CO_2 emissions of 25 per cent by the year 2005. Their application could be classified as *Ordnungspolitik* since the role of government is limited to the definition of the maximum level of emissions and the creation of a market (stock exchange) for the tradable permits. No further interventions are necessary.

(5) Consumer Information (Labelling): Setting up rules for voluntary and obligatory product labelling in order to promote consumer information in respect to ecological characteristics of a product is a form of *Ordnungspolitik* which supports the search for sustainable production and consumption patterns. Standardised obligatory product labels make products comparable for the consumer, whereas voluntary labels strengthen the self-organising capacity of industry: Within a competitive process new environmental standards could be developed – and certified through an ecolabel.

Unresolved issues

The ordoliberal approach as shown is rule orientated, as direct interventions into the market process do not occur. It is an 'indirect' approach. The list of policy proposals also shows that there exists not one single optimal strategy to define a set of rules for sustainable development.[16] A policy-mix is needed. Besides, two major problems still remain unresolved:

• *The Public Choice problem – how to implement Ordnungspolitik?* Policy recommendations of the Freiburg School so far have not changed political decision-making towards an ordoliberal strategy for sustainability. A wide consensus exists among economists (those of the Freiburg School and others) that environmental policy should be based on economic incentives. Still these instruments are not selected within the political decision-

---

[16] In a strict sense all policy recommendations – except for one – do not fully fulfil the ordoliberal criteria. In environmental politics it is difficult to define 'general and abstract' rules "applicable to an unknown and indeterminable number of persons and instances" because natural scientists permanently discover new potential risks that suggest political action (Wegner, 1994). This implies that the institutional framework has to be adjusted in a political *case-by-case decision*. New regulations on the use of natural resources have to be defined (for example, re-use of packaging). New markets for transferable emission permits have to be created (for example, for SO_2, CO_2, and so on). The amounts of tradable emission permits have to be adjusted. The use of specific substances has to be generally prohibited (for example, CFCs). It follows that there is always a risk of the economic and social order (unintentionally) being destabilised by government action re-specifying the institutional setting. As argued above, only *liability law* is not faced with this problem.

making process. Walter Eucken (1952/90) had this problem of political lobbyism in mind when he argued that once a 'competition order' is implemented, economic interest groups could no longer lobby successfully for an interventionist policy which does not promote the common interests of the citizens. Still, he does not explain why a rational political actor should self-constrain his/her set of policy instruments by sticking to the Freiburg policy recommendation.

- *The normative element in Ordnungspolitik – how to weigh the economic, social and ecological aspects?* The implementation of Eucken's principles for a 'competition order' – for environmental policy this means: the assignment of individual property rights to environmental goods along with a sophisticated liability law – does not suffice to reach a sustainable development path. This has been seen also by Eucken who argues that in some cases we have to further specify the set of rules with other policy instruments.[17] But unlimited options exist on how to specify the set of rules. The policy then depends on how we interpret the 'needs' of ecological sustainability. We therefore face the question of how to weigh ecological criteria against social and economic criteria. No scientific criterion exists on how to resolve this conflict – it is a value judgement, which depends on preferences.

The Virginia School

The Constitutional Economists of the Virginia School (Buchanan 1975; Brennan and Buchanan, 1988; Buchanan and Tullock, 1962) developed a methodology for deriving policy recommendations, which resolves both the public-choice problem and the question of how to deal with differing interests or value judgements. Buchanan argues that on a meta-level policy recommendations could be developed which offer benefits to all parties concerned. The recommendations, therefore, might have a chance to be adopted. The major field of research for Constitutional Economists is the institutional setting of the political decision-making process.

James Buchanan's Constitutional Economics is explicitly based on methodological and normative individualism. These 'liberal' assumptions state first that the working properties of institutions have to be explained by the structure of incentives for individual behaviour and second that political action can only be legitimised by agreement of the individuals concerned. At first glance it appears to be difficult to discuss sustainability within the theoretical framework of normative and methodological individualism. Indeed, Buchanan does not deal with this subject in particular. Nevertheless,

---

[17] Eucken (1952/90, p. 302) for example, proposes the prohibition of non-sustainable forest cultivation.

individualism is no obstacle if we focus on the level of rules. Whereas constitutional reforms proposed by liberal economists traditionally focused on the rules for the co-ordination of market transactions, that is, the market order (see Freiburg School), James Buchanan's Constitutional Economics (Virginia School) focuses on the rules for collective entities – in particular: the political order. Based on a Public Choice Analysis of the political decision-making process with politicians modelled as self-interested actors (methodological individualism), constitutional rules are developed which are supposed to make the political decision-making more responsive to citizens' preferences (normative individualism).

The basic idea of Buchanan's theoretical concept is to transform the idea of mutual-gains-from-trade from individual decision-making on economic markets to collective decision-making in the sphere of politics. Whereas in economic markets people agree on the conditions of trade if both parties believe to realise gains-from-trade the citizens of a constituency will agree on a rule restricting their individual behaviour if they believe their own situation will improve. Buchanan argues that collective decisions on changes in the set of rules are legitimate only if they offer such 'mutual-gains-from-agreement,' that is, if they put every single citizen in a better situation than before. The relevant test whether a rule is Pareto-superior in this sense is the actual vote: a proposed change in the set of rules has to reach consensus within society in order to be legitimate. Constitutional Economists therefore look for win-win options. Homann and Pies (1996) argue that this may involve the compensation of those who believe that they will not benefit from a proposed change in the set of rules. To give an example: countries (that is, their citizens) which judge climate stability to be less important than other issues (such as economic growth) or which simply are effected less negatively by global warming may have to be compensated for their commitment to participate within an international CO_2 emission reduction scheme.

Now, how can the Constitutional Economics approach be applied to the question of sustainable development? As stated above, the traditional answer of Constitutional Economists is to develop constitutional reforms that make political decision-making more responsive to citizens' preferences. However, in order to show that such reforms would lead to a sustainable development, we have to take a closer look at the notion of individual preferences. Whenever liberal social scientists argue that politics should be more responsive to individual preferences they have 'informed' preferences in mind. Democracy cannot mean that people vote – rationally or irrationally – 'ignorant' in the sense that they vote for a policy, which they would not opt for if they were better informed. This is particularly important for the domain of environmental policy. Ecological systems are too complex. It is hard for 'normal' citizens to judge for themselves which emission limits to prefer. We have to think also about constitutional arrangement allowing people to form 'informed' preferences. The basic questions then are: How can institutions be designed so that the political decision-making process is responsive to 'informed' (wise, long-term) citizens' preferences? How can we make sure that the arguments of both natural and social scientists will be reflected within the sustainable development decision-making? The Virginia School makes four policy recommendations for constitutional reform based on this reasoning.[18]

Recommendations of the Virginia School
1. Reform of the Electoral System. *Direct Votes on Environmental Objectives*. Direct democratic votes on environmental objectives ('national environmental plans') could promote sustainable development, as it would raise the acceptance of environmental policies. Additionally, the political decision-making would be influenced less by interest groups than today; today's non-transparent mechanisms of political lobbying would be substituted by a public discourse in which the arguments of both natural and social scientists would be discussed. This would increase the chance that decisions are taken on basis of 'better informed' preferences (Cassel, 1998).
2. Reform of the Electoral System. *Proxi-Votes for Parents on Behalf of their Children*. Proxi-votes of parents on behalf of their children could help link present day political decision-making to the interests of future generations. The proposal is based on the assumption that parents tend to vote 'in the interests' of their children. It acknowledges that in a democracy the preferences of present day citizens are the only legitimate point of reference for political decision-making. It may be interpreted as a step towards a liberal concept of intergenerational justice.
3. Reform of the Political Decision-Making. *Transparent Advisory Councils and Participatory Networks*. IFOK (1997) proposes among others reforms with respect to policy advice and citizens participation in the run-up of parliamentary decision-making.
   (a) Government advisory councils should be more transparent and independent than at present in order to effectively improve the transfer of knowledge from natural and social scientists into the political decision-making.
   (b) A professionally managed process of participatory networking among the different groups within society concerned by a legislative project could promote consensus on controversial issues within society.

---

[18] Not listed are proposals, which imply a fundamental restructuring of the political system even if they are challenging from a theoretical point of view such as Hayek's 1979 proposal of a 'model constitution.'

4. Reform of the Federal Order. *Fostering Institutional Competition.* The decentralisation of political competence leads to a competition of different political and theoretical concepts. Institutional competition then is a search process in which knowledge about successful concepts is generated (Gerken and Renner, 1996). Renner and Hannowsky (1998) propose to consider to "decentralise the competence to decentralise competence" within federal entities in order to promote political innovations – in the field of environmental and social policy for example – two areas of policy which in Europe are being more and more centralised. Whenever externalities prevent lower political entities of solving a problem (global warming, for example) institutional competition has to be framed by a common set of rules; that is new forms of intergovernmental co-operation have to go along with the decentralisation of political competence.

CONSTITUTIONAL ECOLOGICAL ECONOMICS – POLITICS BEYOND IDEOLOGY?

The proposal to link Ecological and Constitutional Economics is unusual for Ecological Economists and Constitutional Economists. Often Ecological Economists oppose not only mainstream neoclassical welfare economics but all concepts based on a (normative and/or methodological) individualism such as Constitutional Economics.[19] Besides, not many Constitutional Economists deal with the question of ecological sustainability. In this final section we will explore more deeply why the individualistic 'liberal' concept of Constitutional Economics could provide a fruitful theoretical framework for Ecological Economics.

What is most fascinating about Constitutional Economics is that it allows the separation of theoretical arguments from ideology. A 'good' Constitutional Economics policy proposal must not be single-sided, that is, ideological. It should, to stick with the notion introduced by John Rawls, reach an 'overlapping consensus' (Rawls, 1993). James Buchanan points out that such a consensus could be reached more easily on the level of rules defining the problem-solving mechanisms for future problems rather than on specific issues where we are faced with conflicting interests. For example, both liberal and non-liberal economists could agree upon an institutional reform that put all members of society in a better situation than before. As

---

[19] Daly (1995) does not make a difference between neoclassical economics and economics based on methodological individualism and therewith ignores that there exist theoretical developments within Ecological Economics that oppose neoclassical economics but not methodological individualism.

(general and abstract) rules are "applicable to an unknown and indeterminable number of persons and instances" (Hayek, 1973/93, p. 50) people do not know how they will be personally affected by them. They decide behind a 'veil of ignorance.' (Brennan and Buchanan 1988). Buchanan concludes that in such situations people have a strong interest in opting for wise, just and commonly acceptable rules. Constitutional reforms therefore tend to reflect long-term interests and, if they are perceived as a win-win solution, have a better chance to be implemented within the political decision-making. If we want to promote sustainability we therefore have to adjust the rules of our political order.

Usually, the Constitutional Economists' proposals have an economic bias. Buchanan's proposal of the constitutional budget constraint aims at economic sustainability, not ecological sustainability. In order to check whether Constitutional Economics could be applied to the question of ecological stability we have to take a closer look on its theoretical framework. Of particular use for our purpose is Vanberg and Buchanan's 1994 essay on Interests and Theories in Constitutional Choice. Vanberg and Buchanan argue that preferences for constitutional arrangements consist of two components, personal interests, and theories 'about the world' (1994, p. 168).

Preferences = function (interest, theories)

Whether a certain policy proposal is mutually beneficial or not depends not only on whether people have a common interest in a certain rule setting, but depends to a high degree on whether people share the knowledge about the working properties of the policy options they decide upon. We may have a common interest in rules that promote an informed preference formation of the citizens and that make politics more responsive to those informed preferences, but we may at the same time disagree on the proposals presented for this purpose. We may not share the theories the proposals are based upon. Consensus will be reached among different parties only if they share some common understanding about the working properties of the proposed policy.

We know that within social science – and particularly within Ecological Economics – different theories compete. Many of them claim to explain one and the same reality. Often it is then difficult to separate 'interests' (derived from norms and value judgements) from 'theories.'[20] Vanberg and Buchanan argue that in constitutional choice the situation is different: people decide 'behind a veil' as they cannot anticipate how they will be personally effected by each constitutional arrangements, which may be interpreted as process-oriented problem-solving mechanisms. Hence they are not able to figure out

---

[20] Hegmann (1998) reveals the different normative assumptions environmental economic research programs are based upon.

their personal interest in a certain constitutional arrangement. On the
constitutional level we discuss 'theories without interests.' We discuss the
working properties of alternative rules (theory component) rather than the
pros and cons of conflicting norms and values (interest component); the
discussion then will not be ideological. This implies that it is in principal
possible to reach a consensus within a scientific discourse.

However, things get more difficult once we begin to specify the
constitutional policy recommendations more precisely. The problem is that
the more we specify a proposal, the less it will find consensus because further
normative assumptions have to be introduced.[21] Seeking policy
recommendations that reach unanimous consent, Constitutional Economists
have to cope with this problem. We have already shown the direction of our
effort: we have to (try to) separate interests from theories. This means that we
have to search for common interests and to recognise potential disagreement
in theoretical questions. Whenever we face conflicting interests, we look for a
more general, rule-oriented policy proposal such as those of the Virginia
School. And whenever we face competing theoretical explanations we engage
in a scientific discourse in order to raise "the level of mutually shared
information on the general working properties of alternative rules." (Vanberg
and Buchanan 1994, p. 176) .

The Constitutional Economics Approach, if applied in a fruitful way,
allows to be revealed normative assumptions so that alternative policy
proposals can be rationally discussed. Besides, it shows that policy
recommendations which limit their normative assumptions to a minimum
have a better chance to be implemented than those based on non-commonly
shared norms and values. The proposal of a global scheme of tradable
emission permits based on the principle of intergenerational justice (Daly,
1992) may be morally appealing but non-attractive within the political
decision-making framework. The Constitutional Economic Approach
suggests transforming notions such as intergenerational justice into policy
proposals that seem attractive to all parties concerned. This may imply that
we may succeed in implementing a scheme of tradable emission permits such
as proposed by Daly only if we first have successfully implemented
institutional reforms. It is also important for political decision-making within
our own country to establish incentives to political leaders to adequately
reflect natural scientific knowledge when defining national environmental
objectives. Such a proposal has to be designed in such a way that it seems
attractive to political leaders in other countries, too. Joint implementation and
financial compensations may play a vital role within Constitutional
Ecological Economic recommendation.

---

[21] We could call this the *dilemma of Constitutional Economics.*

A Constitutional Economics Approach to Ecological Economics has a heuristic function helping to structure our arguments. We discuss hypothetical policy options; these are to be understood not as Kantian *categorical* imperatives telling us what we have to do, but rather as *hypothetical* imperatives giving us some advice on what best to do if we want to pursue certain interests. Such an approach could be of great use for Ecological Economics because it focuses on a problem Ecological Economists are faced with more intensely than scientists adhering to mainstream neoclassical economics: the problem coping with non-commonly shared interests and theories. A common theoretical framework which reveals the underlying assumptions of each policy proposal would help to find a common basis within Ecological Economics – a prerequisite for any approach which challenges mainstream theory (Hinterberger, 1997; Norgaard, 1985).

Finally, the Constitutional Economics Approach could help to resolve another problem Ecological Economists are frequently faced with: the problem of not wanting to question democratic institutions while at the same time distrusting them. Based on the liberal assumption that there are no *'wrong preferences'* but that they may be based on *'wrong theories,'* an Ecological Constitutional Economics develops policy proposals that allow a fruitful competition among different theories. These theories should be anchored in natural and social science allowing citizens and political leaders to form 'informed' preferences.

REFERENCES

Bellah, R.N., Madsen, R., Sullivan, W.M., Swidler, A. and Tipton, S.M. 1991. *The Good Society*, New York: Knopf.

Brennan, G. and Buchanan, J. 1988. *The Reason of Rules. Constitutional Political Economy*. Cambridge: Cambridge University Press.

Buchanan, J. 1975. *The Limits of Liberty. Between Anarchy and Leviathan*. Chicago: The University of Chicago Press.

Buchanan, J. and Tullock, G. 1962. *The Calculus of Consent. Logical Foundations of Constitutional Democracy*. Ann Arbor: University of Michigan.

BUND and Misereor (eds.) 1996. *Zukunftsfähiges Deutschland. Ein Beitrag zur einer global nachhaltigen Entwicklung*. Basel: Birkhäuser.

Cassel, S. 1998. 'Direkte Demokratie, Bürgerpräferenzen und die Rolle von Politikberatung.' In Renner, A. and Hinterberger, F. (eds.) *Zukunftsfähigkeit und Neoliberalismus. Zur Vereinbarkeit von Umweltschutz und Wettbewerbswirtschaft*. Baden-Baden: Nomos.

Costanza, R., Daly, H.E. and Bartholomew, J.A. (eds.) 1991. *Ecological Economics: The Science and Management of Sustainability.* New York: Columbia Press.

Daly, H.E. 1977. *Steady-State Econommics.* San Francisco: Freeman and Company.

Daly, H.E. 1992. 'Allocation, Distribution, and Scale: Towards an Economics That is Efficient, Just and Sustainable.' *Ecological Economics* 6, 7–34.

Daly, H.E. 1995. 'Against Free-Trade: Neoclassical and Steady-State Perpectives.' *Journal of Evolutionary Economics* 5, 313–326.

Etzioni, A. 1988. *The Moral Dimension. Toward a New Economics.* New York: Free Press.

Eucken, W. 1952/90. *Grundsätze der Wirtschaftspolitik.* Tübingen: J.C.B. Mohr.

Eucken, W. and Böhm, F. 1948. *Vorwort,* ORDO 1, VII–XI.

Gerken, L. and Renner, A. 1996. *Nachhaltigkeit durch Wettbewerb.* Tübingen: J.C.B. Mohr.

Glasbergen, P. (ed.) 1995. *Managing Environmental Disputes. Network Management as an Alternative.* Dordrecht: Kluwer Academic Publishers.

Gunderson, L.H., Holling, C.S. and Light, S.S. (eds.) 1995. *Barriers and Bridges to the Renewal of Ecosystems and Institutions.* New York: Columbia University Press.

Hayek, F.A. von 1967. 'The Result of Human Action but not of Human Design.' In Hayek, F.A. von (ed.) *Studies in Philosophy, Politics and Economics.* London: Routledge, 96–105.

Hayek, F.A. von 1973/93. *Law, Legislation and Liberty, Rules and Order.* London: Routledge.

Hayek, F.A. von 1976/93, *Law, Legislation and Liberty, The Mirage of Social Justice.* London: Routledge.

Hayek, F.A. von 1979. *Law, Legislation and Liberty, The Political Order of a Free People.* London: Routledge.

Hegmann, H. 1997. 'Differing World-Views and Collective Action: The Case of Research.' *Constitutional Political Economy* 8, 3, 179–194.

Hegmann, H. 1998. 'Wissenssoziologische Aspekte der Verfassungs-ökonomik. Das Beispiel der Nachhaltigkeitsdebatte.' In Renner, A. and Hinterberger, F. (eds.) *Zukunftsfähigkeit und Neoliberalismus. Zur Vereinbarkeit von Umweltschutz und Wettbewerbswirtschaft.* Baden-Baden: Nomos, 175–195.

Hinterberger, F. 1994. 'Biological, Cultural, and Economic Evolution and the Economy/Ecology Relationship.' In Bergh, J. van den and Straaten, J. van der (eds.) *Toward Sustainable Development.* Washington D.C.: Island Press, 57–81.

Hinterberger, F. 1997. 'Another Plea for Pluralism in Ecological Economics.' *ESEE Newsletter*, November 1997.

Hinterberger, F., Luks, F. and Stewen, M. 1998. *Ecological Economic Policy.* London: Routledge.

Hinterberger, F. and Wegner, G. 1996. 'Limited Knowledge and the Precautionary Principle: On the Feasibility of Environmental Policies.' In Bergh, J. van den and Straaten, J. van der (eds.) *Economy and Ecosystems in Change: Analytical and Historical Approaches.* Washington D.C.: Island Press.

Homann, K. and Pies, I. 1996. 'Sozialpolitik für den Markt.' In Pies, I. and Leschke, M. (eds.) *James Buchanans konstitutionelle Ökonomik.* Tübingen: J.C.B. Mohr, 203–239.

IFOK (Institut für Organisationskommunikation) (ed.) 1997. *Bausteine für ein zukunftsfähiges Deutschland.* Wiesbaden: Gabler.

Lippmann, W. 1937. *The Good Society.* Boston: Little, Brown and Co.

Maier-Rigaud, G. 1994. *Umweltpolitik mit Mengen und Märkten. Lizenzen als konstituierendes Element einer ökologischen Marktwirtschaft.* Marburg: Metropolis.

Norgaard, R. 1985. 'Environmental Economics: An Evolutionary Critique and a Plea for Pluralism.' *Journal for Environmental Economics and Management* 12, 382–394.

Norgaard, R. 1994. *Development Betrayed. The End of Progress and a Coevolutionary Revisioning of the Future.* London: Routledge.

Nordhaus, W.D. 1991. To Slow or Not To Slow: The Economics of the Greenhouse Effect. *The Economic Journal* 101, 920–937.

Peacock, A. and Willgerodt, H. 1989. *Germany's Social Market Economy: Origins and Evolution.* London: Macmillan.

Rawls, J. 1993. *Political Liberalism.* New York: Columbia University Press.

Renner, A. 1997. 'La qualification des droits de propriété comme 'Ordnungspolitik': Le cas de la protection de l'environnement, dans: Max Falque / Michel Massenet, droits de propriété et environnement.' Paris: Editions Dalloz, 178–183.

Renner, A. 1998. 'Zukunftsfähiges Deutschland und Ordoliberalismus der Freiburger Schule – zwei gegensätzliche Welten?' In Renner, A. and Hinterberger, F. (eds.) *Zukunftsfähigkeit und Neoliberalismus. Zur Vereinbarkeit von Umweltschutz und Wettbewerbswirtschaft.* Baden-Baden: Nomos, 93–116.

Renner, A. and Hanowsky, D. 1998. *Zur präsenzkonformen Ordnung Europas. Ordnungsgestaltung im Spannungsfeld von Einheit und Vielfalt.* Frankfurt a.M.: Peter Lang.

Sachs, W. and Loske, R. 1996. *Greening the North.* London: Zed Books.

Stewen, M. 1998. 'The Interdependence of Allocation, Distribution, Scale and Stability – A Comment on Herman E. Daly's Vision of An Economics That is Efficient, Just and Sustainable.' *Ecological Economics* forthcoming.

Suchanek, A. 1997. 'Chancen und Grenzen der Implementation umweltverträglicher Verhaltensmuster in der modernen Gesellschaft.' In Sellmann, M. (ed.) *Umweltethik und ihre gesellschaftliche Vermittlung.* Bad Honnef: Katholisch-Soziales Institut der Erzdiözese Köln.

Vanberg, V. and Buchanan, J. 1994. 'Interests and Theories in Constitutional Choice.' In Vanberg, V. (ed.) *Rules and Choice.* London: Routledge.

Wegner, G. 1994. *Marktkonforme Umweltpolitik zwischen Dezisionismus und Selbststeuerung.* Tübingen: J.C.B. Mohr.

Subject Index